Writing Arguments

Why Do You Need This New Edition?

If you're wondering why you should buy this new edition of *Writing Arguments*, here are nine great reasons!

1 A new full-color design visually differentiates key ideas, making reading a user-friendly experience and ensuring it is easier for you to find important information.

2 A new Chapter 8, Analyzing Arguments Rhetorically, shows you how to read arguments critically so you will be able to identify and explain the strategies writers use to persuade their audiences.

3 New Writing Assignments in Parts 1, 2, and 3 on analysis, invention, planning, drafting, and revising include both instruction and samples to guide you as you build your argument skills.

4 New readings and visual arguments on current topics such as immigration, video games, sports, and the connection between gender and math ability model the different argument types your instructor may assign.

5 New student essays include several that are researched to help you see how to integrate researched material into your argument as well as how to cite and document it.

6 New Organization Plan diagrams for various types of arguments show you how to introduce, develop, and conclude your own arguments.

7 New Toulmin Analysis charts represent complicated concepts—such as the Toulmin system of argument—in a visual way, helping you see the underlying conceptual structure of an argument and make effective arguments in your course (Ch. 4, 11–15).

8 Thoroughly revised Chapters 11–15 (Part 4) on different types of arguments have been rewritten to improve clarity and ease of use, removing a language of mathematic variables ("x" and "y") and replacing it with simpler, clearer instruction.

9 Up-to-date MLA and APA citation examples, including examples of the most recent style changes, show you how to correctly cite and document sources in your research papers (App. 2).

Writing Arguments

A Rhetoric with Readings

Concise Edition

Fifth Edition

John D. Ramage
Arizona State University

John C. Bean
Seattle University

June Johnson
Seattle University

Longman

New York   San Francisco   Boston
London   Toronto   Sydney   Tokyo   Singapore   Madrid
Mexico City   Munich   Paris   Cape Town   Hong Kong   Montreal

Acquisitions Editor: Lauren A. Finn
Senior Development Editor: Marion B. Castellucci
Senior Marketing Manager: Sandra McGuire
Senior Supplements Editor: Donna Campion
Senior Media Producer: Stefanie Liebman
Production Manager: Savoula Amanatidis
Project Coordination and Text Design: Elm Street
    Publishing Services

Electronic Page Makeup: Integra Software Services Pvt. Ltd.
Cover Design Manager: John Callahan
Cover Designer: Marie Ilardi
Cover Images: Courtesy of Alamy
Photo Researcher: Rebecca Karamehmedovic
Senior Manufacturing Buyer: Alfred C. Dorsey
Printer and Binder: Courier Corporation—Kendallville
Cover Printer: Lehigh-Phoenix Color Corporation

For permission to use copyrighted material, grateful acknowledgment is made to the copyright holders on pp. 295–296, which are hereby made part of this copyright page.

Library of Congress Cataloging-in-Publication Data

Ramage, John D.
  Writing arguments: a rhetoric with readings/John D. Ramage, John C. Bean, June Johnson.—Concise ed., 5th ed.
    p. cm.
  Includes bibliographical references and index.
  ISBN-13: 978-0-205-66577-8
  ISBN-10: 0-205-66577-2
  1. English language—Rhetoric. 2. Persuasion (Rhetoric) 3. College readers. 4. Report writing.
  I. Bean, John C. II. Johnson, June, 1953— III. Title.
  PE1431.R33 2010
  808'.0427—dc22

                                    2009003685

1 2 3 4 5 6 7 8 9 10—CRK—12 11 10 09

Longman
is an imprint of

www.pearsonhighered.com

Complete Edition
ISBN-13: 978-0-205-64836-8
ISBN-10: 0-205-64836-3

Brief Edition
ISBN-13: 978-0-205-66576-1
ISBN-10: 0-205-66576-4

Concise Edition
ISBN-13: 978-0-205-66577-8
ISBN-10: 0-205-66577-2

Brief Contents

Detailed Contents

Preface

Through several editions, *Writing Arguments* has established itself as the leading college textbook in argumentation. By focusing on argument as dialogue in search of solutions to problems instead of as pro-con debate with winners and losers, *Writing Arguments* treats argument as a process of inquiry as well as a means of persuasion. Users and reviewers have consistently praised the book for teaching the critical thinking skills needed for *writing* arguments: how to analyze the occasion for an argument; how to ground an argument in the values and beliefs of the targeted audience; how to develop and elaborate an argument; and how to respond sensitively to objections and alternative views. The text is available in three versions—a regular edition, which includes an anthology of readings; a brief edition, which offers the complete rhetoric without the anthology; and this concise edition with fewer readings and examples—to support many instructional approaches and course designs. We are pleased that in this fifth concise edition we have made many improvements while retaining the text's signature strengths.

The Big Picture: What's New in the Fifth Edition?

Based on our continuing research into argumentation theory and pedagogy, as well as on the advice of users, we have made significant improvements in the fifth edition that increase the text's flexibility for teachers and its appeal to students. We have made the following major changes:

- **New full-color design and increased focus on visual arguments throughout the text.** The interest level and reader-friendliness of the text have been greatly increased by the new full-color design and by the many new photographs, ads, cartoons, drawings, and other visual arguments that deepen students' encounters with persuasive messages. Each claim-type chapter in Part Four opens with a **visual case**, an example of a type of argument, and includes an **Examining Visual Arguments** feature that asks students to analyze advocacy ads, political cartoons, posters, and other visual arguments.

- **A new Chapter 8 on the rhetorical analysis of arguments.** In response to user requests that we expand the text's treatment of rhetorical analysis of arguments, the new Chapter 8 teaches students to identify a writer's strategies for reaching a targeted audience, to analyze the writer's angle of vision, to evaluate the argument's overall effectiveness for both insider and outsider audiences—and, ultimately, to write a rhetorical analysis of a written text. New Writing Assignment options and a student example increase the text's flexibility for instructors when planning major assignments.

- **Graphic display of concepts.** New **Toulmin Analysis** charts help students see the conceptual framework of an argument and plan argument strategies, and new **Organization Plans** for various types of arguments help students outline and structure their own arguments.

- **Simpler, shorter, and more accessible claim-type chapters (Part Four)** through elimination of the "XY" templates, through new examples, and through substantive tightening. In the previous editions of *Writing Arguments,* we used "X" and "Y" as placeholders in templates to explain a stasis: *Is this X a Y?* or *Does X cause Y?* Although this approach worked for some students and instructors, for others certain passages in these chapters seemed like a math text. In the fifth edition, we have eliminated this language and have adopted a simpler, more straightforward, and clearer approach for explaining each claim type. We have also made these chapters shorter and crisper and have used many new examples and new student essays.

- **A significantly revised Chapter 2, which places the reading of arguments within a context of inquiry and exploration.** Our newly revised Chapter 2, "Argument as Inquiry: Reading and Exploring," combines features of the fourth edition's Chapters 2 and 3. The chapter continues to focus on reading arguments (summary writing, reading to believe and to doubt), but places greater emphasis on argument as inquiry and truth-seeking. A new Writing Assignment, an exploratory essay, is illustrated with a student example, increasing the instructor's options for course planning and providing students with a productive tool for reading arguments and generating ideas.

- **An improved emphasis on writing throughout Part Two with new Writing Assignments.** Writing Assignments now appear in each chapter in Part Two, allowing teachers to coordinate students' reading of Part Two with the development and writing of their own arguments. In addition, Part Two introduces a new Writing Assignment— a "supporting reasons argument"—that focuses on reasons in support of the writer's claim without requiring students to summarize and respond to opposing views.

- **Updated MLA documentation based on the new seventh edition of the *MLA Handbook for Writers of Research Papers* (2009), and updated APA documentation based on the *APA Style Guide to Electronic References* (2007).** In Appendix 2, we briefly explain and show the far-ranging changes in the citing of both print and Web sources according to the new MLA handbook, including the use of italics rather than underscoring and the inclusion of medium of publication in each citation. We also show examples of citations based on the APA's latest style guide for electronic sources.

- **Six new professional readings and five new student essays, chosen for their illustrative power and student interest.** High-interest topics include immigration, women in math and science, video games, and alternative energy. Two of the new student pieces are researched arguments in MLA and APA format.

The Details: What Has Changed in the Fifth Edition?

Our part titles now signal a clear progression from an introduction to the nature of argument (Part One), to writing arguments (Part Two), to analyzing arguments (Part Three), to a deeper understanding of claim types (Part Four). This revised arrangement provides an improved pedagogical framework for the teaching of argument while giving instructors the flexibility to use what they need. In the context of this framework, we have made many changes to the content of each chapter.

Part One, Overview of Argument   Part One (Chapters 1 and 2) has been refocused to emphasize argument as truth-seeking and inquiry and to encourage students to enter a disputed conversation with an open mind, searching for the best solution to a problem.

- Chapter 1, "Argument: An Introduction," has an improved explanation of implicit versus explicit arguments illustrated by the controversy over phthalates in toys. Two implicit visual arguments opposing phthalates (pictures of a baby with a "poison" bib and of a phthalates protest) are juxtaposed with an explicit argument supporting the chemical industry's position. In addition, Chapter 1 has a new class activity analyzing implicit visual arguments and a new role-playing exercise on regulating student self-presentations on Facebook.
- Chapter 2, "Argument as Inquiry: Reading and Exploring" combines elements of Chapter 2 and Chapter 3 from the fourth edition to better explain how to evaluate rhetorical context, read arguments, and explore issues. The chapter's focus on inquiry and exploration is supported by new readings, photos, and cartoons about undocumented workers and illegal immigration. The chapter offers two Writing Assignment options—an argument summary or a new exploratory essay, which is described in detail and illustrated with a new student essay.

Part Two, Writing Arguments   Part Two, which has absorbed the material on writing arguments from the fourth edition's Chapter 3, places increased attention on the writing process. Part Two introduces the classical argument and leads students through a series of writing assignments that help them plan and draft an argument. Each of the chapters in Part Two includes changes as follows:

- Chapter 3, "The Core of an Argument: A Claim with Reasons," introduces the structure of classical argument and the classical appeals of *logos, ethos*, and *pathos* to frame the discussion of the principles of argument. A new Writing Assignment asks students to frame an issue question and produce a working thesis statement.
- In Chapter 4, "The Logical Structure of Arguments" the explanation of the Toulmin system is clarified with examples in graphic form. A new Writing Assignment asks students to use the Toulmin schema to plan details for an argument-in-progress.
- Chapter 5, "Using Evidence Effectively," expands its treatment of visual evidence and includes new exercises on angle of vision and photographs. A new Writing Assignment asks students to write a "supporting reasons" argument, which is illustrated by student writer Carmen Tieu's "Why Violent Video Games Are Good for Girls."
- Chapter 6, "Moving Your Audience: *Ethos, Pathos,* and *Kairos,*" has an improved section on how audience-based reasons enhance *logos, ethos,* and *pathos* and includes a new chart of questions for analyzing an audience. It also contains a new Examining Visual Arguments feature that asks students to analyze the appeals of a

Toyota Prius ad. Its new Writing Assignment asks students to revise a draft for improved focus on *ethos, pathos*, and audience-based reasons.

■ Chapter 7, "Responding to Objections and Alternative Views," has been tightened. The fourth edition's student example of a classical argument ("A Plea for Fair Treatment of Skateboarders") has been moved to this chapter, where the Writing Assignment options are to write either a classical argument or a dialogic argument aimed at conciliation.

Part Three, Analyzing Arguments   Part Three includes a new Chapter 8 on analyzing written arguments along with Chapter 9 on analyzing visual arguments.

■ Chapter 8, "Analyzing Arguments Rhetorically," provides comprehensive instruction to students on how to write a rhetorical analysis of an argument using the theory and principles of argument explained in Part Two. As examples for analysis, it presents two arguments about ethical issues in reproductive technology: Kathryn Jean Lopez's "Egg Heads" and Ellen Goodman's "Womb for Rent—For a Price." The chapter provides our own analysis of Lopez's argument, a student analysis of Goodman's argument, as well as a new Writing Assignment—a rhetorical analysis of an argument.

■ Chapter 9 has been updated with new visual argument examples and provides a new Writing Assignment option: to write a rhetorical analysis of a visual argument.

Part Four, Arguments in Depth: Five Types of Claims   Part Four has been updated and made simpler and more accessible by elimination of the XY templates. In each chapter, the Toulmin analysis of an argument has been clarified with a chart to help students pinpoint the elements of the argument. In each chapter, we have also added an Examining Visual Arguments feature and a new section on identifying audience and determining what's at stake. Numerous other local changes include the following:

■ In Chapter 10, "An Introduction to the Types of Claims," the example of a hybrid argument is now annotated to help students identify the various claim-types used in the essay.

■ In Chapter 11, "Definitional Arguments," we have simplified the vocabulary and eliminated the distinction between definition arguments and what the fourth edition called "simple categorical arguments." The chapter opens with a visual argument—a Conoco ad—and has an Examining Visual Arguments feature analyzing a poster defining fascism.

■ Chapter 12, "Causal Arguments," opens with a new visual case using global warming graphs, has several new cause and effect diagrams, and has an Examining Visual Arguments feature analyzing an Adbuster's ad. The chapter has also been shortened and reorganized to explain causal arguing more crisply. A new student example of a causal argument—a researched and documented paper in APA format—is Julee Christianson's "Why Lawrence Summers Was Wrong."

- Chapter 13, "Resemblance Arguments," opens with a new visual case and includes a new example of a resemblance argument: a pro-gay-marriage cartoon with a letter to the editor in response.
- Chapter 14, "Evaluation and Ethical Arguments," opens with a new visual case (an ad for the movie *A Day without a Mexican*) and includes a new Examining Visual Arguments feature on the *Daily Show*.
- Chapter 15, "Proposal Arguments," opens with a visual argument supporting T. Boone Picken's wind farm proposal and includes a new reading: an MLA-format research paper by student Juan Vazquez, "Why the United States Should Adopt Nuclear Power."

Appendix 2, A Concise Guide to Finding, Evaluating, and Documenting Sources
Appendix 2 has been updated to reflect new MLA and APA guidelines for citations. Other local changes include the following:

- The database search illustrations have been updated, as well as the evaluation of a Web site.
- The MLA Quick Reference Guide includes citations based on the new seventh edition of the *MLA Handbook for Writers of Research Papers* (2009).
- The APA Quick Reference Guide includes updated APA documentation based on the *APA Style Guide to Electronic References* (2007).

What Hasn't Changed?

The Distinguishing Features of *Writing Arguments*

Building on earlier success, we have preserved the signature features of earlier editions praised by students, instructors, and reviewers:

- *Focus throughout on writing arguments.* Grounded in composition theory, this text combines explanations of argument with class-tested discussion tasks, exploratory writing tasks, and sequenced writing assignments aimed at developing skills of writing and critical thinking. This text builds students' confidence in their ability to enter the argumentative conversations of our culture, understand diverse points of view, synthesize ideas, and create their own persuasive texts.
- *Equal focus on argument as a rhetorical act, on understanding the real-world occasions for argument, and on appreciating the rhetorical context and genre of arguments.* Focusing on both the reading and the writing of arguments, the text emphasizes the critical thinking that underlies effective arguments, particularly the skills of critical reading, believing and doubting, empathic listening, active exploring and questioning, and negotiating ambiguity and seeking synthesis.

- *Integration of four different approaches to argument.* We blend several basic approaches to argument to help students craft thoughtful and effective arguments: the Toulmin system as a means of invention and analysis of arguments; the enthymeme as a logical structure rooted in the beliefs and values of the audience; the classical concepts of *logos, pathos, ethos,* and *kairos* as persuasive appeals; and stasis theory (called claim-types) as an aid to inventing and structuring arguments through understanding of generic argumentative moves associated with different categories of claims.
- *Numerous "For Class Discussion" exercises and sequenced Writing Assignments designed to teach critical thinking and build argumentative skills.* All For Class Discussion exercises can be used either for whole class discussions or for collaborative group tasks.
- *Effective student and professional arguments used to illustrate argumentative strategies and stimulate discussion, analysis, and debate.* The text includes 11 essays and 30 visual arguments drawn from the public arena and 12 essays and 2 visual arguments done by students.

Our Approaches to Argumentation

Our interest in argumentation grows out of our interest in the relationship between writing and thinking. When writing arguments, writers are forced to lay bare their thinking processes in an unparalleled way, grappling with the complex interplay between inquiry and persuasion, between issue and audience. In an effort to engage students in the kinds of critical thinking that argument demands, we draw on four major approaches to argumentation:

- *The enthymeme as a rhetorical and logical structure.* This concept, especially useful for beginning writers, helps students "nutshell" an argument as a claim with one or more supporting *because* clauses. It also helps them see how real-world arguments are rooted in assumptions granted by the audience rather than in universal and unchanging principles.
- *The three classical types of appeal*—logos, ethos, *and* pathos. These concepts help students place their arguments in a rhetorical context focusing on audience-based appeals; they also help students create an effective voice and style.
- *Toulmin's system of analyzing arguments.* Toulmin's system helps students see the complete, implicit structure that underlies an enthymeme and develop appropriate grounds and backing to support an argument's reasons and warrants. It also highlights the rhetorical, social, and dialectical nature of argument.
- *Stasis theory concerning types of claims.* This approach stresses the heuristic value of learning different patterns of support for different types of claims and often leads students to make surprisingly rich and full arguments.

Throughout the text, these approaches are integrated and synthesized into generative tools for both producing and analyzing arguments.

Structure of the Text

The text has four main parts and two appendixes. Part One gives an overview of argumentation with an initial focus on argument as inquiry and truth seeking. These first two chapters present our philosophy of argument, showing how argument helps writers clarify their own thinking and connect with the values and beliefs of a questioning audience. By emphasizing argument as a community's search for the best solution to a problem, we invite students to enter arguments with an open mind rather than with their minds already made up. Chapter 2 teaches students to read arguments first by summarizing them fairly (listening) and then by systematically engaging with the writer's ideas through believing and doubting.

Part Two teaches students how to write arguments by applying key principles. Chapters 3 through 5 show that the core of an effective argument is a claim with reasons. These reasons are often stated as enthymemes, the unstated premise of which must sometimes be brought to the surface and supported. In effective arguments, the reasons are audience-based so that the argument proceeds from underlying beliefs, values, or assumptions held by the intended audience. Discussion of Toulmin logic shows students how to discover both the stated and unstated premises of their arguments and how to provide audience-based structures of reasons and evidence to support them. Chapter 6 focuses on *ethos, pathos,* and *kairos* as means of persuasion, while Chapter 7 focuses on strategies for accommodating arguments to different kinds of audiences from sympathetic to neutral to hostile.

Part Three focuses on analyzing arguments. Chapter 8 teaches students to do a rhetorical analysis of a written argument. Chapter 9 focuses on the theory and practice of visual arguments—both images and quantitative data—giving students the tools for analyzing visual arguments and for creating their own.

Part Four discusses five different types of argument: definitional arguments, causal arguments, resemblance arguments, evaluation arguments including ethics, and proposal arguments. These chapters introduce students to recurring strategies of argument that cut across the different category types:

- Criteria-match arguing, in which the writer establishes criteria for making a judgment and argues whether a specific case does or does not meet those criteria
- Causal arguing, in which the writer shows that one event or phenomenon can be linked to others in a causal chain
- Resemblance arguing, in which the writer uses analogy or precedent to shape the writer's view of a phenomenon
- Proposal arguing, in which the writer identifies a problem, presents a proposed solution, and justifies that solution, often using a hybrid of criteria-match, causal, or resemblance strategies.

The appendixes provide important supplemental information useful for courses in argument. Appendix 1 gives an overview of informal fallacies while Appendix 2 presents a concise guide to finding, evaluating, and documenting research sources.

Writing Assignments

The text provides a variety of sequenced Writing Assignments.

- In Part One, the Writing Assignment options are an argument summary or an exploratory essay.
- Part Two includes as options a "supporting-reasons" argument (with earlier scaffolding assignments), a classical argument, a delayed-thesis or Rogerian argument, and an advocacy ad. It also includes "microthemes" for practicing basic argumentative moves (for example, supporting a reason with evidence).
- In Part Three, the Writing Assignment options are a rhetorical analysis of a written argument and a rhetorical analysis of a visual argument.
- Each chapter in Part Four on claim types includes a Writing Assignment option based on the claim type covered in the chapter. (Chapter 15 includes a practical proposal assignment, a researched policy proposal assignment, and an advocacy poster.)

The Instructor's Manual

The Instructor's Manual is written by Tim N. Taylor of Eastern Illinois University. New to the Instructor's Manual are nine detailed sample writing assignments. In addition, the Instructor's Manual has the following features:

- Discussion of planning decisions an instructor must make in designing an argument course: for example, how to use readings, how much to emphasize Toulmin or claim-type theory; how much time to build into the course for invention, peer review of drafts, and other writing instruction; and how to select and sequence assignments.
- Three detailed syllabi showing how *Writing Arguments* can support a variety of course structures and emphases:

   Syllabus #1: This course emphasizes argumentative skills and strategies, uses readings for rhetorical analysis, and asks students to write on issues drawn from their own interests and experience.

   Syllabus #2: This more rigorous course works intensely with the logical structure of argument, the classical appeals, the Toulmin schema, and claim-type theory. It uses readings for rhetorical analysis and for an introduction to the argumentative controversies that students will address in their papers.

   Syllabus #3: This course asks students to experiment with genres of argument (for example, op-ed pieces, visual arguments, white papers, and researched freelance or scholarly arguments) and focuses on students' choice of issues and claim-types.

- For instructors who include Toulmin, an independent, highly teachable introductory lesson on the Toulmin schema, and an additional exercise giving students practice using Toulmin to generate argument frames.

- For new instructors, a helpful discussion of how to sequence writing assignments and how to use a variety of collaborative tasks in the classroom to promote active learning and critical thinking.
- Chapter-by-chapter responses to the For Class Discussion exercises.
- Numerous teaching tips and suggestions placed strategically throughout the chapter material, including several sample quizzes asking students to explain and apply argumentative concepts.
- For instructors who teach visual arguments, suggestions for encouraging students to explore how visual arguments have molded public thinking in historical controversies.
- For instructors who like to use student essays in class exercises and discussions, a number of student essays showing how students responded to assignments in the text. Several of these student pieces exemplify stages of revision.

MyCompLab (www.mycomplab.com)

 The new MyCompLab integrates the market-leading instruction, multimedia tutorials, and exercises for writing, grammar, and research that users have come to expect with a new online composing space and new assessment tools. The result is a revolutionary application that offers a seamless and flexible teaching and learning environment built specifically for writers. Created after years of extensive research and in partnership with composition faculty and students across the country, the new MyCompLab provides help for writers in the context of their writing, with instructor and peer commenting functionality; proven tutorials and exercises for writing, grammar, and research; an e-portfolio; an assignment builder; a bibliography tool; tutoring services; and a gradebook and course management organization created specifically for writing classes. Visit www.mycomplab.com for more information.

Acknowledgments

We are happy for this opportunity to give public thanks to the scholars, teachers, and students who have influenced our approach to composition and argument. We want to thank our talented students who contributed their ideas, research, and time to this edition, especially Michael Banks for his researching and writing about illegal immigration in Chapter 2; Mike Bowersox for dialoguing with us on rhetorical analysis and contributing ideas to Chapter 8; Carmen Tieu for her essay on women and violent video games; Julee Christiansen for her APA research paper on the nature/nurture controversy about women and mathematics; and Juan Vazquez for his MLA-researched white paper on nuclear power. Additionally, we are grateful to all our students whom we have been privileged to teach in our writing classes and to our other students who have enabled us to include their arguments in this text. Their insights and growth as writers have inspired our ongoing study of rhetoric and composition.

We thank too the many users of our texts who have given us encouragement about our successes and offered helpful suggestions for improvements. Particularly, we thank the following scholars and teachers who reviewed this revision of *Writing Arguments* in its various stages:

Diane Abdo, The University of Texas at San Antonio; Shavawn M. Berry, Arizona State University; Christine Caver, The University of Texas at San Antonio; Jo Ann Dadisman, West Virginia University; Josh Gehl, San Jose State University; Linda Gladden, University of South Florida; Laura Gray-Rosendale, Northern Arizona University; Joseph Jones, University of Memphis; Sandy Jordan, University of Houston; Brenda S. Martin, Kansas State University; William B. Matta, McLennan Community College; Elizabeth Metzger, University of South Florida; Gary S. Montano, Tarrant County College; Mary Anne Reiss and her students, Elizabethtown Community and Technical College; Jordan Sanderson, Auburn University; Jeffrey Schneider, Saint Louis Community College—Meramec; Ann Spurlock, Mississippi State University; Carl Runyon, Owensboro Community and Technical College; Amy Tomasi, Roger Williams University; and Pat Tyrer, West Texas A&M University.

We are especially grateful to our editor, Lauren Finn, whose keen understanding of the needs of argument instructors and whose commitment to producing the most useful texts have guided us. We appreciate her support and professional expertise. Finally, we owe our deepest thanks to Marion Castellucci, our development editor, without whom we could not maintain the pace and quality of our textbook revisions. Marion's invaluable mastery of both the big picture and specific dimensions of this work and her calmness, encouragement, and wit have shepherded this project at every point.

As always, we want to conclude by thanking our families. John Bean thanks his wife, Kit, also a professional composition teacher, and his children, Matthew, Andrew,

Stephen, and Sarah, who have grown to adulthood since he first began writing textbooks. June Johnson thanks her husband, Kenneth Bube, a mathematics professor and researcher, and her daughter, Jane Ellen Bube, now completing her high school experience. Ken and Janie have played major roles in the ongoing family analysis of argumentation in the public sphere and of specific arguments on wide-ranging issues. They have also made it possible for her to meet the demands and challenges of continuing to infuse new ideas and material into this text in each revision.

John D. Ramage
John C. Bean
June Johnson

PART ONE
Overview of Argument

These stills from the film *Under the Same Moon* (2007) depict the painful separation and longing for connection of an immigrant mother in the United States and her young son, Carlitos, left behind in Mexico. The telephone booth and the furtive, precious calls symbolize the plight of families divided by economics and immigration policy. The film's appeals to our emotions are discussed in Michael Banks' exploratory essay in Chapter 2, pages 37–42.

1 Argument
An Introduction

At the outset of a book on argument, we ought to explain what an argument is. Instead, we're going to explain why no universally accepted definition is possible. Over the centuries, philosophers and rhetoricians have disagreed about both the meaning of the term and the goals that arguers should set for themselves. Our goal in this opening chapter is to introduce you to some of these controversies as well as to various ways of thinking about argument as a way of helping you become a more powerful arguer.

We begin by asking what we mean by argument, suggesting what argument *isn't* as well as what it is. We then discuss three defining features of argument: It requires writers or speakers to justify their claims, it is both a product and a process, and it combines elements of truth seeking and persuasion. Next, we explore more deeply the relationship between truth seeking and persuasion by asking questions about the nature of "truth" that arguments seek. Finally, we give you an example of a successful arguing process.

What Do We Mean by Argument?

Let's begin by rejecting two popular synonyms for "argument": *fight* and *debate*.

Argument Is Not a Fight or a Quarrel

The word *argument* often connotes anger, as when we say, "I just got in a huge argument with my roommate!" We may picture heated disagreements, rising pulse rates, and slamming doors. We may conjure up images of shouting talk-show guests or fist-banging speakers.

But to our way of thinking, argument doesn't necessarily imply anger. In fact, arguing can be pleasurable. It can be a creative and productive activity that engages our minds and our hearts in conversations with people we respect about ideas that we cherish. For your primary image of argument, we invite you to think not of a shouting match on cable news but of a small group of reasonable people seeking the best solution to a problem. We will return to this image throughout the chapter.

Argument Is Not Pro-Con Debate

Another popular conception of argument is debate—a presidential debate, perhaps, or a high school or college debate tournament, in which, according to one popular dictionary, "opposing speakers defend and attack a given proposition." Although formal debates can develop our critical thinking powers, they stress winning and losing, often to the detriment of cooperative inquiry.

To illustrate the limitations of debate, consider one of our former students, a champion high school debater who spent his senior year debating prison reform. Throughout the year he argued for and against such propositions as "The United States should build more prisons" and "We must find innovative alternatives to prison." One day we asked him, "What do you personally think is the best way to reform prisons?" "I don't know," he replied. "I've never thought about it that way."

Nothing in the atmosphere of pro-con debate had engaged this bright, articulate student in the important process of clarifying his own values and taking a personal stand. As we explain throughout this text, argument entails a desire for truth seeking, not necessarily Truth with a capital T but truth as a desire to find the best solutions to complex problems. Arguers' passionate defenses and relentless probings are not moves in a win-lose game but rather moves toward discovering and promoting the best belief or best course of action.

Arguments Can Be Explicit or Implicit

Before proceeding to some defining features of argument, we should note that arguments can be either explicit or implicit. An *explicit* argument directly states its controversial claim and supports it with reasons and evidence. An *implicit* argument, in contrast, may not look like an argument at all: It may be a bumper sticker, a billboard, a poster, a photograph, a cartoon, a vanity license plate, a slogan on a T-shirt, an advertisement, a poem, or a song lyric. But like an explicit argument, it persuades its audience toward a certain point of view.

Consider the striking photograph in Figure 1.1—a baby wearing a bib labeled "POISON." This photograph enters a conversation about the safety of toys and other baby products sold in the United States, prompted in part by the discovery that a substance used to make plastics pliable and soft—*phthalates* (pronounced "thalates")—may be harmful. Phthalates have been shown to interfere with hormone production in rat fetuses and, based on other rodent studies, may produce cancers and other ailments. Because many baby products contain phthalates—bibs, edges of cribs, rubber duckies, and other soft rubbery toys—parents worry that babies can ingest phthalates by chewing on these items.

The photograph of the baby and bib makes the argumentative claim that baby products are poisonous; the photograph implicitly urges viewers to take action against phthalates. But this photograph is just one voice in a surprisingly complex conversation. Is the bib in fact poisonous? Such questions were debated during a recent campaign to ban the sale of toys containing phthalates in California. A legislative initiative sparked

FIGURE 1.1 Baby and bib

intense lobbying from both child-advocacy groups and toy industry representatives. At issue were a number of scientific questions about the risk posed by phthalates. To what extent do studies on rats apply to humans? How much exposure to phthalates should be considered dangerous? Experiments on rats used large amounts of phthalates—amounts that, according to many scientists, far exceed anything a baby could absorb by chewing on a toy. Another issue raised was the level of health risks a free market society should be willing to tolerate. A U.S. agency generally doesn't ban a substance unless it has been *proven* harmful to humans, not merely suspected of being harmful. In defense of free markets, the toy and chemical industries accused opponents of phthalates of using "junk science" to produce scary—but inaccurate—data.

Our point in summarizing the toxic toy controversy is to demonstrate the persuasive roles of both implicit and explicit arguments. The "Trouble in Toyland" poster in Figure 1.2 is an example of an implicit argument, and the letter on page 5 by Dr. Louis W. Sullivan, Secretary of Health and Human Services under the Clinton administration, makes an explicit argument. Sullivan opposes the bill banning phthalates, claiming that scientific agencies charged with public safety haven't found phthalates harmful. Instead, he supports an alternative "green chemistry initiative" that would make public policy decisions based on "facts, not fear."

FIGURE 1.2 Implicit arguments (the toys and poster) against phthalates

Let the Facts Decide, Not Fear: Ban AB 1108

LOUIS W. SULLIVAN, M.D.

Dear Governor Schwarzenegger:

As a physician and public servant who has worked in the field of medicine and public health all my life, I am writing to urge your veto of AB 1108, a bill that would ban the use of compounds used to make vinyl toys and childcare products soft and flexible. AB 1108 widely misses the mark on the most fundamental underpinning of all good public health policy—sound science.

AB 1108 ignores a recent, comprehensive review of the safety of vinyl toys conducted by the U.S. Consumer Product Safety Commission. The CPSC took a long, hard look at the primary softener used in children's toys and concluded that vinyl toys containing this compound are safe as used. In fact, its experts warned that using substitutes could make toys more brittle and less safe.

The CPSC's conclusions are reinforced by the findings of many scientific bodies around the globe—including the European Union's European Chemicals Bureau, the U.S. National Toxicology Program, and the U.S. Centers for Disease Control and Prevention. At a time when public officials are trying to deal with the serious issue of lead paint in toys imported from China, California lawmakers should not confuse the safety of these soften-ing compounds in vinyl toys with that issue. Signing AB 1108 will do nothing to resolve the lead paint in toys issue.

California needs public health policies based on science. That's why I resoundingly support your Green Chemistry Initiative. This is a coordinated, comprehensive strategy for addressing possible risk from products—in a holistic, science-based fashion—that would serve the interests of California families and their children.

5   I urge you to reject AB 1108 and allow your health and safety experts, not legislators, to make judgments about the chemicals in our environment—based on facts, not fear.

Sincerely,

Louis W. Sullivan, M.D.
U.S. Secretary of Health & Human Services 1989-1993
President Emeritus, Morehouse School of Medicine

■ ■ ■   **FOR CLASS DISCUSSION**   **Implicit and Explicit Arguments**

Any argument, whether implicit or explicit, tries to influence the audience's stance on an issue, moving the audience toward the arguer's claim. Arguments work on us cognitively and psychologically, triggering emotions as well as thoughts and ideas. How would you describe the differences in the way that the toy poster and the letter from Sullivan "work on us"?   ■ ■ ■

The Defining Features of Argument

We turn now to examine arguments in more detail. (Unless we say otherwise, by *argument* we mean explicit arguments that attempt to supply reasons and evidence to support their claims.) This section examines three defining features of such arguments.

Argument Requires Justification of Its Claims

To begin defining argument, let's turn to a humble but universal site of disagreement: the conflict between a parent and a teenager over rules. In what way and in what circum-stances do such conflicts constitute arguments?

Consider the following dialogue:

YOUNG PERSON (*racing for the front door while putting coat on*):   Bye. See you later.

PARENT: Whoa! What time are you planning on coming home?

YOUNG PERSON (*coolly, hand still on doorknob*):   I'm sure we discussed this earlier. I'll be home around two A.M. (*the second sentence, spoken very rapidly, is barely audible.*)

PARENT (*mouth tightening*):   We did *not* discuss this earlier, and you're *not* staying out till two in the morning. You'll be home at twelve.

At this point in the exchange, we have a quarrel, not an argument. Quarrelers exchange antagonistic assertions without any attempt to support them rationally. If the dialogue never gets past the "Yes-you-will/No-I-won't" stage, it either remains a quarrel or degenerates into a fight.

Let us say, however, that the dialogue takes the following turn:

YOUNG PERSON (*tragically*):   But I'm *sixteen years old!*

Now we're moving toward argument. Not, to be sure, a particularly well-developed or cogent one, but an argument all the same. It's now an argument because one of the quarrelers has offered a reason for her assertion. Her choice of curfew is satisfactory, she says, *because* she is sixteen years old.

The parent can now respond in one of several ways that will either advance the argument or turn it back into a quarrel. The parent can simply invoke parental authority ("I don't care—you're still coming home at twelve"), in which case the argument ceases. Or the parent can provide a reason for his or her view ("You will be home at twelve because your dad and I pay the bills around here!"), in which case the argument takes a new turn.

So far we've established two necessary conditions that must be met before we're willing to call something an argument: (1) a set of two or more conflicting assertions and (2) the attempt to resolve the conflict through an appeal to reason. But good argument demands more than meeting these two formal requirements. For an argument to be effective, the arguer must clarify and support the reasons presented.

For example, "But I'm sixteen years old!" is not yet a clear support for the assertion "I should be allowed to set my own curfew." On the surface, Young Person's argument seems absurd. Her parent, of all people, knows precisely how old she is. What makes it an argument is that behind her claim lies an unstated assumption—all sixteen-year-olds are old enough to set their own curfews. What Young Person needs to do now is to support that assumption.* In doing so, she must anticipate the sorts of questions the assumption will raise in the minds of her parent: What is the legal status of sixteen-year-olds? How psychologically mature, as opposed to chronologically mature, is Young Person? What is the actual track record of Young Person in being responsible? Each of these questions will force Young Person to reexamine and clarify her assumptions about the proper degree of autonomy for sixteen-year-olds. And her response to those questions should in turn force the parents to reexamine their assumptions about the dependence of sixteen-year-olds on parental guidance and wisdom. (Likewise, the parents will need to show why "paying the bills around here" automatically gives them the right to set Young Person's curfew.)

As the argument continues, Young Person and Parent may shift to a different line of reasoning. For example, Young Person might say: "I should be allowed to stay out until two A.M. because all my friends get to stay out that late." (Here the unstated assumption is that the rules in this family ought to be based on the rules in other families.) The parent might in turn respond, "But I certainly never stayed out that

---

*In Chapter 4 we will call the assumption underlying a line of reasoning its *warrant.*

late when I was your age"—an argument assuming that the rules in this family should follow the rules of an earlier generation.

As Young Person and Parent listen to each other's points of view (trying to figure out why their initial arguments are unpersuasive), both parties find themselves in the uncomfortable position of having to examine their own beliefs and to justify assumptions that they have taken for granted. Here we encounter one of the earliest senses of the term *to argue,* which is "to clarify." In response to her audience's failure to understand or assent to her view, the arguer must reshape her argument to help her audience "see" her position. In the process she may, perhaps for the first time, come to understand that position herself. Thus Young Person might recast her argument so that it relates more directly to her parent's values:

> I should be allowed to stay out until two A.M. on a trial basis because I need enough space to demonstrate my maturity and show you I won't get into trouble.

The assumption underlying this argument is that it is good to give teenagers freedom to demonstrate their maturity. Because this reason is likely to appeal to her parent's values (the parent wants the daughter to mature) and because it is tempered by the qualifier "on a trial basis" (which reduces some of the threat of Young Person's initial demands), it may prompt productive discussion.

Whether or not Young Person and Parent can work out the best solution, the preceding scenario illustrates how argument leads people to clarify their reasons and provide justifications that can be examined rationally. The scenario also illustrates two specific aspects of argument that we will explore in detail in the next sections: (1) Argument is both a process and a product. (2) Argument combines truth seeking and persuasion.

Argument Is Both a Process and a Product

In the preceding scenario, argument functioned as a *process* whereby two or more parties sought the best solution to a question or problem. But if we stopped the process at a given moment and looked at each person's contribution to the conversation, these contributions would be *products.* In an informal discussion, these products usually are brief, comprising a few sentences. In a more formal setting, such as an open-mike discussion of a campus issue or a PowerPoint presentation at a business meeting, the oral argument might be considerably longer.

Written versions of informal conversations occur online among bloggers or members of chat groups. These messages usually are short and informal, albeit more carefully crafted than real-time oral rejoinders. And as these discussions (or *threads*) play out over several days, you may well see participants' ideas shift and evolve as they negotiate some sort of collectively agreeable view, or perhaps a simple truce.

Written versions of formal speeches may take the form of an academic argument for a college course; a grant proposal; a guest op-ed* piece; a legal brief; a letter to a

---

*Op-ed stands for "opposite-editorial." It is the generic name in journalism for signed arguments that voice the writer's opinion on an issue, as opposed to news stories, which are supposed to report events objectively.

member of Congress; or an article for an organizational newsletter, popular magazine, or professional journal. In such instances, the written argument (a product) enters a conversation (a process)—in this case, a conversation of readers, many of whom will carry on the conversation by writing their own responses or by discussing the writer's views with others.

Argument Combines Truth Seeking and Persuasion

In producing her argument, the writer will find herself continually moving back and forth between truth seeking and persuasion—that is, between questions about the subject matter (What is the best solution to this problem?) and about audience (What reasons and evidence best speak to my audience's values?). Back and forth she'll weave, alternately absorbed in the subject matter of her argument and in the persuasiveness of her argument to her audience.

Rarely is either focus ever completely ignored, but their relative importance shifts during different phases of the argument's development. We could thus place "concern for truthfulness" at one end of a continuum and "concern for persuasiveness" at the other, and fit any argument somewhere along that continuum (see Figure 1.3). At the far truth-seeking end might be an exploratory piece that lays out several alternative approaches to a problem and weighs the strengths and weaknesses of each. At the other end of the continuum would be outright propaganda, such as a political campaign advertisement that reduces a complex issue to sound bites. (At its most blatant, propaganda obliterates truth seeking; it will do anything, including distorting or inventing evidence, to win over an audience.) In the middle ranges of the continuum, writers shift their focuses back and forth between truth seeking and persuasion but with varying degrees of emphasis.

To illustrate the need for a shifting focus, consider the case of Kathleen who, in her college argument course, addressed the definitional question "Should American Sign Language meet the university's foreign language requirement?" Kathleen had taken two years of ASL at a community college. When she transferred to a four-year college, her ASL proficiency was dismissed by the foreign language department chair. "ASL isn't a 'language,'" he said summarily. "It's not equivalent to learning French, German, or Japanese."

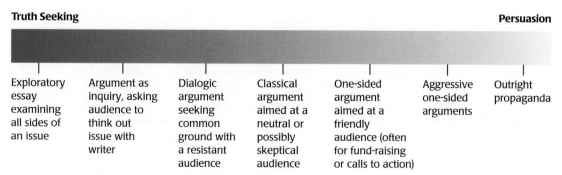

FIGURE 1.3 Continuum of arguments from truth seeking to persuasion

Kathleen disagreed and immersed herself in her argument. In her initial research she focused almost entirely on subject matter, searching for what linguists, neurologists, cognitive psychologists, and sociologists had said about ASL. She was only tacitly concerned with her audience, whom she mostly envisioned as her classmates and those sympathetic to her view. She wrote a well-documented paper, citing several scholarly articles, that made a good case to her classmates (and her professor) that ASL is indeed a distinct language.

Proud of the big red A the professor had placed on her paper, Kathleen decided for a subsequent assignment to write a second paper on ASL—but this time aimed it directly at the chair of foreign languages, petitioning him to accept her ASL proficiency for the foreign language requirement. Now her writing task falls closer to the persuasive end of our continuum. Kathleen once again immersed herself in research, but this time focused not on subject matter—whether or not ASL is a distinct language—but on audience. She researched the history of the foreign language requirement at her college and discovered some of the politics behind it. She also interviewed foreign language teachers to find out what they knew and didn't know about ASL. She discovered that many teachers thought ASL was "easy to learn" and would allow students to avoid the rigors of a "real" foreign language class. Additionally, she learned that foreign language teachers valued immersing students in a foreign culture; in fact, the foreign language requirement was part of her college's effort to create a multicultural curriculum.

This new understanding of her target audience helped Kathleen reconceptualize her argument. Her claim that ASL was a real language (the subject of her first paper) became only one section of her second paper, much condensed and abridged. She added sections showing (1) that learning ASL is difficult (to counter her audience's belief that learning ASL was easy), (2) that the deaf community formed a distinct culture with its own customs and literature (to show how ASL met the goals of multiculturalism), and (3) that the number of transfer students with ASL credits would be negligible (to allay fears that accepting ASL would threaten enrollments in language classes). She ended her argument with an appeal to her college's emphasis—declared in its mission statement—on eradicating social injustice and reaching out to the oppressed. She described the isolation of deaf people in a world where almost no hearing people learn ASL, and she argued that the deaf community on her campus could be integrated more fully into campus life if more students could "talk" with them. Thus all the ideas included in her new argument—the reasons selected, the evidence used, the arrangement and tone—were determined by her primary focus on persuasion.

Our point, then, is that all along the continuum writers are concerned with truth seeking and persuasion, but not necessarily with equal balance. Kathleen could not have written her second paper—aimed specifically at persuading the chair of the foreign language department—if she hadn't first immersed herself in truth-seeking research that convinced her that ASL is indeed a distinct language. Neither paper was better than the other; both fulfilled their purposes and met the needs of their intended audiences. Both involved truth seeking and persuasion, but the first focused primarily on subject matter and the second on audience.

Argument and the Problem of Truth

The tension that we have just examined between truth seeking and persuasion raises an ancient issue in the field of argument: Is the arguer's first obligation to truth or to winning the argument? And just what is the nature of the truth to which arguers are supposed to be obligated?

In Plato's famous dialogues from ancient Greek philosophy, these questions were at the heart of Socrates' disagreement with the Sophists. The Sophists were professional rhetoricians who specialized in training orators to win arguments. Socrates, who valued truth seeking over persuasion and believed that truth could be discovered through philosophic inquiry, opposed the Sophists. For Socrates, Truth resided in the ideal world of forms, and through philosophic rigor humans could transcend the changing, shadowlike world of everyday reality to perceive the world of universals where Truth, Beauty, and Goodness resided. Through his method of questioning his interlocutors, Socrates would gradually peel away layer after layer of false views until Truth was revealed. The good person's duty, Socrates believed, was not to win an argument but to pursue this higher Truth. Socrates distrusted rhetoricians because they were interested only in the temporal power and wealth that came from persuading audiences to the orator's views.

Let's apply Socrates' disagreement with the Sophists to a modern instance. Suppose your community is divided over the issue of raising environmental standards versus keeping open a job-producing factory that doesn't meet new guidelines for waste discharge. The Sophists would train you to argue any side of this issue on behalf of any lobbying group willing to pay for your services. If, however, you followed the spirit of Socrates, you would be inspired to listen to all sides of the dispute, peel away false arguments, discover the Truth through reasonable inquiry, and commit yourself to a Right Course of Action.

But what is the nature of Truth or Right Action in a dispute between jobs and the environment? The Sophists believed that truth was determined by those in power; thus they could enter an argument unconstrained by any transcendent beliefs or assumptions. When Socrates talked about justice and virtue, they could reply contemptuously that these were fictitious concepts invented by the weak to protect themselves from the strong. Over the years, the Sophists' relativist beliefs were so repugnant to people that the term *sophistry* became synonymous with trickery in argument.

However, in recent years the Sophists' critique of a transcendent Universal Truth has been taken seriously by many philosophers, sociologists, and other thinkers who doubt Socrates' confident belief that arguments, properly conducted, necessarily arrive at a single Truth. For these thinkers, as for the Sophists, there are often different degrees of truth and different kinds of truths for different situations or cultures. From this perspective, when we consider questions of interpretation or value, we can never demonstrate that a belief or assumption is true—not through scientific observation, not through reason, and not through religious revelation. We get our beliefs, according to these contemporary thinkers, from the shared assumptions of our particular cultures. We are condemned (or liberated) to live in a pluralistic, multicultural world with competing visions of truth.

If we accept this pluralistic view of the world, do we then endorse the Sophists' radical relativism, freeing us to argue any side of any issue? Or do we doggedly pursue some modern equivalent of Socrates' truth?

Our own sympathies are with Socrates, but we admit to a view of truth that is more tentative, cautious, and conflicted than his. For us, truth seeking does not mean finding the "Right Answer" to a disputed question, but neither does it mean a valueless relativism in which all answers are equally good. For us, truth seeking means taking responsibility for determining the "best answer" or "best solution" to the question for the good of the whole community when taking into consideration the interests of all stakeholders. It means making hard decisions in the face of uncertainty. This more tentative view of truth means that you cannot use argument to "prove" your claim, but only to make a reasonable case for your claim.

To seek truth, then, means to seek the best or most just solution to a problem while observing all available evidence, listening with an open mind to the views of all stakeholders, clarifying and attempting to justify your own values and assumptions, and taking responsibility for your argument. It follows that truth seeking often means delaying closure on an issue, acknowledging the pressure of alternative views, and being willing to change one's mind. Seen in this way, learning to argue effectively has the deepest sort of social value: It helps communities settle conflicts in a rational and humane way by finding, through the dialectic exchange of ideas, the best solutions to problems without resorting to violence or to other assertions of raw power.

■ ■ ■ **FOR CLASS DISCUSSION** **Role-Playing Arguments**

As the following newspaper excerpt shows, social networking Web sites such as MySpace and Facebook create conflicts between free speech and the reputations of persons and institutions in the public domain.

> College students across the country have been cited or disciplined for content they posted on social networking Web sites such as MySpace and Facebook, including such things as criticism of a student government candidate (at the University of Central Florida), complaints about the theater department (Cowley College in Kansas) or vulgar comments about a teaching assistant (Syracuse).
>
> "College administrators are very nervous about this huge new forum," said Greg Lukianoff, president of the Foundation for Individual Rights in Education.
>
> The most nervous of those might be coaches and athletic directors, whose student-athletes are under a more intense public spotlight than the general student body and who usually are required to adhere to more stringent policies and rules of conduct. One distasteful picture of a prominent football player on the Internet could be seen by anybody and might end up on the front page of a newspaper. It's why some athletic departments have stricter policies about such sites and restrict usage as part of individual team rules.

Your task: Imagine holding a campus meeting on the issue of students' free speech rights versus the rights of your college/university and its officials to establish rules and monitor students' online social network pages. You and your classmates play the following roles: (a) a student athlete who has been warned to remove from his Facebook profile a photograph of himself chugging beer at a fraternity party; (b) students who are not on athletic teams but are concerned about institutionally imposed restrictions on students' freedom; (c) a faculty member who feels he has been slandered on a former student's MySpace page; (d) a women's basketball coach who forbids her athletes from having personal online social networking accounts; (e) a tennis coach who establishes clear team policies for postings on students' sites; (f) the athletic director, who is considering buying tracking technology to monitor athletes' online social networking pages; (g) a representative of the American Civil Liberties Union, who supports student rights and free speech; (h) the Dean of Students who is concerned for the reputation of the institution and for the future well-being of students who might be embarrassed by current postings or endangered by disclosing too much personal information.

For additional writing, reading, and research resources, go to www.mycomplab.com.

2 Argument as Inquiry
Reading and Exploring

In the previous chapter, we explained that argument is both a process and a product, both inquiry and persuasion. In this chapter, we focus on inquiry as the entry point into argumentative conversations. How can argument's role as a community's search for the best answers to disputed questions be emphasized? How can arguers participate in a "mingling of minds" and use argument productively to seek answers to problems?

We believe that the best way to reinvigorate argument is to approach the reading and writing of arguments as an exploratory process. To do so means to position ourselves as inquirers as well as persuaders, engaging thoughtfully with alternative points of view, truly listening to other perspectives, examining our own values and assumptions, and perhaps even changing our views. Rhetorician Wayne Booth proposes that when we enter an argumentative conversation we should first ask "When should I change my mind?" rather than "How can I change your mind?"*

In this chapter, we present some practical strategies for reading and exploring arguments in an open-minded and sophisticated way. You will learn to play what rhetorician Peter Elbow calls the believing and doubting game in which a thinker systematically stretches her thinking by willing herself to believe positions that she finds threatening and to doubt positions that she instinctively accepts.† The thinker's goal is to live with questions, to acknowledge uncertainty and complexity, and to resist settling for simple or quick answers. In this chapter, the main exploratory strategies that we propose are these:

- Using a variety of means to find complex, puzzling issues to explore
- Placing a text in its rhetorical context
- Reading to believe an argument's claims
- Reading to doubt an argument's claims
- Thinking dialectically

In this chapter, we show how one student, Michael Banks, jumped into the puzzling, complex problem of illegal immigration and used these strategies to guide his thoughtful exploration of various viewpoints and texts.

---

*Wayne Booth raised these questions in a featured session with Peter Elbow titled "Blind Skepticism vs. the Rhetoric of Assent: Implications for Rhetoric, Argument, and Teaching" at the CCCC Convention, Chicago, Illinois, March 2002.
†Peter Elbow, *Writing without Teachers* (New York: Oxford University Press, 1973), 147–90.

Finding Issues to Explore

The mechanisms by which you enter a controversy will vary, but most likely they will include reflecting on your experiences or reading. Typically, the process goes like this: Through reading or talking with friends, you encounter a contested issue on which you are undecided or a viewpoint with which you disagree. Your curiosity, confusion, or concern then prompts you to learn more about the issue and to determine your own stance. In this section, we examine some strategies you can use to find issues worth exploring.

Do Some Initial Brainstorming

As a first step, make an inventory of issues that interest you. Many of the ideas you develop may become subject matter for arguments that you will write later in this course.

Brainstorming Issues to Explore

What You Can Do	How It Works
Make an inventory of the communities to which you belong. Think about classroom communities; clubs and organizations; residence hall, apartment, neighborhood, or family communities; church/synagogue or work communities; communities related to your hobbies or avocations; your city, state, region, nation, and world communities.	Since arguments arise out of disagreements within communities, you often can think of issues for argument by beginning with a list of the communities to which you belong. Possible prompts to stimulate thinking: ▦ People in this community are always arguing about _____. ▦ Within my work community, Person X believes _____; however, this view troubles me because _____.
Identify controversies within those communities. Think both big and small: ▦ Big issue in world community: What is the best way to prevent destruction of rain forests? ▦ Small issue in dorm community: Should quiet hours be enforced?	To stimulate thinking, use prompts such as these: ▦ Something that really makes me mad about this campus (my apartment life, city government, our society) is _____. ▦ In a recent dorm meeting, I didn't know where I stood on _____. ▦ The situation at _____ could be improved if _____.
Narrow your list to a handful of issues for which you don't have a position; share it with classmates. Identify a few issues you would like to explore more deeply. When you share with classmates, add their issues to yours.	Sharing your list with classmates stimulates more thinking and encourages conversations. The more you explore your views with others, the more ideas you will develop. Good writing grows out of good talking.

(Continued)

What You Can Do	How It Works
Brainstorm a network of related issues. Any given issue is always embedded in a network of other issues. To see how open-ended and fluid an argumentative conversation can be, try connecting one of your issues to a network of other issues including subissues and side issues.	Brainstorm questions that compel you to look at an issue in a variety of ways. For example, if you explored the controversy over whether toys with phthalates should be banned (see Chapter 1), you might generate questions such as these about related issues:

- How dangerous are phthalates?
- Is the testing done on rats adequate or accurate for determining the effects on humans?
- To what extent are controversies over phthalates similar to controversies over steroids, genetically modified foods, or mercury in dental fillings?

Once you've made a list, add to it as new ideas strike you and return to it each time you are given a new argumentative assignment.

Be Open to the Issues All around You

We are surrounded by argumentative issues. Once you get attuned to them, you'll start noticing them everywhere. You will be invited into argumentative conversations by posters, bumper stickers, blog sites, newspaper editorial pages, magazine articles, the sports section, movie reviews, song lyrics, and so forth. When you read or listen, watch for "hot spots"—passages or moments that evoke strong agreement, disagreement, or confusion. To illustrate how arguments are all around us, try the following exercise on the issue of illegal immigration.

■ ■ ■ ■ **FOR CLASS DISCUSSION** Responding to Visual Arguments about Immigration
Suppose you encounter some political cartoons on the United States' problems with illegal immigration (see Figures 2.1 and 2.2). Working individually or in small groups, generate exploratory responses to these questions:

1. What claim is each cartoon making?
2. What background information about the problems of illegal immigration do these cartoons assume?
3. What network of issues do these visual texts suggest?
4. What puzzling questions do these visual texts raise for you?

FIGURE 2.1 Political cartoon on immigration and labor

FIGURE 2.2 Political cartoon on immigrant labor

Explore Ideas by Freewriting

Freewriting is useful at any stage of the writing process. When you freewrite, you put fingers to keyboard (or pen to paper) and write rapidly *nonstop*—usually five to ten minutes at a stretch—without worrying about structure, grammar, or correctness. Your goal is to generate as many ideas as possible without stopping to edit your work. If you can't think of anything to say, write "relax" or "I'm stuck" over and over until new ideas emerge. Here is how Michael Banks did a freewrite in response to the cartoon in Figure 2.1.

Michael's Freewrite

At first when I looked at this cartoon I didn't quite see what it meant. I understood the wall keeping immigrants out, but I didn't connect the $20 minimum wage to the wall. OK. Now I see. The argument is that if the United States raised the minimum wage to $20/hour, then Americans would be willing to do the job that Mexicans now do much cheaper. But that seems to really sidestep the entire issue surrounding immigrant labor—sure, there'd be a lot more Americans willing to work harder if they were earning $20 an hour and getting benefits, but it isn't as if there are a bunch of contractors out there who'd rather pay that than hire an immigrant worker, under the table, for much cheaper. The problem isn't finding someone to work, it's finding someone to work for substandard wages who's still motivated to work hard and for long hours. Hmmm. Relax relax relax relax. I'm really puzzled by the immigration question. I can remember growing up in Southern California that a lot of the low pay work was done by Mexicans. I was in a high school service group that took free lunches to immigrants waiting for work in front of a Home Depot. They would take any kind of job at really low pay, and they seemed like really nice people. Why won't our homeless people or unemployed people in the United States take these low pay jobs? Relax relax. I don't really know whether I agree with the cartoon that it would be best to force immigrants out of the country, but I'm fairly certain that raising the minimum wage for legal workers to $20.00 isn't the way to go about it because that would drive up the price of goods so much nobody could afford to buy anything and the economy would come to a halt. Immigrants are willing to work, hard, for much less than the proposal in the cartoon. They benefit by making more money than they could make in Mexico and Americans benefit by lower prices. Also, the image of the wall raises concerns of mine—I'm aware of organizations like the Border Fence Project that are all about walling off the entire southern border of the country, but it seems like a really ineffective way to enforce the border. I wonder whose "crazy fantasy" this cartoon really depicts.

Explore Ideas by Idea Mapping

Another good technique for exploring ideas is *idea mapping*. When you make an idea map, draw a circle in the center of the page and write some trigger idea—a broad topic, a question, or working thesis statement—in the center of the circle. Then record your ideas on branches and subbranches extending from the center circle. That's a major advantage of "picturing" your thoughts; you can see them as part of an emerging design rather than as strings of unrelated ideas.

Idea maps usually generate more ideas, though less well-developed ones, than freewrites. Figure 2.3 shows an idea map that student Michael Banks created on the issue of illegal immigration after class discussion of the cartoons in Figures 2.1 and 2.2.

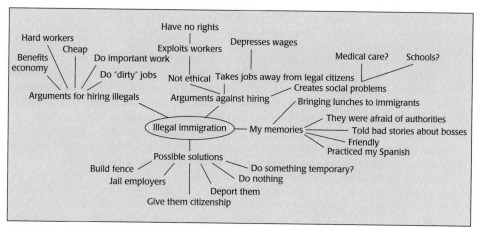

FIGURE 2.3 Michael's Idea Map

Explore Ideas by Playing the Believing and Doubting Game

The believing and doubting game, a term coined by rhetorician Peter Elbow, is an excellent way to imagine views different from your own and to anticipate responses to those views.

- **As a believer, your role is to be wholly sympathetic to an idea.** You must listen carefully to it and suspend all disbelief. You must identify all the ways in which the idea might appeal to different audiences and all the reasons for believing the idea. The believing game can be difficult, even frightening, if you are asked to believe an idea that strikes you as false or threatening.
- **As a doubter, your role is to be judgmental and critical, finding fault with an idea.** The doubting game is the opposite of the believing game. You do your best to find counterexamples and inconsistencies that undermine the idea you are examining. Again, it can be threatening to doubt ideas that you instinctively want to believe.

When you play the believing and doubting game with an assertion, simply write two different chunks; one arguing for the assertion (the believing game) and one opposing it (the doubting game). Freewrite both chunks, letting your ideas flow without censoring. Alternatively, make an idea map with believing and doubting branches. The following is how student writer Michael Banks played the believing and doubting game with the assertion: "Employers of illegal immigrants should be jailed."

Michael's Believing and Doubting Game

Believe: If we really want to stop illegal immigration, then we should jail employers who hire illegals. What draws illegal immigrants to this country is the money they can make, so if the government eliminated these jobs by jailing the employers then illegal immigration would stop. This would be just because employers of illegal immigrants benefit by not having to pay a fair wage and what's more they often do this hiring under the table so that they don't pay taxes. They are breaking laws and deserve to go to jail. By avoiding taxes and not providing medical insurance etc., they cost every American taxpayer more, and it is not fair to law abiding citizens. Employers also often exploit immigrant laborers, because they have nobody to be held accountable to. They also lower the wages of American workers. Their actions can cause rifts in communities already troubled by an influx of immigration. Like anybody else who supports illegal activity, employers of illegal immigrants should be jailed. If employers faced charges for hiring illegal immigrants, it seems likely that there would be much less of a market for the services of immigrant workers. I could see this being a more effective way to combat illegal immigration than building fences or trying to deport them all.

Doubt: Jailing employers of illegal immigration probably would stop some people from hiring undocumented immigrants, but I doubt it would be a reliable long-term solution. Especially for people who only hire a few immigrants at a time, it would likely be hard to prosecute them. Besides, I'm not convinced there is anything necessarily wrong with the employer's actions in hiring undocumented immigrants. If the government cannot enforce its own immigration laws, employers shouldn't be forced to do so for them. Many businesses, especially in agriculture, absolutely depend on good workers who will work long hours in hot fields to pick fruit and vegetables. Employers can't possibly be expected to do background checks on every employee. Moreover, if undocumented workers weren't available, the fruit wouldn't get picked. To send the employers to jail would mean to cause horrible disruption to much of our food supply. We are lucky to have these workers. The United States has a long history of people capitalizing on good business opportunities when the opportunity presents itself, and that's just what illegal immigrants are. It does not make sense to jail people for taking advantage of cheap and motivated labor.

Although Michael sees the injustice of paying workers substandard wages, he also realizes that much of our economy depends on this cheap labor. Playing the believing and doubting game has helped him articulate his doubts and see the issue in more complex terms.

■ ■ ■ **FOR CLASS DISCUSSION**   **Playing the Believing and Doubting Game**
Individual task: Choose one or more of the following controversial claims and play the believing and doubting game with it, through either freewriting or idea mapping.
Group task: Working in pairs, in small groups, or as a whole class, share the results with your classmates.

1. A student should report a fellow student who is cheating on an exam or plagiarizing an essay.
2. Women should be assigned to combat duty equally with men.
3. Illegal immigrants already living in the United States should be granted amnesty and placed on a fast track to U.S. citizenship.   ■ ■ ■

Placing Texts in a Rhetorical Context

In the previous section, we suggested strategies for finding issues and entering argumentative conversations. Once you join a conversation, you typically will read a number of different arguments addressing your selected issue. In this section and the ones that follow, we turn to productive strategies for reading arguments. We begin by explaining the importance of analyzing a text's rhetorical context as a preliminary step prior to reading. In subsequent sections, we explain powerful strategies for reading an argument—reading to believe, reading to doubt, and placing texts in conversation with each other through dialectic thinking.

As you read arguments on a controversy, try to place each text within its rhetorical context. It is important to know, for example, whether a blog that you are reading appears on Daily Kos (a liberal blog site) or on Little Green Footballs (a conservative blog site). To help you reconstruct a reading's rhetorical context, you need to understand the genres of argument as well as the cultural and professional contexts that cause people to write arguments. We'll begin with the genres of argument.

Genres of Argument

To situate an argument rhetorically, you should know something about its genre. A *genre* is a recurring type or pattern of argument such as a letter to the editor, a political cartoon, or the home page of an advocacy Web site. Genres often are categorized by recurring features, formats, and style. The genre of any given argument helps determine its length, tone, sentence complexity, level of informality or formality, use of visuals, kinds of evidence, depth of research, and the presence or absence of documentation. When you do your own Internet research, you should be aware of the original genre of the text you are reading: Was this piece originally a newspaper editorial, a blog, an organizational white paper, a scholarly article, a student paper posted to a Web site, or something else?

In the following chart, we identify most of the genres of argument through which readers and writers carry on the conversations of a democracy.

Genres of Argument

Genre	Explanation and Examples	Stylistic Features
Personal correspondence	▨ Letters or e-mail messages ▨ Often sent to specific decision makers (complaint letter, request for an action)	▨ Style can range from a formal business letter to an informal note
Letters to the editor	▨ Published in newspapers and some magazines ▨ Provide forum for citizens to voice views on public issues	▨ Very short and time sensitive ▨ Often focus in "sound bite" style on one point
Newspaper editorials and op-ed pieces	▨ Published on the editorial or op-ed ("opposite-editorial") pages ▨ Editorials promote views of the newspaper owners/editors ▨ Op-ed pieces, written by professional columnists or guest writers, range from ultraconservative to socialist ▨ Often written in response to political events or social problems in the news	▨ Usually short (500–1000 words) ▨ Vary from explicit thesis-driven arguments to implicit arguments with stylistic flair ▨ Have a journalistic style (short paragraphs) without detailed evidence ▨ Sources usually not documented

(Continued)

Genre	Explanation and Examples	Stylistic Features
Articles in public affairs or niche magazines	▪ Usually written by staff writers or freelancers ▪ Appear in public affairs magazines such as *National Review* or *The Progressive* or in niche magazines such as *Rolling Stone* (popular culture), *Minority Business Entrepreneur* (business), or *The Advocate* (gay and lesbian issues) ▪ Often reflect the political point of view of the magazine	▪ Often have a journalistic style with informal documentation ▪ Frequently include narrative elements rather than explicit thesis-and-reasons organization ▪ Often provide well-researched coverage of various perspectives on a public issue
Articles in scholarly journals	▪ Peer-reviewed articles published by nonprofit academic journals subsidized by universities or scholarly societies ▪ Characterized by scrupulous attention to completeness and accuracy in treatment of data	▪ Usually employ a formal academic style ▪ Include academic documentation and bibliographies ▪ May reflect the biases, methods, and strategies associated with a specific school of thought or theory within a discipline
Legal briefs and court decisions	▪ Written by attorneys or judges ▪ "Friend-of-the-court" briefs often are published by stakeholders to influence appeals courts ▪ Court decisions explain the reasoning of justices (often include minority opinions)	▪ Usually written in legalese, but use a logical reasons-and-evidence structure ▪ Friend-of-the-court briefs sometimes are aimed at popular audiences
Organizational white papers	▪ In-house documents or PowerPoint presentations aimed at influencing policy or giving advice to clients ▪ Sometimes written for external audiences to influence public opinion favorable to the organization ▪ External white papers often are posted on Web sites or sent to legislators	▪ Usually desktop or Web published ▪ Often use graphics and visuals ▪ Vary in style from the dully bureaucratic (satirized in *Dilbert* cartoons) to the cogent and persuasive
Blogs and postings to chat rooms and electronic bulletin boards	▪ Web-published commentaries, usually on specific topics and often intended to influence public opinion ▪ Blogs are gaining influence as alternative to the established media ▪ Reflect a wide range of perspectives	▪ Often blend journalism, personal narrative, and formal argument ▪ Often difficult to determine identity, credentials of blogger ▪ Often provide hyperlinks to related sites on the Web

Genre	Explanation and Examples	Stylistic Features
Public affairs advocacy advertisements	▪ Published as posters, fliers, Web pages, or paid advertisements ▪ Condensed verbal/visual arguments aimed at influencing public opinion ▪ Often have explicit bias and ignore alternative views	▪ Use succinct "sound bite" style ▪ Employ document design, bulleted lists, and visual elements (graphics, photographs, or drawings) for rhetorical effect
Advocacy Web sites	▪ Usually identified by the extension ".org" in the Web site address ▪ Often created by well-financed advocacy groups such as the National Rifle Association or People for the Ethical Treatment of Animals ▪ Reflect the bias of the site owner ▪ (For further discussion of reading and evaluating Web sites, see Appendix 2, pp. 281–285)	▪ Often contain many layers with hyperlinks to other sites ▪ Use visuals and verbal text to create an immediate visceral response favorable to the site owner's views ▪ Ethical sites announce their bias and purpose in an "about us" or "Mission Statement" link on the home page
Visual arguments	▪ Political cartoons, usually drawn by syndicated cartoonists ▪ Other visual arguments (photographs, drawings, graphics, ads), usually accompanied by verbal text	▪ Make strong emotional appeals, often reducing complex issues to one powerful perspective (see Chapter 9)
Speeches and PowerPoint presentations	▪ Political speeches, keynote speeches at professional meetings, informal speeches at hearings, interviews, business presentations ▪ Often made available via transcription in newspapers or on Web sites ▪ In business or government, often accompanied by PowerPoint slides	▪ Usually organized clearly with highlighted claim, supporting reasons, and transitions ▪ Accompanying PowerPoint slides designed to highlight structure, display evidence in graphics, mark key points, and sometimes provide humor
Documentary films	▪ Formerly nonfiction reporting, documentary films now range from efforts to document reality objectively to efforts to persuade viewers to adopt the filmmaker's perspective or take action ▪ Usually cost less to make than commercial films and lack special effects ▪ Cover a wide range of issues	▪ Often use extended visual arguments, combined with interviews and voice-overs, to influence as well as inform viewers ▪ The filmmaker's angle of vision may dominate, or his/her perspective and values may be more subtle

Cultural Contexts: Who Writes Arguments and Why?

A democratic society depends on the lively exchange of ideas—people with different points of view creating arguments for their positions. Now that you know something about the genre of arguments, we ask you to consider who writes arguments and why. The following list identifies the wide range of people who are motivated to write arguments.

- *Lobbyists and advocacy groups* commit themselves to a cause—often with passion—and produce avidly partisan arguments aimed at persuading voters, legislators, government agencies, and other decision makers.
- *Legislators, political candidates, and government officials and their staff* do research and write white papers recommending positions on an issue.
- *Business professionals, labor union leaders, and bankers* often try to influence public opinion in ways that support their interests.
- *Lawyers* write briefs supporting their clients' cases. Sometimes lawyers or legal experts not directly connected to a case, particularly law professors, file friend-of-the-court briefs aimed at influencing the decision of judges.
- *Judges* write court opinions explaining their decisions on a case.
- *Media commentators*—like journalists, editorial writers, syndicated columnists, bloggers, and political cartoonists—produce arguments, filtering them through the perspective of their own political views.
- *Professional freelance or staff writers* compose some of the most thoughtful analyses of public issues for public affairs magazines such as *Atlantic Monthly, The Nation, Ms., The National Review, The New Yorker*, and many others.
- *Think tanks* supply statistical studies and in-depth investigation of problems. These think tanks range across the political spectrum, from conservative (the Hoover Institute, the Heritage Foundation) or libertarian (the Cato Institute) to the centrist or liberal (the Brookings Institution, the Pew Foundation, the Economic Policy Institute).
- *Scholars and academics* play a public role through their scholarly research, contributing data, studies, and analyses to public debates.
- *Independent and commercial filmmakers* often reflect on issues of the day; commercial filmmakers often embed arguments within their dramatic storytelling.
- *Citizens and students.* Engaged citizens influence policy through letters, contributions to advocacy Web sites, guest editorials, blogs, and speeches. Students also write for university communities, present their work at undergraduate research conferences, and influence public opinion by writing to political leaders and decision makers.

Analyzing Rhetorical Context and Genre

The background we have just provided about the writers and genres of argument will help you situate arguments in their rhetorical context. When you encounter any argumentative text, whether reprinted in a textbook or retrieved through your own library and Web research, use the following guide questions to analyze its rhetorical context:

Questions about Rhetorical Context and Genre

1. What genre of argument is this? How do the conventions of that genre help determine the depth, complexity, and even appearance of the argument?
2. Who is the author? What are the author's credentials and what is his/her investment in the issue?
3. What audience is he or she writing for?
4. What motivating occasion prompted the writing? The motivating occasion could be a current event, a crisis, pending legislation, a recently published alternative view, or another ongoing problem.
5. What is the author's purpose? The purpose could range from strong advocacy to inquiring truth seeker (analogous to the continuum from persuasion to truth seeking discussed in Chapter 1, p. 9).
6. What information about the publication or source (magazine, newspaper, advocacy Web site) helps explain the writer's perspective or the structure and style of the argument?
7. What is the writer's angle of vision? By angle of vision, we mean the filter, lens, or selective seeing through which the writer is approaching the issue. What is left out in this argument? What does this author not see? (Chapter 5, pp. 74–80, discusses how angle of vision operates in the selection and framing of evidence.)

This rhetorical knowledge becomes important in helping you select a diversity of voices and genres of argument when you are exploring an issue. Note how Michael Banks makes use of his awareness of rhetorical context in his exploratory paper on pages 37–42.

■ ■ ■   **FOR CLASS DISCUSSION**   Placing Readings in Their Rhetorical Context
Find two recent arguments on the illegal immigration issue. Your arguments should (1) represent different genres and (2) represent different kinds of arguers (syndicated newspaper columnists, bloggers, freelance magazine writers, scholars, and so forth). For each argument, answer the "Questions about Rhetorical Context and Genre" above. Then share your findings with classmates.   ■ ■ ■

Reading to Believe an Argument's Claims

Once you have established the rhetorical context of an argument, you are ready to begin reading. We suggest that you read arguments in the spirit of the believing and doubting game, beginning with "believing," in which you practice what psychologist Carl Rogers calls *empathic listening.* Empathic listening requires that you see the world through the author's eyes, temporarily adopt the author's beliefs and values, and suspend your skepticism and biases long enough to hear what the author is saying.

To illustrate what we mean by reading to believe, we will continue with our example of illegal immigration. The following article, "Amnesty?" by Roman Catholic priest and professor of philosophy John F. Kavanaugh, appeared in the March 10, 2008, issue of *America*, a Jesuit publication that describes itself as "the only national Catholic weekly magazine in the United States." Please read this article carefully in preparation for the exercises and examples that follow.

Amnesty?
Let Us Be Vigilant and Charitable
JOHN F. KAVANAUGH

Let's call her María. She was illegally brought into the United States at the age of 2. Now 27, she is a vital member of her parish and has three young children. María was recently deported to Ciudad Juárez, where, in the last 15 years, 600 young women have been kidnapped, raped, murdered and buried in the desert. Luckily, she was able to find a way into the United States, again illegally, to be with her children. If she is discovered again, she will spend five years in a U.S. federal prison.

My Jesuit friend and neighbor, Dick Vogt, has told me of people like María and many others of the 12 to 14 million "undocumented aliens." She is not necessarily typical of the masses who have illegally entered this country. Some, no doubt, are drunks and dealers; many are incarcerated for other crimes than their immigrant status. But most have come at great risk to their lives, because their lives were already at risk from poverty and displacement. They want to make a living, form a family, and help their families back home.

The Catholic bishops of Mexico pointed out in January that the recent surge of immigration is a direct effect of the North American Free Trade Agreement. Open trade, while benefiting the most powerful and technologically advanced, has threatened poor farmers and their small rural communities. They cannot compete with heavily subsidized U.S. and Canadian producers. It is this phenomenon that drives so many to leave their homeland for a livelihood in the United States, despite, as the bishops put it, "its anti-humane immigration program."

The U.S. bishops, witnessing everything from evictions in California to employment raids in Massachusetts, have stirred the consciences of their dioceses and taken stands in conscience of their own. The bishop of Oklahoma City and 10 of his pastors have publicly professed defiance of a punitive state law that makes felons of all who "aid, assist, or transport any undocumented person." The bishops of Missouri have expressed their alarm over politicians "who vie to see who can be tougher on illegal immigrants." Cognizant of the economic pressures on many families in rural Mexico, they call for a more compassionate, fair, and realistic reform of our immigration system, including education and humanitarian assistance to all children, "without regard to legal status."

There has been some resistance to the bishops' proposals and some resentment. It is reminiscent of the outrage directed by anti-immigrant groups toward last year's immigration reform bill, a very harsh measure that they nonetheless condemned for proposing what they called amnesty.

Some of the resentment is understandable. There are householders, especially on the border, who have had their land and yards trashed. Residents of some towns feel flooded with immigrants they cannot engage or manage. A few businesspersons who have refused to hire undocumented or cheaper labor have lost sales and customers.

But this does not explain the seething hostility that can be read in some nativist opinion columns and popular books or heard on radio talk shows: "They are criminals, felons; and that's that."

"They have broken the law." This is an interesting standard of ethics, justice or charity for a nation that sees itself as Judeo-Christian and humane. It is puzzling that we do not think of the Good Samaritan or of the "least of our brothers and sisters" in Matthew 25, or of the passage from Leviticus that the Missouri bishops quote: "The stranger who sojourns with you shall be to you as the native among you, and you shall love him as yourself."

As for making the law our bottom line, do Christians know how many times Jesus was in trouble with the law? Do they know that the natural law tradition, articulated in the work of Thomas Aquinas, holds an unjust law to be no law at all? Do they forget that our nation was founded upon an appeal to a higher law than positive law, an appeal shared by the labor movement, by Martin Luther King Jr., and by Elizabeth Cady Stanton and Susan B. Anthony?

10 A nation has every right to secure its borders. Unrestrained immigration will hurt our country, the immigrants, and their homeland. So let us indeed protect our borders (even though that will not solve the problem of those who enter legally and overstay their visa). Let us also honestly face the multiple causes of illegal immigration. As an excellent position paper from the Center for Concern notes, illegal immigration involves many factors: trade negotiation, the governments involved, the immigrants who break the law by entering our country, employers who take advantage of them, corporate leaders who profit from them, and consumers who benefit from lower food and service costs.

We must devise ways to offer legal status to anyone who contributes to our common good, whether as a future citizen or a temporary guest worker. If that means using the dirty word "amnesty," so be it.

As to those who sojourn in our midst, let us be vigilant if they are threats and charitable if they are friends. It would be a good, if unusual, move if our legislators had the imagination to call for citizen panels before which an illegal immigrant could request amnesty, leniency, and a path to citizenship based on his or her contribution to the community, solid employment record, faithful payment of taxes, family need, and crime-free record.

Instead of fearing some abstract horde of millions, we might see the faces of people like María and hear their stories. If we turn them away, we will have to face the fact that we are not so much a nation of Judeo-Christian values as a punitive and self-interested people hiding under the protection of lesser, human-made laws.

Summary Writing as a Way of Reading to Believe

One way to show that you have listened well to an article is to summarize its argument in your own words. A summary (also called an abstract, a précis, or a synopsis) presents only a text's major points and eliminates supporting details. Writers often incorporate summaries of other writer's views into their own arguments, either to support their own views or to represent alternative views that they intend to oppose. Summaries can be any length, depending on the writer's purpose, but usually they range from several sentences to one or two paragraphs. To maintain your own credibility, your summary should be as neutral and fair as possible.

To help you write an effective summary, we recommend the following steps:

Step 1: *Read the argument for general meaning.* Don't judge it; put your objections aside; just follow the writer's meaning, trying to see the issue from the writer's perspective. Try to adopt the writer's values and belief system.

Step 2: *Reread the article slowly, writing brief does and says statements for each paragraph (or group of closely connected paragraphs).* A *does* statement identifies a paragraph's function, such as "summarizes an opposing view," "introduces a supporting reason," "gives an example," or "uses statistics to support the previous point." A *says* statement summarizes a paragraph's content. Here are *does* and *says* statements for the first four paragraphs of Kavanaugh's article:

Does/Says Analysis of Kavanaugh's Article

Paragraph 1: *Does:* Uses a vivid example to introduce the injustice of the current treatment of illegal immigrants. *Says:* The U.S. government is separating productive, long-term illegal immigrants from their families, deporting them, exposing them to dangerous conditions, and threatening them with felony charges.

Paragraph 2: *Does:* Puts the problem of illegal immigrants in a larger international context. *Says:* Although some illegal immigrants are involved in criminal activities, most have been pushed here by poverty and loss of opportunity in their own countries and have come to the United States seeking a better life for themselves and their families.

Paragraph 3: *Does:* Further explores the reasons behind the increase in immigration rates. *Says:* Catholic bishops have spoken out against the North American Free Trade Agreement and corporate interests, which have sought their own trade benefits at the expense of poor farmers and rural communities.

Paragraph 4: *Does:* Presents a sketch of Catholic leaders protesting the recent crackdowns on illegal immigrants. *Says:* U.S. bishops are protesting recent punitive laws against illegal immigrants and advocating for "a more compassionate, fair and realistic reform of our immigration system."

■ ■ ■ **FOR CLASS DISCUSSION** Writing *"Does/Says"* Statements

Working individually or in small groups, write *does* and *says* statements for the remaining paragraphs of Kavanaugh's article.   ■ ■ ■

Step 3: *Examine your* does *and* says *statements to determine the major sections of the argument.* Create a list of the major points (and subpoints). If you are visually oriented, you may prefer to make a diagram or flowchart of Kavanaugh's argument.

Step 4: *Turn your list, outline, flowchart, or diagram into a prose summary.* Writers typically do this in one of two ways. Some start by joining all their *says* statements into a lengthy paragraph-by-paragraph summary and then prune it. Others start with a one-sentence summary of the argument's thesis and major supporting reasons and then flesh it out with more supporting ideas. Your goal is to be as neutral as possible by keeping your own response to the writer's ideas out of your summary. You also need to cover all the writer's main points and give them the same emphasis as in the original article.

Step 5: *Revise your summary until it is the desired length and is sufficiently clear, concise, and complete.* In a summary of several hundred words, you often will need transitions to indicate structure and create a coherent flow of ideas: "Kavanaugh's second point is that…" or "Kavanaugh concludes by…." When you incorporate a summary into your own essay, you must distinguish that author's views from your own by using *attributive tags* (expressions such as "Kavanaugh asserts," or "according to Kavanaugh"). You must also put any directly borrowed wording in quotation marks. Finally, you must cite the original author using appropriate conventions for documenting sources.

What follows are two summaries of Kavanaugh's article—a one-paragraph version and a one-sentence version—by student writer Michael Banks.

Michael's One-Paragraph Summary of Kavanaugh's Argument

In his article "Amnesty?" from *America* magazine, John F. Kavanaugh, a Jesuit priest and professor of philosophy at St. Louis University, questions the morality of the current U.S. treatment of undocumented immigrants and advocates for a frank dealing with "the multiple causes of illegal immigration" (27). He points out that most immigrants are not criminals but rather hard-working, family-oriented people. He attributes recent increases in immigration to the North American Free Trade Agreement and the poverty it causes among rural Mexican farmers. Kavanaugh reports that recently U.S. bishops have protested the "anti-humane" treatment of immigrants and called for "compassionate, fair and realistic reform" (26). He also mentions the anti-immigration groups, residents on the border, and business owners who have resisted the bishops and any treatment that resembles "amnesty." Kavanaugh's piece culminates with his argument that a nation that identifies itself as "Judeo-Christian and humane" should follow biblical teaching, "higher law," and the courageous example of leaders such as Martin Luther King, Jr., in challenging unjust laws (27). Admitting that unrestrained immigration would help nobody, Kavanaugh exhorts the country to move constructively toward "legal status for anyone who contributes to our common good" (27) and suggests a radically new solution to the problem: a citizen panel for the review of an immigrant's legal status. He concludes by stating that turning away undocumented immigrants is an immoral act motivated by self-interest.

Work Cited

Kavanaugh, John F. "Amnesty?" *America* 10 Mar. 2008: 8. Rpt. in *Writing Arguments: A Rhetoric with Readings.* John D. Ramage, John C. Bean, and June Johnson. Concise 5th ed. New York: Pearson Longman, 2010. 26–27. Print.

Michael's One-Sentence Summary of Kavanaugh's Argument

In his article in *America*, Jesuit professor of philosophy John F. Kavanaugh questions the morality of the current treatment of undocumented immigrants in the United States, arguing that in a Judeo-Christian nation anyone who contributes positively to their community should be afforded some level of legal status.

Practicing Believing: Willing Your Own Belief in the Writer's Views

Although writing an accurate summary of an argument shows that you have listened to it effectively and understood it, summary writing by itself doesn't mean that you have actively tried to enter the writer's world view. We want to stress the importance of believing the argument. Rhetorician Peter Elbow reminds us that before we critique a text, we should try to "dwell with" and "dwell in" the writer's ideas—play the believing game—in order to "earn" our right to criticize.* To believe a writer and dwell with his or her ideas, find places in the text that resonate positively for you, look for values and beliefs you hold in common (however few), and search for personal experiences and values that affirm his or her argument.

Reading to Doubt

After willing yourself to believe an argument, will yourself to doubt it. When you read as a doubter, you question the writer's logic, evidence and assumptions, and strategies for developing the argument. You also think about what is *not* in the argument by noting what the author has glossed over or left out. You add a new layer of marginal notes, articulating what is bothering you, demanding proof, doubting evidence, challenging the author's assumptions and values, and so forth.

■ ■ ■ **FOR CLASS DISCUSSION**   Raising Doubts about Kavanaugh's Argument
Return now to Kavanaugh's article and read it skeptically. Raise questions, offer objections, and express doubts. Then, working as a class or in small groups, list all the doubts you have about Kavanaugh's argument.   ■ ■ ■

Now that you have doubted Kavanaugh's article, compare your questions and doubts to some raised by student writer Michael Banks.

Michael's Doubts about Kavanaugh's Article

- Kavanaugh's introductory paragraph seems sensational. María's situation is disturbing, but I doubt that every deported immigrant is likely to be "kidnapped, raped, murdered, and buried in the desert" as he seems to be insinuating.
- His argument often seems to be based too much upon vague statements about the opposition. He talks about "some resentment," "some towns," "a few people," and "some hateful columns," but he doesn't provide specifics. He also doesn't provide any specific data about the effects of NAFTA, which seems like something he really should have provided.
- His references to opinion columns and popular books and radio talk shows seem to suggest that the majority of opposition to immigration reform is simplistic and

*Peter Elbow, "Bringing the Rhetoric of Assent and the Believing Game Together—Into the Classroom." In *College English*. 67.4 (March 2005), p. 390.

ignorant. He only pays lip service to a few "understandable" objections. There must be more to the opposition than this. It would be particularly interesting to find an ethical justification for an anti-immigration stance.

■ Perhaps because he's a member of the Society of Jesus, he draws hardly any line at all between church and state. However, most U.S. citizens I know believe that government should be secular. This contrasts harshly with his notion that the U.S. self-identifies as "Judeo-Christian" and limits his audience to people who would probably already agree with him. If we remove religion from the equation, the capitalistic values behind NAFTA and immigration policy seems much more understandable. I would need to investigate the economic impact of illegal immigration. Who really benefits the most from it? Who's really harmed?

These are only some of the objections that might be raised against Kavanaugh's argument. The point here is that doubting as well as believing is a key part of the exploratory process and purpose. *Believing* takes you into the views of others so that you can expand your views and perhaps see them differently and modify or even change them. *Doubting* helps protect you from becoming overpowered by others' arguments and teaches you to stand back, consider, and weigh points carefully. It also leads you to new questions and points you might want to explore further.

Thinking Dialectically

This chapter's final strategy—thinking dialectically to bring texts into conversation with each other—encompasses all the previous strategies and can have a powerful effect on your growth as a thinker and arguer. The term *dialectic* is associated with the German philosopher Georg Wilhelm Friedrich Hegel, who postulated that each thesis prompts an opposing thesis (which he calls an "antithesis") and that the conflict between these views can lead thinkers to a new claim (a "synthesis") that incorporates aspects of both views. Dialectic thinking is the philosophical underpinning of the believing and doubting game, pushing us toward new and better ideas. It means playing ideas against each other, creating a tension that forces you to keep expanding your perspective. It helps you achieve the "mingling of minds" that we discussed in the introduction to this chapter.

As you listen to differing views, try to identify sources of disagreement among arguers, which often fall into two categories: (1) disagreement about the facts of the case and (2) disagreement about underlying values, beliefs, or assumptions. We saw these disagreements in Chapter 1 in the conversation about phthalates in children's toys. At the level of facts, disputants disagreed about the amount of phthalates a baby might ingest when chewing a rubber toy or about the quantity of ingested phthalates needed to be harmful. At the level of values, disputants disagreed on the amount of risk that must be present in a free market economy before a government agency should ban a substance. As you try to determine your own position on an issue, consider what research you might have to do to resolve questions of fact; also try to articulate your own underlying values, beliefs, and assumptions.

Questions to Stimulate Dialectic Thinking

As you consider multiple points of view on an issue, try using the following questions to promote dialectic thinking:

Questions to Promote Dialectic Thinking

1. What would writer A say to writer B?
2. After I read writer A, I thought _____; however, after I read writer B, my thinking on this issue had changed in these ways: _____
3. To what extent do writer A and writer B disagree about facts and interpretations of facts?
4. To what extent do writer A and writer B disagree about underlying beliefs, assumptions, and values?
5. Can I find any areas of agreement, including shared values and beliefs, between writer A and writer B?
6. What new, significant questions do these texts raise for me?
7. After I have wrestled with the ideas in these two texts, what are my current views on this issue?

Responding to questions like these—either through class discussion or through exploratory writing—can help you work your way into a public controversy. Earlier in this chapter, you read John Kavanaugh's article expressing a Catholic, pro-immigrant, anticorporate view of immigrants. Now consider an article expressing a quite different point of view, "Why Blame Mexico?" by freelance journalist Fred Reed, published in *The American Conservative* on March 10, 2008. We ask you to read the article and then use the preceding questions to stimulate dialectic thinking about Kavanaugh versus Reed.

Why Blame Mexico?

FRED REED

To grasp American immigration policy, one needs only remember that the United States frowns on smoking while subsidizing tobacco growers.

We say to impoverished Mexicans, "See this river? Don't cross it. If you do, we'll give you good jobs, drivers licenses, citizenship for your kids born here, school for said kids, public assistance, governmental documents in Spanish for your convenience, and a much better future. There is no penalty for getting caught. Now, don't cross this river, hear?"

How smart is that? We're baiting them. It's like putting out a salt lick and then complaining when deer come. Immigrant parents would be irresponsible not to cross.

The problem of immigration, note, is entirely self-inflicted. The U.S. chose to let them in. It didn't have to. They came to work. If Americans hadn't hired them, they would have gone back.

5   We have immigration because we want immigration. Liberals favor immigration because it makes them feel warm and fuzzy and from a genuine streak of decency. Conservative Republican businessmen favor immigration, frequently *sotto voce*, because they want cheap labor that actually shows up and works.

It's a story I've heard many times—from a landscaper, a construction firm, a junkyard owner, a group of plant nurserymen. "We need Mexicans." You could yell "Migra!" in a lot of restaurants in Washington, and the entire staff would disappear out the back door. Do we expect businessmen to vote themselves out of business? That's why we don't take the obvious steps to control immigration. (A $1,000 a day fine for hiring illegals, half to go anonymously to whoever informed on the employer would do the trick.)

In Jalisco, Mexico, where I live, crossing illegally is regarded as casually as pirating music or smoking a joint and the coyotes who smuggle people across as a public utility, like light rail. The smuggling is frequently done by bribing the border guards, who are notoriously corrupt.

Why corrupt? Money. In the book *De Los Maras a Los Zetas*, by a Mexican journalist, I find an account of a tunnel he knew of that could put 150 illegals a day across the border. (I can't confirm this.) The price of passage is about $2,000 a person. That's $300,000 a day, tax-free. What does a border guard make? (And where can I find a shovel?) The author estimated that perhaps 40 tunnels were active at any given time. Certainly some are. A woman I know says she came up in a restaurant and just walked out the door. Let's hear it for Homeland Security.

There is much noise about whether to grant amnesty. The question strikes me as cosmetic. We are not going to round up millions of people and physically throw them across the border. Whether we should doesn't matter. It's fantasy. Too many people want them here or don't care that they are here or don't want to uproot families who have established new lives here. Ethnic cleansing is ugly. Further, the legal Latino population is just starting to vote. A bumper crop of Mexican-American kids, possessed of citizenship, are growing headlong toward voting age. These people cannot be thrown out, even in principle.

10   People complain that Mexico doesn't seal the borders. Huh? Mexico is a country, not a prison. It has no obligation to enforce American laws that America declines to enforce. Then there was the uproar when some fast-food restaurant in the U.S. began accepting pesos. Why? Mexican border towns accept dollars. Next came outrage against Mexico because its consulates were issuing ID cards to illegals, which they then used to get drivers licenses. Why outrage? A country has every right to issue IDs to its citizens. America doesn't have to accept them. If it does, whose problem is that?

If you want to see a reasonable immigration policy, look to Mexico. You automatically get a 90-day tourist visa when you land. To get residency papers, you need two things apart from photographs, passport, etc. First, a valid tourist visa to show that you entered the country legally. Mexico doesn't do illegal aliens. Second, a demonstrable income of $1,000 a month. You are welcome to live in Mexico, but you are going to pay your own way. Sounds reasonable to me.

You want a Mexican passport? Mexico allows dual citizenship. You (usually) have to be a resident for five years before applying. You also have to speak Spanish. It's the national language. What sense does it make to have citizens who can't talk to anybody?

It looks to me as though America thoughtlessly adopted an unwise policy, continued it until reversal became approximately impossible, and now doesn't like the results. It must be Mexico's fault.

■ ■ ■   **FOR CLASS DISCUSSION**   **Practicing Dialectic Thinking with Two Articles**
Individual task: Freewrite your responses to the preceding questions in which
Kavanaugh is writer A and Reed is writer B. **Group task:** Working as a whole class or in
small groups, share your responses to the two articles, guided by the dialectic questions.   ■ ■ ■

Three Ways to Foster Dialectic Thinking

In this concluding section, we suggest three ways to stimulate and sustain the process
of dialectic thinking: effective discussions in class, over coffee, or online; a reading log
in which you make texts speak to each other; or a formal exploratory essay. We'll look
briefly at each.

Effective Discussions   Good rich talk is one of the most powerful ways to stimulate
dialectic thinking and foster a "mingling of minds." The key is to keep these discussions
from becoming shouting matches or bully pulpits for those who like to dominate the
airtime. Discussions are most productive if people are willing to express different points
of view or to role-play those views for the purpose of advancing the conversation.

Reading Logs   In our own classes, we require students to keep reading logs or journals
in which they use freewriting and idea mapping to explore their own ideas as they
encounter multiple perspectives on an issue. One part of a journal or reading log should
include summaries of each article you read. Another part should focus on your own
dialectic thinking as you interact with your sources while you are reading them. Adapt
the questions for promoting dialectic thinking on page 32.

A Formal Exploratory Essay   A formal exploratory essay tells the story of an
intellectual journey. It is both a way to promote dialectical thinking and a way to
narrate one's struggle to negotiate multiple views. The keys to writing successful
exploratory essays are (1) choosing an issue to explore on which you don't have an
answer or position (or on which you are open to changing your mind); (2) wrestling with
an issue or problem by resisting quick, simple answers and by exploring diverse
perspectives; and (3) letting your thinking evolve and your own stance on the issue grow
out of this exploration.

Exploratory essays can be powerful thinking and writing experiences in their own
right, but they can also be a valuable prewriting tool for a formal argument. Many
instructors assign an exploratory paper as the first stage of a research project—what we
might call a "thesis-seeking" stage. Although often used as part of a research project,
exploratory essays can also be low-stakes reflective pieces narrating the evolution of a
writer's thinking. An exploratory essay includes these thinking moves and parts:

■ The essay is opened and driven by the writer's issue question or research problem—
   not a thesis.
■ The introduction presents the question and shows why it interests the writer, why
   it is significant, and why it is problematic rather than clear-cut or easy to resolve.

- The body of the essay shows the writer's inquiry process. It demonstrates how the writer has kept the question open, sincerely wrestled with different views on the question, accepted uncertainty and ambiguity, and possibly redefined the question in the midst of his or her reading and reflection on multiple perspectives.
- The body of the essay includes summaries of the different views or sources that the writer explored and often includes believing and doubting responses to them.
- In the essay's conclusion, the writer may clarify his or her thinking and discover a thesis to be developed and supported in a subsequent argument. But the conclusion can also remain open because the writer may not have discovered his or her own position on the issue and may acknowledge the need or desire for more exploration.

One of the writing assignment options for this chapter is a formal exploratory paper. Michael Banks's exploratory essay on pages 37–42 shows how he explored different voices in the controversy over illegal immigration.

WRITING ASSIGNMENT An Argument Summary or a Formal Exploratory Essay

Option 1: An Argument Summary   Write a 250-word summary of an argument selected by your instructor. Then write a one-sentence summary of the same argument. Use as models Michael Banks's summaries of John Kavanaugh's argument on immigration (p. 29).

Option 2: A Formal Exploratory Essay   Write an exploratory essay in which you narrate in first-person, chronological order the evolution through time of your thinking about an issue or problem. Rather than state a thesis or claim, begin with a question or problem. Then describe your inquiry process as you worked your way through sources or different views. Follow the guidelines for an exploratory paper shown on pages 34–35 and the organization plan shown in Figure 2.4. When you cite the sources you have considered, be sure to use attributive tags so that the reader can distinguish between your own ideas and those of the sources you have summarized. If you use research sources, use MLA documentation for citing ideas and quotations and for creating a Works Cited at the end. ■

Reading

What follows is Michael Banks' exploratory essay on the subject of illegal immigration. His research begins with the articles by Kavanaugh and Reed that you have already read and discussed. He then moves off in his own direction.

Organization Plan for an Exploratory Essay

Introduction (one to several paragraphs)	• Establish that your question is complex, problematic, and significant. • Show why you are interested in it. • Present relevant background on your issue. Begin with your question or build up to it, using it to end your introductory section.
Body section 1: First view or source	• Introduce your first source and show why you started with it. • Provide rhetorical context and information about it. • Summarize the source's content and argument. • Offer your response to this source, including both believing and doubting points. • Talk about what this source contributes to your understanding of your question: What did you learn? What value does this source have for you? What is missing from this source that you want to consider? Where do you want to go from here?
Body section 2: Second view or source	• Repeat the process with a new source selected to advance the inquiry. • Explain why you selected this source (to find an alternative view, pursue a sub-question, find more data, and so forth). • Summarize the source's argument. • Respond to the source's ideas. Look for points of agreement and disagreement with other sources. • Show how your cumulative reading of sources is shaping your thinking or leading to more questions.
Body sections 3, 4, 5, etc.	• Continue exploring views or sources.
Conclusion	• Wrap up your intellectual journey and explain where you are now in your thinking and how your understanding of your problem has changed. • Present your current answer to your question based on all that you have learned so far, or explain why you still can't answer your question, or explain what research you might pursue further.

FIGURE 2.4

Should the United States Grant Legal Status to Undocumented Immigrant Workers?

MICHAEL BANKS (STUDENT)

Introduction shows the writer's interest and investment in the issue, which, in this case, began with personal experience.

Having grown up in the California Bay Area, I have long been aware of illegal immigration. In high school, I volunteered through a school program to deliver free lunches to Mexican workers waiting for day jobs at popular hiring sites such as local hardware stores. One time we even went out to one of the farm fields to deliver lunches, and some of the workers scattered when they saw us coming. Apparently they thought we were police or immigration officials. Although the relationships were not deep or lasting, I had the opportunity to talk with some of the workers in my stumbling high school Spanish, and they would tell me about some of their bad experiences such as employers who wouldn't pay them what was promised. They had no recourse to file a complaint because they lacked legal status. Our program supervisor often stressed the importance of recognizing the workers as friends or equals rather than as charity cases. I often wondered how they could work with such low wages and still live a dignified life. However, my experiences did not push me to consider deeply the reality of being an illegal immigrant.

Writer presents the problem he is going to investigate. He shows why the problem is complex, significant, and difficult to resolve. The introduction shows his genuine perplexity.

Writer states his research question.

With this background, I entered our class discussions sympathetic towards the immigrants. However, I also recognized that the cheap labor they provided allowed Americans to keep food prices affordable or to find workers for any kind of hard day-labor job such as landscaping or digging up a backyard septic system. I am still not sure whether illegal immigrants are taking away jobs that Americans want, but I do know that I and most of my college friends would not be willing to work low-paying summer jobs picking tomatoes or weeding lettuce. For this exploratory essay, I wanted to look more deeply into this complicated ethical and economic dilemma. I set for myself this question: What is the best way for the United States to handle the problem of illegal immigration?

Writer explains his starting point, introduces his first source, and gives some rhetorical context for it.

Writer summarizes the article.

My exploration began with an article that our instructor assigned to the whole class: "Amnesty?" from *America* magazine by John F. Kavanaugh, a Jesuit priest and professor of philosophy at St. Louis University. In this article, Kavanaugh questions the morality of the current U.S. treatment of undocumented immigrants. He points out that most immigrants are not criminals but rather hard-working, family-oriented people. He attributes recent increases in immigration to the North American Free Trade Agreement and the poverty it causes among rural Mexican farmers. He also notes that anti-immigration groups have a "seething hostility" (27) for these persons and strongly resist any granting of amnesty or legal status. Kavanaugh disagrees with these groups, arguing that a nation that identifies itself as "Judeo-Christian and humane" should follow biblical teaching, "higher law," and the courageous example of leaders such as Martin Luther King, Jr., in challenging unjust laws (27). Although admitting that unrestrained immigration would help nobody, Kavanaugh exhorts the country to give "legal status to anyone who contributes to our common good" (27). He recommends that a citizen panel be used to review an immigrant's status and make recommendations for amnesty.

Writer includes believing and doubting points as he discusses what he learned from this article and how it influenced his thinking on his research question.

I found Kavanaugh's article to be quite persuasive. This article could particularly inspire its Catholic readers, and I too had an easy time agreeing with much of what Kavanaugh says. In fact, he reminded me of the director of my high school outreach program. I like the argument that people who contribute to the community should not be labeled as "illegal" as if they are in the same category as thieves or welfare cheaters. But I wasn't yet convinced that the laws governing immigration were "unjust" in the same way that segregation laws were unjust. It seems to me that a country has the right to control who enters the country, but doesn't have the right to make certain people sit in the back of the bus. So the references to Martin Luther King's fighting unjust laws didn't quite connect with me. So I was still caught in the dilemma. Also, I saw some other major problems with Kavanaugh's argument. First, it may not be fair to apply Judeo-Christian ethics to everyone in the country, especially considering our Constitutional separation of church and state. His appeal to religious beliefs may be appropriate to persuade Christians to volunteer for a cause but not to change a secular nation's laws. Also, his solution of having a citizen panel seemed impractical, especially for handling the number of illegal immigrants. Finally, Kavanaugh doesn't address the economic side of this argument. He didn't help me see what the disadvantages would be to granting amnesty to millions of undocumented workers.

Here the writer doubts the article and challenges some of its ideas.

Writer moves to his next source and provides some rhetorical context, including information about the author.

5   My next article, which the class also read together, was from *The American Conservative* titled "Why Blame Mexico?" by Fred Reed. According to Reed's biographical sketch on the Web ("Fred on Everything: Biography"), Reed is an ex-marine, former scientist, wanderer and world traveler, former law-enforcement columnist for the *Washington Times*, and a freelance journalist currently living in Mexico. He is known for his provocative columns. Reed's article was hard to summarize because it jumps around and is very sarcastic. His overall view is best exemplified by his very first statement: "To grasp American immigration policy, one needs only remember that the United States frowns on smoking while subsidizing tobacco growers" (32). Reed argues that illegal immigration occurs not mainly because there are millions of impoverished Mexicans in need of work, but because liberals feel good about tolerating them and because "[c]onservative Republican businessmen favor immigration...because they want cheap labor that actually shows up and works" (33). Reed points out that Mexico itself is clear and consistent in its

Writer summarizes the article.

own immigration policies: Immigrants into Mexico must possess clear residency papers, must have regular monthly earnings, and must be fluent in Spanish. In contrast to Kavanaugh, who focuses on immigrants, Reed focuses on the Americans who hire them; without Americans wanting cheap labor, immigrants would have no reason to cross the border. He takes it for granted that illegal immigrants should not be given legal status. Reed offers no solutions for the tangled mess of U.S. treatment of illegal immigrants, but underscores the fact that it is this country's self-created problem.

Writer shows his dialectical thinking, as he weighs the ideas of this source against those in his first article. He explores points of disagreement between these two sources.

Reed's article pulled me back away from Kavanaugh's call for amnesty. It made me see more clearly the entangled economic issues. Many American citizens *want* a source of cheap labor. Reed, in contrast, wants to eliminate cheap labor. If we followed the logical path that Reed seems to propose, we'd start jailing employers in order to cut off the job supply. At this point in my research, the status quo seemed to be a better situation. If cheap labor is so important to America's economy and if a low paying job in the United States is better than no job, perhaps some kind of legal status other than amnesty and citizenship would help resolve the situation. My head was spinning because I could picture all my classmates who would disagree with my last sentence! At this point, I felt I needed to explore other approaches to this controversy.

Writer shows how he is wrestling with the ideas in this source.

The day after I read the Reed article, I was talking with a friend, who suggested I watch a recent movie about immigration called *Under the Same Moon*. I figured it would be a fun diversion, if nothing else, and rented it. The movie tells the tale of a nine-year-old boy, Carlitos, who lives with his grandmother until she dies and then sets out to cross the border illegally to find his mother, who has been working several jobs at once as an undocumented immigrant for four years in Los Angeles. The dramatic story—shown from the dual perspective of mother and son—highlights many of the dangers faced by the immigrants themselves: separation from family members and support networks, exploitation by border-crossing agencies, INS raids on job sites, and dangerous jobs such as picking pesticide-coated tomatoes, just to name a few. The main characters' immigrant laborer status also draws attention to the undeniable humanity of immigrants.

Writer explains his movement to his next source.

He summarizes the plot of the film.

This film works powerfully to create sympathy for illegal immigrants but without the explicit religious coating provided by Kavanaugh. I cannot help but admire the sacrifices made by immigrant workers who leave behind children and family in order to try to provide a brighter future for their loved ones. In cases where immigrants are separated from their young children, granting these parents legal status could help unite families more quickly and could ease the great pain that comes with being separated while allowing them the opportunity to forge a better life. On the other hand, families would also be reunited if the parents were sent back to Mexico. The great sympathy I feel for illegal immigrants doesn't necessarily mean that granting amnesty

Writer discusses and analyzes the ideas in the film by presenting believing and doubting points.

Writer mentions problems the source raises for him.

and citizenship is the best solution. While the film evokes compassion for individual immigrants, it does not address the magnitude of the problem.

Writer explains his choice of another film.

A brief summary prepares for his discussion.

I had heard about a number of films about illegal immigration and immigrants' experiences and wanted to continue with another film, so I headed back to Blockbuster and asked one of the workers if he could point me towards a recent documentary on illegal immigration. What I came up with was *A Day Without a Mexican*, a mock documentary, or "mockumentary." The movie's plot imagines the complete disappearance of the entire Latino population in California, both legal and illegal. The state grinds to a complete halt, widespread panic occurs, and homes, restaurants, supermarkets, orchards, farms, schools, and construction services are completely dysfunctional. The story and structure of the film viciously satirize anti-immigrant organizations, the news media, the border patrol, and waffling politicians. I visited the movie's web site to search for further information, as I was curious about its reception. The Latino audience saw this film as a hit; it took in the second best per screen average the weekend it was released in Southern California. According to the general sales manager of Televisa Cine, *A Day Without a Mexican*'s success "underscores that there is not only a broad Hispanic audience who wants to see this film, but also a significant crossover audience," while the director, Sergio Arau, and lead actress/screenwriter, Yareli Arizmendi, add "we still believe we can change the world one screen at a time" ("Missing Jose Found").

Writer presents some information about the rhetorical context of this film, including statements from the directors and details about how it was first received.

Writer demonstrates how he is grappling with the issue of illegal immigration and how this film complicates his views.

10   The film's success at the box office suggests to me that Arau and Arizmendi have revealed the important truth that Latino immigration makes California a better place. The comic film works by exaggeration, but its image of a helpless California without immigrants is easy to believe. Since California, and presumably the rest of the country, relies so heavily upon its immigrants, it would make very little sense to create new immigration policies that made the status quo worse. Perhaps a solution might lie in somehow recognizing the worth of immigrants, as *A Day Without a Mexican* suggests is important, while maintaining the status quo of paying them wages lower than American standards. A moral dilemma remains, however, because this approach places economics above justice.

Writer takes stock of his developing views, sorting out what he has learned so far and what he is currently thinking.

He explains why he thinks he needs to continue exploring the issue and expand the diversity of views he examines.

At this stage, I decided to review some of the possible "solutions" that I had encountered so far to the illegal immigration problem. One solution, based on our valuing the humanity of immigrants, is to offer them amnesty, legal status, and eventual citizenship. Another, based on our valuing the economic benefits of cheap labor, is to keep the status quo. Still another solution is to get rid of illegal aliens altogether either by deporting them or by jailing their employers and thus eliminating their source of income. None of these options appealed to me. In search of another approach, I decided to head for the library to do more research. A friendly reference librarian suggested that I start with a couple of overview articles from *CQ Researcher*. These articles, which I just skimmed, provided some background information, statistical data on immigration, and summaries of different bills before Congress. I found my head swimming with so many little details that I began losing the big picture about an actual direction I wanted to go. However, one idea that kept emerging from the *CQ Researcher* was the possibility of guest worker programs. I decided I wanted to find out more about what these programs were. With the reference librarian's guidance, I used *Academic Search Complete* to find a number of articles on guest worker programs. I also entered "guest worker program" into Google and found a number of bloggers supporting or attacking guest worker programs.

He narrates his research path and explains his selection of sources.

I focused first on an editorial "That's Hospitality" from *The New Republic,* a news commentary magazine that is in the political center, neither dominantly liberal nor conservative. The editorial opposes a congressional bill that would establish a guest worker program wherein businesses could hire foreigners as "guest workers" for up to six years. These workers would be granted temporary legal status, but they would have to return to their home country when the six years were up. Although supporters of the bill called it "humane" and "compassionate," the editorial writer opposes it because it is "un-American." No other group of immigrants, the editorial states, has been treated this way—as second class transients who had no opportunity to make a full life in America. The article compares this proposed guest worker program to similar programs in Europe after WWII, where workers from Eastern Europe or Turkey came to countries like Germany or Netherlands and stayed but never assimilated. What the article supports instead is an alternative bill that grants "temporary worker" status but allows workers to apply for a green card after six years and for citizenship after five more years.

Writer introduces his next source and summarizes it.

This article excited me because it seemed to promote a compromise that turned undocumented workers who were afraid of getting caught and deported into persons with legal status and with the hope of eventually becoming citizens. It shared the pro-immigrant spirit of Kavanaugh and *Under the Same Moon* but didn't directly undermine the economic benefits provided by cheap labor. Rather than offering direct amnesty, it specified a waiting period of at least eleven years before a person could apply for citizenship. Although this article did not specify how the United States might manage the volume and rate of people seeking guest worker and then citizen status, I thought that this proposal would be the position I would like to argue for in a later persuasive paper.

Writer responds to this source and explains the current status of his thinking about his research question. He looks for points of agreement among this source and others he has consulted.

But I decided next to look at the negative side of a guest worker program and was amazed at how many anti-immigration groups hated this bill. One provocative blog "Guest Worker Program Illusion" is by a freelance writer Frosty Wooldridge, who maintains his own website aimed at combating "overpopulation and immigration." According to his blog site he has written hundreds of articles for seventeen national and two international magazines and has been an invited speaker on environmental issues at many universities. Wooldridge favors strict border enforcement and deportation of anyone who has illegally entered the country. He sees all forms of guest worker programs

Writer decides to continue exploring his question by looking at a source that opposes his preceding one. He gives information about the rhetorical context of this source, particularly about the blogger.

He summarizes the ideas in his blog.

Writer shows how this source has challenged the ideas in the preceding source, complicated the issue, and raised important questions for him.

Although he has not fully worked out his answer to his research question, he sums up how his views have evolved. He explains how his reading and thinking have deepened and clarified his views on this issue.

He sketches a path he might follow in further exploration of his question.

as amnesty that will lead to overpopulation and an increasing welfare burden on middle-class Americans who try to provide services for the guest workers. He also argues that the guest workers will suppress wages for American workers. His strategy is to point out all the problems that the guest worker program will open up: Can the guest worker bring his or her family? Will children born to guest workers automatically be U.S. citizens? Must the states provide tax-payer supported schools and hospital services for the guest workers? If so, must the schools be bilingual? Will guest workers pay social security taxes and thus become eligible for social security? Will they be eligible for Workers Compensation if they get hurt on the job? Will their older children get in-state rates at public universities? Will their younger children be covered by child labor laws? Will they actually leave after six years or simply revert back to undocumented illegal status?

15   All these problems raised by Woolridge were never mentioned in the *New Republic* editorial, and they severely dampened my spirits. As I end this exploratory paper, I still have a number of articles left to read and much left to learn, but I think I have a pretty good grasp of what the issues and disagreements are. I definitely think that the plan supporting a guest worker program with the chance of eventual citizenship is the best approach. But it has to be linked with other approaches also, including ways to improve the economies of Mexico and other Latin American countries so that poor people wouldn't have to come to the United States to find work. My hope is that many of the objections raised by Woolridge are solvable. I have realized from my inquiry that my heart is with the immigrants and that I don't share Woolridge's desire to close America off from future immigration.

Works Cited

A Works Cited page in MLA format lists the sources consulted and discussed in this essay.

A Day Without a Mexican. Dir. Sergio Arau. Xenon Pictures, 2004. DVD.

Kavanaugh, John F. "Amnesty?" *America* 10 March 2008: 8. Print.

"Missing Jose Found: Walks His Way to Box Office Success Throughout Southern California." *ADWAM News.* A Day Without a Mexican, n.d. Web. 12 July 2008.

Reed, Fred. "Why Blame Mexico?" *The American Conservative* 10 March 2008: 35. Print.

"That's Hospitality." *New Republic* 17 April 2006: 7. *Academic Search Complete.* Web. 30 August 2008.

Under the Same Moon. Dir. Patricia Riggen. Perf. Adrián Alonso, Kate del Castillo, Eugenio Derbez. Twentieth Century Fox, 2008. DVD.

Woolridge, Frosty. "Guest Worker Program Illusion." *Newswithviews.com.* 2 Dec. 2005. Web. 22 May 2008.

PART TWO

Writing Arguments

This still from the *Tomb Raider* video game series features main character Lara Croft engaged in one of her typical combats with humans, beasts, or supernatural creatures. Lara, an adventurer and archeologist, represents both a sexualized and an empowered woman. Women and violent video games are the focus of student Carmen Tieu's argument developed in Chapters 4–6; however, Carmen explores gender roles from the perspective of a woman playing a "male" video game, *Halo*.

3 The Core of an Argument
A Claim with Reasons

In Part One, we explained that argument combines truth seeking with persuasion. By highlighting the importance of exploration and inquiry, Part One emphasizes the truth-seeking dimension of argument. The suggested writing assignments in Part One include a variety of exploratory tasks ranging from freewriting to playing the believing and doubting game to writing a formal exploratory essay. In Part Two, we show you how to convert your exploratory ideas into a thesis-governed classical argument that uses effective reasons and evidence to support its claims. Each chapter in Part Two focuses on a key skill or idea needed for responsible and effective persuasion.

The Structure of a Classical Argument

Classical argument is patterned after the persuasive speeches of ancient Greek and Roman orators. In traditional Latin terminology, the main parts of a persuasive speech are the *exordium,* in which the speaker gets the audience's attention; the *narratio,* which provides needed background; the *propositio,* which is the speaker's claim or thesis; the *partitio,* which forecasts the main parts of the speech; the *confirmatio,* which presents the speaker's arguments supporting the claim; the *confutatio,* which summarizes and rebuts opposing views; and the *peroratio,* which concludes the speech by summing up the argument, calling for action, and leaving a strong, lasting impression.

Let's go over the same territory again using more contemporary terms. We provide an organization plan showing the structure of a classical argument in Figure 3.1, which shows these typical sections:

- **The introduction.** Writers of classical argument typically begin with an attention grabber such as a memorable scene, illustrative story, or startling statistic. They continue the introduction by focusing the issue—often by stating it directly as a question or by briefly summarizing opposing views—and providing needed background and context. They conclude the introduction by presenting their claim (thesis statement) and forecasting the argument's structure.
- **The presentation of the writer's position.** The presentation of the writer's position is usually the longest part of a classical argument. Here writers present the reasons and evidence supporting their claims, typically

Organization Plan for an Argument with a Classical Structure

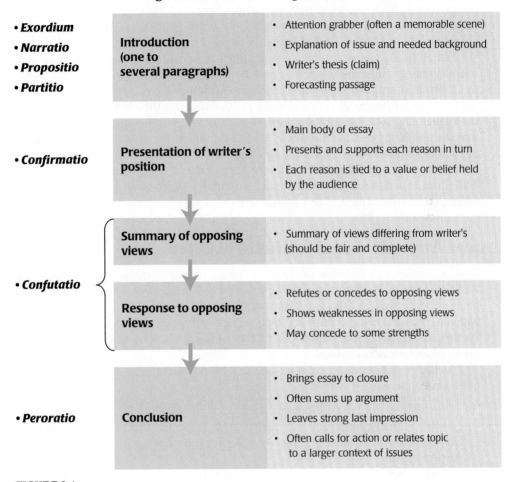

• *Exordium* • *Narratio* • *Propositio* • *Partitio*	**Introduction (one to several paragraphs)**	• Attention grabber (often a memorable scene) • Explanation of issue and needed background • Writer's thesis (claim) • Forecasting passage
• *Confirmatio*	**Presentation of writer's position**	• Main body of essay • Presents and supports each reason in turn • Each reason is tied to a value or belief held by the audience
• *Confutatio*	**Summary of opposing views**	• Summary of views differing from writer's (should be fair and complete)
	Response to opposing views	• Refutes or concedes to opposing views • Shows weaknesses in opposing views • May concede to some strengths
• *Peroratio*	**Conclusion**	• Brings essay to closure • Often sums up argument • Leaves strong last impression • Often calls for action or relates topic to a larger context of issues

FIGURE 3.1

choosing reasons that tie into their audience's values, beliefs, and assumptions. Usually each reason is developed in its own paragraph or sequence of paragraphs.

■ **The summary and critique of alternative views.** When summarizing and responding to opposing views, writers have several options. If there are several opposing arguments, writers may summarize all of them together and then compose a single response, or they may summarize and respond to each argument in turn. As we explain in Chapter 7, writers may respond to opposing views either by refuting them or by conceding to their strengths and shifting to a different field of values.

■ **The conclusion.** Finally, in their conclusion, writers sum up their argument, often calling for some kind of action, thereby creating a sense of closure and leaving a strong final impression.

In this organization, the body of a classical argument has two major sections—the one presenting the writer's position and the other summarizing and critiquing alternative views. Figure 3.1 and our discussion have the writer's position coming first, but it is possible to reverse that order. (In Chapter 7 we consider the factors affecting this choice.)

For all its strengths, the classical argument may not always be your most persuasive strategy. In some cases, you may be more effective by delaying your thesis, by ignoring alternative views altogether, or by showing great sympathy for opposing views (see Chapter 7). Even in these cases, however, the classical argument is a useful planning tool. Its call for a thesis statement and a forecasting statement in the introduction helps you see the whole of your argument in miniature. And by requiring you to summarize and consider opposing views, classical argument alerts you to the limits of your position and to the need for further reasons and evidence. As we will show, the classical argument is a particularly persuasive mode of argument when you address a neutral or undecided audience.

Classical Appeals and the Rhetorical Triangle

Besides developing a template or structure for an argument, classical rhetoricians analyzed the ways that effective speeches persuaded their audiences. They identified three kinds of persuasive appeals—*logos, ethos,* and *pathos.* These appeals can be understood within a rhetorical context illustrated by a triangle with points labeled *message, writer or speaker,* and *audience* (see Figure 3.2). Effective arguments pay attention to all three points on this *rhetorical triangle.*

As Figure 3.2 shows, each point on the triangle corresponds to one of the three persuasive appeals:

- *Logos* (Greek for "word") focuses attention on the quality of the message—that is, on the internal consistency and clarity of the argument itself and on the logic of its reasons and support. The impact of *logos* on an audience is referred to as its *logical appeal.*
- *Ethos* (Greek for "character") focuses attention on the writer's character as it is projected in the message. It refers to the credibility of the writer or speaker. *Ethos* often is conveyed through the tone and style of the message, through the care with which the writer considers alternative views, and through the writer's investment in his or her claim. In some cases, it's also a function of the writer's reputation for honesty and expertise independent of the message. The impact of *ethos* on an audience is referred to as its *ethical appeal* or *appeal from credibility.*
- *Pathos* (Greek for "suffering" or "experience") focuses attention on the values and beliefs of the intended audience. Often associated with emotional appeal, *pathos* appeals more specifically to an audience's imaginative sympathies—their capacity to feel and see what the writer feels and sees. Thus, when we turn the abstractions of logical discourse into a tangible and immediate story, we are making a pathetic appeal. Although appeals to *logos* and *ethos* can further an audience's intellectual assent to our claim, appeals to *pathos* engage the imagination and feelings, moving the audience to a deeper appreciation of the argument's significance.

Message
LOGOS: *How can I make the argument internally consistent and logical? How can I find the best reasons and support them with the best evidence?*

Audience
PATHOS: *How can I make the reader open to my message? How can I best appeal to my reader's values and interests? How can I engage my reader emotionally and imaginatively?*

Writer or Speaker
ETHOS: *How can I present myself effectively? How can I enhance my credibility and trustworthiness?*

FIGURE 3.2 The rhetorical triangle

A related rhetorical concept, connected to the appeals of *logos*, *ethos*, and *pathos*, is that of *kairos*, from the Greek word for "right time," "season," or "opportunity." This concept suggests that for an argument to be persuasive its timing must be effectively chosen and its tone and structure in right proportion or measure. You may have had the experience of composing an argumentative e-mail and then hesitating before clicking the "send" button. Is this the right moment to send this message? Is my audience ready to hear what I'm saying? Would my argument be more effective if I waited for a couple of days? If I send this message now, should I change its tone and content? This attentiveness to the unfolding of time is what is meant by *kairos*. We will return to this concept in Chapter 7, when we consider *ethos* and *pathos* in more depth.

Given this background on the classical appeals, let's turn now to *logos*—the logic and structure of arguments.

Issue Questions as the Origins of Argument

At the heart of any argument is a controversial question, or issue question, that gives rise to alternative answers. Any topic area, such as "the labeling of genetically engineered foods" or "racial profiling," has embedded within it a number of issue questions. Thus the topic area "abortion" gives rise to issue questions such as "Should abortion be legal?", "Should the federal government underwrite the cost of abortion?", and "When does a fetus become a human being?" Each of these issue questions opens up one strand of the complex debate on abortion.

Difference between an Issue Question and an Information Question

Of course, not all questions are issue questions. Some may simply call for more information, not argument. Keeping this distinction in mind, consider the following two questions:

> How does the teenage pregnancy rate in the United States compare with the rate in Sweden? If the rates are different, why?

Although both questions seem to call for information rather than for argument, we believe that the second one would be an issue question if reasonable people disagreed on the answer. Thus, different writers might agree that the teenage pregnancy rate in the United States is four times higher than the rate in Sweden. But they might disagree about why. One writer might emphasize Sweden's practical, secularized sex education courses in the schools, leading to more consistent use of contraceptives among Swedish teenagers. Another writer might point to the higher use of oral contraceptives among teenage girls in Sweden (partly a result of Sweden's generous national health program) and to less reliance on condoms for preventing pregnancy. Another might argue that moral decay in the United States is at fault. Thus, underneath the surface of what looks like a simple explication of the "truth" is really a controversy.

How to Identify an Issue Question

To determine if a given question is an issue question or an information question, examine the role it calls you to play in relation to your audience. If the question asks you to be a teacher providing new information or knowledge, then it is probably an information question. But if the question asks you to be an advocate, persuading your audience toward your point of view in a controversy, then it is probably an issue question. Sometimes context will determine if a given question is an issue question or an information question. Consider the following examples:

- How does a diesel engine work? (Almost surely an information question, posed by an audience of learners who regard you as a teacher.)
- What is the most cost-effective way to produce diesel fuel from crude oil? (This would be an information question if experts agreed on the answer and you were teaching this knowledge to new learners. But if experts disagreed—imagine a roomful of petroleum engineers seeking ways to reduce the production costs of diesel fuel—it would be an issue question.)
- Should the tax on diesel fuel be reduced? (A slam-dunk issue question sure to provoke controversy in almost any context.)

■ ■ ■ **FOR CLASS DISCUSSION**   **Information Questions versus Issue Questions**
Working as a class or in small groups, decide whether the following questions are information questions or issue questions. Some questions could be either, depending on the context. For such questions, create a hypothetical context that justifies your choice.

1. What is the percentage of U.S. public schools that are failing?
2. What causes U.S. public schools to fail?
3. What techniques for interrogating prisoners of war are permitted according to current military codes?
4. Is playing loud music 24 hours a day over prison loudspeakers an instance of torture?
5. What is the effect of violent TV shows on children?

Difference between a Genuine Argument and a Pseudo-Argument

While every argument features an issue question with alternative answers, not every dispute over answers is a rational argument. Rational arguments require two additional factors: (1) reasonable participants who operate within the conventions of reasonable behavior and (2) potentially shareable assumptions that can serve as a starting place or foundation for the argument. Lacking one or both of these conditions, disagreements remain stalled at the level of pseudo-arguments.

Pseudo-Arguments: Fanatical Believers and Fanatical Skeptics   A reasonable argument assumes the possibility of growth and change; disputants may modify their views as they acknowledge strengths in an alternative view or weaknesses in their own. Such growth becomes impossible—and argument degenerates to pseudo-argument—when disputants are fanatically committed to their positions. Consider the case of the fanatical believer or the fanatical skeptic.

Fanatical believers believe that their claims are true because they say so, period. Often fanatical believers follow a party line, their ideological convictions shaped by their favorite, not-to-be-disputed texts, Web sites, blogs, or radio shows. Once you've pushed their buttons on global warming, abortion, gun control, gay marriage, or some other issue, you can expect a barrage of never-changing pronouncements. Disagreeing with a fanatical believer is like ordering the surf to quiet down. The only response is another crashing wave.

The fanatical skeptic, in contrast, dismisses the possibility of proving anything. So what if the sun has risen every day of recorded history? That's no proof that it will rise tomorrow. Short of absolute proof, which never exists, fanatical skeptics accept nothing. In a world where the most we can hope for is increased audience adherence to our ideas, the fanatical skeptic demands an ironclad logical demonstration of our claim's rightness. In the presence of fanatical believers or skeptics, then, genuine argument is impossible.

Another Source of Pseudo-Arguments: Lack of Shared Assumptions   A reasonable argument is difficult to conduct unless the participants share common assumptions on which the argument can be grounded. Like axioms in geometry, these shared assumptions serve as the starting point for the argument. Consider the following conversation, in which Randall refuses to accept Rhonda's assumptions.

RHONDA: Smoking should be banned because it causes cancer.

RANDALL: So it causes cancer. What's so bad about that?

RHONDA: Don't be perverse, Randy. Cancer causes suffering and death.

RANDALL: Rhonda, my dear girl, don't be such a twinkie. Suffering and death are just part of the human condition.

RHONDA: But that doesn't make them desirable, especially when they can be avoided.

RANDALL: Perhaps in particular cases they're avoidable for a while, but in the long run, we all suffer and we all die, so who cares if smoking causes what's inevitable anyway?

This, we would suggest, is a doomed argument. Without any shared assumptions (for example, that cancer is bad, that suffering should be minimized and death delayed), there's no "bottom" to this argument, just an endless regress of reasons based on more reasons. While calling assumptions into question is a legitimate way to deepen and complicate our understanding of an issue, the unwillingness to accept any assumption makes argument impossible.

Lack of shared assumptions often dooms arguments about purely personal opinions—for example, someone's claim that opera is boring or that pizza is better than nachos. Of course, a pizza versus nachos argument might be possible if the disputants agreed on a criterion such as the value of balanced nutrition. For example, a nutritionist could argue that pizza is better than nachos because it provides more balanced nutrients per calorie. But if one of the disputants responds, "Nah, nachos are better than pizza because nachos taste better," then he makes a different assumption—"My sense of taste is better than your sense of taste." This is a wholly personal standard, an assumption that others are unable to share.

■ ■ ■   **FOR CLASS DISCUSSION**   Reasonable Arguments versus Pseudo-Arguments
The following questions can all be answered in alternative ways. However, not all of them will lead to reasonable arguments. Try to decide which questions will lead to reasonable arguments and which will lead only to pseudo-arguments.

1. Are *Star Wars* films good science fiction?
2. Is postmodern architecture beautiful?
3. Should cities subsidize professional sports venues?
4. Is this abstract oil painting by a monkey smearing paint on a canvas a true work of art?
5. Are nose rings and tongue studs attractive?   ■ ■ ■

Frame of an Argument: A Claim Supported by Reasons

In writing an argument, you take a position on an issue and support it with reasons and evidence. You state your position in the form of a claim, which functions as the thesis statement of your argument. A claim should provide a one-sentence answer to the issue question. Your task, then, is to make a claim and support it with reasons and evidence, which together comprise your argument's framework.

What Is a Reason?

A reason is a claim used to support another claim. Reasons are usually linked to their claims with words like *because, thus, since, consequently,* and *therefore* to underscore their logical connection.

Let's take an example. In one of our recent classes, a female naval ROTC student argued that women should be allowed to serve on submarines. A heated discussion quickly followed, expanding into the more general issue of whether women should be allowed to join military combat units. Here are frameworks the class developed for two alternative positions on that issue:

One View

CLAIM: Women should be barred from military combat units.

REASON 1:   Most women don't have the strength or endurance for combat roles.

REASON 2:   Women haven't been socialized into fighters and wouldn't have the "Kill them with a bayonet" spirit that men can get.

REASON 3:   Women would be less reliable to a combat unit if they became pregnant or had to care for infants or small children.

Alternative View

CLAIM: Women should be allowed to join military combat units.

REASON 1:   Millions of women are stronger and more physically fit than most men; women selected for combat duty would have the strength and endurance for the job.

REASON 2:   The image of women as combat soldiers would help society overcome harmful gender stereotyping.

REASON 3:   Women are already seeing direct combat in the Iraq war, where there are no front lines.

REASON 4:   Women would have more opportunities for career advancement in the military if they could serve in combat units.

REASON 5:   Allowing women to serve in combat units promotes equal rights.

Formulating a list of reasons in this way breaks your argumentative task into a series of subtasks. In the previous example, there are five different lines of reasoning a writer might pursue. A writer might use all five or select only two or three, depending on which reasons would most persuade the intended audience. Each line of reasoning would be developed in its own separate section of the argument.

We can summarize the gist of this section as follows: The frame of an argument consists of a claim (the thesis statement of the essay), which is supported by one or more reasons, which are in turn supported by evidence or sequences of further reasons.

Expressing Reasons in *Because* Clauses

There are many ways to express the logical connection between a reason and a claim. Our language is rich in ways of stating *because* relationships:

- Women shouldn't be allowed to join combat units because they don't have the strength or endurance for combat roles.
- Women don't have the strength or endurance for combat roles. Therefore women should not be allowed to join combat units.
- Women don't have the strength or endurance for combat roles, so they should not be allowed to join combat units.
- One reason why women should not be allowed to join combat units is that they don't have the strength or endurance for combat roles.

But even though logical relationships can be stated in various ways, writing out one or more *because* clauses remains the most succinct way to clarify an argument for oneself. We therefore suggest that sometime in the writing process you create a *working thesis statement* that summarizes your main reasons as *because* clauses attached to your claim. Some writers compose their working thesis statement before they write their rough draft. Others discover their thesis as they write. Still others compose their working thesis statement in mid-draft in order to rein in an argument headed off in too many directions. Some wait until the very end, using their thesis statement to check the unity of the final product.

No matter when you write your working thesis statement, you will find doing so both thought provoking and frustrating. On the plus side, composing *because* clauses can be a powerful discovery tool, causing you to think of many different kinds of arguments to support your claim. But often it is difficult to wrestle your ideas into *because* clauses, which sometimes seem overly tidy for the complex network of ideas you are trying to work with. In the end, though, constructing a scale-model version of your argument in your working thesis statement is immensely helpful and worth the effort.

■ ■ ■ **FOR CLASS DISCUSSION** Developing Claims and Reasons

Try the following group exercise to help you see how writing *because* clauses can be a discovery procedure.

Divide into small groups. Each group member should contribute an issue that he or she might like to explore. Discussing one person's issue at a time, help each member develop a claim supported by several reasons. Express each reason as a *because* clause. Then write out the working thesis statement for each person's argument by attaching the *because* clauses to the claim. Finally, try to create *because* clauses in support of an alternative claim for each issue. Recorders should select two or three working thesis statements from the group to present to the class as a whole. ■ ■ ■

WRITING ASSIGNMENT An Issue Question and Working Thesis Statements

Decide on an issue and a claim for a classical argument that you would like to write. Create a one-sentence question that summarizes the controversial issue that your claim addresses. Then draft a working thesis statement for your proposed argument. Organize the thesis as a claim using bulleted *because* clauses for reasons. You should have at least two reasons, but it is okay to have three or four. In addition, include an "opposing thesis statement"—a claim with *because* clauses for an alternative position on your issue.

Recall that in Part One we emphasized exploratory writing as a way of resisting closure and helping you wrestle with multiple perspectives. Now we ask you to begin a process of closure by developing a thesis statement that nutshells your argument into a claim with supporting reasons. However, as we emphasize throughout this text, drafting itself is an *exploratory process*. Writers almost always discover new ideas when they write a first draft; as they take their writing project through multiple drafts, their views may change substantially. Often, in fact, honest writers can switch positions on an issue by discovering that a counterargument is stronger than their own. So the working thesis statement that you submit for this assignment may change substantially once you begin to draft.

In this chapter, as well as in Chapters 4 and 5, we will follow the process of student writer Carmen Tieu as she constructed an argument on violent video games. During earlier exploratory writing, she wrote about a classroom incident in which her professor had described video game playing as gendered behavior (overwhelmingly male). The professor indicated his dislike for such games, pointing to their antisocial, dehumanizing values. In her freewrite, Carmen described her own enjoyment of violent videogames—particularly first-person shooter games—and explored the pleasure that she derived from beating boys at Halo. She knew that she wanted to write an argument on this issue. What follows is Carmen's submission for this assignment.

Carmen's Issue Question and Working Thesis Statements

Issue Question: Should girls be encouraged to play first-person shooter video games?

My claim: First-person shooter (FPS) video games are great activities for girls

- because beating guys at their own game is empowering for girls
- because being skilled at FPS games frees girls from feminine stereotypes
- because they give girls a different way of bonding with males
- because they give girls new insights into a male subculture

Opposing claim: First-person shooter games are a bad activity for anyone, especially girls

- because they promote antisocial values like indiscriminate killing
- because they amplify the bad macho side of male stereotypes
- because they waste valuable time that could have been spent on something constructive
- because FPS games could encourage women to see themselves as objects ■

For additional writing, reading, and research resources, go to www.mycomplab.com.

The Logical Structure of Arguments

4

In Chapter 3, you learned that the core of an argument is a claim supported by reasons and that these reasons often can be stated as *because* clauses attached to a claim. In the present chapter we examine the logical structure of arguments in more depth.

An Overview of *Logos:* What Do We Mean by the "Logical Structure" of an Argument?

As you will recall from our discussion of the rhetorical triangle, *logos* refers to the strength of an argument's support and its internal consistency. *Logos* is the argument's logical structure. But what do we mean by "logical structure"?

Formal Logic versus Real World Logic

First of all, what we *don't* mean by logical structure is the kind of precise certainty you get in a philosophy class in formal logic. Logic classes deal with symbolic assertions that are universal and unchanging, such as "If all ps are qs and if r is a p, then r is a q." This statement is logically certain so long as p, q, and r are pure abstractions. But in the real world, p, q, and r turn into actual things, and the relationships among them suddenly become fuzzy.

For example, p might be a class of actions called "sexual harassment," and q could be the class "actions that justify dismissal from a job." If r is the class "telling off-color stories," then the logic of our p–q–r statement suggests that telling off-color stories (r) is an instance of sexual harassment (p), which in turn is an action justifying dismissal from one's job (q). Now, most of us would agree that sexual harassment is a serious offense that might well justify dismissal from a job. In turn, we might agree that telling off-color stories, if the jokes are sufficiently raunchy and are inflicted on an unwilling audience, constitutes sexual harassment. But few of us would want to say categorically that all people who tell off-color stories are harassing their listeners and ought to be fired. Most of us would want to know the particulars of the case before making a final judgment.

The Role of Assumptions

A key difference, then, between formal logic and real-world argument is that real-world arguments are not grounded in abstract, universal statements. Rather, as we shall see, they must be grounded in beliefs, assumptions, or values granted by the audience. A second important difference is that in real-world arguments these beliefs, assumptions, or values often are unstated. So long as writer and audience share the same assumptions, then it's fine to leave them unstated. But if these underlying assumptions aren't shared, the writer has a problem. To illustrate the nature of this problem, consider one of the arguments we introduced in the last chapter.

> Women should be allowed to join combat units because the image of women in combat would help eliminate gender stereotypes.

On the face of it, this is a plausible argument. But the argument is persuasive only if the audience agrees with the writer's assumption that it is a good thing to eliminate gender stereotyping.

The writer assumes that gender stereotyping (for example, seeing men as the fighters who are protecting the women and children back home) is harmful and that society would be better off without such fixed gender roles. But what if you believed that some gender roles are biologically based, divinely intended, or otherwise culturally essential and that society should strive to maintain these gender roles rather than dismiss them as "stereotypes"? If such were the case, you might believe as a consequence that our culture should socialize women to be nurturers, not fighters, and that some essential trait of "womanhood" would be at risk if women served in combat. If these were your beliefs, the argument wouldn't work for you because you would reject its underlying assumption. To persuade you with this line of reasoning, the writer would have to show not only how women in combat would help eliminate gender stereotypes but also why these stereotypes are harmful and why society would be better off without them.

The Core of an Argument: The Enthymeme

The previous core argument ("Women should be allowed to join combat units because the image of women in combat would help eliminate gender stereotypes") is an incomplete logical structure called an *enthymeme*. Its persuasiveness depends on an unstated assumption or belief that the audience must accept. To complete the enthymeme and make it effective, the audience must willingly supply a missing premise—in this case, that gender stereotypes are harmful and should be eliminated. The Greek philosopher Aristotle showed how successful enthymemes, which he considered the main underlying structure of argument, root the speaker's argument in assumptions, beliefs, or values held by the audience. If the audience is unwilling to supply the missing premise, then the argument fails. Our point is that successful arguments depend both on what the arguer says and on what the audience already has in mind.

To clarify the concept of the enthymeme, let's go over this same territory again more slowly, examining what we mean by "incomplete logical structure." The original claim with *because* clause is an enthymeme. It combines a claim ("Women should be allowed to join combat units") with a reason expressed as a *because* clause ("because the image of women in combat would help eliminate gender stereotypes"). To render this enthymeme logically complete, you must supply an unstated assumption—that gender stereotypes are harmful and should be eliminated. If your audience accepts this assumption, then you have a starting place on which to build an effective argument. If your audience doesn't accept this assumption, then you must supply another argument to support it, and so on until you find common ground with your audience. To sum up:

1. Claims are supported with reasons. You can usually state a reason as a *because* clause attached to a claim (see Chapter 3).
2. A *because* clause attached to a claim is an incomplete logical structure called an enthymeme. To create a complete logical structure from an enthymeme, the unstated assumption (or assumptions) must be articulated.
3. To serve as an effective starting point for the argument, this underlying assumption should be a belief, value, or principle that the audience grants.

Let's illustrate this structure by putting the previous example into schematic form.

ENTHYMEME

CLAIM Women should be allowed to join combat units

REASON because the image of women in combat would help eliminate gender stereotypes.

Audience must supply this assumption ──────────→

UNDERLYING ASSUMPTION
Gender stereotypes are harmful and should be eliminated.

■ ■ ■   **FOR CLASS DISCUSSION**   Identifying Underlying Assumptions
Working individually or in small groups, identify the underlying assumption the audience must supply in order to make the following enthymemes persuasive.

Example

Enthymeme: Rabbits make good pets because they are gentle.

Underlying assumption: Gentle animals make good pets.

1. We shouldn't elect Joe as committee chair because he is too bossy.
2. Airport screeners should use racial profiling because doing so will increase the odds of stopping terrorists.

3. Racial profiling should not be used by airport screeners because it violates a person's civil rights.
4. We should strengthen the Endangered Species Act because doing so will preserve genetic diversity on the planet.
5. The Endangered Species Act is too stringent because it severely damages the economy.

Adopting a Language for Describing Arguments: The Toulmin System

Understanding a new field usually requires us to learn a new vocabulary. Luckily, the field of argument requires us to learn a mere handful of new terms. A particularly useful set of argument terms, one we'll be using occasionally throughout the rest of this text, comes from philosopher Stephen Toulmin. In the 1950s, Toulmin rejected the prevailing models of argument based on formal logic in favor of a very audience-based courtroom model.

Toulmin's courtroom model differs from formal logic in that it assumes that (1) all assertions and assumptions are contestable by "opposing counsel" and that (2) all final "verdicts" about the persuasiveness of the opposing arguments will be rendered by a neutral third party, a judge or jury. As writers, keeping in mind the "opposing counsel" forces us to anticipate counterarguments and to question our assumptions. Keeping in mind the judge and jury reminds us to answer opposing arguments fully, without rancor, and to present positive reasons for supporting our case as well as negative reasons for disbelieving the opposing case. Above all else, Toulmin's model reminds us not to construct an argument that appeals only to those who already agree with us. In short, it helps arguers tailor arguments to their audiences.

The system we use for analyzing arguments combines Toulmin's language with Aristotle's concept of the enthymeme. It builds on the system you have already been practicing. We simply need to add a few key terms from Toulmin. The first term is Toulmin's *warrant,* the name we will now use for the underlying assumption that turns an enthymeme into a complete logical structure. For example:

ENTHYMEME

CLAIM Women should be allowed to join combat units

REASON because the image of women in combat would help eliminate gender stereotypes.

Audience must accept this warrant ⟶

WARRANT
Gender stereotypes are harmful and should be eliminated.

Toulmin derives his term *warrant* from the concept of "warranty" or "guarantee." The warrant is the value, belief, or principle that the audience has to hold if the soundness of the argument is to be guaranteed or warranted. Thus the warrant— once accepted by the audience—"guarantees" the soundness of the argument.

But arguments need more than claims, reasons, and warrants. These are simply one-sentence statements—the frame of an argument, not a developed argument. To give body and weight to our arguments and make them convincing, we need what Toulmin calls *grounds* and *backing*. Let's start with grounds. Grounds are the supporting evidence that cause an audience to accept your reason. Grounds are facts, data, statistics, causal links, testimony, examples, anecdotes—the blood and muscle that flesh out the skeletal frame of your enthymeme. Toulmin suggests that grounds are "what you have to go on" in an argument—the stuff you can point to and present before a jury. Here is how grounds fit into our emerging argument schema.

ENTHYMEME

CLAIM Women should be allowed to join combat units

REASON because the image of women in combat would help eliminate gender stereotypes.

Grounds support the reason → **GROUNDS**

- Examples showing how the image of women in combat gear packing a rifle, driving a tank, firing a machine gun from a foxhole, or radioing in artillery would counter the prevailing stereotypes of woman as soft and nuturing.

- Arguments showing how the shock impact of these combat images would help eliminate gender stereotypes.

In many cases, successful arguments require just these three components: a claim, a reason, and grounds. If the audience already accepts the underlying assumption behind the reason (the warrant), then the warrant can safely remain in the background unstated and unexamined. But if there is a chance that the audience will question or doubt the warrant, then the writer needs to back it up by providing an argument in its support. *Backing* is the argument that supports the warrant. It may require no more than one or two sentences or as much as a major section in your argument. Its goal is to persuade the audience to accept the warrant. How *backing* is added to our schema is shown at the top of page 60.

Toulmin's system next asks us to imagine how a resistant audience would try to refute our argument. Specifically, the adversarial audience might challenge our reason and grounds by showing how letting women become combat soldiers wouldn't

WARRANT

Gender stereotypes are harmful and should be eliminated.

BACKING

Backing supports the warrant

• Arguments showing why gender stereotypes are harmful.

  • Macho male stereotypes keep men from developing their nurturing side.

  • Girly-girl stereotypes hinder women from developing power and autonomy.

• Examples of benefits that would come from eliminating gender stereotypes such as promoting equality between genders

do much to end gender stereotyping. Or the adversary might attack our warrant and backing by showing how some gender stereotypes are worth keeping.

In the case of the argument supporting women in combat, an adversary might offer one or more of the following rebuttals:

Writer must anticipate these attacks from skeptics

ENTHYMEME

CLAIM Women should be allowed to join combat units

REASON because the image of women in combat would eliminate gender stereotypes.

GROUNDS

• Examples showing how the image of women in combat gear packing a rifle, driving a tank, firing a machine gun from a foxhole, or radioing in artillery would counter the prevailing stereotypes of women as soft and nurturing.

• Arguments showing how the shock impact of these combat images would help eliminate gender stereotypes.

CONDITIONS OF REBUTTAL

A skeptic can attack the reason and grounds

Arguments that letting women serve in combat wouldn't eliminate gender stereotypes

• Few women would join combat units.

• Those who did would be considered freaks.

• Most girls would still identify with Barbie dolls, not women as combat soldiers.

WARRANT

Gender stereotypes are harmful and should be eliminated.

BACKING

• Arguments showing why gender stereotypes are harmful

  • Macho male stereotypes keep men from developing their nurturing side

  • Girly-girl stereotypes hinder women from developing power and autonomy

• Examples of benefits that would come from eliminating gender stereotypes such as promoting equality between genders

CONDITIONS OF REBUTTAL

A skeptic can attack the warrant and backing

Arguments showing that it is important to maintain traditional distinctions between men and women

• These role differences are biologically determined, divinely inspired, or otherwise important culturally.

• Women's strength is in nurturing, not fighting.

• Nature of womanhood would be sullied by putting women in combat.

As this example shows, adversarial readers can question an argument's reasons and grounds or its warrant and backing or sometimes both. Conditions of rebuttal remind writers to look at their arguments from the perspective of skeptics.

Toulmin's final term, used to limit the force of a claim and indicate the degree of its probable truth, is *qualifier*. The qualifier reminds us that real-world arguments almost never prove a claim. We may say things like "very likely," "probably," or "maybe" to indicate the strength of the claim we are willing to draw from our grounds and warrant. Thus if there are exceptions to your warrant or if your grounds are not very strong, you will have to qualify your claim. For example, you might say, "Except in rare cases, women should not be allowed in combat units." In our future displays of the Toulmin scheme, we will omit the qualifiers—but you should always remember that no argument is one hundred percent persuasive.

■ ■ ■   **FOR CLASS DISCUSSION**   Using the Toulmin Schema

Working individually or in small groups, imagine you have to write arguments developing the enthymemes listed in the "For Class Discussion" exercise on pages 57–58. Use the Toulmin schema to help determine what you need to consider when developing each enthymeme. We suggest you try a four-box diagram structure as a way of visualizing the schema. We have applied the Toulmin schema to the first enthymeme: "We shouldn't elect Joe as committee chair because he is too bossy."

ENTHYMEME

CLAIM We shouldn't elect Joe as committee chair
REASON because he is too bossy.

GROUNDS

Evidence of Joe's bossiness

• Examples of the way he dominates meetings—doesn't call on people, talks too much

• Testimony about his bossiness from people who have served with him on committees

• Anecdotes about his abrasive style

CONDITIONS OF REBUTTAL

Attacking the reason and grounds

Evidence that Joe is not bossy or is only occasionally bossy

• Counterevidence showing his collaborative style

• Testimony from people who have liked Joe as a leader and claim he isn't bossy; testimony about his cooperativeness and kindness

• Testimony that anecdotes about Joe's bossiness aren't typical

---

WARRANT

Bossy people make bad committee chairs.

BACKING

Problems caused by bossy committee chairs

• Bossy people don't inspire cooperation and enthusiam.

• Bossy people make others angry.

• Bossy people tend to make bad decisions because they don't incorporate advice from others

---

CONDITIONS OF REBUTTAL

Attacking the warrant and backing

• Arguments that bossiness can be a good trait

  • Sometimes bossy people make good chairpersons.

  • Argument that this committee needs a bossy person who can make decisions and get things done.

• Argument that Joe has other traits of good leadership that outweigh his bossiness

Using Toulmin's Schema to Determine a Strategy of Support

So far we have seen that a claim, a reason, and a warrant form the frame for a line of reasoning in an argument. Most words in an argument, however, are devoted to grounds and backing.

For an illustration of how a writer can use the Toulmin schema to generate ideas for an argument, consider the following case. In 2005, the Texas house of representatives passed a bill banning "sexually suggestive" cheerleading. Across the nation, late-night TV comics poked fun at the bill, while newspaper editorialists debated its wisdom and constitutionality. In one of our classes, however, several students—including one who had earned a high school varsity letter in competitive cheerleading—defended the bill by contending that provocative dance moves hurt the athletic image of cheerleading. In the following example, which draws on ideas developed in class discussion, we create a hypothetical student writer (we'll call her Chandale) who argues in defense of the Texas bill. Chandale's argument is based on the following enthymeme:

> The cheerleading bill to ban suggestive dancing is good because it promotes a view of female cheerleaders as athletes rather than exotic dancers.

Chandale used the Toulmin schema to brainstorm ideas for developing her argument. Here are her notes:

Chandale's Planning Notes Using the Toulmin Schema

Enthymeme: The cheerleading bill to ban suggestive dancing is good because it promotes a view of female cheerleaders as athletes rather than exotic dancers.
Grounds: First, I've got to use evidence to show that cheerleaders are athletes.

- Cheerleaders at my high school are carefully chosen for their stamina and skill after exhausting two-week tryouts.
- We begin all practices with a mile run and an hour of warm-up exercises—also expected to work out on our own for at least an hour on weekends and on days without practice.
- We learned competitive routines and stunts consisting of lifts, tosses, flips, catches, and gymnastic moves. This requires athletic ability! We'd practice these stunts for hours each week.
- Throughout the year cheerleaders have to attend practices, camps, and workshops to learn new routines and stunts.
- Our squad competed in competitions around the state.
- Competitive cheerleading is a growing movement across the country—the University of Maryland has made it a varsity sport for women.
- Skimpy uniforms and suggestive dance moves destroy this image by making women eye candy like the Dallas Cowboys cheerleaders.

Warrant: It is a good thing to view female cheerleaders as athletes.

Backing: Now I need to make the case that it is good to see cheerleaders as athletes rather than as eye candy.

- Athletic competition builds self-esteem, independence, a powerful sense of achievement—contributes to health, strength, conditioning.
- Competitive cheerleading is one of the few sports where teams are made up of both men and women. (Why is this good? Should I use this?)
- The suggestive dance moves turn women into sex objects whose function is to be gazed at by men—suggests that women's value is based on their beauty and sex appeal.
- We are talking about HIGH SCHOOL cheerleading—very bad early influence on girls to model themselves on Dallas Cowboys cheerleaders or sexy MTV videos of rock stars.
- Junior high girls want to do what senior high girls do—suggestive dance moves promote sexuality way too early.

Conditions of Rebuttal: Would anybody try to rebut my reasons and grounds that cheerleading is an athletic activity?

- No. I think it is obvious that cheerleading is an athletic activity once they see my evidence.
- However, they might not think of cheerleading as a sport. They might say that the University of Maryland just declared it a sport as a cheap way to meet Title IX federal rules to have more women's sports. I'll have to make sure that I show this is really a sport.
- They also might say that competitive cheerleading shouldn't be encouraged because it is too dangerous—lots of serious injuries including paralysis have been caused by mistakes in doing flips, lifts, and tosses. If I include this, maybe I could say that other sports are dangerous also—and it is in fact danger that makes this sport so exciting.

Would anyone doubt my warrant and backing that it is good to see female cheerleaders as athletes?

- Yes, all those people who laughed at the Texas legislature think that people are being too prudish and that banning suggestive dance moves violates free expression. I'll need to make my case that it is bad for young girls to see themselves as sex objects too early.

The information that Chandale lists under "grounds" is what she sees as the facts of the case—the hard data she will use as evidence to support her contention that cheerleading is an athletic activity. The paragraph that follows shows how this argument might look in written form.

First Part of Chandale's Argument

Although late-night TV comedians have made fun of the Texas legislature's desire to ban "suggestive" dance moves from cheerleading routines, I applaud this bill because it promotes a healthy view of female cheerleaders as athletes rather than show girls. I was lucky enough to attend a high school where cheerleading is a sport, and I earned a varsity letter as a cheerleader. To get on my high school's cheerleading squad, students have to go through an exhausting two-week tryout of workouts and instruction in the basic routines; then they are chosen based on their stamina and skill. Once on the squad, cheerleaders begin all practices with a mile run and an hour of grueling warm-up exercises and are expected to exercise on their own on weekends. As a result of this regimen, cheerleaders achieve and maintain a top level of physical fitness. In addition, to get on the squad, students must be able to do handstands, cartwheels, handsprings, high jumps, and the splits. Each year the squad builds up to its complex routines and stunts consisting of lifts, tosses, flips, catches, and gymnastic moves that only trained athletes can do. In tough competitions at the regional and state levels, the cheerleading squad demonstrates its athletic talent. This view of cheerleading as a competitive sport is also spreading to colleges. As reported recently in a number of newspapers, the University of Maryland has made cheerleading a varsity sport, and many other universities are following suit. Athletic performance of this caliber is a far cry from the sexy dancing that many high school girls often associate with cheerleading. By banning suggestive dancing in cheerleading routines, the Texas legislature creates an opportunity for schools to emphasize the athleticism of cheerleading.

As you can see, Chandale has plenty of evidence for arguing that competitive cheerleading is an athletic activity quite different from sexy dancing. But how effective is this argument as it stands? Is this all she needs? The Toulmin schema encourages writers to include—if needed for the intended audience—explicit support for their warrants as well as attention to conditions for rebuttal. Because the overwhelming national response to the Texas law was ridicule at the perceived prudishness of the legislators, Chandale decides to expand her argument as follows:

Continuation of Chandale's Argument

Whether we see cheerleading as a sport or as sexy dancing is an important issue for women. The erotic dance moves that many high school cheerleaders now incorporate into their routines show that they are emulating the Dallas Cowboys cheerleaders or pop stars on MTV. Our already sexually saturated culture (think of the suggestive clothing marketed to little girls) pushes girls and women to measure their value by their beauty and sex appeal. It would be far healthier, both physically and psychologically, if high school cheerleaders were identified as athletes. For women and men both, competitive cheerleading can build self-esteem, pride in teamwork, and a powerful sense of achievement, as well as promote health, strength, and fitness.

Some people might object to competitive cheerleading by saying that cheerleading isn't really a sport. Some have accused the University of Maryland of making cheerleading a varsity sport only as a cheap way of meeting Title IX requirements. But anyone who has watched competitive cheerleading, and imagined what it would be like to be thrown thirty feet into the air, knows instinctively that this is a sport indeed. In fact, other persons might object to competitive cheerleading because it is too dangerous with potential for very severe injuries including paralysis. Obviously the sport is dangerous—but so are many sports, including football, gymnastics, diving, or trampoline. The danger and difficulty of the sport is part of its appeal. Part of what can make cheerleaders as athletes better role models for girls than cheerleaders as erotic dancers is the courage and training needed for success. Of course, the Texas legislators might not have had athleticism in mind when they banned suggestive dancing. They might only have been promoting their vision of morality. But at stake are the role models we set for young girls. I'll pick an athlete over a Dallas Cowboys cheerleader every time.

Our example suggests how a writer can use the Toulmin schema to generate ideas for an argument. For evidence, Chandale draws primarily on her personal experiences as a cheerleader/athlete and on her knowledge of popular culture. She also draws on her reading of several newspapers articles about the University of Maryland's making cheerleading a varsity sport. (In an academic paper rather than a newspaper editorial, she would need to document these sources through formal citations.) Although many arguments depend on research, many can be supported wholly or in part from your own personal experiences, so don't neglect the wealth of evidence from your own life when searching for data. A more detailed discussion of evidence in arguments occurs in Chapter 5.

■ ■ ■   **FOR CLASS DISCUSSION**   Reasons, Warrants, and Conditions of Rebuttal

   1. Working individually or in small groups, consider ways you could use evidence to support the stated reason in each of these following partial arguments.

     a. Another reason to oppose a state sales tax is that it is so annoying.

     b. Rap music has a bad influence on teenagers because it promotes disrespect for women.

     c. Professor X is an outstanding teacher because he (she) generously spends so much time outside of class counseling students with personal problems.

   2. Now create arguments to support the warrants in each of the partial arguments in exercise 1. The warrants for each of the arguments are stated below.

     a. Support this warrant: We should oppose taxes that are annoying.

     b. Support this warrant: It is bad to promote disrespect for women.

     c. Support this warrant: Time spent counseling students with personal problems is an important criterion for identifying outstanding teachers.

   3. Using Toulmin's conditions of rebuttal, work out a strategy for refuting either the stated reasons or the warrants or both in each of the preceding arguments.   ■ ■ ■

The Power of Audience-based Reasons

As we have seen, both Aristotle's concept of the enthymeme and Toulmin's concept of the warrant focus on the arguer's need to create what we will now call "audience-based reasons." Whenever you ask whether a given piece of writing is persuasive, the immediate rejoinder should always be "Persuasive to whom?" What seems like a good reason to you may not be a good reason to others. Finding audience-based reasons means finding arguments whose warrants the audience will accept—that is, arguments effectively rooted in your audience's beliefs and values.

To illustrate the difference between writer-based and audience-based reasons, let's consider how one student, Gordon Adams, petitioned his university to waive the math requirement for his undergraduate pre-law degree. In making his case to his university's standards committee, he used the following enthymeme:

> I should be exempted from the algebra requirement because in my chosen field of law I will have no need for algebra.

The warrant for Gordon's argument is that general education requirements should be based on career utility (that is, if a course isn't needed for a particular student's career, it shouldn't be required).

In our discussions of this case with students and faculty, students generally vote to support Gordon's request, whereas faculty members generally vote against it. And in fact, his university's standards committee rejected Gordon's petition, thus delaying his entry into law school.

Why do faculty members and students differ on this issue? Mainly they differ because faculty members reject Gordon's warrant that general education requirements should serve students' individual career interests. Most faculty members believe that general education courses, including math, provide a base of common learning that links us to the past and teaches us modes of understanding that remain useful through-out life. Gordon's argument thus challenges one of college professors' most cherished beliefs—that the liberal arts and sciences are innately valuable. Further, it threatens his immediate audience, the committee, with a possible flood of student requests to waive other general education requirements on the grounds of their irrelevance to a particular career choice.

How might Gordon have created a more persuasive argument? In our view, Gordon might have prevailed had he accepted the faculty's belief in the value of the math requirement and argued that he had fulfilled the "spirit" of that requirement through alternative means. He could have based his argument on an enthymeme like this:

> I should be exempted from the algebra requirement because my previous job experience has already provided me with equivalent mathematical knowledge.

Following this audience-based approach, Gordon would drop all references to algebra's uselessness for lawyers and discuss the mathematical savvy he acquired on the job. This argument would honor faculty values and reduce faculty members' fears of setting a bad precedent. Few students are likely to have Gordon's background, and those who did could apply for a similar exemption without threatening the system. Again, this argument may not have won, but it would have gotten a more sympathetic hearing.

■ ■ ■ **FOR CLASS DISCUSSION**   **Audience-based Reasons**
Working in groups, decide which of the two reasons offered in each instance would be more persuasive to the specified audience. Be prepared to explain your reasoning to the class. Write out the implied warrant for each *because* clause and decide whether the specific audience would likely grant it.

1. *Audience*: people who advocate a pass/fail grading system on the grounds that present grading system is too competitive

   a. We should keep the present grading system because it prepares people for the dog-eat-dog pressures of the business world.

   b. We should keep the present grading system because it tells students that certain standards of excellence must be met if individuals are to reach their full potential.

2. *Audience*: young people ages fifteen to twenty-five

   a. You should become a vegetarian because an all-vegetable diet will help you lower your cholesterol.

   b. You should become a vegetarian because that will help eliminate the suffering of animals raised in factory farms.

3. *Audience*: conservative proponents of "family values"

   a. Same-sex marriages should be legalized because doing so will promote public acceptance of homosexuality.

   b. Same-sex marriages should be legalized because doing so will make it easier for gay people to establish and sustain long-term, stable relationships.

WRITING ASSIGNMENT: Plan of an Argument's Details

This assignment asks you to return to the working thesis statement you created for the brief writing assignment in Chapter 3. From that thesis statement, extract one of your enthymemes (your claim with one of your because clauses). Write out the warrant for your enthymeme. Then use the Toulmin schema to brainstorm the details you might use (grounds, backing, conditions of rebuttal) to convert your enthymeme into a fleshed out argument. Use as your model Chandale's planning notes on pages 62–63.

Like the brief assignment for Chapter 3, this is a process-oriented brainstorming task aimed at helping you generate ideas for one part of your classical argument. You might end up changing your ideas substantially as you compose the actual argument. What follows is Carmen's submission for this assignment. ■

Carmen's Plan for Part of an Argument

Enthymeme: First-person shooter (FPS) video games are great activities for girls because playing these games gives girls new insights into male subculture.

Grounds: I've got to show the insights I learned into male subculture.

- The guys who play these videogames are intensely competitive.
  - They can play for hours without stopping—intense concentration.
  - They don't multi-task—no small talk during the games; total focus on playing.
  - They take delight in winning at all costs—they boast with every kill; they call each other losers.

■ They often seem homophobic or misogynist.

  ■ They put each other down by calling opponents "gay," "faggot," "wussy," "pussy," or other similar names that are totally obscene.

  ■ They associate victory with being macho.

Warrant: It is beneficial for a girl to get these insights into male subculture.

Backing: How can I show these benefits?

■ Although I enjoy winning at FPS games, as I girl I feel alienated from this male subculture.

■ I'm glad that I don't feel the need to put everyone else down.

■ It was a good learning experience to see how girls' way of bonding is very different from boys; girls tend to be nicer to each other rather than insulting each other.

■ The game atmosphere tends to bring out these traits; guys don't talk this way so much when they are doing other things.

■ This experience helped me see why men might progress faster than women in a competitive business environment—they seem programmed to crush each other and they devote enormous energy to the process.

■ What else can I say? I need to think about this further.

Conditions of Rebuttal: Would anybody try to rebut my reasons and grounds?

■ I think my evidence is pretty convincing that males put each other down, concentrate intensely, use homophobic or misogynist insults, etc.

■ However, some guys might say "Hey, I don't talk that way," etc.

■ Maybe people would say that my sample is biased.

Would anyone try to rebut my warrant and backing?

■ Skeptics might say that girls are just as mean to each other as guys are but they display their meanness in a different way.

Using Evidence Effectively 5

In Chapters 3 and 4, we introduced you to the concept of *logos*—the logical structure of reasons and evidence in an argument. In this chapter, we explain in more detail how to use evidence. By *evidence,* we mean all the verifiable information a writer might use as support for an argument, such as facts, observations, examples, cases, testimony, experimental findings, survey data, statistics, and so forth. In Toulmin's terms, evidence is part of the *grounds* or *backing* of an argument in support of reasons or warrants.

We begin by explaining some general principles for the persuasive use of evidence. Next we describe and illustrate various kinds of evidence and then present a rhetorical way to think about evidence, particularly the way writers select and frame evidence to support the writer's reasons while simultaneously guiding and limiting what the reader sees. We conclude the chapter by suggesting strategies to help you gather evidence for your arguments, including advice on conducting interviews and using questionnaires.

The Persuasive Use of Evidence

Consider a target audience of educated, reasonable, and careful readers who approach an issue with healthy skepticism, open-minded but cautious. What demands would such readers make on a writer's use of evidence? To begin to answer that question, let's look at some general principles for using evidence persuasively.

Apply the STAR Criteria to Evidence

Our open-minded but skeptical audience would first of all expect your evidence to meet what rhetorician Richard Fulkerson calls the STAR criteria:*

Sufficiency: Is there enough evidence?

Typicality: Is the chosen evidence representative and typical?

---

*Richard Fulkerson, *Teaching the Argument in Writing* (Urbana: National Council of Teachers of English, 1996), 44–53. In this section, we are indebted to Fulkerson's discussion.

Accuracy: Is the evidence accurate and up-to-date?

Relevance: Is the evidence relevant to the claim?

Let's examine each in turn.

Sufficiency of Evidence   How much evidence you need is a function of your rhetorical context. In a court trial, opposing attorneys often agree to waive evidence for points that aren't in doubt in order to concentrate on contested points. The more a claim is contested or the more your audience is skeptical, the more evidence you may need to present. If you provide too little evidence, you may be accused of *hasty generalization* (see Appendix One), a reasoning fallacy in which a person makes a sweeping conclusion based on only one or two instances. On the other hand, if you provide too much evidence, your argument may become overly long and tedious. You can guard against having too little or too much evidence by appropriately qualifying the claim your evidence supports.

> **Strong claim:** Working full time seriously harms a student's grade point average. [much data needed—probably a combination of examples and statistical studies]
>
> **Qualified claim:** Working full time often harms a student's grade point average. [a few representative examples may be enough]

Typicality of Evidence   Whenever you select data, readers need to believe the data are typical and representative rather than extreme instances. Suppose that you want to argue that students can combine full-time work with full-time college and cite the case of your friend Pam who pulled a straight-A grade average while working forty hours per week as a night receptionist in a small hotel. Your audience might doubt the typicality of Pam's case since a night receptionist often can use work hours for studying. What about more typical jobs, they'll ask, where you can't study while you work?

Accuracy of Evidence   Data can't be used ethically unless they are accurate and up-to-date, and they can't be persuasive unless the audience believes in the writer's credibility. As a writer, you must be scrupulous in using the most recent and accurate data you can find. Faith in the accuracy of a writer's data is one function of *ethos*—the audience's confidence in the writer's credibility and trustworthiness (see Chapter 6, p. 89).

Relevance of Evidence   Finally, evidence will be persuasive only if the reader considers it relevant to the contested issue. Consider the following student argument: "I deserve an A in this course because I worked exceptionally hard." The student then cites substantial evidence of how hard he worked—a log of study hours, copies of multiple drafts of papers, testimony from friends, and so forth. Such evidence is ample support for the claim "I worked very hard" but is irrelevant to the claim that "I deserve an A."

Use Sources Your Readers Trust

Another way to enhance the persuasiveness of your evidence is to choose data, whenever possible, from sources you think your readers will trust. Because questions of fact often are at issue in arguments, readers may be skeptical of certain sources. When you research an issue, you soon get a sense of who the participants in the conversation are and what their reputations tend to be. Knowing the political biases of sources and the extent to which a source has financial or personal investment in the outcome of a controversy will also help you locate data sources that both you and your readers can trust. Citing a peer-reviewed scholarly journal is often more persuasive than citing an advocacy Web site. Similarly, citing a conservative magazine such as the *National Review* may be unpersuasive to liberal audiences, just as citing a Sierra Club publication may be unpersuasive to conservatives. (See Appendix 2 for discussion of how to evaluate research sources.)

Rhetorical Understanding of Evidence

In the previous section, we presented some general principles for the effective use of evidence. We now want to deepen your understanding of how evidence persuades by asking you to consider more closely the rhetorical context in which evidence operates. We'll look first at the kinds of evidence used in arguments and then show you how writers select and frame evidence for persuasive effect.

Kinds of Evidence

Writers have numerous options for the kinds of evidence they can use in an argument, ranging from personal experience data to research findings to hypothetical examples. To explain these options, we present a series of charts that categorize different kinds of evidence, illustrate how each kind might be worked into an argument, and add comments about the strengths and limitations of each.

Data from Personal Experience   One powerful kind of evidence comes from personal experience:

Example	Strengths And Limitations
Despite recent criticism that Ritalin is overprescribed for attention deficit and hyperactivity disorder, it can often seem like a miracle drug. My little brother is a perfect example. Before he was given Ritalin he was a terror in school…[tell the "before" and "after" story of your little brother]	▪ Personal examples help readers identify with writer; they show writer's personal connection to issue. ▪ Vivid stories capture imagination. ▪ Skeptics may argue that personal examples are insufficient (writer is guilty of hasty generalization), not typical, or not adequately scientific or verifiable.

Data from Observation or Field Research   You can also develop evidence from personally observing a phenomenon or from doing your own field research:

Example	Strengths And Limitations
The intersection at 5th and Montgomery is particularly dangerous because pedestrians almost never find a comfortable break in the heavy flow of cars. On April 29, I watched fifty-seven pedestrians cross the street. Not once did cars stop in both directions before the pedestrian stepped off the sidewalk onto the street. [Continue with observed data about danger.]	■ Field research gives feeling of scientific credibility. ■ It increases typicality by expanding database beyond one example. ■ It enhances *ethos* of writer as personally invested and reasonable. ■ Skeptics may point to flaws in how observations were conducted, showing how data are insufficient, inaccurate, or nontypical.

Data from Interviews, Questionnaires, Surveys   You can also gather data by interviewing stakeholders in a controversy, creating questionnaires, or doing surveys.

Example	Strengths and Limitations
Another reason to ban laptops from classrooms is the extent to which laptop users disturb other students. In a questionnaire distributed to 50 students in my residence hall, a surprising 60 percent said that they were annoyed by fellow students' sending emails, paying their bills, or surfing the Web while pretending to take notes in class. Additionally, I interviewed five students, who gave me specific examples of how these distractions interfere with learning. [Report the examples.]	■ Interviews, questionnaires, and surveys enhance sufficiency and typicality of evidence by expanding database beyond experiences of one person. ■ Quantitative data from questionnaires and surveys often increase scientific feel of argument. ■ Surveys and questionnaires often uncover local or recent data not available in published research. ■ Interviews can provide engaging personal stories enhancing *pathos*. ■ Skeptics can raise doubts about research methodology, questionnaire design, or typicality of interview subjects.

Data from Library or Internet Research   For many arguments, evidence is derived from reading, particularly from library or Internet research. Appendix 2 helps you conduct effective research and incorporate research sources into your arguments:

Example	Strengths and Limitations
The belief that a high carbohydrate–low fat diet is the best way to lose weight has been challenged by research conducted by Walter Willett and his colleagues in the department of nutrition in the Harvard School of Public Health. Willett's research suggests that complex carbohydrates such as pasta and potatoes spike glucose levels, increasing risk of diabetes. Additionally, some fats—especially monounsaturated and polyunsaturated fats found in nuts, fish, and most vegetable oils—help lower "bad" cholesterol levels (45).	▪ Researched evidence is often powerful, especially when sources are respected by your audience. ▪ Researched data may take the form of facts, examples, summaries of research studies, quotations from experts, and so forth. ▪ Skeptics might doubt the accuracy of facts, the credentials of a source, or the research design of a study. They might also cite studies with different results. ▪ Skeptics might raise doubts about sufficiency, typicality, or relevance of your research data.

Testimony   Writers frequently use testimony when direct data are either unavailable or highly technical or complex. Testimonial evidence can come from research or from interviews:

Example	Strengths and Limitations
Although the Swedish economist Bjorn Lomborg claims that acid rain is not a significant problem, many environmentalists disagree. According to David Bellamany, president of the Conservation Foundation, "Acid rain does kill forests and people around the world, and it's still doing so in the most polluted places, such as Russia" (qtd. in BBC News).	▪ By itself, testimony generally is less persuasive than direct data. ▪ Persuasiveness can be increased if source has impressive credentials, which the writer can state through attributive tags. ▪ Skeptics might undermine testimonial evidence by questioning credentials of source, showing source's bias, or quoting a countersource.

Statistical Data   Many contemporary arguments rely heavily on statistical data, often supplemented by visual graphics such as tables, pie charts, and graphs. (See Chapter 9 for a discussion of the use of graphics in argument.)

Example	Strengths and Limitations
Americans are delaying marriage at a surprising rate. In 1970, 85 percent of Americans between the ages of 15 and 29 were married. In 2000, however, only 54 percent were married (U.S. Census Bureau).	▪ Statistics can give powerful snapshots of aggregate data from a wide database. ▪ They often are used in conjunction with graphics (see pp. 156–159). ▪ They can be calculated and displayed in different ways to achieve different rhetorical effects, so readers must be wary (see pp. 79–80). ▪ Skeptics might question statistical methods, research design, and interpretation of data.

Hypothetical Examples, Cases, and Scenarios Arguments occasionally use hypothetical examples, cases, or scenarios, particularly to illustrate conjectured consequences of an event or to test philosophical hypotheses.

Example	Strengths and Limitations
Consider what might happen if we continue to use biotech soybeans that are resistant to herbicides. The resistant gene, through cross-pollination, might be transferred to an ordinary weed, creating an out-of-control superweed that herbicides couldn't kill. Such a superweed could be an ecological disaster.	▪ Scenarios have strong imaginative appeal. ▪ They are persuasive only if they seem plausible. ▪ A scenario narrative often conveys a sense of inevitability, even if the actual scenario is unlikely; hence, rhetorical effect may be illogical. ▪ Skeptics might show implausibility of the scenario or offer an alternative scenario.

Reasoned Sequence of Ideas Sometimes arguments are supported with a reasoned sequence of ideas rather than with concrete facts or other forms of empirical evidence. The writer's concern is to support a point through a logical progression of ideas. Such arguments are conceptual, supported by linked ideas, rather than evidential. This kind of support occurs frequently in arguments and often is intermingled with evidentiary support.

Example	Strengths and Limitations
Embryonic stem cell research, despite its promise in fighting diseases, may have negative social consequences. This research encourages us to place embryos in the category of mere cellular matter that can be manipulated at will. Currently we place animals in this category when we genetically alter them for human purposes such as engineering pigs to grow more human-like heart valves for use in transplants. Placing human embryos in the same category by treating them as material that can be altered and destroyed at will may benefit society materially, but this quest for greater knowledge and control involves a reclassifying of embryos that could potentially lead to a devaluing of human life.	▪ These sequences often are used in causal arguments to show how causes are linked to effects or in definitional or values arguments to show links among ideas. ▪ They have great power to clarify values and show the belief structure upon which a claim is founded. ▪ They can sketch out ideas and connections that would otherwise remain latent. ▪ Their effectiveness depends on the audience's acceptance of each link in the sequence of ideas. ▪ Skeptics might raise objections at any link in the sequence, often by pointing to different values or outlining different consequences.

Angle of Vision and the Selection and Framing of Evidence

You can increase your ability to use evidence effectively—and to analyze how other arguers use evidence—by becoming more aware of a writer's rhetorical choices when using evidence to support a claim. When writers select evidence for an argument, they

EXAMINING VISUAL ARGUMENTS

Angle of Vision

Because of nationally reported injuries and near-death experiences resulting from stage diving and crowd surfing at rock concerts, many cities have tried to ban mosh pits. Critics of mosh pits have pointed to the injuries caused by crowd surfing and to the ensuing lawsuits against concert venues. Meanwhile supporters cite the almost ecstatic enjoyment of crowd-surfing rock fans who seek out concerts with "festival seating."

These photos display different angles of vision toward crowd-surfing. Suppose you were writing a blog in support of crowd surfing. Which image would you include in your posting? Why? Suppose alternatively that you were blogging against mosh pits, perhaps urging local officials to outlaw them. Which image would you choose? Why?

Analyze the visual features of these photographs in order to explain how they are constructed to create alternative angles of vision on mosh pits.

Crowd surfing in a mosh pit

An alternative view of a mosh pit

are guided by an "angle of vision" determined by their underlying beliefs, values, or purposes. (Instead of "angle of vision," we could also use other words or metaphors such as *perspective, bias, lens,* or *filter*—all terms that suggest that our way of seeing the world is shaped by our values and beliefs.) A writer's angle of vision, like a lens or filter, helps determine what stands out for that writer in a field of data—that is, what data are important or trivial, significant or irrelevant, worth focusing on or worth ignoring.

To illustrate the concept of selective seeing, consider how two hypothetical speakers might select different data about homeless people when making speeches to their city council. The first speaker argues that the city should increase its services to the homeless. The second asks the city to promote tourism more aggressively. Their differing angles of vision will cause the two speakers to select different data about the homeless and to frame these data in different ways. (Our use of the word "frame" derives metaphorically from a window frame or a camera's viewfinder. When you look through a frame, some part of your field of vision is blocked off, while the material appearing in the frame is emphasized. Through framing, a writer maximizes the reader's focus on some data, minimizes the reader's focus on other data, and otherwise guides the reader's vision and response.)

Because the first speaker wants to increase the council's sympathy for the homeless, she frames homeless people positively by telling the story of one homeless man's struggle to find shelter and nutritious food. Her speech focuses primarily on the low number of tax dollars devoted to helping the homeless. In contrast, the second speaker, using data about lost tourist income, might frame the homeless as "panhandlers" by telling the story of obnoxious, urine-soaked winos who pester shoppers for handouts. As arguers, both speakers want their audience to see the homeless from their own angles of vision. Consequently, lost tourist dollars don't show up at all in the first speaker's argument while the story of a homeless man's night in the cold doesn't show up in the second speaker's argument. As this example shows, writers select and frame evidence to bring the reader's view of the subject into alignment with the writer's angle of vision. The writer selects and frames evidence to limit and control what the reader sees.

■ ■ ■   **FOR CLASS DISCUSSION**   Creating an Angle of Vision by Selecting Evidence

Suppose your city has scheduled a public hearing on a proposed city ordinance to ban mosh pits at rock concerts. (See p. 75, where we introduced this issue.) Among the possible data available to various speakers for evidence are the following:

- Some bands, like Nine Inch Nails, specify festival seating that allows a mosh pit area.
- A female mosher writing on the Internet says: "I experience a shared energy that is like no other when I am in the pit with the crowd. It is like we are all a bunch of atoms bouncing off of each other. It's great. Hey, some people get that feeling from basketball games. I get mine from the mosh pit."
- A student conducted a survey of fifty students on her campus who had attended rock concerts in the last six months. Of the respondents, 80 percent thought that mosh pits should be allowed at concerts.
- Narrative comments on these questionnaires included the following:
  - Mosh pits are a passion for me. I get an amazing rush when crowd surfing.
  - I don't like to be in a mosh pit or do crowd surfing. But I love festival seating and like to watch the mosh pits. For me, mosh pits are part of the ambience of a concert.
  - I know a girl who was groped in a mosh pit, and she'll never do one again. But I have never had any problems.
  - Mosh pits are dangerous and stupid. I think they should be outlawed.

- If you are afraid of mosh pits, just stay away. It is ridiculous to ban them because they are totally voluntary. They should just post big signs saying, "City assumes no responsibility for accidents occurring in mosh pit area."
- A teenage girl suffered brain damage and memory loss at a 1998 Pearl Jam concert in Rapid City, South Dakota. According to her attorney, she hadn't intended to bodysurf or enter the mosh pit but "got sucked in while she was standing at its fringe."
- There were twenty-four concert deaths recorded in 2001, most of them in the area closest to the stage where people are packed in.
- A twenty-one-year-old man suffered cardiac arrest at a Metallica concert in Indiana and is now in a permanent vegetative state. Because he was jammed into the mosh pit area, nobody noticed he was in distress.
- In 2005, a blogger reported breaking his nose on an elbow while another described having his lip ring pulled out. Another blogger on the same site described having his lip nearly sliced off by the neck of a bass guitar. The injury required seventy-eight stitches. In May 2008, fifty people were treated at emergency rooms for mosh pit injuries acquired at a Bamboozle concert in New Jersey.

Tasks: Working individually or in small groups, complete the following tasks:

1. Compose two short speeches from different angles of vision—one supporting the proposed city ordinance to ban mosh pits and one opposing it. How you use these data is up to you, but be able to explain your reasoning in the way you select and frame them. Share your speeches with classmates.
2. After you have shared examples of different speeches, explain the approaches that different classmates employed. What principle of selection was used? If arguers included evidence contrary to their positions, how did they handle it, respond to it, minimize its importance, or otherwise channel its rhetorical effect?

Rhetorical Strategies for Framing Evidence

What we hope you learned from the preceding exercise is that an arguer's angle of vision causes the arguer to select evidence from a wide field of data and then frame these data through rhetorical strategies that emphasize some data, minimize others, and guide the reader's response. Now that you have a basic idea of what we mean by framing evidence, here are some strategies writers can use to guide what the reader sees and feels.

Strategies for Framing Evidence

- *Controlling the space given to supporting versus contrary evidence*: Depending on their audience and purpose, writers can devote most of their space to supporting evidence and minimal space to contrary evidence (or omit it entirely). Thus, those arguing in favor of mosh pits may have used lots of evidence supporting mosh pits, including enthusiastic quotations from concertgoers, while omitting (or summarizing very rapidly) the data about the dangers of mosh pits.

■ *Emphasizing a detailed story versus presenting lots of facts and statistics:* Often, writers can choose to support a point with a memorable individual case or with aggregate data such as statistics or lists of facts. A memorable story can have a strongly persuasive effect. For example, to create a negative view of mosh pits, a writer might tell the heartrending story of a teenager suffering permanent brain damage from being dropped on a mosh pit floor. In contrast, a supporter of mosh pits might tell the story of a happy music lover turned on to the concert scene by the rush of crowd surfing. A different strategy is to use facts and statistics rather than case narratives—for example, data about the frequency of mosh pit accidents, financial consequences of lawsuits, and so forth. The single narrative case often has a more powerful rhetorical effect, but it is always open to the charge that it is an insufficient or nonrepresentative example. Vivid anecdotes make for interesting reading, but by themselves they may not be compelling logically. In contrast, aggregate data, often used in scholarly studies, can provide more compelling logical evidence but sometimes make the prose wonkish and dense.

■ *Providing contextual and interpretive comments when presenting data:* When citing data, writers can add brief contextual or interpretive comments that act like lenses over the readers' eyes to help them see the data from the writer's perspective. Suppose you want to support mosh pits, but want to admit that mosh pits are dangerous. You could make that danger seem irrelevant or inconsequential by saying: "It is true that occasional mosh pit accidents happen, just as accidents happen in any kind of recreational activity from swimming to weekend softball games." The concluding phrase frames the danger of mosh pits by comparing them to other recreational accidents that don't require special laws or regulations. The implied argument is this: banning mosh pits because of an occasional accident would be as silly as banning recreational swimming because of occasional accidents.

■ *Putting contrary evidence in subordinate positions:* Just as a photographer can place a flower at the center of a photograph or in the background, a writer can place a piece of data in a subordinate clause or main clause of a sentence. Note how the structure of the following sentence minimizes the fact that mosh pit accidents are rare: "Although mosh pit accidents are rare, the danger to the city of multimillion-dollar liability lawsuits means that the city should nevertheless ban them for reasons of fiscal prudence." The factual datum that mosh pit accidents are rare is summarized briefly and tucked away in a subordinate "*although* clause," while the writer's own position is elaborated in the main clause where it receives grammatical emphasis. A writer with a different angle of vision might say, "Although some cities may occasionally be threatened with a lawsuit, serious accidents resulting from mosh pits are so rare that cities shouldn't interfere with the desires of music fans to conduct concerts as they please."

■ *Choosing labels and names that guide the reader's response to data:* One of the most subtle ways to control your reader's response to data is to choose labels and names that prompt them to see the issue as you do. If you like mosh pits, you might refer to the seating arrangements in a concert venue as "festival seating, where concert-goers have the opportunity to create a free-flowing mosh pit." If you don't like mosh pits, you might refer to the seating arrangements as "an accident-inviting use of empty space where rowdies can crowd together, slam into each other, and occasionally punch and kick." The labels you choose, along with the connotations of the words you select, urge your reader to share your angle of vision.

■ *Using images (photographs, drawings) to guide the reader's response to data:* Another strategy for moving your audience toward your angle of vision is to include a photograph or drawing that portrays a contested issue from your perspective. You've already tried your hand at selecting mosh pit photographs that make arguments through their angle of vision. (See Evaluating Visual Arguments on p. 75). Most people agree that the first photo supports a positive view of mosh pits. The crowd looks happy and relaxed (rather than rowdy or out of control), and the young woman lifted above the crowd smiles broadly, her body relaxed, her arms extended. In contrast, the second photo emphasizes muscular men and threatens danger rather than harmony. The crowd seems on the verge of turning ugly. (See Chapter 9 for a complete discussion of the use of visuals in argument.)

■ *Revealing the value system that determines the writer's selection and framing of data:* Ultimately, how a writer selects and frames evidence is linked to the system of values that organize his or her argument. If you favor mosh pits, you probably favor maximizing the pleasure of concertgoers, promoting individual choice, and letting moshers assume the risk of their own behavior. If you want to forbid mosh pits, you probably favor minimizing risks, protecting the city from lawsuits, and protecting individuals from the danger of their own out-of-control actions. Sometimes you can foster connections with your audience by openly addressing your underlying values that you hope your audience shares with you. You can often frame your selected data by stating explicitly the values that guide your argument.

Special Strategies for Framing Statistical Evidence

Numbers and statistical data can be framed in so many ways that this category of evidence deserves its own separate treatment. By recognizing how writers frame numbers to support the story they want to tell, you will always be aware that other stories are also possible. Ethical use of numbers means that you use reputable sources for your basic data, that you don't invent or intentionally distort numbers for your own purposes, and that you don't ignore alternative points of view. Here are some of the choices writers make when framing statistical data:

■ *Raw numbers versus percentages.* You can alter the rhetorical effect of a statistic by choosing between raw numbers or percentages. In summer 2002, many American parents panicked over what seemed like an epidemic of child abductions. If you cited the raw number of these abductions reported in the national news, this number, although small, could seem scary. But if you computed the actual percentage of American children who were abducted, that percentage was so infinitesimally small as to seem insignificant. You can apply this framing option directly to the mosh pit case. To emphasize the danger of mosh pits, you can say that twenty deaths occurred at rock concerts in a given year. To minimize this statistic, you could compute the percentage of deaths by dividing this number by the total number of persons who attended rock concerts during the year, certainly a number in the several millions. From the perspective of percentages, the death rate at concerts is extremely low.

■ *Median versus mean.* Another way to alter the rhetorical effect of numbers is to choose between the median and the mean. The mean is the average of all numbers on a list. The median is the middle number when all the numbers are arranged sequentially from high to low. In 2006, the mean annual income for retired families in the United States was $41,928—not a wealthy amount but enough to live on comfortably if you owned your own home. However, the median income was only $27,798, a figure that gives you a much more striking picture of income distribution among older Americans. This median figure means that half of all retired families in the United States had annual incomes of $27,798 or less. The much higher mean income indicates that many retired Americans are quite wealthy. This wealth raises the average of all incomes (the mean) but doesn't effect the median.

■ *Unadjusted versus adjusted numbers.* Suppose your boss told you that you were getting a 5 percent raise. You might be happy—unless inflation rates were running at 6 percent. Economic data can be hard to interpret across time unless the dollar amounts are adjusted for inflation. This same problem occurs in other areas. For example, comparing grade point averages of college graduates in 1970 versus 2009 means little unless one can somehow compensate for grade inflation.

■ *Base point for statistical comparisons.* In 2008, the stock market was in precipitous decline if one compared 2008 prices with 2000 prices. However, the market still seemed vigorous and healthy if one compared 2008 against 2002. One's choice of the base point for a comparison often makes a significant rhetorical difference.

■ ■ ■   **FOR CLASS DISCUSSION**   Using Strategies to Frame Statistical Evidence

A proposal to build a new ballpark in Seattle yielded a wide range of statistical arguments. All of the following statements are reasonably faithful to the same facts:

■ The ballpark would be paid for by raising the sales tax from 8.2 percent to 8.3 percent over a twenty-year period.
■ The sales tax increase is one-tenth of 1 percent.
■ This increase represents $750 per five-person family over the twenty-year period of the tax.
■ For a family building a new home in the Seattle area, this tax will increase building costs by $200.
■ This is a $250 million tax increase for the residents of the Seattle area.

How would you describe the costs of the proposed ballpark if you opposed the proposal? How would you describe the costs if you supported the proposal?   ■ ■ ■

Gathering Evidence

We conclude this chapter with some brief advice on ways to gather evidence for your arguments. We begin with a list of brainstorming questions that may help you think of possible sources for evidence. We then provide suggestions for conducting interviews and creating surveys and questionnaires, since these powerful sources often are overlooked by students.

Creating a Plan for Gathering Evidence

As you begin contemplating an argument, you can use the following checklist to help you think of possible sources for evidence.

A Checklist for Brainstorming Sources of Evidence

- What personal experiences have you had with this issue? What details from your life or the lives of your friends, acquaintances, or relatives might serve as examples or other kinds of evidence?
- What observational studies would be relevant to this issue? How could you gather data by observing people, events, or other phenomena or by doing field or laboratory research?
- Who could you interview to provide insights or expert knowledge on this issue?
- What questions about your issue could be addressed in a survey or questionnaire?
- What evidence could you gather by doing library research, including a licensed database search for articles in magazines, newspapers, and scholarly journals? (See Appendix 1.)
- What evidence could you find by doing a rhetorically savvy search of Internet and Web sources? (See Appendix 2.)

Gathering Data from Interviews

Conducting interviews is a useful way not only to gather expert testimony and important data but also to learn about alternative views. To make interviews as productive as possible, determine your purpose in advance. Prepare by doing background reading so that you will be informed on the issue, establish your credibility, and build a bridge between you and your source. It is also a good idea to formulate questions in advance, but be ready to move in unexpected directions if the interview opens up new territory. As part of your professional demeanor, be sure to have with you all the necessary supplies (notepaper, pens, pencils, perhaps a tape recorder, if your interviewee is willing). Take brief but clear notes, recording the main ideas and being accurate with quotations. Ask for clarification of any points you don't understand. Immediately after the interview, while your memory is still fresh, rewrite your notes more fully and completely.

When you use interview data in your writing, put quotation marks around any direct quotations. In most cases, you will also want to identify your source by name and indicate his or her title or credentials—whatever will convince the reader that this person's remarks are to be taken seriously.

Gathering Data from Surveys or Questionnaires

A well-constructed survey or questionnaire can provide lively, current data for your argument. To give you useful information and avoid charges of bias, you will want to include a range of questions, including both closed-response questions and open-response questions. Closed-response questions, asking participants to check a box or number on a scale, yield quantitative data that you can report statistically, perhaps in tables or graphs. Open-response questions elicit varied responses and often short narratives that allow participants to offer their own input. These may contribute new insights to your perspective on the issue. Make your questionnaire clear and easy to complete and explain your purpose at the outset. Respondents usually are more willing to participate if they know how the knowledge gained from the questionnaire or survey will benefit others. Also seek a random sample of respondents. For example, if a questionnaire about the university library went only to dorm residents, then you wouldn't learn how commuting students felt. When you have collected the questionnaires or finished the survey interviews, tally the usable data and summarize responses.

WRITING ASSIGNMENT A Microtheme or a Supporting-Reasons Argument

Option 1: A Microtheme   Write a one- or two-paragraph argument in which you support one of the following enthymemes, using evidence from personal experience, field observation, interviews, or data from a brief questionnaire or survey. Most of your microtheme should support the stated reason with evidence. However, also include a brief passage supporting the implied warrant. The opening sentence of your microtheme should be the enthymeme itself, which serves as the thesis statement for your argument. (Note: If you disagree with the enthymeme's argument, recast the claim or the reason to assert what you want to argue.)

1. Reading fashion magazines can be detrimental to teenage girls because such magazines can produce an unhealthy focus on beauty.
2. Surfing the Web might harm your studying because it causes you to waste time.
3. Service-learning courses are valuable because they allow you to test course concepts within real-world contexts.
4. Summer internships in your field of interest, even without pay, are the best use of your summer time because they speed up your education and training for a career.
5. Any enthymeme (a claim with a *because* clause) of your choice that can be supported without library or Internet research. (The goal of this microtheme is to give you practice using data from personal experience or from brief field research.) You may want to have your instructor approve your enthymeme in advance.

Option 2: A Supporting-Reasons Argument   Write an argument that uses at least two reasons to support your claim. Your argument should include all the features of a classical argument except the section on summarizing and responding to opposing views, which we will cover in Chapter 7. This assignment builds on the brief writing assignments in Chapter 3 (create a thesis statement for an argument) and Chapter 4 (brainstorm support for one of your enthymemes using the Toulmin schema). We now ask you to expand your argument frame into a complete essay.

A *supporting-reasons* argument is our term for a classical argument without a section that summarizes and responds to opposing views. Even though alternative views aren't dealt with in detail, the writer usually summarizes an opposing view briefly in the introduction to provide background on the issue being addressed. Follow the explanations and organization chart for a classical argument as shown on pages 44–46, but omit the section called "summary and critique of opposing views."

Like a complete classical argument, a supporting-reasons argument has a thesis-governed structure in which you state your claim at the end of the introduction, begin body paragraphs with clearly stated reasons, and use effective transitions throughout to keep your reader on track. In developing your own argument, place your most important, persuasive, or interesting reason last, where it will have the greatest impact on your readers. This kind of tightly organized structure is sometimes called a *self-announcing* or *closed-form* structure because the writer states his or her claim before beginning the body of the argument and forecasts the structure that is to follow. In contrast, an *unfolding* or *open-form* structure doesn't give away the writer's position until late in the essay. (We discuss delayed thesis arguments in Chapter 7.)

In writing a self-announcing argument, students often ask how much of the argument to summarize in the thesis statement. Consider your options:

- You might announce only your claim:

  Women should be allowed to join combat units.

- You might forecast a series of parallel reasons:

  Women should be allowed to join combat units for several reasons.

- You might forecast the actual number of reasons:

  Women should be allowed to join combat units for five reasons.

- Or you might forecast the whole argument by including your *because clauses* with your claim:

  Women should be allowed to join combat units because they are physically capable of doing the job; because the presence of women in combat units would weaken gender stereotypes; because they are already seeing combat in Iraq; because opening combat units to women would expand their military career opportunities; and because it would advance the cause of civil rights.

This last thesis statement forecasts not only the claim, but also the supporting reasons that will serve as topic sentences for key paragraphs throughout the body of the paper.

No formula can tell you exactly how much of your argument to forecast in the introduction. The only general rule is this: Readers sometimes feel insulted by too much forecasting. In writing a self-announcing argument, forecast only what is needed for clarity. In short arguments, readers often need only your claim. In longer arguments, however, or in especially complex ones, readers appreciate your forecasting the complete structure of the argument (claim with reasons). ∎

Reading

What follows is Carmen Tieu's supporting-reasons argument. Carmen's earlier explorations for this assignment are shown at the end of Chapters 3 and 4.

Why Violent Video Games Are Good for Girls

CARMEN TIEU (STUDENT)

It is ten o'clock P.M., game time. My entire family knows by now that when I am home on Saturday nights, ten P.M. is my gaming night when I play my favorite first-person shooter games, usually *Halo 3,* on Xbox Live. Seated in my mobile chair in front of my family's 42-inch flat screen HDTV, I log onto Xbox Live. A small message in the bottom of the screen appears with the words "Kr1pL3r is online," alerting me that one of my male friends is online and already playing. As the game loads, I send Kr1pL3r a game invite, and he joins me in the pre-game room lobby.

In the game room lobby, all the players who will be participating in the match are chatting aggressively with each other: "Oh man, we're gonna own you guys so bad." When a member of the opposing team notices my gamer tag, "embracingapathy," he begins to insult me by calling me various degrading, gay-associated names: "Embracing apa-what? Man, it sounds so emo. Are you some fag? I bet you want me so bad. You're gonna get owned!" Players always assume from my gamer tag that I am a gay male, never a female. The possibility that I am a girl is the last thing on their minds. Of course, they are right that girls seldom play first-person shooter games. Girls are socialized into activities that promote togetherness and talk, not high intensity competition involving fantasized shooting and killing. The violent nature of the games tends to repulse girls. Opponents of violent video games typically hold that these games are so graphically violent that they will influence players to become amoral and sadistic. Feminists also argue that violent video games often objectify women by portraying them as sexualized toys for men's gratification. Although I understand these objections, I argue that playing first-person shooter games can actually be good for girls.

First, playing FPS games is surprisingly empowering because it gives girls the chance to beat guys at their own game. When I first began playing *Halo 2,* I was horrible. My male friends constantly put me down for my lack of skills, constantly telling me that I was awful, "but for a girl, you're good." But it didn't take much practice until I learned to operate the two joy sticks with precision and with quick instinctual reactions. While guys and girls can play many physical games together, such as basketball or touch football, guys will always have the advantage because on average they are taller, faster, and stronger than females. However, when it comes to video games, girls can compete equally because physical strength isn't required, just quick reaction time and manual dexterity—skills that women possess in abundance. The adrenaline rush that I receive from beating a bunch of testosterone-driven guys at something they supposedly excel at is exciting; I especially savor the look of horror on their faces when I completely destroy them.

Since female video gamers are so rare, playing shooter games allows girls to be freed from feminine stereotypes and increases their confidence. Culture generally portrays females as caring, nonviolent, and motherly beings who are not supposed to enjoy FPS games with their war themes and violent killings. I am in no way rejecting these traditional female values since I myself am a compassionate, tree-hugging vegan. But I also like to break these stereotypes. Playing video games offers a great way for females to break the social mold of only doing "girly" things and introduces them to something that males commonly enjoy. Playing video games with sexist males has also helped me become more outspoken. Psychologically, I can stand up to aggressive males because I know that I can beat them at their own game. The confidence I've gotten from excelling at shooter games may have even carried over into the academic arena because I am majoring in chemical engineering and have no fear whatsoever of intruding into the male-dominated territory of math and science. Knowing that I can beat all the guys in my engineering classes at *Halo* gives me that little extra confidence boost during exams and labs.

5   Another reason for girls to play FPS games is that it gives us a different way of bonding with guys. Once when I was discussing my latest *Halo 3* matches with one of my regular male friends, a guy whom I didn't know turned around and said, "You play *Halo*? Wow, you just earned my respect." Although I was annoyed that this guy apparently didn't respect women in general, it is apparent that guys will talk to me differently now that I can play video games. From a guy's perspective I can also appreciate why males find video games so addicting. You get joy from perfecting your skills so that your high-angle grenade kills become a thing of beauty. While all of these skills may seem trivial to some, the acknowledgment of my skills from other players leaves me with a perverse sense of pride in knowing that I played the game better than everyone else. Since I have started playing, I have also noticed that it is much easier to talk to males about lots of different subjects. Talking video games with guys is a great ice-breaker that leads to different kinds of friendships outside the realm of romance and dating.

Finally, playing violent video games can be valuable for girls because it gives them insights into a disturbing part of male subculture. When the testosterone starts kicking in, guys become blatantly homophobic and misogynistic. Any player, regardless of gender, who cannot play well (as measured by having a high number of kills and a low number of deaths) is made fun of by being called gay, a girl, or worse. Even when some guys finally meet a female player, they will also insult her by calling her a lesbian or an ugly fat chick that has no life. Their insults towards the girl will dramatically increase if she beats them because they feel so humiliated. In their eyes, playing worse than a girl is embarrassing because girls are supposed to be inept at FPS games. Whenever I play *Halo* better than my male friends, they often comment on how "it makes no sense that we're getting owned by Carmen."

When males act like such sexist jerks it causes one to question if they are always like this. My answer is no because I know, first hand, that when guys like that are having one-on-one conversations with a female, they show a softer side, and the macho side goes away. They don't talk about how girls should stay in the kitchen and make them dinner, but rather how they think it is cool that they share a fun, common interest with a girl. But when they are in a group of males their fake, offensive macho side comes out. I find this phenomenon troubling because it shows a real problem in the way boys are socialized. To be a real "man" around other guys, they have to put down women and gays in activities involving aggressive behavior where men are supposed to excel. But they don't become macho and aggressive in activities like reading and writing, which they think of as feminine. I've always known that guys are more physically aggressive than women, but until playing violent video games I had never realized how this aggression is related to misogyny and homophobia. Perhaps these traits aren't deeply ingrained in men but come out primarily in a competitive male environment. Whatever the cause, it is an ugly phenomenon, and I'm glad that I learned more about it. Beating guys at FPS games has made me a more confident woman while being more aware of gender differences in the way men and women are socialized. I joined the guys in playing *Halo,* but I didn't join their subculture of ridiculing women and gays.

For additional writing, reading, and research resources, go to www.mycomplab.com

Moving Your Audience:
Ethos, Pathos, and *Kairos*

6

In Chapters 4 and 5 we focused on *logos*—the logical structure of reasons and evidence in argument. Even though we have treated *logos* in its own chapters, an effective arguer's concern for *logos* is always connected to *ethos* and *pathos* (see the rhetorical triangle introduced in Chapter 3, p. 47). By seeking audience-based reasons—so that an arguer connects her message to the assumptions, values, and beliefs of her audience—she appeals also to *ethos* and *pathos* by enhancing the reader's trust and by triggering the reader's sympathies and imagination. In this chapter, we turn specifically to *ethos* and *pathos*. We also introduce you to a related rhetorical concept, *kairos,* which concerns the timeliness, fitness, and appropriateness of an argument for its occasion.

Ethos and *Pathos* as Persuasive Appeals: An Overview

To see how *logos, ethos,* and *pathos* work together to create an impact on the reader, consider the different impacts of the following arguments, all having roughly the same logical appeal:

1. People should adopt a vegetarian diet because doing so will help prevent the cruelty to animals caused by factory farming.
2. If you are planning to eat chicken tonight, please consider how much that chicken suffered so that you can have a tender and juicy meal. Commercial growers cram the chickens so tightly together into cages that they never walk on their own legs, see sunshine, or flap their wings. In fact, their beaks must be cut off to keep them from pecking each other's eyes out. One way to prevent such suffering is for more people to become vegetarians.
3. People who eat meat are no better than sadists who torture other sentient creatures to enhance their own pleasure. Unless you enjoy sadistic tyranny over others, you have only one choice: Become a vegetarian.
4. People committed to justice might consider the extent to which our love of eating meat requires the agony of animals. A visit to a modern chicken factory—where chickens live their entire lives in tiny darkened coops without room to spread their wings—might raise doubts about our right to inflict such suffering on sentient creatures. Indeed, such a visit might persuade us that vegetarianism is a more just alternative.

87

Each argument has roughly the same logical core:

ENTHYMEME

CLAIM People should adopt a vegetarian diet

REASON because doing so will help prevent the cruelty to animals caused by factory farming.

GROUNDS

• Evidence of suffering in commercial chicken farms, where chickens are crammed together and lash out at one another

• Evidence that only widespread adoption of vegetarianism will end factory farming

WARRANT

If we have an alternative to making animals suffer, we should use it.

But the impact of each argument varies. The difference between arguments 1 and 2, most of our students report, is the greater emotional power of 2. Whereas argument 1 refers only to the abstraction "cruelty to animals," argument 2 paints a vivid picture of chickens with their beaks cut off to prevent their pecking each other blind. Argument 2 makes a stronger appeal to *pathos* (not necessarily a stronger argument), stirring feelings by appealing simultaneously to the heart and to the head.

The difference between arguments 1 and 3 concerns both *ethos* and *pathos*. Argument 3 appeals to the emotions through highly charged words like *torture, sadists,* and *tyranny*. But argument 3 also draws attention to its writer, and most of our students report not liking that writer very much. His stance is self-righteous and insulting. In contrast, argument 4's author establishes a more positive *ethos*. He establishes rapport with members of his audience by assuming they are committed to justice and by qualifying his argument with conditional terms such as *might* and *perhaps*. He also invites sympathy for his problem—an appeal to *pathos*—by offering a specific description of chickens crammed into tiny coops.

Which of these arguments is best? They all have appropriate uses. Arguments 1 and 4 seem aimed at receptive audiences reasonably open to exploration of the issue. Arguments 2 and 3 seem designed to shock complacent audiences or to rally a group of True Believers. Even argument 3, which is too abusive to be effective in most instances, might work as a rallying speech at a convention of animal liberation activists.

Our point thus far is that *logos, ethos,* and *pathos* are different aspects of the same whole, different lenses for intensifying or softening the light beam you project onto the screen. Every choice you make as a writer affects in some way each of the three appeals. The rest of this chapter examines these choices in more detail.

How to Create an Effective *Ethos:* The Appeal to Credibility

The ancient Greek and Roman rhetoricians recognized that an argument will be more persuasive if the audience trusts the speaker. Aristotle argued that such trust resides within the speech itself, not in the prior reputation of the speaker. In the speaker's manner and delivery; in tone, word choice, and arrangement of reasons; and in the sympathy with which the speaker treats alternative views, he or she creates a trustworthy persona. Aristotle called the impact of the speaker's credibility the appeal from *ethos*. How does a writer create credibility? We suggest three ways:

- **Be knowledgeable about your issue.** The first way to gain credibility is to *be* credible—that is, to argue from a strong base of knowledge, to have at hand the examples, personal experiences, statistics, and other empirical data needed to make a sound case. If you have done your homework, you will command the attention of most audiences.
- **Be fair.** Besides being knowledgeable about your issue, you need to demonstrate fairness and courtesy to alternative views. Because true argument can occur only where persons may reasonably disagree with one another, your *ethos* will be strengthened if you demonstrate that you understand and empathize with other points of view. There are times, of course, when you may appropriately scorn an opposing view. But these times are rare, and they mostly occur when you address audiences predisposed to your view. Demonstrating empathy to alternative views is generally the best strategy.
- **Build a bridge to your audience.** A third means of establishing credibility—building a bridge to your audience—has been treated at length in our earlier discussion of audience-based reasons. By grounding your argument in shared values and assumptions, you demonstrate your goodwill and enhance your image as a trustworthy person respectful of your audience's views. We mention audience-based reasons here to show how this aspect of *logos*—finding the reasons most rooted in the audience's values—also affects your *ethos* as a person respectful of your readers' views.

How to Create *Pathos:* The Appeal to Beliefs and Emotions

Although commonly defined as an "appeal to the emotions," *pathos* evokes effects that are subtler and more complex than the word *emotions* suggests. Because our understanding of something is a matter of feeling as well as perceiving, *pathos* can evoke nonlogical, but not necessarily nonrational, ways of knowing. When used effectively and ethically, pathetic appeals reveal the fullest human meaning of an issue, helping us walk in the writer's shoes. That is why arguments often are improved through the use of sensory details that allow us to see the reality of a problem or through stories that make specific cases and instances come alive. *Pathos* touches the heart and mind simultaneously.

Although it is difficult to classify all the ways that writers can create appeals from *pathos,* we will focus on five strategies: concrete language; specific examples and illustrations; narratives; word connotations, metaphors, and analogies; and visual images.

Use Concrete Language

Concrete language can increase the liveliness, interest level, and personality of one's prose and typically heightens *pathos* in an argument. Consider the differences between the first and second drafts of the following student argument:

First Draft

People who prefer driving a car to taking a bus think that taking the bus will increase the stress of the daily commute. Just the opposite is true. Not being able to find a parking spot when in a hurry to work or school can cause a person stress. Taking the bus gives a person time to read or sleep, etc. It could be used as a mental break.

Second Draft (with Concrete Language)

Taking the bus can be more relaxing than driving a car. Having someone else behind the wheel gives people time to chat with friends or cram for a test. They can balance their checkbooks, do homework, doze off, read the daily newspaper, or get lost in a novel rather than foaming at the mouth looking for a parking space.

In the second draft, specific details enliven the prose by creating images that trigger positive feelings. Who wouldn't want some free time to doze off or to get lost in a novel?

Use Specific Examples and Illustrations

Specific examples and illustrations serve two purposes in an argument: They provide evidence that supports your reasons; simultaneously, they give your argument presence and emotional resonance. Note the flatness of the following draft, arguing for the value of multicultural studies in a university core curriculum:

First Draft

Another advantage of a multicultural education is that it will help us see our own culture in a broader perspective. If all we know is our own heritage, we might not be inclined to see anything bad about this heritage because we won't know anything else. But if we study other heritages, we can see the costs and benefits of our own heritage.

Now note the increase in "presence" when the writer adds a specific example.

Second Draft (Example Added)

Another advantage of multicultural education is that it raises questions about traditional Western values. For example, owning private property (such as buying your own home) is part of the American dream and is a basic right guaranteed in our Constitution. However, in studying the beliefs of American Indians, students are confronted with a very different view of private property. When the U.S. government sought to buy land in the Pacific Northwest from Chief Sealth, he is alleged to have replied:

> The president in Washington sends words that he wishes to buy our land. But how can you buy or sell the sky? The land? The idea is strange to us. If we do not own the freshness of the air and the sparkle of the water, how can you buy them?...We are part of the earth and it is part of us....This we know: The earth does not belong to man, man belongs to the earth.

> Our class was shocked by the contrast between traditional Western views of property and Chief Sealth's views. One of our best class discussions was initiated by this quotation from Chief Sealth. Had we not been exposed to a view from another culture, we would have never been led to question the "rightness" of Western values.

The writer begins his revision by evoking a traditional Western view of private property, which he then questions by shifting to Chief Sealth's vision of land as open, endless, and as unobtainable as the sky. Through the use of a specific example, the writer brings to life his previously abstract point about the benefit of multicultural education.

Use Narratives

A particularly powerful way to evoke *pathos* is to tell a story that either leads into your claim or embodies it implicitly and that appeals to your readers' feelings and imagination. Brief narratives—whether real or hypothetical—are particularly effective as opening attention grabbers for an argument. To illustrate how an introductory narrative (either a story or a brief scene) can create pathetic appeals, consider the following first paragraph to an argument opposing jet skis:

> I dove off the dock into the lake, and as I approached the surface I could see the sun shining through the water. As my head popped out, I located my cousin a few feet away in a rowboat waiting to escort me as I, a twelve-year-old girl, attempted to swim across the mile-wide, pristine lake and back to our dock. I made it, and that glorious summer day is one of my most precious memories. Today, however, no one would dare attempt that swim. Jet skis have taken over this small lake where I spent many summers with my grandparents. Dozens of whining jet skis crisscross the lake, ruining it for swimming, fishing, canoeing, rowboating, and even waterskiing. More stringent state laws are needed to control jetskiing because it interferes with other uses of lakes and is currently very dangerous.

This narrative makes a case for a particular point of view toward jet skis by winning our identification with the writer's experience. She invites us to relive that experience with her while she also taps into our own treasured memories of summer experiences that have been destroyed by change.

Opening narratives to evoke *pathos* can be powerfully effective, but they are also risky. If they are too private, too self-indulgent, too sentimental, or even too dramatic and forceful, they can backfire on you. If you have doubts about an opening narrative, read it to a sample audience before using it in your final draft.

Choose Words, Metaphors, and Analogies with Appropriate Connotations

Another way of appealing to *pathos* is to select words, metaphors, or analogies with connotations that match your aim. We have already described this strategy in Chapter 5 in our discussion of the "framing" of evidence (pp. 74–80). By using words with particular connotations, a writer guides readers to see the issue through the writer's angle of vision. Thus if you want to create positive feelings about a recent city council decision, you can call it "bold and decisive"; if you want to create negative feelings, you can call it "haughty and autocratic." Similarly, writers can use favorable or unfavorable metaphors and analogies to evoke different imaginative or emotional responses. A tax bill might be viewed as a "potentially fatal poison pill" or as "unpleasant but necessary economic medicine." In each of these cases, the words create an emotional as well as intellectual response.

■ ■ ■   **FOR CLASS DISCUSSION**   Incorporating Appeals to *Pathos*
Outside class, rewrite the introduction to one of your previous papers (or a current draft) to include more appeals to *pathos*. Use any of the strategies for giving your argument presence: concrete language, specific examples, narratives, metaphors, analogies, and connotative words. Bring both your original and your rewritten introductions to class. In pairs or in groups, discuss the comparative effectiveness of these introductions in trying to reach your intended audience.   ■ ■ ■

Use Images for Emotional Appeal

One of the most powerful ways to engage an audience emotionally is to use photos or other images (see Chapter 9 for a full discussion of the persuasive power of images). Although many written arguments do not lend themselves to visual illustrations, we suggest that when you construct arguments you consider the potential of visual support. Imagine that your argument will appear in a newspaper or magazine where space is provided for one or two visuals. What photographs or drawings might help persuade your audience toward your perspective?

When images work well, they are analogous to the verbal strategies of concrete language, specific illustrations, narratives, and connotative words. The challenge in using visuals is to find material that is straightforward enough not to require elaborate explanations, that is timely and relevant, and that clearly adds impact to a specific part of your argument. As an example, suppose you are writing an argument supporting fundraising efforts to help third-world countries. To add a powerful appeal to *pathos*, you might consider incorporating into your argument the photograph shown in Figure 6.1—

a Haitian woman walking on a rickety bridge over a vast garbage heap in a Haitian slum. This image, which appeared in the *New York Times* in summer 2002, creates an almost immediate emotional and imaginative response.

■ ■ ■ **FOR CLASS DISCUSSION** Analyzing Images as Appeals to *Pathos*

Working in small groups or as a whole class, share your responses to the following questions:

1. How would you describe the emotional/imaginative impact of the photograph of Haitian poverty?
2. Many appeals for helping third-world countries show pictures of big-bellied, starving children during a famine, often in Africa. How is your response to Figure 6.1 similar to or different from the commonly encountered pictures of starving children? How is its story about the ravages of poverty different from the stories of starving children?

FIGURE 6.1 La Saline, a slum in Port-au-Prince, Haiti   ■ ■ ■

Kairos—The Timeliness and Fitness of Arguments

To increase your argument's effectiveness, you need to consider not only its appeals to *logos, ethos,* and *pathos,* but also its *kairos*—that is, its timing, its appropriateness for the occasion. In Greek, *kairos* means "right time," "season," or "opportunity." To

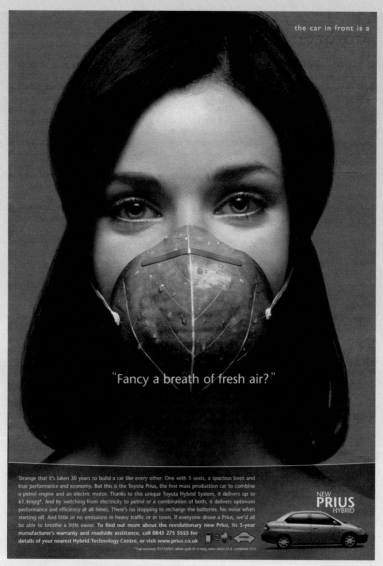

Logos, Ethos, Pathos, and Kairos

Increasing sales of Toyota's Prius, a hybrid car with an engine that runs on both electricity and gasoline, confirm Toyota's leadership in the automobile industry's search for more energy-efficient cars. As this advertisement for the Prius shows, energy efficient cars are connected to a constellation of issues, including the need to decrease carbon emissions because of pollution-caused health problems and environmental concern for cleaner energy.

How does ad attempt to move its audience by tapping into these issues? Analyze ad's appeals to *logos, ethos, pathos* and *kairos*.

think *kairotically* is to be attuned to the total context of a situation in order to act in the right way at the right moment. By analogy, consider a skilled baserunner who senses the right moment to steal second or a wise teacher who senses the right moment to praise or critique a student's performance. *Kairos* reminds us that a rhetorical situation is not stable and fixed, but evolves as events unfold or as audiences experience the psychological ebbs and flows of attention and care. Here are examples that illustrate the range of insights contained by the term *kairos*:

- If you write a letter to the editor of a newspaper, you usually have a one- or two-day window before a current event becomes "old news" and is no longer interesting. An out-of-date letter will be rejected, not because it is poorly written or argued, but because it misses its *kairotic* moment.
- A group has decided to protest your university's on-campus residency requirement for all students except seniors. This group has designed a poster—portraying the university administration as greedy corporate capitalists exploiting students—to be hung all over campus during a fund-raising weekend when alumni and donors are likely to be on campus. The fund-raising weekend creates a *kairotic* moment for the posters, but some members of the group wonder if the poster is fair. After all, successful fund-raising benefits students as well as faculty and administrators. How could the poster be redesigned to emphasize student unhappiness with the residency requirement without creating such a negative view of university administrators? Here, *kairos* concerns the appropriateness of the message for the moment.

As you can see from these examples, *kairos* concerns questions about the timing, fitness, appropriateness, and proportions of a message within an evolving rhetorical context. There are no rules to help you determine the *kairotic* moment for your argument, but being attuned to *kairos* will help you "read" your audience and rhetorical situation in a dynamic way.

■ ■ ■ **FOR CLASS DISCUSSION**   **Analyzing an Argument's Appeals**
Your instructor will select an argument for analysis. Working in small groups or as a whole class, analyze the assigned argument first from the perspective of *kairos* and then from the perspective of *logos, ethos,* and *pathos.*   ■ ■ ■

How Audience-based Reasons Enhance
Logos, Ethos, and *Pathos*

We conclude this chapter by returning to the concept of audience-based reasons that we introduced in Chapter 4. Audience-based reasons enhance *logos* because they are built on underlying assumptions (warrants) that the audience is likely to accept. But they also enhance *ethos* and *pathos* by helping the writer identify with the audience, entering into their beliefs and values. To consider the needs of your audience, you can ask yourself the following questions:

Questions for Analyzing Your Audience

What to Ask	Why to Ask It
1. Who is your audience?	Your answer will help you think about audience-based reasons.
2. How much does your audience know or care about your issue?	Your answer can especially affect your introduction and conclusion. The less the audience knows, the more background you will have to provide.
3. What is your audience's current attitude toward your issue?	Your answer will help you decide the structure and tone of your argument.
4. What will be your audience's likely objections to your argument?	Your answers will help determine the content of your argument and will alert you to extra research you may need.
5. What values, beliefs, or assumptions about the world do you and your audience share?	Your answer will help you find common ground with your audience.

To see how a concern for audience-based reasons can enhance *ethos* and *pathos*, suppose that you support racial profiling (rather than random selection) for determining who receives intensive screening at airports. Suppose further that you are writing a guest op-ed column for a liberal campus newspaper and imagine readers repulsed by the notion of racial profiling (as indeed you are repulsed too in most cases). It's important from the start that you understand and acknowledge the interests of those opposed to your position. Middle Eastern men, the most likely candidates for racial profiling, will object to your racial stereotyping, which lumps all people of Arabic or Semitic appearance into the category "potential terrorists." African Americans and Hispanics, frequent victims of racial profiling by police in U.S. cities, may object to further extension of this hated practice. Also, most political liberals, as well as many moderates and conservatives, may object to the racism inherent in selecting people for airport screening on the basis of ethnicity.

What shared values might you use to build bridges to those opposed to racial profiling at airports? You need to develop a strategy to reduce your audience's fears and to link your reasons to their values. Your thinking might go something like this:

Problem: How can I create an argument rooted in shared values? How can I reduce fear that racial profiling in this situation endorses racism or will lead to further erosion of civil liberties?

Bridge-building goals: I must try to show that my argument's goal is to increase airline safety by preventing terrorism like that of 9/11/01. My argument must show my respect for Islam and for Arabic and Semitic people. I must also show my rejection of racial profiling as normal police practice.

Possible strategies:

- Stress the shared value of protecting innocent people from terrorism.

- Show how racial profiling significantly increases the efficiency of secondary searches. (If searches are performed at random, then we waste time and resources searching those statistically unlikely to be terrorists.)

- Argue that airport screeners must also use indicators other than race to select individuals for searches (for example, traits that might indicate a domestic terrorist).

- Show my respect for Islam.

- Show sympathy for people selected for searching via racial profiling and acknowledge that this practice would normally be despicable except for the extreme importance of airline security, which overrides personal liberties in this case.

- Show my rejection of racial profiling in situations other than airport screening—for example, stopping African Americans for traffic violations more often than whites and then searching their cars for drugs or stolen goods.

These thinking notes about your audience allow you to develop a plan for your argument.

FOR CLASS DISCUSSION   Planning an Audience-based Argumentative Strategy

Working individually or in small groups, plan an audience-based argumentative strategy for one or more of the following cases. Follow the thinking process used by the writer of the racial profiling argument: (1) state several problems that the writer must solve to reach the audience, and (2) develop possible solutions to those problems.

1. An argument for the right of software companies to continue making and selling violent video games: Aim the argument at parents who oppose their children's playing these games.
2. An argument to reverse grade inflation by limiting the number of As and Bs a professor can give in a course: Aim the argument at students who fear getting lower grades.
3. An argument supporting the legalization of cocaine: Aim your argument at readers of *Reader's Digest,* a conservative magazine that supports the current war on drugs.

WRITING ASSIGNMENT Revising a Draft for *Ethos, Pathos,* and Audience-based Reasons

Part 1: Choose an argument that you have previously written or are currently drafting. Revise the argument with explicit focus on increasing its appeals to *ethos, pathos,* and *logos* via audience-based reasons. Consider especially how you might improve *ethos* by building bridges to the audience or improve *pathos* through concrete language, specific examples, metaphors, or connotations of words. Imagine also how you might include an effective photograph or other image. Finally, consider the extent to which your reasons are audience-based.

Part 2: Attach to your revision a self-reflective letter explaining the choices you made in your revision. Describe the changes you made and explain how or why these changes are intended to enhance your argument's effectiveness at moving its audience. ■

PEARSON

For additional writing, reading, and research resources, go to www.mycomplab.com.

Responding to Objections and Alternative Views

In the previous chapter, we discussed strategies for moving your audience through appeals to *ethos, pathos,* and *kairos.* In this chapter, we examine strategies for addressing opposing or alternative views—whether to omit them, refute them, concede to them, or incorporate them through compromise and conciliation. We show you how your choices about structure, content, and tone may differ depending on whether your audience is sympathetic, neutral, or resistant to your views. The strategies explained in this chapter will increase your flexibility as an arguer and enhance your chance of persuading a wide variety of audiences.

One-Sided, Multisided, and Dialogic Arguments

Arguments are said to be one-sided, multisided, or dialogic:

- *A one-sided argument* presents only the writer's position on the issue without summarizing and responding to alternative viewpoints.
- *A multisided argument* presents the writer's position, but also summarizes and responds to possible objections and alternative views.
- *A dialogic argument* has a much stronger component of inquiry, where the writer presents himself as uncertain or searching, where the audience is considered a partner in the dialogue, and where the writer's purpose is to seek common ground perhaps leading to a consensual solution to a problem. (See our discussion in Chapter 1 of argument as truth seeking versus persuasion, pp. 9–10.)

One-sided and *multisided* arguments often take an adversarial stance in that the writer regards alternative views as flawed or wrong and supports his own claim with a strongly persuasive intent. Although multisided arguments can be adversarial, they can also be made to feel dialogic, depending on the way the writer introduces and responds to alternative views.

How can one determine the kind of argument that would be most effective in a given case? As a general rule, one-sided arguments are effective primarily for people who already agree with the writer's claim. They tend to strengthen the convictions of those already in the writer's camp, but alienate those who aren't. For those initially opposed to a writer's claim, a multisided argument shows that the writer has considered other views and thus reduces some initial hostility. An especially interesting effect can occur with neutral or undecided audiences. In the short run, one-sided arguments often are persuasive to a neutral audience, but in the long run multisided arguments have more staying power. Neutral audiences who've heard only one side of an issue tend to change their minds when they hear alternative arguments. By anticipating and rebutting opposing views, a multisided argument diminishes the surprise and force of subsequent counterarguments. If we move from neutral to highly resistant audiences, adversarial approaches—even multisided ones—are seldom effective because they increase hostility and harden the differences between writer and reader. In such cases, more dialogic approaches have the best chance of establishing common ground for inquiry and consensus.

In the rest of this chapter, we will show you how your choice of writing one-sided, multisided, or dialogic arguments is a function of how you perceive your audience's resistance to your views as well as your level of confidence in your own views.

Determining Your Audience's Resistance to Your Views

When you write an argument, you must always consider your audience's point of view. One way to imagine your relationship to members of your audience is to place them on a scale of resistance ranging from "strongly supportive" of your position to "strongly opposed" (see Figure 7.1). At the "accord" end of this scale are like-minded people who basically agree with your position on the issue. At the "resistance" end are those who strongly disagree with you, perhaps unconditionally, because their values, beliefs, or assumptions sharply differ from your own. In between lies a range of opinions. Close to your position will be those leaning in your direction but with less conviction than you. Close to the resistance position will be those basically opposed to your view but willing to listen to your argument and perhaps willing to acknowledge some of its strengths. In the middle are those undecided people who are still sorting out their feelings, seeking additional information, and weighing the strengths and weaknesses of alternative views.

Seldom, however, will you encounter an issue in which the range of disagreement follows a simple line from accord to resistance. Resistant views often fall into different categories so that no single line of argument appeals to all those whose views differ from your own. You have to identify not only your audience's resistance to your ideas but also the causes of that resistance.

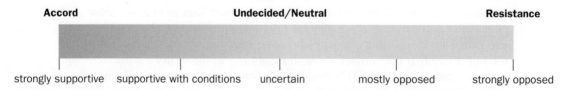

Accord	Undecided/Neutral	Resistance

| strongly supportive | supportive with conditions | uncertain | mostly opposed | strongly opposed |

FIGURE 7.1 Scale of resistance

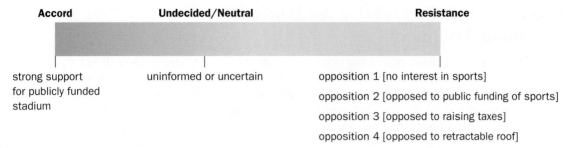

FIGURE 7.2 Scale of resistance, baseball stadium issue

Consider, for example, the issues surrounding publicly financed sports stadiums. In one city, a ballot initiative asked citizens to raise sales taxes to build a new retractable-roof stadium for its baseball team. Supporters of the initiative faced a complex array of resisting views (see Figure 7.2). Opponents of the initiative could be placed into four categories. Some simply had no interest in sports, cared nothing about baseball, and saw no benefit in building a huge publicly financed sports facility. Another group loved baseball, followed the home team passionately, but was philosophically opposed to subsidizing rich players and owners with taxpayer money. This group argued that the whole sports industry needed to be restructured so that stadiums were paid for out of sports revenues. Still another group was opposed to tax hikes in general. It focused on the principle of reducing the size of government and of using tax revenues only for essential services. Finally, another powerful group supported baseball and supported the notion of public funding of a new stadium but opposed the kind of retractable-roof stadium specified in the initiative. This group wanted an old-fashioned, open-air stadium like Baltimore's Camden Yards or Cleveland's Jacobs Field.

Writers supporting the initiative found it impossible to address all these resisting audiences at once. A supporter of the initiative who wanted to aim an argument at sports haters could stress the spin-off benefits of a new ballpark (the new ballpark would attract tourist revenue, renovate the deteriorating Pioneer Square neighborhood, create jobs, make sports lovers more likely to vote for public subsidies of the arts, and so forth). But these arguments were irrelevant to those who wanted an open-air stadium, who opposed tax hikes categorically, or who objected to public subsidy of millionaires.

The baseball stadium example illustrates that it is not always easy to adapt your argument to your audience's position on the scale of resistance. Yet identifying your audience is important because writers need a stable vision of their audience before they can determine an effective content, structure, and tone for an argument.

Sometimes as a writer you will simply need to "invent" your audience—that is, to assume that a certain category of readers will be your primary audience. Making this decision gives you a stable base from which to create audience-based reasons and to craft an appropriate tone and structure. The next sections show how you can adjust your arguing strategy depending on whether you imagine your audience as supportive, neutral, or hostile.

Appealing to a Supportive Audience: One-sided Argument

One-sided arguments commonly occur when an issue isn't highly contested and the writer's aim is merely to put forth a new or different point of view. When an issue is contested, however, one-sided arguments are used mainly to stir the passions of supporters—to convert belief into action by inspiring a party member to contribute to a senator's campaign or a bored office worker to sign up for a change-your-life weekend seminar.

Typically, appeals to a supportive audience are structured as one-sided arguments that either ignore opposing views or reduce them to "enemy" stereotypes. Filled with motivational language, these arguments list the benefits that will ensue from your donations to the cause and the horrors just around the corner if the other side wins. One of the authors of this text received a fund-raising letter from an environmental lobbying group declaring, "It's crunch time for the polluters and their pals on Capitol Hill." The "corporate polluters" and "anti-environment politicians," the letter continues, have "stepped up efforts to roll back our environmental protections—relying on large campaign contributions, slick PR firms and well-heeled lobbyists to get the job done before November's election." This letter makes the reader feel part of an in-group of good guys fighting big business "polluters." Nothing in the letter examines environmental issues from a business perspective or attempts to examine alternative views fairly. Since the intended audience already believes in the cause, nothing in the letter invites readers to consider the issues more complexly. Rather, the goal is to solidify support, increase the fervor of belief, and inspire action. Most appeal arguments make it easy to act, ending with a toll-free phone number to call, a Web site to visit, a tear-out postcard to send in, or a congressperson's address to write to.

Appealing to a Neutral or Undecided Audience: Classical Argument

The in-group appeals that motivate an already supportive audience can repel a neutral or undecided audience. Because undecided audiences are like jurors weighing all sides of an issue, they distrust one-sided arguments that caricature other views. Generally the best strategy for appealing to undecided audiences is the classical argument described in Chapter 3 (pp. 44–46). What characterizes the classical argument is the writer's willingness to summarize opposing views fairly and to respond to them openly—either by trying to refute them or by conceding to their strengths and then shifting to a different field of values. Let's look at these strategies in more depth.

Summarizing Opposing Views

The first step toward responding to opposing views in a classical argument is to summarize them fairly. Follow the *principle of charity*, which obliges you to avoid loaded, biased, or "straw man" summaries that oversimplify or distort opposing arguments, making them easy to knock over.

Consider the difference between an unfair and a fair summary of an argument. In the following example, a supporter of genetically engineered foods intends to refute the argument of organic food advocate Lisa Turner, who opposes all forms of biotechnology.

Unfair Summary of Turner's Argument

In a biased article lacking scientific understanding of biotechnology, natural foods huckster Lisa Turner parrots the health food industry's party line that genetically altered crops are Frankenstein's monsters run amok. She ignorantly claims that consumption of biotech foods will lead to worldwide destruction, disease, and death—ignoring the wealth of scientific literature showing that genetically modified foods are safe. Her misinformed attacks are scare tactics aimed at selling consumers on overpriced "health food" products to be purchased at boutique organic food stores.

Fair Summary of Turner's Argument

In an article appearing in a nutrition magazine, health food advocate Lisa Turner warns readers that much of our food today is genetically modified using gene-level techniques that differ completely from ordinary crossbreeding. She argues that the potential, unforeseen, harmful consequences of genetic engineering offset the possible benefits of increasing the food supply, reducing the use of pesticides, and boosting the nutritional value of foods. Turner asserts that genetic engineering is imprecise, untested, unpredictable, irreversible, and also uncontrollable because of animals, insects, and winds.

In the unfair summary, the writer distorts and oversimplifies Turner's argument, creating a straw man argument that is easy to knock over because it doesn't make the opponent's best case. In contrast, a fair summary follows the "principle of charity," allowing the strength of the opposing view to come through clearly.

Refuting Opposing Views

Once you have summarized an opposing view, you can either refute it or concede to its strengths. In refuting an opposing view, you attempt to convince readers that its argument is logically flawed, inadequately supported, or based on erroneous assumptions or wrong values. In Toulmin's terms, you can refute (1) the writer's stated reason and grounds, (2) the writer's warrant and backing, or (3) both.

For example, suppose you want to refute the following argument: "We shouldn't elect Joe as chairperson because he is too bossy." One way to refute this argument is to rebut the stated reason and grounds:

I disagree with you that Joe is bossy. In fact, Joe is very unbossy. He's a good listener who is willing to compromise, and he involves others in decisions. The example you cite for his being bossy wasn't typical. It was a one-time circumstance that doesn't represent his normal behavior. [The writer could then provide examples of Joe's cooperative nature.]

Or you could concede that Joe is bossy but rebut the argument's warrant that bossiness is a bad trait:

> I agree that Joe is bossy, but in this circumstance bossiness is just the trait we need. This committee hasn't gotten anything done for six months, and time is running out. We need a decisive person who can come in, get the committee organized, assign tasks, and get the job done.

Let's now illustrate these strategies in a more complex situation. Consider the controversy inspired by a *New York Times Magazine* article entitled "Recycling Is Garbage." Its author, John Tierney, argued that recycling is not environmentally sound and that it is cheaper to bury garbage in a landfill than to recycle it. In criticizing recycling, Tierney argued that recycling wastes money; he provided evidence that "every time a sanitation department crew picks up a load of bottles and cans from the curb, New York City loses money." A number of environmentalists responded angrily to Tierney's argument, challenging either his reason, his warrant, or both. Those refuting the reason offered counterevidence showing that recycling isn't as expensive as Tierney claimed. Those refuting the warrant said that even if the costs of recycling are higher than burying wastes in a landfill, recycling still benefits the environment by reducing the amount of virgin materials taken from nature. These critics, in effect, offered a new warrant: Saving the earth's resources takes precedence over economic costs.

Strategies for Rebutting Evidence

Whether you are rebutting an argument's reasons or its warrant, you will frequently need to question a writer's use of evidence. Here are some strategies you can use:

- *Deny the truth of the data.* Arguers can disagree about the facts of a case. If you have reasons to doubt a writer's facts, call them into question.
- *Cite counterexamples and countertestimony.* You often can rebut an argument based on examples or testimony by citing counterexamples or countertestimony, which deny the conclusiveness of the original data.
- *Cast doubt on the representativeness or sufficiency of examples.* Examples are powerful only if the audience feels that they are representative and sufficient. Many environmentalists complained that John Tierney's attack on recycling was based too largely on data from New York City and that it didn't accurately take into account the more positive experiences of other cities and states. When data from outside New York City were examined, the cost-effectiveness and positive environmental impact of recycling seemed more apparent.
- *Cast doubt on the relevance or recency of examples, statistics, or testimony.* The best evidence is up-to-date. In a rapidly changing universe, data even a few years out-of-date are often ineffective. For example, as the demand for recycled goods increases, the cost of recycling will be reduced. Out-of-date statistics will skew any argument about the cost of recycling. Another problem with data is their

occasional lack of relevance. For example, in arguing that an adequate ozone layer is necessary for preventing skin cancer, it is not relevant to cite statistics on the alarming rise of lung cancer.

■ *Call into question the credibility of an authority.* If an opposing argument is based on testimony, you can undermine its persuasiveness if you show that the person cited lacks up-to-date or relevant expertise in the field. (This procedure is different from the *ad hominem* fallacy discussed in Appendix 1 because it attacks not the personal character of the authority but the authority's expertise on a specific matter.)

■ *Question the accuracy or context of quotations.* Evidence based on testimony is frequently distorted by being either misquoted or taken out of context. Often scientists will qualify their findings heavily, but these qualifications will be omitted by the popular media. You can thus attack the use of a quotation by putting it in its original context or by restoring the qualifications accompanying the quotation in its original source.

■ *Question the way statistical data were produced or interpreted.* Chapter 9 provides fuller treatment of how to question statistics. In general, you can rebut statistical evidence by calling into account how the data were gathered, treated mathematically, or interpreted. It can make a big difference, for example, whether you cite raw numbers or percentages or whether you choose large or small increments for the axes of graphs.

Conceding to Opposing Views

In writing a classical argument, a writer must sometimes concede to an opposing argument rather than refute it. Sometimes you encounter portions of an argument that you simply can't refute. For example, suppose you support the legalization of hard drugs such as cocaine and heroin. Adversaries argue that legalizing hard drugs will increase the number of drug users and addicts. You might dispute the size of their numbers, but you reluctantly agree that they are right. Your strategy in this case is not to refute the opposing argument but to concede to it by admitting that legalization of hard drugs will promote heroin and cocaine addiction. Having made that concession, your task is then to show that the benefits of drug legalization still outweigh the costs you have just conceded.

As this example shows, the strategy of a concession argument is to switch from the field of values employed by the writer you disagree with to a different field of values more favorable to your position. You don't try to refute the writer's stated reason and grounds (by arguing that legalization will *not* lead to increased drug usage and addiction) or his warrant (by arguing that increased drug use and addiction is not a problem). Rather, you shift the argument to a new field of values by introducing a new warrant, one that you think your audience can share (that the benefits of legalization— eliminating the black market and ending the crime and violence associated with procurement of drugs—outweigh the costs of increased addiction). To the extent that opponents of legalization share your desire to stop drug-related crime, shifting to this new field of values is a good strategy. Although it may seem that you weaken your own position by conceding to an opposing argument, you may actually strengthen it by increasing your credibility and gaining your audience's goodwill. Moreover, conceding to one part of an opposing argument doesn't mean that you won't refute other parts of that argument.

Appealing to a Resistant Audience: Dialogic Argument

Whereas classical argument is effective for neutral or undecided audiences, it is often less effective for audiences strongly opposed to the writer's views. Because resisting audiences hold values, assumptions, or beliefs widely different from the writer's, they often are unswayed by classical argument, which attacks their world view too directly. On many values-laden issues such as abortion, gun control, gay rights, or the role of religion in the public sphere, the distance between a writer and a resisting audience can be so great that argument seems impossible. In these cases, the writer's goal may simply be to open dialogue by seeking common ground—that is, by finding places where the writer and audience agree. For example, pro-choice and a pro-life advocates may never agree on a woman's right to an abortion, but they might share common ground in wanting to reduce teenage pregnancy. There is room, in other words, for conversation, if not for agreement.

Because of these differences in basic beliefs and values, the goal of dialogic argument is seldom to convert resistant readers to the writer's position. The best a writer can hope for is to reduce somewhat the level of resistance, perhaps by increasing the reader's willingness to listen as preparation for future dialogue. In fact, once dialogue is initiated, parties who genuinely listen to each other and have learned to respect each others' views might begin finding solutions to shared problems.

The dialogic strategies we explain in this section—the delayed-thesis strategy and Rogerian strategy—are aimed at promoting understanding between a writer and a resistant audience. They work to disarm hostility by showing the writer's respect for alternative views and by lessening the force with which the writer presents his or her own views.

Delayed-Thesis Argument

In many cases, you can reach a resistant audience by using a *delayed-thesis* structure in which you wait until the end of your argument to reveal your thesis. Classical argument asks you to state your thesis in the introduction, support it with reasons and evidence, and then summarize and refute opposing views. Rhetorically, however, it is not always advantageous to tell your readers where you stand at the start of your argument or to separate yourself so definitively from alternative views. For resistant audiences, it may be better to keep the issue open, delaying the revelation of your own position until the end of the essay.

To illustrate the different effects of classical versus delayed-thesis arguments, we invite you to read a delayed-thesis argument by nationally syndicated columnist Ellen Goodman. The article appeared shortly after the nation was shocked by a brutal gang rape in New Bedford, Massachusetts, in which a woman was raped on a pool table by patrons of a local bar.*

---

*The rape was later the subject of an Academy Award—winning movie, *The Accused*, starring Jodie Foster.

Minneapolis Pornography Ordinance

ELLEN GOODMAN

Just a couple of months before the pool-table gang rape in New Bedford, Mass., *Hustler* magazine printed a photo feature that reads like a blueprint for the actual crime. There were just two differences between *Hustler* and real life. In *Hustler,* the woman enjoyed it. In real life, the woman charged rape.

There is no evidence that the four men charged with this crime had actually read the magazine. Nor is there evidence that the spectators who yelled encouragement for two hours had held previous ringside seats at pornographic events. But there is a growing sense that the violent pornography being peddled in this country helps to create an atmosphere in which such events occur.

As recently as last month, a study done by two University of Wisconsin researchers suggested that even "normal" men, prescreened college students, were changed by their exposure to violent pornography. After just ten hours of viewing, reported researcher Edward Donnerstein, "the men were less likely to convict in a rape trial, less likely to see injury to a victim, more likely to see the victim as responsible." Pornography may not cause rape directly, he said, "but it maintains a lot of very callous attitudes. It justifies aggression. It even says you are doing a favor to the victim."

If we can prove that pornography is harmful, then shouldn't the victims have legal rights? This, in any case, is the theory behind a city ordinance that recently passed the Minneapolis City Council. Vetoed by the mayor last week, it is likely to be back before the Council for an overriding vote, likely to appear in other cities, other towns. What is unique about the Minneapolis approach is that for the first time it attacks pornography, not because of nudity or sexual explicitness, but because it degrades and harms women. It opposes pornography on the basis of sex discrimination.

5   University of Minnesota Law Professor Catherine MacKinnon, who co-authored the ordinance with feminist writer Andrea Dworkin, says that they chose this tactic because they believe that pornography is central to "creating and maintaining the inequality of the sexes.... Just being a woman means you are injured by pornography."

They defined pornography carefully as, "the sexually explicit subordination of women, graphically depicted, whether in pictures or in words." To fit their legal definition it must also include one of nine conditions that show this subordination, like presenting women who "experience sexual pleasure in being raped or...mutilated...." Under this law, it would be possible for a pool-table rape victim to sue *Hustler.* It would be possible for a woman to sue if she were forced to act in a pornographic movie. Indeed, since the law describes pornography as oppressive to all women, it would be possible for any woman to sue those who traffic in the stuff for violating her civil rights.

In many ways, the Minneapolis ordinance is an appealing attack on an appalling problem. The authors have tried to resolve a long and bubbling conflict among those who have both a deep aversion to pornography and a deep loyalty to the value of free speech.

"To date," says Professor MacKinnon, "people have identified the pornographer's freedom with everybody's freedom. But we're saying that the freedom of the pornographer is the subordination of women. It means one has to take a side."

But the sides are not quite as clear as Professor MacKinnon describes them. Nor is the ordinance.

Even if we accept the argument that pornography is harmful to women—and I do—then we must also recognize that anti-Semitic literature is harmful to Jews and racist literature is harmful to blacks. For that matter, Marxist literature may be harmful to government policy. It isn't just women versus pornographers. If women win the right to sue publishers and producers, then so could Jews, blacks, and a long list of people who may be able to prove they have been harmed by books, movies, speeches or even records. The Manson murders, you may recall, were reportedly inspired by the Beatles.

10   We might prefer a library or book store or lecture hall without *Mein Kampf* or the Grand Whoever of the Ku Klux Klan. But a growing list of harmful expressions would inevitably strangle freedom of speech.

This ordinance was carefully written to avoid problems of banning and prior restraint, but the right of any woman to claim damages from pornography is just too broad. It seems destined to lead to censorship.

What the Minneapolis City Council has before it is a very attractive theory. What MacKinnon and Dworkin have written is a very persuasive and useful definition of pornography. But they haven't yet resolved the conflict between the harm of pornography and the value of free speech. In its present form, this is still a shaky piece of law.

Consider now how this argument's rhetorical effect would be different if Ellen Goodman had revealed her thesis in the introduction, using the classical argument form. Here is how this introduction might have looked:

Goodman's Introduction Rewritten in Classical Form

Just a couple of months before the pool-table gang rape in New Bedford, Mass., *Hustler* magazine printed a photo feature that reads like a blueprint for the actual crime. There were just two differences between *Hustler* and real life. In *Hustler,* the woman enjoyed it. In real life, the woman charged rape. Of course, there is no evidence that the four men charged with this crime had actually read the magazine. Nor is there evidence that the spectators who yelled encouragement for two hours had held previous ringside seats at pornographic events.

But there is a growing sense that the violent pornography being peddled in this country helps to create an atmosphere in which such events occur. One city is taking a unique approach to attack this problem. An ordinance recently passed by the Minneapolis City Council outlaws pornography not because it contains nudity or sexually explicit acts, but because it degrades and harms women. Unfortunately, despite the proponents' good intentions, the Minneapolis ordinance is a bad law because it has potentially dangerous consequences.

Even though Goodman's position can be grasped more quickly in this classical form, our students generally find the original delayed-thesis version more effective. Why is this? Most people point to the greater sense of complexity and surprise in the delayed-thesis version, a sense that comes largely from the delayed discovery of the writer's position. The classical version immediately labels the ordinance a "bad law," but the original version withholds judgment, inviting the reader to examine the law more sympathetically and to identify with the position of those who drafted it. Rather than distancing herself from those who see pornography as a violation of women's rights, Goodman shares with her readers her own struggles to think through these issues, thereby persuading us of her genuine sympathy for the ordinance and for its feminist proponents. In the end, her delayed thesis renders her final rejection of the ordinance not only more surprising but more convincing.

Clearly, then, a writer's decision about when to reveal her thesis is critical. Revealing the thesis early makes the writer seem more hard-nosed, more sure of her position, more confident about how to divide the ground into friendly and hostile camps, more in control. Delaying the thesis, in contrast, complicates the issues, increases reader sympathy for more than one view, and heightens interest in the tension among alternative views and in the writer's struggle for clarity.

Rogerian Argument

An even more powerful strategy for addressing resistant audiences is a conciliatory strategy often called *Rogerian argument,* named after psychologist Carl Rogers, who used this strategy to help people resolve differences.* Rogerian argument emphasizes "empathic listening," which Rogers defined as the ability to see an issue sympathetically from another person's perspective. He trained people to withhold judgment of another person's ideas until after they listened attentively to the other person, understood that person's reasoning, appreciated that person's values, respected that person's humanity—in short, walked in that person's shoes. What Carl Rogers understood is that traditional methods of argumentation are threatening. Because Rogerian argument stresses the psychological as well as logical dimensions of argument, and because it emphasizes reducing threat and building bridges rather than winning an argument, it is particularly effective for dealing with emotionally laden issues.

Under Rogerian strategy, the writer reduces the sense of threat in her argument by showing that *both writer and resistant audience share many basic values.* Instead of attacking the audience as wrongheaded, the Rogerian writer respects her audience's views and demonstrates an understanding of the audience's position before presenting her own position. Finally, the Rogerian writer seldom asks the audience to capitulate entirely to the writer's side—just to shift somewhat toward the writer's views. By acknowledging that she has already shifted toward the audience's views, the writer

---

*See Carl Rogers's essay "Communication: Its Blocking and Its Facilitation" in his book *On Becoming a Person* (Boston: Houghton, 1961), 329–37. For a fuller discussion of Rogerian argument, see Richard Young, Alton Becker, and Kenneth Pike, *Rhetoric: Discovery and Change* (New York: Harcourt, 1972).

makes it easier for the audience to accept compromise. All of this negotiation ideally leads to a compromise between—or better, a synthesis of—the opposing positions.

The key to successful Rogerian argument, besides the art of listening, is the ability to point out areas of agreement between the writer's and reader's positions. For example, if you support a woman's right to choose abortion and you are arguing with someone completely opposed to abortion, you're unlikely to convert your reader but you might reduce the level of resistance. You begin this process by summarizing your reader's position sympathetically, stressing your shared values. You might say, for example, that you also value babies; that you also are appalled by people who treat abortion as a form of birth control; that you also worry that the easy acceptance of abortion diminishes the value society places on human life; and that you also agree that accepting abortion lightly can lead to lack of sexual responsibility. Building bridges like these between you and your readers makes it more likely that they will listen to you when you present your own position.

In its emphasis on establishing common ground, Rogerian argument has much in common with recent feminist theories of argument. Many feminists criticize classical argument as rooted in a male value system and tainted by metaphors of war and combat. Thus, classical arguments, with their emphasis on assertion and refutation, typically are praised for being "powerful," "forceful," or "disarming." The writer "defends" his position and "attacks" his "opponent's" position using facts and data as "ammunition" and reasons as "big guns" to "blow away" his opponent's claim. According to some feminists, viewing argument as war can lead to inauthenticity, posturing, and game playing. Writers who share this distrust of classical argumentation often find Rogerian argument appealing because it stresses self-examination, clarification, and accommodation rather than refutation. Rogerian argument is more in tune with win-win negotiation than with win-lose debate.

An example of a student's Rogerian argument is shown on pages 114–115.

WRITING ASSIGNMENT A Classical Argument or a Dialogic Argument Aimed at Conciliation

Option 1: A Classical Argument   Write a classical argument following the explanations in Chapter 3, pages 44–46, using the guidelines for developing such an argument throughout Chapters 3–7. Depending on your instructor's preferences, this argument could focus on a new issue, or it could be a final stage of an argument-in-progress throughout Part Two. This assignment expands the supporting-reasons assignment from Chapter 5 by adding sections that summarize opposing views and respond to them through refutation or concession. For an example of a classical argument, see "'Half-Criminals' or Urban Athletes? A Plea for Fair Treatment of Skateboarders," by David Langley (p. 111).

Option 2: A Dialogic Argument Aimed at Conciliation   Write a dialogic argument aimed at a highly resistant audience. A good approach is to argue against a popular cultural practice or belief that you think is wrong, or argue for an action or belief that you think is right even though it will be highly unpopular. In other words, your claim must be controversial so that you can anticipate considerable resistance to your views. This assignment invites you to stand up for something you believe in—even though your view will be highly contested. Your goal is to persuade your audience toward your position or toward a conciliatory compromise. In writing and revising your argument, draw on appropriate strategies from Chapters 6 and 7. From Chapter 6, consider strategies for increasing your appeals to *ethos* and *pathos*. From Chapter 7, consider strategies for appealing to highly resistant audiences through delayed-thesis or Rogerian approaches. Your instructor may ask you to attach to your argument a self-reflective letter explaining and justifying the choices you made for appealing to your audience and accommodating their views. For an example of a Rogerian argument written in response to this assignment, see Rebekah Taylor's "Letter to Jim" on page 114. ■

Readings

Our first student essay illustrates a classical argument. This essay grew out of a class discussion about alternative sports, conflicts between traditional sports and newer sports (downhill skiing versus snowboarding), and middle-age prejudices against groups of young people.

"Half-Criminals" or Urban Athletes? A Plea for Fair Treatment of Skateboarders
(A Classical Argument)
DAVID LANGLEY (STUDENT)

For skateboarders, the campus of the University of California at San Diego is a wide-open, huge, geometric, obstacle-filled, stair-scattered cement paradise. The signs posted all over campus read, "No skateboarding, biking, or rollerblading on campus except on Saturday, Sunday, and holidays." I have always respected these signs at my local skateboarding spot. On the first day of 1999, I was skateboarding here with my hometown skate buddies and had just landed a trick when a police officer rushed out from behind a pillar, grabbed me, and yanked me off my board. Because I didn't have my I.D. (I had emptied my pockets so I wouldn't bruise my legs if I fell—a little trick of the trade), the officer started treating me like a criminal. She told me to spread my legs and put my hands on my head. She frisked me and then called in my name to police headquarters.

"What's the deal?" I asked. "The sign said skateboarding was legal on holidays."

"The sign means that you can only *roll* on campus," she said.

But that's *not* what the sign said. The police officer gave one friend and me a warning. Our third friend received a fifty-dollar ticket because it was his second citation in the last twelve months.

5 Like other skateboarders throughout cities, we have been bombarded with unfair treatment. We have been forced out of known skate spots in the city by storeowners and police, kicked out of every parking garage in downtown, compelled to skate at strange times of day and night, and herded into crowded skateboard parks. However, after I was searched by the police and detained for over twenty minutes in my own skating sanctuary, the unreasonableness of the treatment of skateboarders struck me. Where are skateboarders supposed to go? Cities need to change their unfair treatment of skateboarders because skateboarders are not antisocial misfits as popularly believed, because the laws regulating skateboarding are ambiguous, and because skateboarders are not given enough legitimate space to practice their sport.

Possibly because to the average eye most skateboarders look like misfits or delinquents, adults think of us as criminal types and associate our skateboards with antisocial behavior. But this view is unfair. City dwellers should recognize that skateboards are a natural reaction to the urban environment. If people are surrounded by cement, they are going to figure out a way to ride it. People's different environments have always produced transportation and sports to suit the conditions: bikes, cars, skis, ice skates, boats, canoes, surfboards. If we live on snow, we are going to develop skis or snowshoes to move around. If we live in an environment that has flat panels of cement for ground with lots of curbs and stairs, we are going to invent an ingeniously designed flat board with wheels. Skateboards are as natural to cement as surfboards are to water or skis to snow. Moreover, the resulting sport is as healthful, graceful, and athletic. A fair assessment of skateboarders should respect our elegant, nonpolluting means of transportation and sport, and not consider us hoodlums.

A second way that skateboarders are treated unfairly is that the laws that regulate skateboarding in public places are highly restrictive, ambiguous, and open to abusive application by police officers. My being frisked on the UCSD campus is just one example. When I moved to Seattle to go to college, I found the laws in Washington to be equally unclear. When a sign says "No Skateboarding," that generally means you will get ticketed if you are caught skateboarding in the area. But most areas aren't posted. The general rule then is that you can skateboard so long as you do so safely without being reckless. But the definition of "reckless" is up to the whim of the police officer. I visited the front desk of the Seattle East Precinct and asked them exactly what the laws against reckless skateboarding meant. They said that skaters are allowed on the sidewalk as long as they travel at reasonable speed and the sidewalks aren't crowded. One of the officers explained that if he saw a skater sliding down a handrail with people all around, he would definitely arrest the skater. What if there were no people around, I asked? The officer admitted that he might arrest the lone skater anyway and not be questioned by his superiors. No wonder skateboarders feel unfairly treated.

One way that cities have tried to treat skateboarders fairly is to build skateboard parks. Unfortunately, for the most part these parks are no solution at all. Most parks were designed by nonskaters who don't understand the momentum or gravity pull associated with the movement of skateboards. For example, City Skate, a park below the Space Needle in Seattle, is very appealing to the eye, but once you start to ride it you realize that the transitions and the verticals are all off, making it unpleasant and even dangerous to skate there. The Skate Park in Issaquah, Washington, hosts about thirty to fifty skaters at a time. Collisions are frequent and close calls, many. There are simply too many people in a small area. The people who built the park in Redmond, Washington, decided to make a huge wall in it for graffiti artists "to tag on" legally. They apparently thought they ought to throw all us teenage "half-criminals" in together. At this park, young teens are nervous about skating near a gangster "throwing up his piece," and skaters become dizzy as they take deep breaths from their workouts right next to four or five cans of spray paint expelling toxins in the air.

Of course, many adults probably don't think skateboarders deserve to be treated fairly. I have heard the arguments against skateboarders for years from parents, storeowners, friends, police officers, and security guards. For one thing, skateboarding tears up public and private property, people say. I can't deny that skating leaves marks on handrails and benches, and it does chip cement and granite. But in general skateboarders help the environment more than they hurt it. Skateboarding places are not littered or tagged up by skaters. Because skaters need smooth surfaces and because any small object of litter can lead to painful accidents, skaters actually keep the environment cleaner than the average citizen does. As for the population as a whole, skateboarders are keeping the air a lot cleaner than many other commuters and athletes such as boat drivers, car drivers, and skiers on ski lifts. In the bigger picture, infrequent repair of curbs and benches is cheaper than attempts to heal the ozone.

10   We skateboarders aren't going away, so cities are going to have to make room for us somewhere. Here is how cities can treat us fairly. We should be allowed to skate when others are present as long as we skate safely on the sidewalks. The rules and laws should be clearer so that skaters don't get put into vulnerable positions that make them easy targets for tickets. I do support the opening of skate parks, but cities need to build more of them, need to situate them closer to where skateboarders live, and need to make them relatively wholesome environments. They should also be designed by skateboarders so that they are skater-friendly and safe to ride. Instead of being treated as "half-criminals," skaters should be accepted as urban citizens and admired as athletes; we are a clean population, and we are executing a challenging and graceful sport. As human beings grow, we go from crawling to walking; some of us grow from strollers to skateboards.

To illustrate a conciliatory or Rogerian approach to an issue, we show you student writer Rebekah Taylor's argument written in response to this assignment. Rebekah chose to write a Rogerian argument in the form of a letter. An outspoken advocate for animal rights on her campus, Rebekah addressed her letter to an actual friend, Jim, with whom she had had many long philosophical conversations when she attended a different college. Note how Rebekah "listens" empathically to her friend's position on eating meat and proposes a compromise action.

A Letter to Jim
(A Rogerian Argument)
REBEKAH TAYLOR (STUDENT)

Dear Jim,

I decided to write you a letter today because I miss our long talks. Now that I have transferred colleges, we haven't had nearly enough heated discussions to satisfy either of us. I am writing now to again take up one of the issues we vehemently disagreed on in the past—meat-based diets.

Jim, I do understand how your view that eating meat is normal differs from mine. In your family, you learned that humans eat animals, and this view was reinforced in school where the idea of the food pyramid based on meat protein was taught and where most children had not even heard of vegetarian options. Also, your religious beliefs taught that God intended humans to have ultimate dominion over all animals. For humans, eating meat is part of a planned cycle of nature. In short, you were raised in a family and community that accepted meat-based diets as normal, healthy, and ethically justifiable whereas I was raised in a family that cared very deeply for animals and attended a church that frequently entertained a vegan as a guest speaker.

Let me now briefly reiterate for you my own basic beliefs about eating animals. As I have shared with you, my personal health is important to me, and I, along with other vegetarians and vegans, believe that a vegetarian diet is much more healthy than a meat diet. But my primary motivation is my deep respect for animals. I have always felt an overpowering sense of compassion for animals and forceful sorrow and regret for the injuries that humans inflict upon them. I detest suffering, especially when it is forced upon creatures that cannot speak out against it. These deep feelings led me to become a vegetarian at the age of 5. While lying in bed one night, I looked up at the poster of a silky-white harbor seal that had always hung on my wall. As I looked at the face of that seal, I made a connection between that precious animal on my wall and the animals that had been killed for the food I ate every day. In the dim glow of my Strawberry Shortcake night light, I promised those large, dark seal eyes that I would never eat animals again. Seventeen years have passed now and that promise still holds true. Every day I feel more dedicated to the cause of animal rights around the world.

I know very well that my personal convictions are not the same as yours. However, I believe that we might possibly agree on more aspects of this issue than we realize. Although we would not be considered by others as allies on the issue of eating meat, we do share a common enemy—factory farms. Although you eat animal products and I do not, we both share a basic common value that is threatened by today's factory farms. We both disapprove of the unnecessary suffering of animals.

5   Though we might disagree on the morality of using animals for food at all, we do agree that such animals should not be made to suffer. Yet at factory farms, billions of animals across the world are born, live, and die in horribly cramped, dark, and foul-smelling barns.

None of these animals knows the feeling of fresh air, or of warm, blessed sunlight on their backs. Most do not move out of their tight, uncomfortable pens until the day that they are to be slaughtered. At these factory farms, animals are processed as if they were inanimate objects, with no regard for the fact that they do feel fear and pain.

It is because of our shared opposition to animal suffering that I ask you to consider making an effort to buy meat from small, independent local farmers. I am told by friends that all supermarkets offer such meat options. This would be an easy and effective way to fight factory farms. I know that I could never convince you to stop eating meat, and I will never try to force my beliefs on you. As your friend, I am grateful simply to be able to write to you so candidly about my beliefs. I trust that regardless of what your ultimate reaction is to this letter, you will thoughtfully consider what I have written, as I will thoughtfully consider what you write in return.

Sincerely,

Rebekah

For additional writing, reading, and research resources, go to www.mycomplab.com

PART THREE
Analyzing Arguments

This advocacy poster fuses three big contemporary public controversies over environmentalism, sustainability, and vegetarianism. What tactics does this poster use to appeal to viewers' emotions and dramatize its claim that meat-eating is destroying the world? Chapters 8 and 9 provide guidance for conducting rhetorical analyses of verbal and visual texts that work in a complex way, as this one does.

117

8 Analyzing Arguments Rhetorically

In Part Two of this book, we explained thinking and writing strategies for composing your own arguments. Now in Part Three, we show you how to use your new rhetorical knowledge to conduct in-depth analyses of other people's arguments. To analyze an argument rhetorically means to examine closely how it is composed and what makes it an effective or ineffective piece of persuasion. A rhetorical analysis identifies the text under scrutiny, summarizes its main ideas, presents some key points about the text's rhetorical strategies for persuading its audience, and elaborates on these points.

Becoming skilled at analyzing arguments rhetorically will provide multiple payoffs. Rhetorical analysis will help you develop your ability to read complex texts critically; speak back to texts from your own insights; apply the strategies of effective argumentation to your own arguments; and prepare you as a citizen to distinguish sound, ethical arguments from manipulative, unreasonable ones. By themselves, rhetorical analyses are common assignments in courses in critical thinking and argument. Rhetorical analysis also plays a major role in constructing arguments. Writers often work into their own arguments summaries and rhetorical analyses of other people's arguments—particularly in sections dealing with opposing views. This chapter focuses on the rhetorical analysis of written arguments; Chapter 9 equips you to analyze visual arguments.

Thinking Rhetorically about a Text

The suggested writing assignment for this chapter is to write your own rhetorical analysis of an argument selected by your instructor (see p. 128). This section will help you get started by showing you what it means to think rhetorically about a text.

Before we turn directly to rhetorical analysis, we should reconsider the key word "rhetoric." In popular usage, *rhetoric* often means empty or deceptive language, as in the phrase, "Well, that's just rhetoric." Another related meaning of rhetoric is decorative or artificial language. Most contemporary rhetoricians, however, adopt a larger view of rhetoric articulated by Greek philosopher Aristotle: the art of determining what will be persuasive in every situation. Focusing on this foundational meaning of rhetoric, this chapter will show you how to analyze a writer's motivation, purpose, and rhetorical choices for persuading a targeted audience.

Most of the knowledge and skills you will need to write an effective rhetorical analysis have already been provided in Parts One and Two. You have already learned how to place a text in its rhetorical context (Chapter 2), and from Chapters 3–7, you already are familiar with such key rhetorical concepts as audience-based reasons; the STAR criteria for evidence; and the classical appeals of *logos, ethos,* and *pathos.* This chapter prepares you to apply these argument concepts to the arguments you encounter.

Questions for Rhetorical Analysis

Conducting a rhetorical analysis asks you to bring to bear on an argument your knowledge of argument and your repertoire of reading strategies. The questions in the following table can help you examine an argument in depth. Although a rhetorical analysis will not include answers to all these questions, using some of them in your thinking stages can give you a thorough understanding of the argument while helping you generate insights for your own rhetorical analysis essay.

Questions for Rhetorical Analysis

What to Focus On	Questions to Ask	Applying These Questions
The kairotic moment and writer's motivating occasion	▪ What motivated the writer to produce this piece? ▪ What social, cultural, political, legal, or economic conversations does this argument join?	▪ Is the writer responding to a bill pending in Congress, a recent speech by a political leader, or a local event that provoked controversy? ▪ Is the writer addressing cultural trends such as the impact of science or technology on values or on some other cultural change?
Rhetorical context: Writer's purpose and audience	▪ What is the writer's purpose? ▪ Who is the intended audience? ▪ What assumptions, values, or beliefs would readers have to hold to find this argument persuasive? ▪ How well does the text suit its particular audience and purpose?	▪ Is the writer trying to change readers' views by offering a new interpretation of a phenomenon, calling readers to action, trying to muster votes, or inspiring further investigations? ▪ Does the audience share a political or religious orientation with the writer?
Rhetorical context: Writer's identity and angle of vision	▪ Who is the writer and what do you know about his/her profession, background, and expertise in the subject? ▪ How does the writer's personal history, education, gender, ethnicity, age, class, sexual orientation, and political leaning influence the angle of vision? ▪ What is emphasized and what is omitted in this text? ▪ How much does the writer's angle of vision dominate the text?	▪ Is the writer a scholar, researcher, scientist, policymaker, politician, professional journalist, or citizen blogger? ▪ Is the writer affiliated with conservative or liberal, religious or lay publications? ▪ Is the writer forcefully advocating a stance or adopting a more inquiry-based mode? ▪ What points of view and pieces of evidence are "not seen" by this writer?

(Continued)

Questions for Rhetorical Analysis

What to Focus On	Questions to Ask	Applying These Questions
Rhetorical context: Genre	▪ What is the argument's original genre? ▪ What is the original medium of publication? How does the genre and its place of publication influence its content, structure, and style?	▪ How popular or scholarly, informal or formal is this genre? ▪ Does the genre allow for in-depth or only sketchy coverage of an issue? (See Chapter 2, pp. 21–23, for detailed explanations of genre.)
Logos **of the argument**	▪ What is the argument's claim, either explicitly stated or implied? ▪ What are the main reasons in support of the claim? Are the reasons audience-based? ▪ How effective is the writer's use of evidence? How is the argument supported and developed? ▪ How well has the argument recognized and responded to alternative views?	▪ Is the core of the argument clear and soundly developed? Or do readers have to unearth or reconstruct the argument? ▪ Is the argument one-sided, multisided, or dialogic? ▪ Does the argument depend on assumptions the audience might not share? ▪ What evidence does the writer employ? Does this evidence meet the STAR criteria? (see pp. 69–70)
Ethos **of the argument**	▪ What *ethos* does the writer project? ▪ How does the writer try to seem credible and trustworthy to the intended audience? ▪ How knowledgeable does the writer seem in recognizing opposing or alternative views and how fairly does the writer respond to them?	▪ If you are impressed or won over by this writer, what has earned your respect? ▪ If you are filled with doubts or skepticism, what has caused you to question this writer? ▪ How important is the character of the writer in this argument?
Pathos **of the argument**	▪ How effective is the writer in using audience-based reasons? ▪ How does the writer use concrete language, word choice, narrative, example, and analogies to tap readers' emotions, values, and imaginations?	▪ What examples, connotative language, and uses of narrative or analogy stand out for you in this argument? ▪ Would you say this argument relies heavily on appeals to *pathos*? Or is this argument more brainy and logical?
Writer's style	▪ How do the writer's language choices and sentence length and complexity contribute to the impact of the argument? ▪ How well does the writer's tone (attitude toward the subject) suit the argument?	▪ How readable is this argument? ▪ Is the argument formal, scholarly, journalistic, informal, or casual? ▪ Would you describe the tone as serious, mocking, humorous, exhortational, confessional, urgent, or something else?

What to Focus On	Questions to Ask	Applying These Questions
Design and visual elements	■ How do design elements—layout, font sizes and styles, and use of color—influence the effect of the argument? (See Chapter 9 for a detailed discussion of these elements.) ■ How do graphics, images, or other visuals contribute to the persuasiveness of the argument?	■ Do design features contribute to the logical or the emotional/imaginative appeals of the argument? ■ How would this argument benefit from visuals and graphics or some different document design?
Overall persuasiveness of the argument	■ What features of this argument contribute most to making it persuasive or not persuasive for its target audience and for you yourself? ■ How would this argument be received by different audiences? ■ What features contribute to the rhetorical complexity of this argument? ■ What is particularly memorable, disturbing, or problematic about this argument? ■ What does this argument contribute to its kairotic moment and the argumentative controversy of which it is a part?	■ For example, are appeals to *pathos* legitimate and suitable? Does the quality and quantity of the evidence help to build a strong case or fall short? ■ What specifically would count as a strength for the target audience? ■ If you differ from the target audience, how do you differ and where does the argument derail for you? ■ What gaps, contradictions, or unanswered questions are you left with? ■ How does this argument indicate that it is engaged in a public conversation? How does it "talk" to other arguments you have read on this issue?

An Illustration of Rhetorical Analysis

To illustrate rhetorical analysis in this section and in the student example at the end of the chapter, we will use two articles on reproductive technology—a subject that continues to generate arguments in the public sphere. By "reproductive technology" we mean scientific advances in the treatment of infertility such as egg and sperm donation, artificial insemination, *in vitro* fertilization, surrogate motherhood, and so forth. Our first article, from a decade ago, springs from the early and increasing popularity of these technological options. Our second article—to be used later in our student example—responds to the recent globalization of this technology.

Read the following article, "Egg Heads" by Kathryn Jean Lopez, and then proceed to the discussion questions that follow. Lopez's article was originally published in the September 1, 1998, issue of the *National Review*, a biweekly conservative news commentary magazine.

Egg Heads

KATHRYN JEAN LOPEZ

Filling the waiting room to capacity and spilling over into a nearby conference room, a group of young women listen closely and follow the instructions: Complete the forms and return them, with the clipboard, to the receptionist. It's all just as in any medical office. Then they move downstairs, where the doctor briefs them. "Everything will be pretty much normal," she explains. "Women complain of skin irritation in the local area of injection and bloating. You also might be a little emotional. But, basically, it's really bad PMS."

This is not just another medical office. On a steamy night in July, these girls in their twenties are attending an orientation session for potential egg donors at a New Jersey fertility clinic specializing in in-vitro fertilization. Within the walls of IVF New Jersey and at least two hundred other clinics throughout the United States, young women answer the call to give "the gift of life" to infertile couples. Egg donation is a quietly expanding industry, changing the way we look at the family, young women's bodies, and human life itself.

It is not a pleasant way to make money. Unlike sperm donation, which is over in less than an hour, egg donation takes the donor some 56 hours and includes a battery of tests, ultrasound, self-administered injections, and retrieval. Once a donor is accepted into a program, she is given hormones to stimulate the ovaries, changing the number of eggs matured from the usual one per month up to as many as fifty. A doctor then surgically removes the eggs from the donor's ovary and fertilizes them with the designated sperm.

Although most programs require potential donors to undergo a series of medical tests and counseling, there is little indication that most of the young women know what they are getting themselves into. They risk bleeding, infection, and scarring. When too many eggs are matured in one cycle, it can damage the ovaries and leave the donor with weeks of abdominal pain. (At worst, complications may leave her dead.) Longer term, the possibility of early menopause raises the prospect of future regret. There is also some evidence of a connection between the fertility drugs used in the process and ovarian cancer.

5   But it's good money—and getting better. New York's Brooklyn IVF raised its "donor compensation" from $2,500 to $5,000 per cycle earlier this year in order to keep pace with St. Barnabas Medical Center in nearby Livingston, New Jersey. It's a bidding war. "It's obvious why we had to do it," says Susan Lobel, Brooklyn IVF's assistant director. Most New York—area IVF programs have followed suit.

Some infertile couples and independent brokers are offering even more for "reproductive material." The International Fertility Center in Indianapolis, Indiana, for instance, places ads in the *Daily Princetonian* offering Princeton girls as much as $35,000 per cycle. The National Fertility Registry, which, like many egg brokerages, features an online catalogue for couples to browse in, advertises $35,000 to $50,000 for Ivy League eggs. While donors are normally paid a flat fee per cycle, there have been reports of higher payments to donors who produce more eggs.

College girls are the perfect donors. Younger eggs are likelier to be healthy, and the girls themselves frequently need money—college girls have long been susceptible to classified ads offering to pay them for acting as guinea pigs in medical research. One 1998 graduate of the University of Colorado set up her own website to market her eggs. She had watched a television show on egg donation and figured it "seemed like a good thing to do"—especially since she had spent her money during the past year to help secure a country-music record deal. "Egg donation would help me with my school and music expenses while helping an infertile couple with a family." Classified ads scattered throughout cyberspace feature similar offers.

The market for "reproductive material" has been developing for a long time. It was twenty years ago this summer that the first test-tube baby, Louise Brown, was born. By 1995, when the latest tally was taken by the Centers for Disease Control, 15 percent of mothers in this country had made use of some form of assisted-reproduction technology in conceiving their children. (More recently, women past menopause have begun to make use of this technology.) In 1991 the American Society for Reproductive Medicine was aware of 63 IVF programs offering egg donation. That number had jumped to 189 by 1995 (the latest year for which numbers are available).

Defenders argue that it's only right that women are "compensated" for the inconvenience of egg donation. Brooklyn IVF's Dr. Lobel argues, "If it is unethical to accept payment for loving your neighbor, then we'll have to stop paying babysitters." As long as donors know the risks, says Glenn McGee of the University of Pennsylvania's Center for Bioethics, this transaction is only "a slightly macabre version of adoption."

10   Not everyone is enthusiastic about the "progress." Egg donation "represents another rather large step into turning procreation into manufacturing," says the University of Chicago's Leon Kass. "It's the dehumanization of procreation." And as in manufacturing, there is quality control. "People don't want to say the word any more, but there is a strong eugenics issue inherent in the notion that you can have the best eggs your money can buy," observes sociology professor Barbara Katz Rothman of the City University of New York.

The demand side of the market comes mostly from career-minded baby-boomers, the frontierswomen of feminism, who thought they could "have it all." Indeed they *can* have it all—with a little help from some younger eggs. (Ironically, feminists are also among its strongest critics; *The Nation*'s Katha Pollitt has pointed out that in egg donation and surrogacy, once you remove the "delusion that they are making babies for other women," all you have left is "reproductive prostitution.")

Unfortunately, the future looks bright for the egg market. Earlier this year, a woman in Atlanta gave birth to twins after she was implanted with frozen donor eggs. The same technology has also been successful in Italy. This is just what the egg market needed, since it avoids the necessity of coordinating donors' cycles with recipients' cycles. Soon, not only will infertile couples be able to choose from a wider variety of donor offerings, but in some cases donors won't even be needed. Young women will be able to freeze their own eggs and have them thawed and fertilized once they are ready for the intrusion of children in their lives.

There are human ovaries sitting in a freezer in Fairfax, Virginia. The Genetics and IVF Institute offers to cut out and remove young women's ovaries and cryopreserve the egg-containing tissue for future implantation. Although the technology was originally designed to give the hope of fertility to young women undergoing treatment for cancer, it is now starting to attract the healthy. "Women can wait to have children until they are well established in their careers and getting a little bored, sometime in their forties or fifties," explains Professor Rothman. "Basically, motherhood is being reduced to a good leisure-time activity."

Early this summer, headlines were made in Britain, where the payment of egg donors is forbidden, when an infertile couple traveled to a California clinic where the woman could be inseminated with an experimental hybrid egg. The egg was a combination of the recipient's and a donor's eggs. The clinic in question gets its eggs from a Beverly Hills brokerage, the Center for Surrogate Parenting and Egg Donation, run by Karen Synesiou and Bill Handel, a radio shock-jock in Los Angeles. Miss Synesiou recently told the London *Sunday Times* that she is "interested in redefining the family. That's why I came to work here."

15   The redefinition is already well under way. Consider the case of Jaycee Buzzanca. After John and Luanne Buzzanca had tried for years to have a child, an embryo was created for them, using

sperm and an egg from anonymous donors, and implanted in a surrogate mother. In March 1995, one month before the baby was born, John filed for divorce. Luanne wanted child support from John, but he refused—after all, he's not the father. Luanne argued that John is Jaycee's father legally. At this point the surrogate mother, who had agreed to carry a baby for a stable two-parent household, decided to sue for custody.

Jaycee was dubbed "Nobody's Child" by the media when a California judge ruled that John was not the legal father nor Luanne the legal mother (neither one was genetically related to Jaycee, and Luanne had not even borne her). Enter Erin Davidson, the egg donor, who claims the egg was used without her permission. Not to be left out, the sperm donor jumped into the ring, saying that his sperm was used without his permission, a claim he later dropped. In March of this year, an appeals court gave Luanne custody and decided that John is the legal father, making him responsible for child support. By contracting for a medical procedure resulting in the birth of a child, the court ruled, a couple incurs "the legal status of parenthood." (John lost an appeal in May.) For Jaycee's first three years on earth, these people have been wrangling over who her parents are.

In another case, William Kane left his girlfriend, Deborah Hect, 15 vials of sperm before he killed himself in a Las Vegas hotel in 1991. His two adult children (represented by their mother, his ex-wife) contested Miss Hect's claim of ownership. A settlement agreement on Kane's will was eventually reached, giving his children 80 percent of his estate and Miss Hect 20 percent. Hence she was allowed three vials of his sperm. When she did not succeed in conceiving on the first two tries, she filed a petition for the other 12 vials. She won, and the judge who ruled in her favor wrote, "Neither this court nor the decedent's adult children possess reason or right to prevent Hect from implementing decedent's pre-eminent interest in realizing his 'fundamental right' to procreate with the woman of his choice." One day, donors may not even have to have lived. Researchers are experimenting with using aborted female fetuses as a source of donor eggs.

And the market continues to zip along. For overseas couples looking for donor eggs, Bill Handel has the scenario worked out. The couple would mail him frozen sperm of their choice (presumably from the recipient husband); his clinic would use it to fertilize donor eggs, chosen from its catalogue of offerings, and reply back within a month with a frozen embryo ready for implantation. (Although the sperm does not yet arrive by mail, Handel has sent out embryos to at least one hundred international customers.) As for the young women at the New Jersey clinic, they are visibly upset by one aspect of the egg-donation process: they can't have sexual intercourse for several weeks after the retrieval. For making babies, of course, it's already obsolete.

■ ■ ■   **FOR CLASS DISCUSSION**   Identifying Rhetorical Features

Working in groups, develop responses to the following questions:

1. How does Lopez appeal to *logos*? What is her main claim and what are her reasons? What does she use for evidence? What ideas would you have to include in a short summary?

2. What appeals to *pathos* does Lopez make in this argument? How well are these suited to the conservative readers of the *National Review*?

3. How would you characterize Lopez's *ethos*? Does she seem knowledgeable and credible? Does she seem fair to stakeholders in this controversy?

4. Choose an additional focus from the "Questions for Rhetorical Analysis" on pages 120–121 to apply to "Egg Heads." How does this question expand your understanding of Lopez's argument?

5. What strikes you as problematic, memorable, or disturbing in this argument?   ■ ■ ■

A Rhetorical Analysis of "Egg Heads"

Now that you have identified some of the rhetorical features of "Egg Heads," we offer our own notes for a rhetorical analysis of this argument.

Rhetorical Context   As we began our analysis, we reconstructed the rhetorical context in which "Egg Heads" was published. In the late 1990s, a furious debate about egg donation rippled through newspapers, popular journalism, Web sites, and scholarly commentary. This debate had been kicked off by several couples placing ads in the newspapers of the country's most prestigious colleges, offering up to $50,000 for the eggs of brilliant, attractive, athletic college women. Coinciding with these consumer demands, advances in reproductive technology provided an increasing number of complex techniques to surmount the problem of infertility, including fertilizing eggs in Petri dishes and implanting these into women through surgical procedures. These procedures could use either a couple's own eggs and sperm or donated eggs and sperm. All these social and medical factors created the kairotic moment for Lopez's article and motivated her to protest the increasing use of these procedures.

Genre and Writer   When we considered the genre and writer of this article and its site of publication, we noted that this article appeared in the *National Review*, which describes itself as "America's most widely read and influential magazine and web site for Republican/conservative news, commentary, and opinion" (www.nationalreview.com). According to our internet search, Kathryn Jean Lopez is known nationally as a conservative journalist writing on social and political issues. Currently editor of *National Review Online*, she has also been published in *The Wall Street Journal*, *New York Post*, and *Washington Times*. This information told us that in her article "Egg Heads," Lopez is definitely on home territory, aiming her article at a conservative audience.

Logos   Turning to the *logos* of Lopez's argument, we decided that the logical structure of Lopez's argument is clear throughout the article. Her claim is that egg donation and its associated reproductive advances have harmful, long-reaching consequences for society. She argues that egg donation and reproductive technology represent bad scientific developments for society because they are potentially harmful to the long-range health of egg donors and because they are dehumanizing. She states a version of this last point at the end of the second paragraph: "Egg donation is a quickly expanding industry, changing the way we look at the family, young women's bodies, and human life itself" (122).

    The body of her article elaborates on each of these reasons. In developing her reason that egg donation endangers donors, Lopez lists the risks but doesn't supply supporting evidence about the frequency of these problems: damage to the ovaries, persistent pain, early menopause, possible ovarian cancer, and even death. She supports her claim about "the expanding industry" by showing how the procedures have become commercialized. To show the popularity of these procedures as well as their commercial value, she quotes a variety of experts such as directors of *in vitro* clinics, fertility centers, bioethicists, and the American Society for Reproductive Medicine. She also cleverly bolsters her own case by showing where even liberal cultural critics agree with her views about the big ethical questions raised by the reproductive technology business. In addition to quoting experts, Lopez has sprinkled impressive numbers and vivid examples throughout the body of her argument, which give her argument momentum as it progresses from the potential harm to young egg donors to a number of case studies that depict increasingly disturbing ethical problems.

Pathos   Much of the impact of this argument, we noted, comes from Lopez's appeals to *pathos*. By describing in detail the waiting rooms for egg donors at fertility clinics, Lopez relies heavily on pathetic appeals to move her audience to see the physical and social dangers of egg donation. She conveys the growing commercialism of reproductive technology by giving readers an inside look at the egg donation process as these young college women embark on the multi-step process of donating their eggs. These young women, she suggests in her title "Egg Heads," are largely unaware of the potential physical dangers to themselves and of the ethical implications and consequences of their acts. She asserts that they are driven largely by the desire for money. Lopez also appeals to *pathos* in her choice of emotionally loaded and often cynical language that creates an angle of vision opposing reproductive technology: "turning procreation into manufacturing"; "reproductive prostitution"; "the intrusion of children in their lives"; "motherhood...reduced to a leisure-time activity"; "aborted female fetuses as a source of donor egg"; and intercourse as an "obsolete" way "to make babies" (123–124).

Audience   Despite Lopez's success at spotlighting serious medical and ethical questions, her lack of attention to alternative views and the alarmism of her language caused us to wonder: who might find this argument persuasive and who would challenge it? What is noticeably missing from her argument is the perspective of infertile couples hoping for a baby. Pursuing our question, we decided that a very provocative feature of this argument—one worthy of deeper analysis—is the disparity between how well this argument is suited to its target audience and yet how unpersuasive it is for readers who do not share the assumptions, values, and beliefs of this primary audience.

To Lopez's credit, she has attuned her reasons to the values and concerns of her conservative readers of the *National Review* who believe in traditional families, gender differences, and gender roles. Lopez's choice and orchestration of evidence are intended to play to her audience's fears that science has fallen into the hands of those who have little regard for the sanctity of the family or traditional motherhood. For example, in playing strongly to the values of her conservative readers, Lopez belabors the physical, social, and ethical dangers of egg donation, mentioning worst case scenarios; however, these appeals to *pathos* will most likely strike other readers who do some investigation into reproductive technology as overblown. She emphasizes the commercialism of the process as her argument moves from college girls as egg donors to a number of sensationalist case studies that depict intensifying ethical ambiguity. In other words, both the *logos* and *pathos* of her argument skillfully focus on details that tap her target audience's values and beliefs and feed their fears and revulsion.

Use of Evidence   For a broader or skeptical audience, the alarmism of Lopez's appeals to *pathos*, her use of atypical evidence, and her distortion of the facts weaken the *logos* and *ethos* of her argument. First, Lopez's use of evidence fails to measure up to the STAR criteria (that evidence should be **s**ufficient, **t**ypical, **a**ccurate, and **r**elevant). She characterizes all egg donors as young women seeking money, but she provides little evidence that egg donors are only out to make a buck. She also paints these young women as short-sighted, uninformed, and foolish. Lopez weakens her *ethos* by not considering the young women who have researched the process and who may be motivated, at least in part, by compassion. Lopez also misrepresents the people who are using egg donation, placing them all into two groups: (1) wealthy couples eugenically seeking designer babies and (2) feminist career women. She directs much of her criticism toward this latter group: "The demand side of the market comes mostly from career-minded baby boomers, the frontierswomen of feminism, who thought they could have it all" (123). However, readers who do a little research on their own, as we did, will learn that infertility affects one in seven couples; that it is often a male and female problem, sometimes caused by an incompatibility between the husband's and wife's reproductive material; and that most couples who take the big step of investing in these expensive efforts to have a baby have been trying to get pregnant for a number of years. Rather than being casual about having children, they are often deeply desirous of children and depressed about their inability to conceive. In addition, far from being the sure thing and quick fix that Lopez suggests, reproductive technology has a success rate of only 50 percent overall and involves a huge investment of time, money, and physical discomfort for women receiving donor eggs.

Another way that Lopez violates the STAR criteria is her choice of extreme cases. For readers outside her target audience, her argument appears riddled with straw man and slippery slope fallacies. (See Appendix 1 on Informal Fallacies). Here are some specific instances of extreme, atypical cases:

- her focus on career women casually and selfishly using the service of young egg donors;
- the notorious case of Jaycee Buzzanca dubbed "Nobody's Child" because her adoptive parents who commissioned her creation divorced before she was born;
- the legal contest between a dead man's teen girlfriend and his ex-wife and adult children over his vials of sperm; and
- the idea of taking eggs from aborted girl fetuses.

By keeping invisible the vast majority of ordinary couples who come to fertility clinics out of desperation, Lopez uses extreme cases to create a "Brave New World" intended to evoke a vehement rejection of these reproductive advances. Skeptical readers would offer the alternative view of the sad, ordinary couples of all ages sitting week after week in fertility clinics, hoping to conceive a child through the "miracle" of these reproductive advances and grateful to the young women who have contributed their eggs.

Conclusion   In short, we concluded that Lopez's angle of vision, although effectively in sync with her conservative readers of the *National Review*, exaggerates and distorts her case against these reproductive advances. Lopez's traditional values and slanting of the evidence undermine her *ethos*, limit the value of this argument for a wider audience, and compel that audience to seek out alternative views for a more complete view of egg donation.

WRITING ASSIGNMENT A Rhetorical Analysis

Write a thesis-driven rhetorical analysis essay in which you examine the rhetorical effectiveness of an argument specified by your instructor. Unless otherwise stated direct your analysis to an audience of your classmates. In your introduction, establish the argumentative conversation to which this argument is contributing. Briefly summarize the argument and present your thesis highlighting two or more rhetorical features of the argument that you find central to the effectiveness or ineffectiveness of this argument. To develop and support your own points, include textual evidence—in the form of examples or short quotations—from the argument. Use attributive tags to distinguish your ideas from those of the writer of the article. Use MLA documentation to cite points and quotations in your essay and in a Works Cited list at the end. Think of your rhetorical analysis as a way to shine a spotlight on important aspects of this argument and make the argument understandable and interesting for your readers.

A student paper written for this assignment is shown at the end of this chapter—Zachary Stumps's analysis of Ellen Goodman's "Womb for Rent."

Generating Ideas for Your Rhetorical Analysis

To develop ideas for your essay, you might follow these suggested steps:

Steps for Writing a Rhetorical Analysis

Step	How to Do It
Familiarize yourself with the article you are analyzing.	Read your article several times. Divide it into sections to understand its structure.
Place the article in its rhetorical context.	Follow the strategies in Chapter 2 and use the "Questions for Rhetorical Analysis" on pages 120–121.
Summarize the article.	Follow the steps in Chapter 2 on pages 27–29. You may want to produce a longer summary of 150–200 words as well as a short one-sentence summary.
Reread the article, identifying "hot spots."	Note hot spots in the article—points that impress you, disturb you, confuse you, or puzzle you.
Use the "Questions for Rhetorical Analysis" on page 119.	Choose several of these questions and freewrite responses to them.
From your notes and freewriting, identify the focus for your analysis.	Choose several features of the article that you find particularly important and that you want to discuss in depth in your essay. Identify points that will bring something new to your readers and that will help them see this article with new understanding. You may want to list your ideas and then look for ways to group them together around main points.
Write a thesis statement for your essay.	Articulate your important points of interest in one or two sentences that will set up these points clearly for your audience.

In finding a meaningful focus for your rhetorical analysis essay, you will need to create a focusing thesis statement that avoids wishy-washy formulas such as, "This argument has some strengths and some weaknesses." To avoid a vapid thesis statement, focus on the complexity of the argument, the writer's strategies for persuading the target audience, and the features that might impede its persuasiveness for skeptics. The below thesis statements try to articulate how their writers see the inner workings of these arguments as well as the arguments' contribution to their public conversations.

Examples of Thesis Statements for Rhetorical Analysis Essays

Lopez's angle of vision, although effectively in sync with her conservative readers of the *National Review*, exaggerates and distorts her case against these reproductive advances, weakening her *ethos* and the value of her argument for a wider audience. *[This is the thesis we would use if we were writing a stand-alone essay on Lopez.]*

In his editorial, "Why Blame Mexico?" published in *The American Conservative*, Fred Reed's irony and hard-hitting evidence undercut his desire to contrast the United States' hypocritical and flawed immigration policies with Mexico's successful ones.

In his editorial, "Amnesty?" in the Jesuit news commentary *America*, John F. Kavanaugh makes a powerful argument for his Catholic and religious readers; however, his proposal based on ethical reasoning may fail to reach other readers.

To make your rhetorical analysis of your article persuasive, you will need to develop each of the points stated or implied in your thesis statement using textual evidence, including short quotations. Your essay should show how you have listened carefully to the argument you are analyzing, summarized it fairly, and probed it deeply.

Organizing Your Rhetorical Analysis

A stand-alone rhetorical analysis can be organized as shown in the following table. ∎

Organization Plan for a Rhetorical Analysis of an Argument

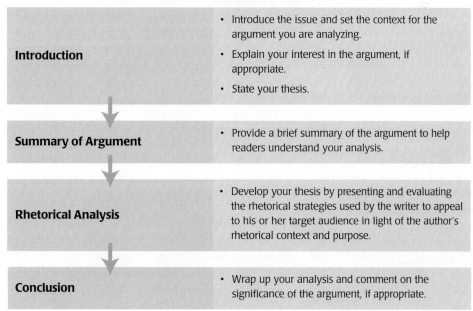

Introduction	• Introduce the issue and set the context for the argument you are analyzing. • Explain your interest in the argument, if appropriate. • State your thesis.
Summary of Argument	• Provide a brief summary of the argument to help readers understand your analysis.
Rhetorical Analysis	• Develop your thesis by presenting and evaluating the rhetorical strategies used by the writer to appeal to his or her target audience in light of the author's rhetorical context and purpose.
Conclusion	• Wrap up your analysis and comment on the significance of the argument, if appropriate.

Readings

Our first reading is by journalist Ellen Goodman, whose columns are syndicated in U.S. newspapers by the Washington Post Writers Group. This column, which appeared in 2008, is analyzed rhetorically by student Zachary Stumps in our second reading.

Womb for Rent—For a Price

ELLEN GOODMAN

BOSTON—By now we all have a story about a job outsourced beyond our reach in the global economy. My own favorite is about the California publisher who hired two reporters in India to cover the Pasadena city government. Really.

There are times as well when the offshoring of jobs takes on a quite literal meaning. When the labor we are talking about is, well, labor.

In the last few months we've had a full nursery of international stories about surrogate mothers. Hundreds of couples are crossing borders in search of lower-cost ways to fill the family business. In turn, there's a new coterie of international workers who are gestating for a living.

Many of the stories about the globalization of baby production begin in India, where the government seems to regard this as, literally, a growth industry. In the little town of Anand, dubbed "The Cradle of the World," 45 women were recently on the books of a local clinic. For the production

and delivery of a child, they will earn $5,000 to $7,000, a decade's worth of women's wages in rural India.

5   But even in America, some women, including Army wives, are supplementing their income by contracting out their wombs. They have become surrogate mothers for wealthy couples from European countries that ban the practice.

This globalization of baby-making comes at the peculiar intersection of a high reproductive technology and a low-tech work force. The biotech business was created in the same petri dish as Baby Louise, the first IVF baby. But since then, we've seen conception outsourced to egg donors and sperm donors. We've had motherhood divided into its parts from genetic mother to gestational mother to birth mother and now contract mother.

We've also seen the growth of an international economy. Frozen sperm is flown from one continent to another. And patients have become medical tourists, searching

for cheaper health care whether it's a new hip in Thailand or an IVF treatment in South Africa that comes with a photo safari thrown in for the same price. Why not then rent a foreign womb?

I don't make light of infertility. The primal desire to have a child underlies this multinational Creation, Inc. On one side, couples who choose surrogacy want a baby with at least half their own genes. On the other side, surrogate mothers, who are rarely implanted with their own eggs, can believe that the child they bear and deliver is not really theirs.

As one woman put it, "We give them a baby and they give us much-needed money. It's good for them and for us." A surrogate in Anand used the money to buy a heart operation for her son. Another raised a dowry for her daughter. And before we talk about the "exploitation" of the pregnant woman, consider her alternative in Anand: a job crushing glass in a factory for $25 a month.

10   Nevertheless, there is—and there should be—something

uncomfortable about a free market approach to baby-making. It's easier to accept surrogacy when it's a gift from one woman to another. But we rarely see a rich woman become a surrogate for a poor family. Indeed, in Third World countries, some women sign these contracts with a fingerprint because they are illiterate.

For that matter, we have not yet had stories about the contract workers for whom pregnancy was a dangerous occupation, but we will. What obligation does a family that simply contracted for a child have

to its birth mother? What control do—should—contractors have over their "employees" lives while incubating "their" children? What will we tell the offspring of this international trade?

"National boundaries are coming down," says bioethicist Lori Andrews, "but we can't stop human emotions. We are expanding families and don't even have terms to deal with it."

It's the commercialism that is troubling. Some things we cannot sell no matter how good "the deal." We cannot, for example, sell ourselves into slavery. We cannot sell

our children. But the surrogacy business comes perilously close to both of these deals. And international surrogacy tips the scales.

So, these borders we are crossing are not just geographic ones. They are ethical ones. Today the global economy sends everyone in search of the cheaper deal as if that were the single common good. But in the biological search, humanity is sacrificed to the economy and the person becomes the product. And, step by step, we come to a stunning place in our ancient creation story. It's called the marketplace.

Our second reading shows how student writer Zachary Stumps analyzed the Ellen Goodman article.

A Rhetorical Analysis of Ellen Goodman's "Womb for Rent—For a Price"

ZACHARY STUMPS (STUDENT)

Introduction provides context and poses issue to be addressed

With her op-ed piece "Womb for Rent—For a Price," published in the *Seattle Times* on April 11, 2008 (and earlier in the *Boston Globe*), syndicated columnist Ellen Goodman enters the murky debate about reproductive technology gone global. Since Americans are outsourcing everything else, "Why not then rent a foreign womb?" (130) she asks.

Provides background on Goodman

Goodman, a Pulitzer Prize–winning columnist for the Washington Post Writers Group, is known for helping readers understand the "tumult of social change and its impact on families," and for shattering "the mold of men writing exclusively about politics" ("Ellen Goodman"). This op-ed piece continues her tradition of examining social change from the perspective of family issues.

Summarizes the op-ed piece

Goodman launches her short piece by asserting that one of the most recent and consequential "jobs" to be outsourced is having babies. She explains how the "globalization of baby production" is thriving because it brings together the reproductive desires of people in developed countries and the bodily resources of women in developing countries like India. Briefly tracing how both reproductive technology and medical tourism have taken advantage of global possibilities, Goodman acknowledges that the thousands of dollars Indian women earn by carrying the babies of foreign couples represent a much larger income than these women could earn in any other available jobs. After appearing to legitimize this global exchange, however, Goodman shifts to her ethical concerns by raising some moral questions that she says are not being addressed in this trade. She concludes with a full statement of her claim that this global surrogacy is encroaching on human respect and dignity, exploiting business-based science, and turning babies into products.

Thesis paragraph

In this piece, Goodman's delay of her thesis has several rhetorical benefits: it gives Goodman space to present the perspective of poor women, enhanced by her appeals to *pathos*, and it invites readers to join her journey into the complex contexts of this issue; however, this strategy is also risky because it limits the development of her own argument.

Develops first point in thesis: use of pathos *in exploring perspective of poor women*

Instead of presenting her thesis up front, Goodman devotes much of the first part of her argument to looking at this issue from the perspective of foreign surrogate mothers. Using the strategies of *pathos* to evoke sympathy for these women, she creates a compassionate and progressively minded argument that highlights the benefits to foreign surrogate mothers. She cites factual evidence showing that the average job for a woman in Anand, India, yields a tiny "$25 a month" gotten through the hard work of "crushing glass in a factory," compared to the "$5,000 to $7,000" made carrying a baby to term (130). To carry a baby to term for a foreign couple represents "a decade's worth of women's wages in rural India" (130). Deepening readers' understanding of these women, Goodman cites one woman who used her earnings to finance her son's heart operation and another who paid for her daughter's dowry. In her fair presentation of these women, Goodman both builds her own positive *ethos* and adds a dialogic dimension to her argument by helping readers walk in the shoes of otherwise impoverished surrogate mothers.

Develops second point in thesis: the complex contexts of this issue—outsourcing and medical tourism

The second rhetorical benefit of Goodman's delayed thesis is that she invites readers to explore this complex issue of global surrogacy with her before she declares her own view. To help readers understand and think through this issue, she relates it to two other familiar global topics: outsourcing and medical tourism. First, she introduces foreign surrogacy as one of the latest forms of outsourcing: "This globalization of baby-making comes at the peculiar intersection of a high reproductive technology and a low-tech work force" (130). Presenting these women as workers, she explains that women in India are getting paid for "the production and delivery of a child" (130) that is analogous to the production and delivery of sneakers or bicycle parts.

Goodman also sets this phenomenon in the context of global medical tourism. If people can pursue lower-cost treatment for illnesses and health conditions in other countries, why shouldn't an infertile couple seeking to start a family not also have such access to these more affordable and newly available means? This reasoning provides a foundation for readers to begin understanding the many layers of the issue.

Shows how the delayed-thesis structure creates two perspectives in conflict

The result of Goodman's delayed-thesis strategy is that the first two-thirds of this piece seem to justify outsourcing surrogate motherhood. Only after reading the whole op-ed piece can readers see clearly that Goodman has been dropping hints about her view all along through her choice of words. Although she clearly sees how outsourcing surrogacy can help poor women economically, her use of market language such as "production," "delivery," and "labor" carry a double meaning. On first reading of this op-ed piece, readers don't know if Goodman's punning is meant to be catchy and entertaining or serves another purpose. This other purpose becomes clear in the last third of the article when Goodman forthrightly asserts her criticism of the commercialism of the global marketplace that promotes worldwide searching for a "cheaper deal": "humanity is sacrificed to the economy and the person becomes the product" (131). This is a bold and big claim, but does the final third of her article support it?

Restates the third point in his thesis: lack of space limits development of Goodman's argument.

In the final five paragraphs of this op-ed piece, Goodman begins to develop the rational basis of her argument; however, the brevity of the op-ed genre and her choice not to state her view openly initially have left Goodman with little space to develop her own claim. The result is that she presents some profound ideas very quickly. Some of the ethically complex ideas she introduces but doesn't explore much are these:

- The idea that there are ethical limits on what can be "sold"
- The idea that surrogate motherhood might be "dangerous work"
- The idea that children born from this "international trade" may be confused about their identities.

Discusses examples of ideas raised by Goodman but not developed

Goodman simply has not left herself enough space to develop these issues and perhaps leaves readers with questions rather than with changed views. I am particularly struck by several questions. Why have European countries banned surrogacy in developing countries and why has the United States not banned this practice? Does Goodman intend to argue that the United States should follow Europe's lead? She could explore more how this business of finding illiterate women to bear children for the wealthy continues to exploit third-world citizens much as sex tourism exploits women in the very same countries. It seems to perpetuate a tendency for the developed world to regard developing countries as a poor place of lawlessness where practices outlawed in the rest of the world (e.g. child prostitution, slave-like working conditions) are somehow tolerable. Goodman could have developed her argument more to state explicitly that a woman who accepts payment for bearing a baby becomes an indentured servant to the family. Yet another way to think of this issue is to see that the old saying of "a bun in the oven" is more literal than metaphoric when a woman uses her womb as a factory to produce children, a body business not too dissimilar to the commercialism of prostitution. Goodman only teases readers by mentioning these complex problems without producing an argument.

Conclusion

Still, although Goodman does not expand her criticism of outsourced surrogate motherhood or explore the issues of human dignity and rights, this argument does introduce the debate on surrogacy in the global marketplace, raise awareness, and begin to direct the conversation toward a productive end of seeking a responsible, healthy, and ethical future. Her op-ed piece lures readers into contemplating deep, perplexing ethical and economic problems and lays a foundation for readers to create an informed view of this issue.

Works Cited

Uses MLA format to list sources cited in the essay

"Ellen Goodman." *Postwritersgroup.com*. Washington Post Writer's Group, 2008. Web. May 19, 2008.

Goodman, Ellen. "Womb for Rent—For a Price." *Seattle Times* 11 April 2008: B6. Rpt. in *Writing Arguments*. John D. Ramage, John C. Bean, and June Johnson. Concise 5th ed. New York: Pearson Longman, 2010. Print.

For additional writing, reading, and research resources, go to www.mycomplab.com

Analyzing Visual Arguments

9

To see how images can make powerful arguments, consider the rhetorical persuasiveness of the "polar bear" marching in a small town parade (Figure 9.1). Sponsored by local environmentalists advocating action against global warming, the polar bear uses arguments from *logos* (drawing on audience knowledge that climate change threatens polar bears), *pathos* (evoking the bears' vulnerability), and *ethos* (conveying the commitment of the citizens group). Delighting children and adults alike, the bear created a memorable environmental argument.

This chapter is aimed at increasing your ability to analyze visual arguments and use them rhetorically in your own work. We begin with some basic components of document and visual design. We then examine genres of visual argument ranging from posters to Web pages, explain how you can use visuals in your own arguments, and conclude by explaining how to display numeric data graphically.

FIGURE 9.1 A visual argument about climate change

Understanding Design Elements in Visual Argument

To understand how visual images can produce an argument, you need to understand the design elements that work together to create a visual text.

The Components of Visual Design

There are four basic components of visual design: use of type, use of space and layout, use of color, and use of images. The most important considerations in using these design components are shown in Table 9.1.

As Table 9.1 suggests, in arguments that don't use images and graphics the writer's primary visual concern is document design. In planning how the document will look, the writer hopes to make it easy to read (choosing plain, conventional typefaces); to meet the readers' expectations for format (double-spacing manuscripts, following expected genre conventions if the argument is to be desktop published); and to provide appropriate structural cues that highlight points and guide the reader through the argument (using

TABLE 9.1 Components of Visual Design

Design Component	Key Variables	Key Principles
Use of type	▪ Font style ranging from conservative (Times New Roman, Courier) to playful and decorative (*Zapf Chancery* and other specialty fonts) ▪ Font size ▪ Variables for emphasis (**boldface**, *italics*, underlining, ALL CAPS)	▪ Choose *display type* (sans serif—without the little extensions on letters—like Century Gothic and Ariel) for headings, titles, and slogans. ▪ Choose *body type* (serif—with the little extensions on letters—like Times New Roman and Courier New) for long documents and main text. ▪ Make type functional and appealing by using only two or three typestyles per document. ▪ Use consistent patterns of type to indicate relationships among items. ▪ Choose type to project a specific impression. To create a formal, businesslike impression, as in scholarly publications, use a structured combination of serif and sans serif type. To create an informal look, as in popular magazine publications and highly visual posters and fliers, use sans serif and specialty type.
Use of space and layout	▪ Page size and type of paper ▪ Proportion of text to white space ▪ Arrangement of text on page (space, margins, columns, size of paragraphs, spaces between paragraphs, justification of margins) ▪ Use of highlighting elements such as bulleted lists, tables, sidebars, boxes ▪ Use headings and other means of breaking text into visual units	▪ Use layout to make documents highly readable and to guide readers with structural clues (headings, paragraph breaks, and bulleted lists). ▪ Focus on creating meaning and coherence with layout. ▪ For academic arguments, use simple, functional layouts. For popular magazine arguments and visual arguments, vary the layout and make the page visually attractive. However, for visual arguments, avoid clutter and confusion by limiting the amount of text and the number of visual items on a page.

Design Component	Key Variables	Key Principles
Use of color	• Variations in font color for effect • Use of color in images and graphics • Use of background tints and colored shading	• Use color to meet audience and genre expectations (minimal use of color in academic arguments and often lavish color in popular magazines). • For visual arguments, use color functionally (to indicate relationships) or decoratively (to create visual appeal). • For visual arguments, decide whether color will be used to make images look documentary-like (realistic), to create symbolic associations (for example, psychedelic colors and the 1960s), or to create a specific aesthetic effect (for example, pleasing, disturbing, or soothing).
Images and graphics	• Photographs • Drawings • Numeric graphics	• For visual arguments, consider how the image will work in the argument: to convey an idea, illustrate a point, evoke an emotional response. • For all arguments, consider how to establish the relationship between the image or graphic and the verbal text. (Images and graphics are described in detail later in this chapter.)

headings, paragraph breaks, bulleted lists). But in moving from verbal-only arguments to arguments that use visual elements for direct persuasive effect—for example in producing a flier, poster, or one-page newspaper advertisement—the writer can make creative use of all the elements of visual design.

Because using images and graphics effectively is especially challenging, we devote the rest of this chapter to explaining how images and graphics can be incorporated into visual arguments. We treat the use of photographs and drawings in the next main section and the use of quantitative graphics in the final section.

Analysis of a Visual Argument Using Type and Spatial Elements

To illustrate the persuasive power of type and layout, we ask you to consider Figure 9.2 on page 138, which shows an advocacy ad sponsored by a coalition of organizations aimed at fighting illegal drugs.

This ad, warning about the dangers of the drug Ecstasy, uses different sizes of type and layout to present its argument. The huge word "Ecstasy" first catches the reader's attention. The first few words at the top of the ad, exuding pleasure, lull the reader with the congruence between the pleasurable message and the playful type. Soon, however, the reader encounters a dissonance between the playful type and the meaning of the words: "dehydrate," "hallucinate," "paranoid," and "dead" name unpleasant ideas. By the end of the ad, readers realize they have been led through a downward progression of ideas beginning with the youth culture's belief that Ecstasy creates wonderfully positive feelings and ending with the ad's thesis that Ecstasy leads to paranoia, depression, and death. The playful informality of the font styles and the unevenly scattered layout of the type convey the seductiveness and unpredictability of the drug. The ad concedes

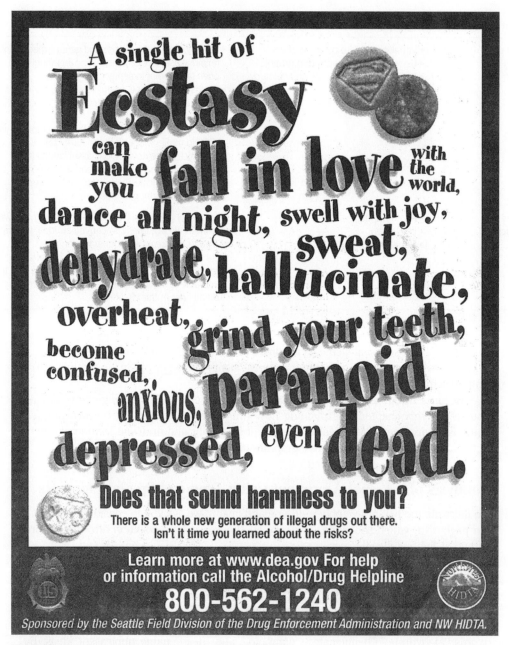

FIGURE 9.2 Advocacy advertisement warning against Ecstasy

that the first effects are falling "in love with the world" but implies that what comes next is increasingly dark and dangerous. At the end of the ad, in the lines of type near the bottom, the message and typestyle are congruent again. The question "Does that sound harmless to you?" marks a shift in type design and layout. The designer composed this section of the ad in conventional fonts centered on the page in a rational, businesslike fashion. This type design signals a metaphoric move from the euphoria of Ecstasy to the ordered structure of everyday reality, where the reader can now consider rationally the drug's harm. The information at the bottom of the ad identifies the ad's sponsors and gives both a Web address and a telephone number to call for more information about Ecstasy and other illegal drugs.

The Compositional Features of Photographs and Drawings

Now that we have introduced you to the four major elements of visual design—type, layout, color, and images—we turn to an in-depth discussion of photographic images and drawings. Used with great calculation in product advertisements, photos and drawings can be used with equal shrewdness in posters, fliers, advocacy ads, and Web sites. Although such images often are made to seem spontaneous and "natural," they are almost always composed: designers consciously select the details of staging and composition as well as manipulate camera techniques (filters, camera angle, lighting) and digital or chemical development techniques (airbrushing, merging of images). For example, public officials often try to control the effect of photographs by creating "photo-ops" (photographing opportunities), wherein news photographers are allowed to photograph an event only during certain times and from certain angles. Political photographs appearing in newspapers often are press releases officially approved by the politician's staff. (See the campaign photographs later in this chapter on page 145.)

To analyze a photograph or drawing, or to create visual images for your own arguments, you need to think both about the composition of the image and about the camera's relationship to the subject. Since drawings produce a perspective on a scene analogous to that of a camera, design considerations for photographs can be applied to drawings as well. The following list of questions can guide your analysis of any persuasive image.

- *Type of photograph or drawing:* Is the image documentary-like (representing a real event), fictionlike (intended to tell a story or dramatize a scene), or conceptual (illustrating or symbolizing an idea or theme)? The two photos of mosh pits—a girl shown crowd surfing and an unruly, almost menacing mosh pit crowd (Chapter 5, page 75)—are documentary photos capturing real events in action. In contrast, the drawing of the lizards in the Earthjustice ad in Figure 9.3 is both a fictional narrative telling a story and a conceptual drawing illustrating a theme.
- *Distance from the subject:* Is the image a close-up, medium shot, or long shot? Close-ups tend to increase the intensity of the image and suggest the importance of the subject; long shots tend to blend the subject into the background. In the images of Carlito and his mother from *Under the Same Moon* (p. 1), the close-ups of the two characters allows you to read the emotions on their faces and emphasize their importance. In contrast, the photograph of the young woman crossing the bridge in Haiti on page 93 is a long-range shot showing her blending into the poverty-stricken background, suggesting the devastating effect of poverty.
- *Orientation of the image and camera angle:* Is the camera (or artist) positioned in front of or behind the subject? Is it positioned below the subject, looking up (a low-angle shot)? Or is it above the subject, looking down (a high-angle shot)? Front-view shots,

Just then, the three lizards
came home and found Goldilocks
eating their porridge...

IT'S JUST NOT THE SAME WITHOUT BEARS.

Once upon a time there were over 100,000 grizzly bears in the lower 48 states. Now, there are less than a thousand grizzly bears left. The health of the grizzly is dependent on vast, undisturbed, wild lands. When bears disappear, other species will follow. Bears are such an important part of our wilderness, history, and culture that it's hard to imagine a world without them in the picture.

Grizzly bears are a threatened species, protected by the Endangered Species Act. But some special interests are pushing the U.S. Fish and Wildlife Service to remove Yellowstone grizzlies from the endangered species list. Why? They want to open up wild lands around Yellowstone

National Park to destructive logging, mining, off-road vehicle use, and development.

You can help protect our wilderness and grizzly bears. Please take a moment to contact Secretary Bruce Babbitt, Department of Interior, 1849 C St. NW, Washington DC 20240, or email Bruce_Babbitt@os.doi.gov – Tell him to keep grizzly bears on the Endangered Species List and that grizzly bears need more protection, not less.

Earthjustice Legal Defense Fund is working tirelessly to protect the grizzly bears and the wilderness they stand for. If we all work together, the grizzly bears will live happily ever after.

HELP KEEP BEARS IN THE PICTURE

www.earthjustice.org

EARTHJUSTICE
LEGAL DEFENSE FUND
1-800-584-6460

designed by **Sustain**

FIGURE 9.3 Earthjustice advocacy ad

such as the one of the baby in Figure 1.1 (p. 4), tend to emphasize the people being photographed. In contrast, rear-view shots often emphasize the scene or setting. A low-angle perspective tends to make the subject look superior and powerful, whereas a high-angle perspective can reduce the size and—by implication—the importance of the subject. A level angle tends to imply equality. The high-angle shot of the girl in the mosh pit emphasizes the superiority of the camera and the harmlessness of the mosh pit (p. 75). In contrast, the low-angle perspective of the lizards in the Earthjustice advocacy ad in Figure 9.3 emphasizes the power of the lizards and the inferiority of the viewer.

- *Point of view:* Does the camera or artist stand outside the scene and create an objective effect as in the Haiti photograph on page 93? Or is the camera or artist inside the scene as if the photographer or artist is an actor in the scene, creating a subjective effect as in the drawing of the lizards in the Earthjustice ad?
- *Use of color:* Is the image in color or in black and white? Is this choice determined by the restrictions of the medium (the publication can't afford color, as in many newspaper photographs) or is it the conscious choice of the photographer or artist? Are the colors realistic or muted? Have special filters been used (a photo made to look old through the use of brown tints)? The bright colors in the lizard and Goldilocks drawing in the Earthjustice ad resemble illustrations in books for children. The subdued colors in the *Tomb Raider* video game image on page 43 are intended to look natural and neutral.
- *Compositional special effects:* Is the entire image clear and realistic? Is any portion of it blurred? Is it blended with other realistic or nonrealistic images (a car ad that blends a city and a desert; a body lotion ad that merges a woman and a cactus)? Is the image an imitation of some other famous image such as a classic painting (as in parodies)? The Earthjustice ad is a conscious imitation of a children's picture book.
- *Juxtaposition of images:* Are several different images juxtaposed, suggesting relationships between them? Juxtaposition can suggest sequential or causal relationships or can metaphorically transfer the identity of a nearby image or background to the subject (as when a bath soap is associated with a meadow). This technique frequently is used in public relations to shape viewers' perceptions of political figures as when presidential candidate Barack Obama was photographed under a large American flag (see p. 145) to counter Republican party charges that he was not "American enough."
- *Manipulation of images:* Are staged images made to appear real, natural, documentary-like? Are images altered with airbrushing? Are images actually composites of a number of images (for instance, using images of different women's bodies to create one perfect model in an ad or film)? Are images cropped for emphasis? What is left out? Are images downsized or enlarged? For an example of a staged photo intended to look natural, see the baby and bib photo on page 4. Note how the baby is silhouetted to remove all background.
- *Settings, furnishings, props:* Is the photo or drawing an outdoor or indoor scene? What is in the background and foreground? What furnishings and props—such as furniture, objects in a room, pets, and landscape features—help create the scene? What social associations of class, race, and gender are attached to these settings and

props? Note, for example, how the designers of the Toyota Prius ad on page 94 used a cabbage leaf as a prop. The leaf suggests a gas mask as well as the Prius's claim to be green.

■ *Characters, roles, actions:* Does the photo or drawing tell a story? Are the people in the scene models? Are the models instrumental (acting out real-life roles) or are they decorative (extra and included for visual or sex appeal)? What are the facial expressions, gestures, and poses of the people? What are the spatial relationships of the figures? (Who is in the foreground, center, and background? Who is large and prominent?) What social relationships are implied by these poses and positions? In the "Save the Children" advocacy ad in Figure 9.4, the pose of the mother and child—each completely absorbed in adoration of the other—tells the story of the bonds of love between mothers and babies.

■ *Presentation of images:* Are there multiple separate images? If so, how are they related? Are the images large in proportion to verbal text? How are images labeled? How does the text relate to the image(s)? Does the image illustrate the text? Does the text explain or comment on the image? For example, the image of the masked woman dominates the Toyota Prius ad on page 94, while the type— and the tiny image of the car—are confined to the bottom of the ad. (You might consider why the ad maker places text at the bottom and image at the top rather than the reverse.)

An Analysis of a Visual Argument Using Images

As an example of a visual argument using an image, consider the Save the Children advocacy ad, which appeared in *Newsweek,* in Figure 9.4. Type, layout, color, and image are skillfully and harmoniously combined, but the image dominates; the verbal text interprets and applies the ideas conveyed by the image. The layout of the ad divides the page into three main parts, giving central focus to the image of the mother standing and looking into the eyes of the child she is holding in her arms. The blank top panel leads readers to look at the image. Two color panels, mauve behind the child and rose behind the mother, also highlight the two figures, isolate them in time and space, and concentrate the readers' attention on them. The large type in the black borders ("SHE'S THE BEST QUALIFIED TEACHER FOR HER CHILDREN" and "IMAGINE IF SHE HAD AN EDUCATION") frames the image, attracts readers' eyes, and plants the main idea in readers' minds: mothers should be equipped to teach their children.

This image skillfully blends familiar, universal ideas—a mother's love for her child and the tenderness and strength of this bond—with unfamiliar, foreign associations: a mother and child from a third-world country, wearing the traditional clothing of their country depicted by the mother's head scarf and the elaborate design on her sleeve. In addition to the familiar–unfamiliar dynamic, a universal–particular dynamic also operates in this ad. This woman and baby are *every* mother and child (after all, we don't know exactly where she is from), but they are also from some specific third-world country. The two figures have been posed to conjure up Western paintings and statues of the Madonna and Christ child. With this pose, the ad intends that readers

FIGURE 9.4 Save the Children advocacy ad

will connect with this image of motherly love and devotion and respond by supporting the Every Mother/Every Child campaign. Color in this ad also accents the warm, cozy, hopeful impression of the image; pink in Western culture is a feminine color often associated with women and babies. In analyzing the photographic image, you should note what is *not* shown: any surroundings, any indication of housing or scenery, any concrete sense of place or culture.

The text of the ad interprets the image, provides background information, and seeks to apply the ideas and feelings evoked by the image to urge readers to action. The image, without either the large type or the smaller type, does convey an idea as well as elicit sympathy from readers, but the text adds meaning to the image and builds on those impressions and applies them.

The ad designer could have focused on poverty, illiteracy, hunger, disease, and high mortality rates but instead chose to evoke positive feelings of identification and to convey hopeful ideas. While acknowledging their cultural difference from this mother and child, readers recognize their common humanity and are moved to "give mothers and children the best chance to survive and thrive." The large amounts of blank space in this ad help to convey that the main points here are important, serious, elemental, but also simple—as if the ad has gotten to the heart of the matter. The bottom panel of the ad gives readers the logo and name of the organization, Save the Children, and a phone number and Web address to use to show their support.

■ ■ ■ **FOR CLASS DISCUSSION**   Analyzing Photos Rhetorically

1. The techniques for constructing photos come into play prominently in news photography. In this exercise, we ask you to examine four photographs of American presidential campaigns. Working individually or in groups, study the four photos in Figures 9.5 through 9.8, and then answer the following questions:

   a. What do you think is the dominant impression of each photo? In other words, what is each photo's implicit argument?

   b. What camera techniques and compositional features do you see in each photo?

   c. What image of the candidates do these photographs attempt to create for citizens and voters?

2. Three of these photographs (of Reagan, Clinton, and Obama) are mostly successful in promoting the image intended by their campaigns. But one of the photographs (of Democratic candidate John Kerry in 1994, running against George W. Bush) is an example of a photograph that backfired. Republicans reversed the intended impact of the photograph and used it to ridicule Kerry.

   a. What is the intended effect of the Kerry photograph, which is from a windsurfing video showing Kerry zigzagging across the water?

   b. How might the photograph produce an unintended effect that opens the candidate to ridicule from the opposing party? (Suggestion: Enter the following keywords into your Web search engine: "Kerry windsurfing photo.")

FIGURE 9.5 Ronald Reagan at his California ranch home

FIGURE 9.6 Presidential candidate John Kerry windsurfing

FIGURE 9.7 Incumbent President Bill Clinton in a campaign ad

FIGURE 9.8 Presidential candidate Barack Obama with the American flag

3. The poster shown in Figure 9.9 is for the documentary film *Wal-Mart: The High Cost of Low Prices*, produced in 2005 by filmmaker and political activist Robert Greenwald. According to its Web site, the movie features "the deeply personal stories and everyday lives of families and communities struggling to survive in a Wal-Mart world."

FIGURE 9.9 Poster for *Wal-Mart: The High Cost of Low Prices*

Working individually or in groups, answer the following questions:

a. What compositional features and drawing techniques do you see in this image? What is striking or memorable about the visual features?

b. How would you state the argument made by this image?

c. The effect of this image derives partly from what cultural analysts call "intertextuality." By this term, analysts mean the way a viewer's reading of an image depends on familiarity with a network of "connected" images—in this case, familiarity with posters for *Godzilla* films from the 1950s as well as with Wal-Mart's conventional use of the smiley face. How does this drawing use viewers' cultural knowledge of Godzilla and smiley faces to create an image of Wal-Mart? Why is this monster wearing a suit? Why does it have five or more arms? Why is this monster destroying a suburb or housing area rather than a city of skyscrapers? In short, what does it retain of conventional Godzilla images, what does it change, and why? Similarly, how is the monster's smiley face similar to and different from the traditional Wal-Mart smiley face?

The Genres of Visual Arguments

We have already mentioned that verbal arguments today frequently are accompanied by photographs or drawings that contribute to the text's persuasive appeal. For example, a verbal argument promoting U.N. action to help AIDS victims in Africa might be accompanied by a photograph of a dying mother and child. However, some genres of argument are dominated by visual elements. In these genres, the visual design carries most of the argumentative weight; verbal text is used primarily for labeling, for focusing the argument's claim, or for commenting on the images. In this section, we describe specifically these highly visual genres of argument.

Posters and Fliers

To persuade audiences, an arguer might create a poster designed for placement on walls or kiosks or a flier to be passed out on street corners. Posters dramatically attract and direct viewers' attention toward one subject or issue. They often seek to rally supporters, promote a strong stance on an issue, and call people to action. For example, during World War II, posters asked Americans to invest in war bonds and urged women to join the workforce to free men for active combat. During the Vietnam War, famous posters used slogans such as "Make Love Not War" or "Girls say yes to boys who say no" to increase national resistance to the war.

The hallmark of an effective poster is the way it focuses and encodes a complex meaning in a verbal-visual text, often with one or more striking images. These images are often symbolic—for example, using children to symbolize family and home, a soaring bird to symbolize freedom, or three firefighters raising the American flag over the World Trade Center rubble in September 2001 to symbolize American heroism, patriotism, and resistance to terrorism. These symbols derive potency from the values they share with their target audience. Posters tend to use words sparingly, either as slogans or as short, memorable directives. This terse verbal text augments the message encoded in an eye-catching, dominant image.

As an example of a contemporary poster, consider the poster on page 117, which is a call to stop eating red meat in order to protect Earth. This poster uses compositional special effects, depicting Earth from outer space against the backdrop of the Milky Way. The grain, color, and texture of pieces of red meat are superimposed over the continents where viewers expect to see the familiar greens and browns of Earth's surface. The impact of the poster is intensified by the big bite that has been taken out of North America. The substitution of meat for land and the presence of the bitten-out piece of Earth convey the message of immediate destruction. Framing this image of Earth on the top and bottom are a question and an imperative phrased in casual but confrontational language: "Think you can be a meat-eating environmentalist? Think again." The summary caption of the poster urges readers to become vegetarians. As you can see, this poster tries to shock and push readers toward a more radical environmentalism—one without meat.

Fliers and brochures often use visual elements similar to those in posters. An image might be the top and center attraction of a flier or the main focus of the front cover of a brochure. However, unlike posters, fliers and brochures offer additional space for verbal arguments, which often present the writer's claim supported with bulleted lists of reasons. Sometimes pertinent data and statistics, along with testimony from supporters, are placed in boxes or sidebars.

Public Affairs Advocacy Advertisements

Public affairs advocacy advertisements share with posters an emphasis on visual elements, but they are designed specifically for publication in newspapers and magazines and, in their persuasive strategies, are directly analogous to product advertisements. Public affairs advocacy ads are usually sponsored by a corporation or an advocacy organization and often have a more time-sensitive message than posters and a more immediate and defined target audience. Designed as condensed arguments aimed at influencing public opinion on civic issues, these ads are characterized by their brevity, audience-based appeals, and succinct, soundbite style. Often, in order to sketch out their claim and reasons clearly and concisely, they employ headings and subheadings, bulleted lists, different sizes and styles of type, and a clever, pleasing layout on the page. They usually have some attention-getting slogan or headline like "MORE KIDS ARE GETTING BRAIN CANCER. WHY?" or "STOP THE TAX REVOLT JUGGERNAUT!"

The balance between verbal and visual elements in an advocacy advertisement varies. Some advocacy ads are verbal only, with visual concerns focused on document design (for example, an "open letter" from the president of a corporation appearing as a full-page newspaper ad). Other advocacy ads are primarily visual, using images and other design elements with the same shrewdness as product advertisements. We looked closely at advocacy ads when we examined the Ecstasy ad, the Earthjustice ad, and the Save the Children ad (Figures 9.2, 9.3, and 9.4).

As another example of a public affairs advocacy ad, consider the ad in Chapter 15, page 257, that attempts to counter the influence of the pro-life movement's growing campaign against abortion. As you can see, this ad is dominated by one stark image: a question mark formed by the hook of a coat hanger. The shape of the hook draws the reader's eye to the concentrated type centered below it. The hook carries most of the weight of the argument. Simple, bold, and harsh, the image of the hanger—tapping readers' cultural knowledge—evokes the dangerous experience of illegal abortions performed crudely by nonmedical people in the dark back streets of cities. The ad wants viewers to think of the dangerous last resorts that desperate women would have to turn to if they could not obtain abortions legally. The hanger itself creates a visual pun: as a question mark, it conveys the ad's dilemma about what will happen if abortions are made illegal. As a coat hanger, it provides the ad's frightening answer to the printed question—desperate women will return to back-street abortionists who use coat hangers as tools.

■ ■ ■ **FOR CLASS DISCUSSION** *Analyzing an Advocacy Ad Rhetorically*
Reexamine the public affairs advocacy ad shown in Figure 9.3. This ad, sponsored by Earthjustice, defends the presence of grizzly bears in Yellowstone National Park as well as other wilderness areas in the Rocky Mountains. In our classes, this ad has yielded lively discussion of its ingenuity and complexity.

Working individually or in groups, conduct your own examination of this ad using the following questions:

1. What visual features of this ad immediately attract your eyes? What principles for effective use of type, layout, color, and image does this ad exemplify?
2. What is the core argument of this ad?
3. Why did Earthjustice use the theme of Goldilocks? How do the lizards function in this ad? Why does the ad *not* have any pictures of grizzlies or bears of any kind?
4. How would you design an advocacy ad for the preservation of grizzly bears? What visuals would you use?

■ ■ ■

Cartoons

An especially charged kind of visual argument is the political cartoon. Although you are perhaps not likely to create your own political cartoons, it is useful to understand how cartoonists use visual and verbal elements to convey their message. Political cartoons often are mini-narratives, portraying an issue dramatically, compactly, and humorously. They employ images and a few well-chosen words to dramatize conflicts and problems. Using caricature, exaggeration, and distortion, cartoonists distill an issue down to an image that boldly reveals the creator's perspective and subsequent claim on a civic issue. The purpose of political cartoons usually is satirical. Because they are so condensed and often connected to current affairs, political cartoons are particularly dependent on the audience's background knowledge of cultural and political events. When political cartoons work well, through their perceptive combination of images and words, they flash a brilliant, clarifying light on a perspective or provide a new lens on an issue, often giving readers a shock of insight.

As an illustration, note the Benson cartoon in Figure 9.10, which first appeared in the *Arizona Republic*. The *kairotic* moment for this piece is the national debate about baseball players' using steroids to blast more home runs or add velocity to their fastballs. Some athletes and sports commentators have accepted the use of steroids, seeing them

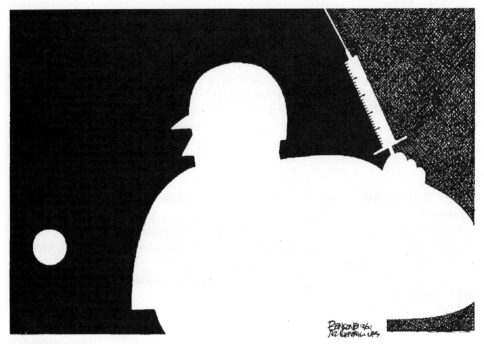

FIGURE 9.10 Cartoon protesting baseball players' use of steroids
Source: By permission of Steve Benson and Creators Syndicate, Inc.

as logical outcomes of other performance enhancers such as Ritalin for concentration or botox for beauty. Others challenge the use of performance-enhancing drugs, citing health dangers to users, unfairness to nonusers, and loss of integrity to sports. In this wordless cartoon, Benson conjures up this controversy; the hefty batter and hypodermic needle substituting for a bat imply that this tampering with drugs and the great American tradition of baseball is abnormal, dangerous, and scary.

■ ■ ■ **FOR CLASS DISCUSSION**   **Analyzing Cartoons Rhetorically**

1. Cartoons often sum up a worldview in a single image. Consider the political cartoons on immigration on page 17. What mini-narrative do the cartoons convey? What are the cartoons arguing? How do the cartoons use caricature, exaggeration, or distortion to convey their perspective?

2. Cartoons can provide insight into how the public is lining up on issues. Choose a current issue, such as athletes' use of steroids, homeland security, reforming social security, army recruitment, or stem cell research. Then, using a cartoon index such as Daryl Cagle's Pro Cartoonists Index (http://www.cagle.com) or a Web search of your own, find several cartoons that capture different perspectives on your issue. What is the mini-narrative, the main claim, and the use of caricature, exaggeration, or distortion in each? How is *kairos,* or timeliness, important to each cartoon?   ■ ■ ■

Web Pages

So far we have only hinted at the influence of the World Wide Web in accelerating use of visual images in argument. The hypertext design of Web pages, along with their complex intermixture of text and image, has changed the way many writers think of argument. The home page of an advocacy site, for example, often has many features of a poster argument with hypertext links to galleries of images on the one hand, and to verbal arguments on the other. These verbal arguments themselves often contain photographs, drawings, and graphics. The strategies discussed in this chapter for analyzing and interpreting visual texts also apply to Web pages. Consider, for example, the "AAS Goals" page for Athletes Against Steroids (Figure 9.11).

FIGURE 9.11 "About Us" page from Athletes Against Steroids Web site

This advocacy site announces its purpose in the black and red type in the center of the Web page. The bottom half of the page briefly summarizes the problem with steroids and then outlines its objectives. The links on the left side of the page announce the range, depth, and relevance of material on steroid use posted on this site. Under the masthead for the organization, the quotation from President Bush's 2004 State of the Union Address conveys that steroid use is a national problem needing immediate attention. Each page on this Web site follows the same basic design with subtle variations. How do the layout and use of color support the *ethos* of this site and its appeal to *pathos*? They could have made the page much more dramatic with scary pictures, but they chose this more understated design. Do you agree with their choice?

Because the Web is such an important tool in research, we have placed our main discussion of Web sites in Appendix 2, pages 279–285. On these pages you will find our explanations for reading, analyzing, and evaluating Web sites.

Constructing Your Own Visual Argument

The most common visual arguments you are likely to create are posters and fliers, public affairs advocacy ads, and possibly Web pages. You may also decide that in longer verbal arguments the use of visuals or graphics could clarify your points while adding visual variety to your paper. The following guidelines will help you apply your understanding of visual elements in the construction of your own visual arguments.

Guidelines for Creating Visual Arguments

1. *Genre*: Determine where this visual argument is going to appear (bulletin board, passed out as a flier, a one-page magazine or newspaper spread, or as a Web page).
2. *Audience-based appeals*: Determine your target audience.
   - What values and background knowledge of your issue can you assume your audience has?
   - What specifically do you want your audience to think or do after reading your visual argument?
   - If you are promoting a specific course of action (sign a petition, send money, vote for or against a bill, attend a meeting), how can you make that request clear and direct?
3. *Core of your argument*: Determine what clear claim and reasons will form the core of your argument; decide if this claim and these reasons will be explicitly stated or implicit in your visuals and slogans.
   - How much verbal text will you use?
   - If the core of your argument will be largely implicit, how can you still make it readily apparent and clear for your audience?

4. *Visual design*: What visual design and layout will grab your audience's attention and be persuasive?

   ▪ How can font sizes and styles, layout, and color be used in this argument to create a strong impression?

   ▪ What balance and harmony can you create between the visual and verbal elements of your argument? Will your verbal element be a slogan, express the core of the argument, or summarize and comment on the image(s)?

5. *Use of images*: If your argument lends itself to images, what photo or drawing would support your claim or have emotional appeal? (If you want to use more than one image, be careful not to clutter your page and confuse your message. Simplicity and clarity are important.)

   ▪ What image would be memorable and meaningful to your audience? Would a photo or a drawing be most effective?

   ▪ Will your image(s) be used to provide evidence for your claim or illustrate a main idea, evoke emotions, or enhance your credibility and authority?

As an example of a poster argument created by a student, consider Leah Johnson's poster in Figure 9.12. Intended for bulletin boards and kiosks around her college campus, Johnson's work illustrates how a writer can use minimal but well-chosen verbal text, layout, and images to convey a rhetorically effective argument. (That is Leah herself in the photograph.) In this ad, Leah is joining a national conversation about alcohol abuse on college campuses and is proposing a safe way of handling her university's weekly social get-together for older students, "Thirsty Thursdays." Notice how Leah in this visual argument has focused on her claim and reasons without seeing the need to supply evidence.

■ ■ ■ **FOR CLASS DISCUSSION**   Developing Ideas for a Poster Argument

This exercise asks you to do the thinking and planning for a poster argument to be displayed on your college or university campus. Choose an issue that is controversial on your campus (or in your town or city), and follow the Guidelines for Creating Visual Arguments on pages 152–153 to envision the view you want to advocate on that issue. What might be the core of your argument? Who is your target audience? Are you representing a group, club, or other organization? What image(s) might be effective in attracting and moving this audience? Possible topics for issues might be commuter parking; poor conditions in the computer lab; student reluctance to use the counseling center; problems with dorm life, financial aid programs, or intramural sports; ways to improve orientation programs for new students, work-study programs, or travel-abroad opportunities; or new initiatives such as study groups for the big lecture courses or new service-learning opportunities.

■ ■ ■

Drink and Then Drive?
Jeopardize My Future?

- Arrest
- Financial Problems (fines up to $8,125)
- Increased Insurance Rates
- License Suspension
- Criminal Conviction
- Incarceration
- Serious Injury or Death

or
Designate a Driver?

It's a no-brainer.
Join your Senior Class at Thirsty Thursday, but
designate a driver.

FIGURE 9.12 Student poster argument promoting the use of designated drivers

Using Information Graphics in Arguments

Besides images in the form of photographs and drawings, writers often use quantitative graphics to support arguments using numbers. In Chapter 5, we introduced you to the use of quantitative data in arguments. We discussed the persuasiveness of numbers and showed you ways to use them responsibly in your arguments.

(See pp. 79–80.) With the advent of spreadsheet and presentation programs, today's writers often create and import quantitative graphics into their documents. These visuals—such as tables, pie charts, and line or bar graphs—can have great rhetorical power by making numbers tell a story at a glance. In this section, we'll show you how quantitative graphics can make numbers "speak." We'll also show you how to incorporate graphics into your text and reference them effectively.

How Tables Contain a Variety of Stories

Data used in arguments usually have their origins in raw numbers collected from surveys, questionnaires, observational studies, scientific experiments, and so forth. Through a series of calculations, the numbers are combined, sorted, and arranged in a meaningful fashion, often in detailed tables. Some of the tables published by the U.S. Census Bureau, for example, contain dozens of pages. The more dense the table, the more their use is restricted to statistical experts who pore over them to analyze their meanings. More useful to the general public are midlevel tables contained on one or two pages that report data at a higher level of abstraction.

Consider, for example, Table 9.2, published by the U.S. Census Bureau in its document "America's Families and Living Arrangements: Population Characteristics" based on the 2000 census. This table shows the marital status of people fifteen years of age and older, broken into gender and age groupings, in March 2000. It also provides comparative data on the "never married" percent of the population in March 2000 and March 1970.

Take a few moments to peruse the table and be certain you know how to read it. You read tables in two directions: from top to bottom and from left to right. Always begin with the title, which tells you what the table contains and includes elements from both the vertical and horizontal dimensions of the table. In this case, the vertical dimension presents demographic categories for people "15 years old and over": for both sexes, for males, and for females. Each of these gender categories is subdivided into age categories. The horizontal dimension provides information about "marital status." Seven of the columns give total numbers (reported in thousands) for March 2000. The eighth column gives the "percent never married" for March 2000, while the last column gives the "percent never married" for March 1970. To make sure you know how to read the table, pick a couple of rows at random and say to yourself what each number means. For example, the first row under "Both sexes" gives total figures for the entire population of the United States ages fifteen and older. In March 2000, there were 213,773,000 persons fifteen and older (remember that the numbers are presented in thousands). Of these, 113,002,000 were married and living with their spouses. As you continue across the columns, you'll see that 2,730,000 persons are married but not living with their spouses (a spouse might be stationed overseas or in prison; or a married couple might be maintaining a "commuter marriage" with separate households in different cities). Continuing across the columns, you'll see that 4,479,000 persons were separated from their spouses; 19,881,000 were divorced; 13,665,000 were widowed; and an additional 60,016,000 were never married. In the next-to-the-last column, the number of

TABLE 9.2 Marital status of people 15 years and over: March 1970 and March 2000 (In thousands)

Characteristic	Total	March 2000 — Number						Percent never married	March 1970 percent never married[a]
		Married spouse present	Married spouse absent	Separated	Divorced	Widowed	Never married		
Both sexes									
Total 15 years old and over..........	213,773	113,002	2,730	4,479	19,881	13,665	60,016	28.1	24.9
15 to 19 years old..........	20,102	345	36	103	64	13	19,541	97.2	93.9
20 to 24 years old..........	18,440	3,362	134	234	269	11	14,430	78.3	44.5
25 to 29 years old..........	18,269	8,334	280	459	917	27	8,255	45.2	14.7
30 to 34 years old..........	19,519	11,930	278	546	1,616	78	5,071	26.0	7.8
35 to 44 years old..........	44,804	29,353	717	1,436	5,967	399	6,932	15.5	5.9
45 to 54 years old..........	36,633	25,460	492	899	5,597	882	3,303	9.0	6.1
55 to 64 years old..........	23,388	16,393	308	441	3,258	1,770	1,218	5.2	7.2
65 years old and over..........	32,620	17,827	485	361	2,193	10,484	1,270	3.9	7.6
Males									
Total 15 years old and over..........	103,113	56,501	1,365	1,818	8,572	2,604	32,253	31.3	28.1
15 to 19 years old..........	10,295	69	3	51	29	3	10,140	98.5	97.4
20 to 24 years old..........	9,208	1,252	75	70	101	-	7,710	83.7	54.7
25 to 29 years old..........	8,943	3,658	139	170	342	9	4,625	51.7	19.1
30 to 34 years old..........	9,622	5,640	151	205	712	15	2,899	30.1	9.4
35 to 44 years old..........	22,134	14,310	387	585	2,775	96	3,981	18.0	6.7
45 to 54 years old..........	17,891	13,027	255	378	2,377	157	1,697	9.5	7.5
55 to 64 years old..........	11,137	8,463	158	188	1,387	329	612	5.5	7.8
65 years old and over..........	13,885	10,084	197	171	849	1,994	590	4.2	7.5
Females									
Total 15 years old and over..........	110,660	56,501	1,365	2,661	11,309	11,061	27,763	25.1	22.1
15 to 19 years old..........	9,807	276	33	52	35	10	9,401	95.9	90.3
20 to 24 years old..........	9,232	2,110	59	164	168	11	6,720	72.8	35.8
25 to 29 years old..........	9,326	4,676	141	289	575	18	3,627	38.9	10.5
30 to 34 years old..........	9,897	6,290	127	341	904	63	2,172	21.9	6.2
35 to 44 years old..........	22,670	15,043	330	851	3,192	303	2,951	13.0	5.2
45 to 54 years old..........	18,742	12,433	237	521	3,220	725	1,606	8.6	4.9
55 to 64 years old..........	12,251	7,930	150	253	1,871	1,441	606	4.9	6.8
65 years old and over..........	18,735	7,743	288	190	1,344	8,490	680	3.6	7.7

[a]The 1970 percentages include 14-year-olds, and thus are for 14+ and 14–19.

Source: U.S. Census Bureau, Current Population Survey, March 2000.

never-married persons is converted to a percentage: 28.1 percent. Finally, the last column shows the percentage of never-married persons in 1970: 24.9 percent. These last two columns show us that the number of unmarried people in the United States rose 3.2 percentage points since 1970.

Now that you know how to read the table, peruse it carefully to see the kinds of stories it tells. What does the table show you, for example, about the percentage of married persons ages 25–29 in 1970 versus 2000? What does it show about different age-related patterns of marriage in males and females? By showing you that Americans are waiting much later in life to get married, a table like this initiates many causal questions for analysis and argument. What happened in American culture between 1970 and 2000 to explain the startling difference in the percentage of married persons within, say, the 20–24 age bracket? In 2000, only 22 percent of persons in this age bracket were married (we converted "unmarried" to "married" by subtracting 78.3 from 100). However, in 1970, 55 percent of people in this age bracket were married.

Using a Graph to Tell a Story

Table 9.2, as we have seen, tells the story of how Americans are postponing marriage until later in life. However, one has to read the table carefully, poring over it like a sleuth, to tease out the story from the dense columns of numbers. To focus on a key story and make it powerfully immediate, you can create a graphic.

Bar Graphs   Suppose, for example, that you are writing an argument in which you want to show that the percentage of married women in age groups 20–29 has dropped significantly since 1970. You could tell this story through a simple bar graph (Figure 9.13).

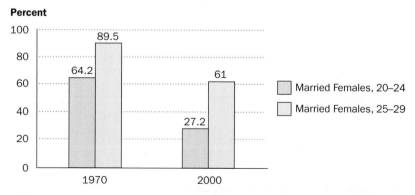

FIGURE 9.13 Percentage of married females, ages 20–29, 1970 and 2000

Source: U.S. Census Bureau, *Current Population Survey*, March 2000.

Bar graphs use bars of varying length, extending either horizontally or vertically, to contrast two or more quantities. As with any graphic presentation, you must create a comprehensive title. In the case of bar graphs, titles tell readers what is being compared to what. Most bar graphs also have legends, which explain what the different features on the graph represent. Bars are typically distinguished from each other by use of different colors, shades, or patterns of cross-hatching. The special power of bar graphs is that they can help readers make quick comparisons between different groups across a variable such as time.

Pie Charts   Another vivid kind of graphic is a pie chart, which depicts different percentages of a total (the pie) in the form of slices. Pie charts are a favorite way of depicting noteworthy patterns in the way parts of a whole are divided up. Suppose, for example, you wanted your readers to notice the high percentage of widows among women ages 65 and older. To do so, you could create a pie chart (Figure 9.14) based on the data in the last row of Table 9.2.

As you can see from Figure 9.14, a pie chart can demonstrate at a glance how the whole of something is divided into segments. The effectiveness of pie charts diminishes as you add more slices. In most cases, you'll begin to confuse readers if you include more than five or six slices.

Line Graphs   Another powerful quantitative graphic is a line graph, which converts numerical data into a series of points on a grid and connects them to create flat, rising,

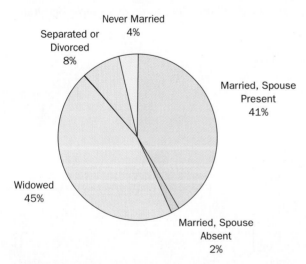

FIGURE 9.14 Marital status of females, ages 65 and older, 2000

Source: U.S. Census Bureau, *Current Population Survey*, March 2000.

or falling lines. The result gives us a picture of the relationship between the variables represented on the horizontal and vertical axes.

Suppose you wanted to tell the story of the rising number of separated/divorced women in the U.S. population. Using Table 9.2, you can calculate the percent of separated/divorced females in 2000 by adding the number of separated females (2,661,000) and the number of divorced females (11,309,000) and dividing that sum by the total number of females (110,660,000). The result is 12.6 percent. You can make the same calculations for 1990, 1980, and 1970 by looking at U.S. census data from those years (available on the Web or in your library). The resulting line graph is shown in Figure 9.15.

To determine what this graph is telling you, clarify what's represented on the two axes. By convention, the horizontal axis of a graph contains the predictable, known variable that has no surprises—what researchers call the "independent variable." In this case, the horizontal axis represents the years 1970–2000 arranged predictably in chronological order. The vertical axis contains the unpredictable variable that forms the graph's story—what researchers call the "dependent variable"—in this case the percentage of divorced females. The ascending curve tells the story at a glance.

Note that with line graphs the steepness of a slope (and hence the rhetorical effect) can be manipulated by the intervals chosen for the vertical axis. Figure 9.15

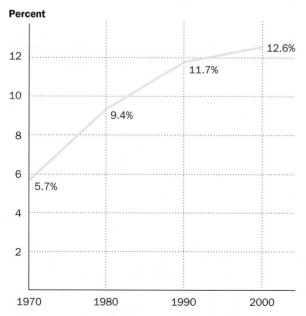

FIGURE 9.15 Percentage of females age 15 and older who are separated or divorced, 1970–2000

Source: U.S. Census Bureau, *Current Population Survey,* March 2000.

shows vertical intervals of 2 percent. The slope could be made less dramatic by choosing intervals of, say, 10 percent and more dramatic by choosing intervals of 1 percent.

Incorporating Graphics into Your Argument

Today writers working with quantitative data usually use graphing software that automatically creates tables, graphs, or charts from data entered into the cells of a spreadsheet. For college papers, some instructors may allow you to make your graphs with pencil and ruler and paste them into your document.

Designing the Graphic When you design your graphic, your goal is to have a specific rhetorical effect on your readers, not to demonstrate all the bells and whistles available on your software. Adding extraneous data in the graph or chart or using such features as three-dimensional effects can often call attention away from the story you are trying to tell. Keep the graphic as uncluttered and simple as possible and design it so that it reinforces the point you are making in your text.

Numbering, Labeling, and Titling Graphics In newspapers and popular magazines, writers often include graphics in boxes or sidebars without specifically referring to them in the text itself. However, in academic or workplace writing, graphics are always labeled, numbered, titled, and referred to directly in the text. By convention, tables are listed as "Tables," while line graphs, bar graphs, pie charts, or any other kind of drawings or photographs are labeled "Figures." Suppose you create a document that includes four graphics—a table, a bar graph, a pie chart, and an imported photograph. The table would be labeled Table 1. The rest of the graphics would be labeled Figure 1, Figure 2, and Figure 3.

In addition to numbering and labeling, every graphic needs a comprehensive title that explains fully what information is displayed. Look back over the tables and figures in this chapter and compare their titles to the information in the graphics. In a line graph showing changes over time, for example, a typical title will identify the information on both the horizontal and vertical axes and the years covered. Bar graphs also have a "legend" explaining how the bars are coded, if necessary. When you import the graphic into your own text, be consistent in where you place the title—either above the graphic or below it.

Referencing the Graphic in Your Text Academic and professional writers follow a referencing convention called *independent redundancy*. The general rule is this: The graphic should be understandable without the text; the text should be understandable without the graphic; the text should repeat the most important information in the graphic. Suppose, for example, you are writing an argument saying that social services for the elderly is a women's issue as well as an age issue and you want to use a pie chart you have constructed. In your text, you would reference this chart and then repeat its key information as shown in Figure 9.16.

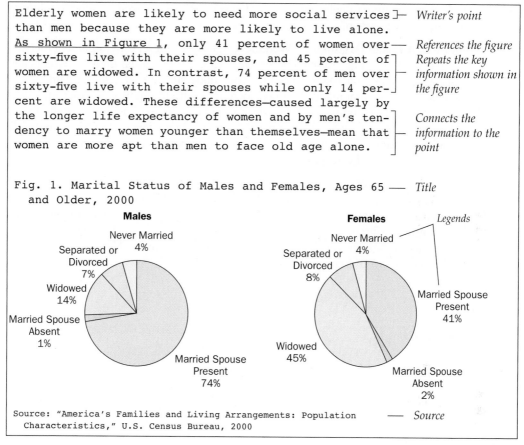

Elderly women are likely to need more social services ⎤— *Writer's point*
than men because they are more likely to live alone.
<u>As shown in Figure 1</u>, only 41 percent of women over—— *References the figure*
sixty-five live with their spouses, and 45 percent of ⎤ *Repeats the key*
women are widowed. In contrast, 74 percent of men over ⎬— *information shown in*
sixty-five live with their spouses while only 14 per- ⎥ *the figure*
cent are widowed. These differences—caused largely by ⎦
the longer life expectancy of women and by men's ten- ⎤ *Connects the*
dency to marry women younger than themselves—mean that ⎬— *information to the*
women are more apt than men to face old age alone. ⎦ *point*

Fig. 1. Marital Status of Males and Females, Ages 65 —— *Title*
   and Older, 2000

Males   **Females**   *Legends*

Never Married   Never Married
4%   4%
Separated or   Separated or
Divorced   Divorced
7%   8%
Widowed   Married Spouse
14%   Present
                                                                 41%
Married Spouse
Absent
1%   Widowed
                                             45%
         Married Spouse   Married Spouse
         Present   Absent
         74%   2%

Source: "America's Families and Living Arrangements: Population —— *Source*
   Characteristics," U.S. Census Bureau, 2000

FIGURE 9.16 Excerpt from a student paper with referenced graphic

WRITING ASSIGNMENT A Visual Argument Rhetorical Analysis, a Poster Argument, or a Microtheme Using Quantitative Data

Option 1: A Rhetorical Analysis of a Visual Argument   Write a thesis-driven rhetorical analysis essay in which you examine the rhetorical effectiveness of a visual argument, either one of the visual arguments in this text or one specified by your instructor. Unless otherwise stated, direct your analysis to an audience of your class-mates. In your introduction, establish the argumentative conversation to which this argument is contributing. Briefly summarize the argument and describe the visual text. Present your thesis, highlighting two or more rhetorical features of the argument you find central to the effectiveness or ineffectiveness of this argument. To develop and support your points, you will need to include visual features and details (such as color, design, camera angle, framing, and special effects) as well as short quotations from any verbal parts of the argument.

Option 2: A Poster Argument   Working with the idea for a poster argument that you explored in the For Class Discussion on page 153, use the visual design concepts and principles presented on pages 152–153, your understanding of visual argument and the genre of poster arguments, and your own creativity to produce a poster argument that can be displayed on your campus or in your town or city. Try out the draft of your poster argument on people who are part of your target audience. Based on these individuals' suggestions for improving the clarity and impact of this visual argument, prepare a final version of your poster argument.

Option 3: A Microtheme Using a Quantitative Graphic   Write a microtheme that tells a story based on data you select from Table 9.2 or from some other table provided by your instructor or located by you. Include in your microtheme at least one quantitative graphic (table, line graph, bar graph, pie chart), which should be labeled and referenced according to standard conventions. Use as a model the short piece shown in Figure 9.16 on page 161. ∎

For additional writing, reading, and research resources, go to www.mycomplab.com

PART FOUR

Arguments in Depth

Five Types of Claims

A shortage of body organs and long waiting lists have motivated some people to make personal appeals to the public on billboards like this one. In Chapter 14, a reading asks you to think about the evaluation and ethical issues involved in advertising for organs and in the selling and trading of body organs.

10 An Introduction to the Types of Claims

In Part One, we showed how argument involves both persuasion and inquiry. In Part Two, we examined the internal structure of arguments and showed how persuasive writers link their arguments to the beliefs and values of their audiences. We also showed how writers can vary their content, structure, and style to reach audiences offering varying degrees of resistance to the writers' views. In Part Three, we explained how to analyze arguments rhetorically.

Now in Part Four, we examine arguments in depth by explaining five types of claims and by showing how each type has its own characteristic patterns of development and support. Because almost all arguments use one or more of these types of claims as basic argumentative "moves" or building blocks, knowing how to develop each claim type will advance your skills in argument. The types of claims we examine in Part Four are related to an ancient rhetorical concept called *stasis*, from a Greek term meaning "stand" as in "to take a *stand* on something." There are many competing theories of stasis, so no two rhetoricians discuss stasis in exactly the same way. But all the theories have valuable components in common.

In Part Four we present our own version of stasis theory or, to use more ordinary language, our own approach to argument based on the types of claims. Understanding types of claims will pay off for you in two ways:

- It will help you focus an argument, generate ideas for it, and structure it persuasively.
- It will increase your flexibility as an arguer by showing you how most arguments are hybrids of different claim types working together.

An Overview of the Types of Claims

To appreciate what a study of claim types can do, imagine one of those heated but frustrating arguments in which the question at issue keeps shifting. Everyone talks at cross-purposes, each speaker's point unconnected to the previous speaker's. Suppose your heated discussion is about the use of steroids. You might get such a discussion back on track if one person says: "Hold it for a moment. What are we actually arguing about here? Are we arguing about whether steroids are a health risk or whether steroids should be banned from sports? These are two different issues. We can't debate both at once." Whether she recognizes it or not, this person is applying the concept of claim types to get the argument focused.

To understand how claim types work, let's return to the concept of stasis. A stasis is an issue or question that focuses a point of disagreement. You and your audience might agree on the answer to question A and so have nothing to argue about. Likewise, you might agree on the answer to question B. But on question C, you disagree. Question C constitutes a stasis where you and your audience diverge. It is the place where disagreement begins, where as an arguer you take a stand against another view. Thus, you and your audience might agree that steroids, if used carefully under a physician's supervision, pose few long-term health risks but still disagree on whether steroids should be banned from sports. This last issue constitutes a stasis, the point where you and your audience part company.

Rhetoricians have discovered that the kinds of questions that divide people have classifiable patterns. In this text, we identify five broad types of claims—each type originating in a different kind of question. The following chart gives you a quick overview of these five types of claims, each of which is developed in more detail in subsequent chapters. It also shows you a typical structure for each type of argument. Note that the first three claim types concern questions of truth or reality whereas the last two concern questions of value. You'll appreciate the significance of this distinction as this chapter progresses.

Claims about Reality, Truth, or the Way Things Are

Claim Type and Generic Question	Examples of Issue Questions	Typical Methods for Structuring an Argument
Definition arguments: *In which category does this thing belong?* Chapter 11	▪ Is sleep deprivation torture? ▪ Is an expert video game player an athlete?	▪ Create a definition that establishes criteria for the category. ▪ Use examples to show how the contested case meets the criteria.
Causal arguments: *What are the causes or consequences of this event or phenomenon?* Chapter 12	▪ What are the causes of autism? ▪ What might be the consequences of requiring a national I.D. card?	▪ Explain the links in a causal chain going from cause to effect. [or] ▪ Speculate about causes (consequences) or propose a surprising cause (consequence).
Resemblance arguments: *To what is this thing similar?* Chapter 13	▪ Is opposition to gay marriage like opposition to interracial marriage? ▪ Is steroid use to improve strength similar to LASIK surgery to improve vision?	▪ Let the analogy or precedent itself create the desired rhetorical effect. [or] ▪ Elaborate on the relevant similarities between the given case and the analogy or precedent.

Claims about Values

Claim Type and Generic Question	Examples of Issue Questions	Typical Methods for Structuring an Argument
Evaluation arguments: *What is the worth or value of this thing?* Chapter 14	■ Is behavior modification a good therapy for anxiety? ■ Is it ethical to use steroids in sports?	■ Establish the criteria for a "good" or "ethical" member of this class or category. ■ Use examples to show how the contested case meets the criteria.
Proposal arguments: *Should we take this proposed action?* Chapter 15	■ Should the United State enact a single-payer health care system? ■ To solve the problem of prison overcrowding, should we legalize possession of drugs?	■ Make the problem vivid for the audience. ■ Explain your proposed action to solve the problem. ■ Justify your solution by showing how it is motivated by principle, by good consequences, or by resemblance to a previous action the audience approves.

■ ■ ■ **FOR CLASS DISCUSSION**   Identifying Types of Claims

Working as a whole class or in small groups, read the following questions and decide which claim type is represented by each. Sometimes the claim types overlap or blend together, so if you think the question fits two different categories, explain your reasoning.

1. Should overnight camping be permitted in this state park?
2. Is taking Adderall to increase concentration for an exam a form of cheating?
3. Will an increase in gas taxes lead to a reduction in road congestion?
4. Is depression a learned behavior?
5. Were the terrorist attacks of September 11, 2001, more like Pearl Harbor (an act of war) or more like an earthquake (a natural disaster)?
6. How effective is acupuncture in reducing morning sickness?
7. Is acupuncture quackery or real medicine?
8. Should cities use tax dollars to fund professional sports arenas?
9. Are Mattel toy factories sweatshops?
10. Why are couples who live together before marriage more likely to divorce than couples who don't live together?

■ ■ ■

Using Claim Types to Focus an Argument and Generate Ideas: An Example

Having provided an overview of the types of claims, we now show you some of the benefits of this knowledge. First of all, understanding claim types will help you focus an argument by asking you to determine what's at stake between you and your audience.

Where do you and your audience agree and disagree? What are the questions at issue? Second, it will help you generate ideas for your argument by suggesting the kinds of reasons, examples, and evidence you'll need.

To illustrate, let's take a hypothetical case—one Isaac Charles Little (affectionately known as I. C. Little), who desires to chuck his contact lenses and undergo LASIK procedure to cure his nearsightedness. LASIK, the common name for laser in-situ keratomileusis, is a surgical treatment for myopia. Sometimes known as "flap and zap" surgery, it involves using a laser to cut a thin layer of the cornea and then flattening it. It's usually not covered by insurance and is quite expensive.

I. C. Little has two different arguments he'd like to make: (1) he'd like to talk his parents into helping him pay for the procedure, and (2) he'd like to join with others who are trying to convince insurance companies that the LASIK procedure should be covered under standard medical insurance policies. In the discussions that follow, note how the five types of claims can help I. C. identify points of disagreement for each audience and simultaneously suggest lines of argument for persuading each one. Note, too, how the questions at issue vary for each audience.

Making the LASIK Argument to Parents

First, imagine what might be at stake in I. C.'s discussions with his parents. Here is how thinking about claim types will help him generate ideas:

- *Definition argument:* Because I. C.'s parents will be concerned about the safety of LASIK surgery, the first stasis for I. C.'s argument is a question about categories: is LASIK a safe procedure? I. C.'s mom has read about serious complications from LASIK and has heard that ophthalmologists prefer patients to be at least in their mid-twenties or older, so I. C. knows he will have to persuade her that LASIK is safe for twenty-year-olds.
- *Causal argument:* Both parents will question I. C.'s underlying motivation for seeking this surgery. "Why do you want this procedure?" they will ask. (I. C.'s dad, who has worn eyeglasses all his life, will not be swayed by cosmetic desires. "If you don't like contacts," he will say, "just wear glasses.") Here, I. C. needs to argue the good consequences of LASIK. Permanently correcting his nearsightedness will improve his quality of life and even his academic and professional options. I. C. decides to emphasize his desire for an active, outdoor life, and especially his passion for water sports, where his need for contacts is a serious handicap. He is even thinking of majoring in marine biology, so LASIK surgery would help him professionally. He says that wearing scuba equipment is easier without worrying about contact lenses or corrective goggles.
- *Resemblance argument:* I. C. can't think of any resemblance questions at issue.
- *Evaluation argument:* When the plusses and minuses are weighed, is LASIK a good way to treat nearsightedness? Is it also a good way for the parents to spend family money? Would the results of the surgery be beneficial enough to justify the cost and the risks? In terms of costs, I. C. might argue that even though the procedure is initially expensive (from $1,000 to $4,000), over the years he will

save money by not needing glasses or contacts. The convenience of seeing well in the water and not being bothered by glasses or contacts while hiking and camping constitutes a major benefit. (Even though he thinks he'll look cooler without glasses, he decides not to mention the cosmetic benefits because his dad thinks wearing glasses is fine.)

■ *Proposal argument:* Should I. C.'s parents pay for a LASIK procedure to treat their son's nearsightedness? (All the previous points of disagreement are sub-issues related to this overarching proposal issue.)

What this example shows is that writers often need to argue issues of reality/truth in order to make claims about values. In this particular case, I. C. would need to convince his parents that (1) the procedure is safe (definition argument), (2) the consequences of the procedure would be beneficial recreationally and professionally (causal argument), and (3) the benefits outweigh the costs (evaluation argument). Only then would I. C. be able to persuade his parents that (4) he should have LASIK surgery with their financial help (proposal claim). Almost all arguments combine subarguments in this way so that lower-order claims provide supporting materials for addressing higher-order claims.

Making the LASIK Argument to Insurance Companies

The previous illustration focused on parents as audience. If we now switch audiences, we can use our claim types to identify different questions at issue. Let's suppose I. C. wants to persuade insurance companies to cover the LASIK procedure. He imagines his primary audience as insurance company executives, along with the general public and state legislators, who may be able to influence them. Again, I. C. generates ideas by considering the claim types.

■ *Definition argument:* For this audience, the issue of safety is no longer relevant. (They share I. C.'s belief that LASIK is a safe procedure.) What's at stake is another definition issue: Should lasik be considered "cosmetic surgery" (as insurance companies contend) or "medically justifiable surgery" (as I. C. contends)? This definitional question constitutes a major stasis. I. C. wants to convince his audience that LASIK belongs in the category of "medically justifiable surgery" rather than "cosmetic surgery." He will need to define "medically justifiable surgery" in such a way that LASIK can be included.

■ *Causal argument:* What will be the consequences to insurance companies and to the general public of making insurance companies pay for LASIK? Will there be an overwhelming crush of claims for LASIK surgery? Will there be a corresponding decrease in claims for eye exams, contacts, and glasses? What will happen to the cost of insurance?

■ *Resemblance argument:* Does LASIK more resemble a facelift (not covered by insurance) or plastic surgery to repair a cleft palate (covered by insurance)?

- *Evaluation argument:* Would it be good for society as a whole if insurance companies had to pay for LASIK?
- *Proposal argument:* Should insurance companies be required to cover LASIK?

As this analysis shows, the questions at issue change when you consider a different audience. Now, the chief question at issue is definition: Is LASIK cosmetic surgery or medically justifiable surgery? I. C. does not need to argue that the surgery is safe (a major concern for his parents); instead he must establish criteria for "medically justifiable surgery" and then argue that LASIK meets these criteria. Again, note how the higher-order issues of value depend on resolving one or more lower-order issues of truth/reality.

Note also that any of the claim type examples described above could be used as the major focus of an argument. If I. C. were not concerned about a values issue (his proposal claims), he might tackle only a reality/truth issue. He could, for example, focus an entire argument on a definition question about categories: "Is LASIK safe?" (an argument requiring him to research the medical literature). Likewise, he could write a causal argument focusing on what might happen to optometrists and eyeglass manufacturers if the insurance industry decided to cover LASIK.

The key insight here is that when you develop an argument, you may have to work through issues of reality and truth before you can tackle a values issue and argue for change or action. Before you embark on writing an evaluation or proposal argument, you must first consider whether you need to resolve a lower-order claim based on reality/truth.

Hybrid Arguments: How Claim Types Work Together in Arguments

As the LASIK example shows, hybrid arguments can be built from different claim types. A writer might develop a proposal argument with a causal subargument in one section, a resemblance subargument in another section, and an evaluation subargument in still another section. Although the overarching proposal argument follows the typical structure of a proposal, each of the subsections follows a typical structure for its own claim type.

Some Examples of Hybrid Arguments

The following examples show how these combinations of claim types can play out in actual arguments.

For more examples of these kinds of hybrid arguments, see Chapter 15, pages 254–256, where we explain how lower-order claims about truth/reality can support higher-order claims about values.

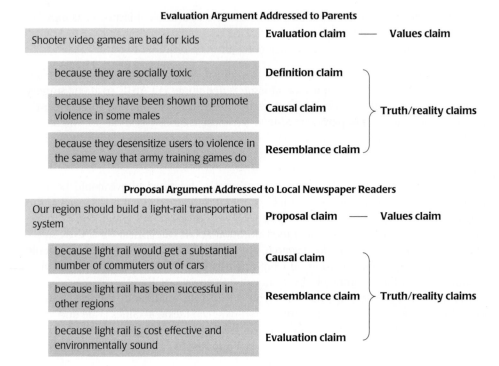

Evaluation Argument Addressed to Parents

Shooter video games are bad for kids	Evaluation claim —— Values claim
because they are socially toxic	Definition claim
because they have been shown to promote violence in some males	Causal claim
because they desensitize users to violence in the same way that army training games do	Resemblance claim

Truth/reality claims

Proposal Argument Addressed to Local Newspaper Readers

Our region should build a light-rail transportation system	Proposal claim —— Values claim
because light rail would get a substantial number of commuters out of cars	Causal claim
because light rail has been successful in other regions	Resemblance claim
because light rail is cost effective and environmentally sound	Evaluation claim

Truth/reality claims

■ ■ ■ **FOR CLASS DISCUSSION**   Exploring Different Claim Types and Audiences

Select an issue familiar to most members of the class—perhaps a current campus issue or an issue prominent in the local or national news—and generate possible issue questions and arguments using the claim types. Take as your models our discussion of I. C. Little's arguments about LASIK surgery. Consider how a writer or speaker might address two different audiences on this issue with a different purpose for each audience.   ■ ■ ■

An Extended Example of a Hybrid Argument

As the previous examples illustrate, different claim types often serve as building blocks for larger arguments. We ask you now to consider a more extended example. Read the following op-ed piece arguing the proposal claim that "New York City should ban car alarms." Note how the reasons are different claim-type subarguments that develop the overall proposal claim.

As you can see, the thesis of Friedman's op-ed piece is a proposal claim, and the article follows the typical problem-solution structure of proposal arguments. Although the whole argument follows a proposal shape, the individual pieces—the various subarguments that support the main argument—comprise different kinds of claim types with their own characteristic structures.

All That Noise for Nothing

AARON FRIEDMAN

Main proposal claim: City Council should ban alarms

Early next year, the New York City Council is supposed to hold a final hearing on legislation that would silence the most hated of urban noises: the car alarm. With similar measures having failed in the past, and with Mayor Michael R. Bloomberg withholding his support for the latest bill, let's hope the Council does right by the citizens it represents.

Reason 1: A definitional claim supported with examples. Can alarms belong in the category of things that harass

Every day, car alarms harass thousands of New Yorkers—rousing sleepers, disturbing readers, interrupting conversations and contributing to quality-of-life concerns that propel many weary residents to abandon the city for the suburbs. According to the Census Bureau, more New Yorkers are now bothered by traffic noise, including car alarms, than by any other aspect of city life, including crime or the condition of schools.

Reason 2: An evaluation claim

So there must be a compelling reason for us to endure all this aggravation, right? Amazingly, no. Many car manufacturers, criminologists and insurers agree that car alarms are ineffective. When the nonprofit Highway Loss Data Institute surveyed insurance-claims data from 73 million vehicles nationwide in 1997, they concluded that cars with alarms "show no overall reduction in theft losses" compared with cars without alarms.

Criteria and evidence supporting the evaluation claim

There are two reasons they don't prevent theft. First, the vast majority of blaring sirens are false alarms, set off by passing traffic, the jostling of urban life or nothing at all. City dwellers quickly learn to disregard these cars crying wolf; a recent national survey by the Progressive Insurance Company found that fewer than 1 percent of respondents would call the police upon hearing an alarm.

5   In 1992, a car alarm industry spokesman, Darrell Issa (if you know his name that's because he would later spearhead the recall of Gov. Gray Davis in California), told the New York City Council that an alarm is effective "only in areas where the sound causes the dispatch of the police or attracts the owner's attention." In New York, this just doesn't happen.

Car alarms also fail for a second reason: they are easy to disable. Most stolen cars are taken by professional car thieves, and they know how to deactivate an alarm in just a few seconds.

Reason 3: A causal claim developed with causal links

Perversely, alarms can encourage more crime than they prevent. The New York Police Department, in its 1994 booklet "Police Strategy No. 5," explains how alarms (which "frequently go off for no apparent reason") can shatter the sense of civility that makes a community safe. As one of the "signs that no one cares," the department wrote, car alarms "invite both further disorder and serious crime."

I've seen some of my neighbors in Washington Heights illustrate this by taking revenge on alarmed cars: puncturing tires, even throwing a toaster

Humorous resemblance claim, sums up problem

Main proposal claim restated as evaluation claim and supported by three criteria

oven through a windshield. False alarms enrage otherwise lawful citizens, and alienate the very people car owners depend on to call the police. In other words, car alarms work about as well as fuzzy dice at deterring theft while irritating entire neighborhoods.

The best solution is to ban them, as proposed by the sponsors of the City Council legislation, John Liu and Eva Moskowitz. The police could simply ticket or tow offending cars. This would be a great improvement over the current laws, which include limiting audible alarms to three minutes—something that has proved to be nearly impossible to enforce.

10   Car owners could easily comply: more than 50 car alarm installation shops throughout the city have already pledged to disable alarms at no cost, according to a survey by the Center for Automotive Security Innovation.

And there is a viable alternative. People worried about protecting their cars can buy what are called silent engine immobilizers. Many European cars and virtually every new General Motors and Ford vehicle use the technology, in which a computer chip in the ignition key communicates with the engine. Without the key, the only way to steal the car is to tow it away, something most thieves don't have the time for. In the meantime, the rest of us could finally get some sleep.

Thus writers enlist other claim-type subarguments in building main arguments. This knowledge can help you increase your flexibility and effectiveness as an arguer. It encourages you to become skilled at four different kinds of arguers' "moves": (1) providing examples and evidence to support a simple categorical claim; (2) using a criteria match strategy to support a definition or evaluation claim; (3) showing links in a causal chain to support a cause/consequence claim; or (4) using analogies and precedents to support a resemblance claim.

In the following chapters, we discuss each of the claim types in more detail, showing you how they work and how you can develop skills and strategies for supporting each type of claim.

For additional writing, reading, and research resources, go to www.mycomplab.com

Definitional Arguments

11

CASE 2 Is a Frozen Embryo a Person or Property?

An infertile couple conceived several embryos in a test tube and then froze the fertilized embryos for future use. During the couple's divorce, they disagreed about the disposition of the embryos. The woman wanted to use the frozen embryos to try to get pregnant, and the man wanted to destroy them. When the courts were asked to decide what should be done with the embryos, several questions of definition arose. Should the frozen embryos be categorized as "persons," thus becoming analogous to children in custody disputes? Or should they be divided up as "property," with the man getting half and the woman getting the other half? Or should a new legal category be created for them that regards them as more than property but less than actual persons? The judge decided that frozen embryos "are not, strictly speaking, either 'persons' or 'property,' but occupy an interim category that entitles them to special respect because of their potential for human life."*

An Overview of Arguments about Definition

Definition arguments are arguments about what category something belongs to. They are among the most common argument types you will encounter. They occur whenever you claim that a particular person, thing, act, or phenomenon belongs (or does not belong) within a certain category. Here are some examples of claims involving categories and definitions:

Claim	Specific Phenomenon	Category
Piping loud rap music into a prison cell twenty-four hours a day constitutes torture.	Constant loud rap music	Torture
Graffiti is often art, rather than vandalism.	Graffiti	Art
My swerving off the road while trying to slap a bee on my windshield does not constitute "reckless driving."	Swerving off the road while killing a bee	Not "reckless driving"

Much is at stake when we place things into categories, because the category that something belongs to can have real consequences. For example, if you favor growing biotech corn, you want to place it in the broad category "corn" and keep the term "genetically engineered" off food labels. If you oppose it, you might classify it as "Frankenfood." Thus the categories we choose are really implicit mini-arguments with subtle but powerful consequences.

Consider the competing categories proposed for whales in an international controversy occasioned by the desire of traditional whaling nations to resume commercial whaling. What category does a whale belong to? Some arguers place whales in the category "sacred animals" that should never be killed because of their intelligence, beauty, grace, and power. Others categorize whales as a "renewable food resource" like tuna, crabs, cattle, and chickens. Others worry whether the kinds of whales being hunted are an "endangered species"—a category that argues for the preservation of whale stocks but not necessarily for a ban on controlled hunting of individual whales. Each of these whaling arguments places whales in a different category that implicitly urges the reader to adopt that category's perspective on whaling.

---

*See Vincent F. Stempel, "Procreative Rights in Assisted Reproductive Technology: Why the Angst?" *Albany Law Review* 62 (1999), 1187.

The Rule of Justice: "Things in the Same Category Should Be Treated the Same Way"

As you can see, how we define a given word can have significant implications for people who must either use the word or have the word used on them. To ensure fairness, philosophers refer to the *rule of justice,* which states that "beings in the same essential category should be treated in the same way." For example, it makes a huge difference to detainees in Guantanamo Bay, Cuba, whether they are classified as "prisoners of war" or as "unlawful combatants." In the first case, they have considerable rights under the Geneva Conventions, including the right to be released and returned to their native country when the war is over. In the latter case, they seem to have few—if any—rights, and may be held indefinitely without charges. Or, to take a more familiar example, if a professor says that absence from an exam can be excused only for emergencies, is attending your best friend's wedding considered an emergency? How about missing an exam because your car wouldn't start? Although your interests might be best served by a broad definition of emergency, your professor, in the desire to be just to all students, might benefit from a narrow definition.

The rule of justice becomes even harder to apply when we consider contested cases marked by growth or slow change through time. When does an Internet poker player become a compulsive gambler? When does a fetus become a human person? Although we may be able arbitrarily to choose a particular point and declare that "human person" means a fetus at conception, or at three months, or at birth, in the everyday world the distinction between egg and person (or between Friday night poker playing and compulsive gambling) seems an evolution—not a sudden and definitive step. Nevertheless, our language requires an abrupt shift between categories. In short, applying the rule of justice often requires us to adopt a digital approach to reality (switches are either on or off, either a fetus is a human person or it is not), whereas our sense of life is more analogical (there are numerous gradations between on and off, there are countless shades of gray between black and white).

As we can see by the preceding examples, the promise of language to fix what psychologist William James called "the buzz and confusion of the world" into an orderly set of categories turns out to be elusive. In most definitional debates, an argument, not a quick trip to the dictionary, is required to settle the matter.

■ ■ ■ **FOR CLASS DISCUSSION**   **Applying the Rule of Justice**

Suppose your landlord decides to institute a "no pets" rule. The rule of justice requires that all pets have to go—not just your neighbor's barking dog, but also Mrs. Brown's cat, the kids' hamster downstairs, and your own pet tarantula. That is, all these animals have to go unless you can argue that some of them are not "pets" for purposes of a landlord's "no pets" rule.

1. Working in small groups or as a whole class, define *pets* by establishing the criteria an animal would have to meet to be included in the category "pets." Consider your landlord's "no pets" rule as the cultural context for your definition.

2. Based on your criteria, which of the following animals is definitely a pet that would have to be removed from the apartment? Based on your criteria, which animals could you exclude from the "no pets" rule? How would you make your argument to your landlord?
   - a German shepherd dog
   - a tiny, well-trained lapdog
   - a canary
   - a tarantula
   - a small housecat
   - a gerbil in a cage
   - a tank of tropical fish

Types of Definitional Arguments

Categorical claims shift from implied mini-arguments to explicit extended arguments whenever the arguer supplies reasons and evidence that a given phenomenon does—or does not—belong in a certain category. Such arguments can be divided into two kinds: (1) *simple categorical arguments* in which the writer and an audience agree on the meaning of the category, and (2) *definitional arguments* in which there is a dispute about the boundaries of the category and hence of its definition.

Simple Categorical Arguments A categorical argument can be said to be "simple" if there is no disagreement about the definition of the category. For example, suppose you oppose electing Joe as committee chair "because he is too bossy." Your supporting reason ("Joe is too bossy") is a simple categorical claim. You assume that everyone agrees what *bossy* means; the point of contention is whether Joe is or is not bossy. To support your claim, you would supply examples of Joe's bossiness. To refute it, someone else might supply counterexamples of Joe's cooperative and kind nature.

As shown in the following chart, the basic procedure for supporting (or rebutting) a simple categorical claim is to supply examples and other data that show how the contested phenomenon fits or doesn't fit into the category:

Strategies for Supporting or Rebutting Simple Categorical Claims

Categorical claim	Strategies for supporting claim	Strategies for rebutting claim
Joe is too bossy.	Show examples of his bossy behavior (for example, his poor listening skills, his shouting at people, his making decisions without asking the committee).	Show counterexamples revealing his ability to listen and create community; re-interpret bossiness as leadership behavior, putting Joe in a better light.

Categorical claim	Strategies for supporting claim	Strategies for rebutting claim
Low-carb diets are dangerous.	Cite studies showing the dangers; explain how low-carb diets produce dangerous substances in the body; explain their harmful effects.	Show design problems in the scientific studies; cite studies with different findings; cite counterexamples of people who lost weight on low-carb diets with no bad health effects.
Little Green Footballs is a conservative blog.	Give examples of the conservative views it promotes; show the conservative leanings of pundits often cited on the blog.	Give examples from the blog that don't fit neatly into a conservative perspective.

■ ■ ■ **FOR CLASS DISCUSSION** Supporting and Rebutting Categorical Claims

Working individually or in small groups, consider how you would support the following categorical claims. What examples or other data would convince readers that the specified case fits within the named category? Then discuss ways you might rebut each claim.

1. Sport utility vehicles are environmentally unfriendly.
2. Nelly is a gangsta rapper.
3. Americans today are obsessed with their appearance.
4. College football coaches are overpaid.
5. Competitive cheerleading is physically risky.

■ ■ ■

Definitional Arguments Simple categorical arguments morph into definitional arguments whenever stakeholders disagree about the boundaries of a category. Suppose in the previous exercise that you had said, "Well, that depends on how you define 'gangsta rapper' or 'overpaid.'" The need to define these terms adds a new layer of complexity to arguments about categories. To understand definitional arguments, one must distinguish between cases where definitions are *needed* and cases where definitions are *disputed*. Many arguments require a definition of key terms. If you are arguing, for example, that therapeutic cloning might lead to cures for various diseases, you would probably need to define *therapeutic cloning* and distinguish it from *reproductive cloning*. Writers regularly define key words for their readers by providing synonyms, by citing a dictionary definition, by stipulating a definition, or by some other means.

In the rest of this chapter, we focus on arguments in which the meaning of a key term is disputed. Consider, for example, the environmental controversy over the definition of *wetland*. Section 404 of the federal Clean Water Act provides for federal protection of wetlands but leaves the task of defining *wetland* to administrative agencies and the courts. Currently about 5 percent of the land surface of the contiguous forty-eight states is potentially affected by the wetlands provision, and 75 percent of this land is privately owned. Efforts to define *wetland* have created a battleground between pro-environment and pro-development (or pro–private property rights) groups. Farmers, homeowners, and developers often want a narrow definition so that

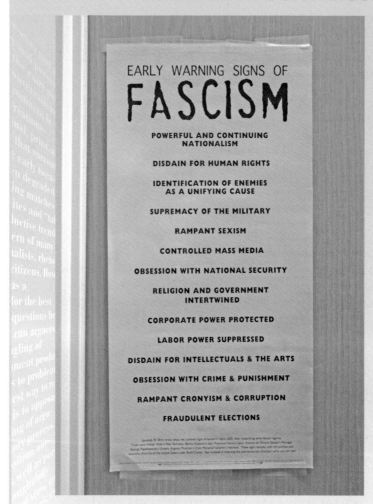

EARLY WARNING SIGNS OF

FASCISM

POWERFUL AND CONTINUING NATIONALISM

DISDAIN FOR HUMAN RIGHTS

IDENTIFICATION OF ENEMIES AS A UNIFYING CAUSE

SUPREMACY OF THE MILITARY

RAMPANT SEXISM

CONTROLLED MASS MEDIA

OBSESSION WITH NATIONAL SECURITY

RELIGION AND GOVERNMENT INTERTWINED

CORPORATE POWER PROTECTED

LABOR POWER SUPPRESSED

DISDAIN FOR INTELLECTUALS & THE ARTS

OBSESSION WITH CRIME & PUNISHMENT

RAMPANT CRONYISM & CORRUPTION

FRAUDULENT ELECTIONS

A Definitional Claim

A professor taped this poster to her office door in the mid-2000s when the country was divided over President Bush's policies, especially the war on terrorism. By stating criteria for "fascism," this poster makes an implied definitional argument that the United States is exhibiting "early warning signs" of fascism. To what extent do you think that the United States meets or does not meet the criteria for "early warning signs" of fascism?

more property is available for commercial or private use. Environmentalists favor a broad definition in order to protect different habitat types and maintain the environmental safeguards that wetlands provide (control of water pollution, spawning grounds for aquatic species, floodwater containment, and so forth).

The problem is that defining *wetland* is tricky. For example, one federal regulation defines a wetland as any area that has a saturated ground surface for twenty-one consecutive days during the year. But how would you apply this law to a pine flatwood ecosystem that was wet for ten days this year but thirty days last year? And how should the courts react to lawsuits claiming that the regulation itself is either too broad or too narrow? It is easy to see why the wetlands controversy provides hefty incomes for lawyers and congressional lobbyists.

The Criteria-Match Structure of Definitional Arguments

As the wetlands example suggests, definitional arguments usually have a two-part structure—(1) a definition part that tries to establish the boundaries of the category (What do we mean by *wetland?*) and (2) a match part that argues whether a given case meets that definition (Does this thirty-acre parcel of land near Swan Lake meet the criteria for a wetland?). To describe this structure, we use the term *criteria-match*. Here is an example:

▪ *Definitional issue:* In a divorce proceeding, is a frozen embryo a "person" or "property"?

Criteria part: What criteria must be met for something to be a "person"?

Match part: Does a frozen embryo meet these criteria?

Developing the Criteria-Match Structure for a Definitional Argument

To show how a definitional issue can be developed into a claim with supporting reasons, let's look more closely at this example:

▪ *Definitional issue:* For purposes of my feeling good about buying my next pair of running shoes, is the Hercules Shoe Company a socially responsible company?

Criteria part: What criteria must be met for a company to be deemed "socially responsible"?

Match part: Does the Hercules Shoe Company meet these criteria?

Let's suppose you work for a consumer information group that wishes to encourage patronage of socially responsible companies while boycotting irresponsible ones. Your group's first task is to define *socially responsible company*. After much discussion and research, your group establishes three criteria a company must meet to be considered socially responsible:

> *Your definition:* A company is socially responsible if it (1) avoids polluting the environment, (2) sells goods or services that contribute to the well-being of the community, and (3) treats its workers justly.

The criteria section of your argument would explain and illustrate these criteria. The match part of the argument would then try to persuade readers that a specific company does or does not meet the criteria. A typical thesis statement might be as follows:

> *Your thesis statement:* Although the Hercules Shoe Company is nonpolluting and provides a socially useful product, it is not a socially responsible company because it treats workers unjustly.

Toulmin Framework for a Definitional Argument

Here is how the core of the Hercules definitional argument could be displayed in Toulmin terms. Note how the criteria established in your definition serve as warrants for your argument.

As this Toulmin schema illustrates, the writer's argument needs to contain a criteria section (warrant and backing) showing that just treatment of workers is a criterion for social responsibility and a match section (stated reason and grounds) showing that the Hercules Shoe Company does not treat its workers justly. The conditions of rebuttal help the writer imagine alternative views and see places where opposing views need to be acknowledged and rebutted.

Toulmin Analysis of the Hercules Shoe Company Argument

ENTHYMEME

CLAIM The Hercules Shoe Company is not a socially responsible company

REASON because it treats workers unjustly.

GROUNDS

Evidence of unjust treatment:

- Evidence that the company manufactures its shoes in East Asian sweatshops

- Evidence of the inhumane conditions in these shops

- Evidence of hardships imposed on displaced American workers

WARRANT

Socially responsible companies treat workers justly.

BACKING

- Arguments showing that just treatment of workers is right in principle and also benefits society

- Arguments that capitalism helps society as a whole only if workers achieve a reasonable standard of living, have time for leisure, and are not exploited

CONDITIONS OF REBUTTAL

Attacking reasons and grounds

- Possible counterevidence that the shops maintain humane working conditions

- Possible questioning of statistical data about hardships on displaced workers

CONDITIONS OF REBUTTAL

Attacking warrant and backing

Justice needs to be considered from an emerging nation's standpoint:

- The wages paid workers are low by American standards but are above average by East Asian standards.

- Displacement of American workers is part of the necessary adjustment of adapting to a global economy and does not mean that a company is unjust.

■ ■ ■   **FOR CLASS DISCUSSION**   Identifying Criteria and Match Issues

Consider the following definitional claims. Working as individuals or in small groups, identify the criteria issue and the match issue for each of the following claims.

> *Example:* A Honda assembled in Ohio is (is not) an American-made car.
>
> *Criteria Part:* What criteria have to be met before a car can be called "American made"?
>
> *Match Part:* Does a Honda assembled in Ohio meet these criteria?

1. American Sign Language is (is not) a "foreign language" for purposes of a college graduation requirement.
2. Burning an American flag is (is not) constitutionally protected free speech.
3. Bungee jumping from a crane is (is not) a "carnival amusement ride" subject to state safety inspections
4. A Mazda Miata is (is not) a true sports car.
5. A race car driver is (is not) a true athlete.

■ ■ ■

Kinds of Definitions

In this section, we discuss two methods of definition: Aristotelian and operational.

Aristotelian Definitions

Aristotelian definitions, regularly used in dictionaries, define a term by placing it within the next larger class or category and then showing the specific attributes that distinguish the term from other terms within the same category. For example, according to a legal dictionary, *robbery* is "the felonious taking of property" (next larger category) that differs from other acts of theft because it seizes property "through violence or intimidation." Legal dictionaries often provide specific examples to show the boundaries of the term. Here is one example:

> There is no robbery unless force or fear is used to overcome resistance. Thus, surreptitiously picking a man's pocket or snatching something from him without resistance on his part is *larceny,* but not robbery.

Many states specify degrees of robbery with increasingly heavy penalties. For example, *armed robbery* involves the use of weapons to threaten the victim. In all cases, *robbery* is distinguished from the lesser crime of *burglary* in which no force or intimidation is involved.

As you can see, an Aristotelian definition of a term identifies specific attributes or criteria that enable you to distinguish it from other members of the next larger class. We created an Aristotelian definition in our example about socially responsible companies. A socially responsible company, we said, is any company (next larger class) that meets three criteria: (1) It doesn't pollute the environment; (2) it creates goods or services that promote the well-being of the community; and (3) it treats its workers justly.

Operational Definitions

In some rhetorical situations, particularly those arising in the physical and social sciences, writers need precise definitions that can be measured empirically and are not subject to problems of context and disputed criteria. A social scientist studying the effects of television on aggression in children needs a precise, measurable definition of *aggression.* Typically, she might measure aggression by counting the number of blows a child gives to an inflatable bobo doll over a fifteen-minute period when other play options are available. In our wetlands example, a federal authority created an operational definition of *wetland:* A wetland is a parcel of land that has a saturated ground surface for twenty-one consecutive days during the year. Such definitions are useful because they are precisely measurable, but they are also limited because they omit criteria that may be unmeasurable but important. Thus, we might ask whether it is adequate to define a *superior student* as someone with a 3.5 GPA or higher or a *successful sex-education program* as one that results in a 25 percent reduction in teenage pregnancies. What important aspects of a superior student or a successful sex-education program are not considered in these operational definitions?

Conducting the Criteria Part of a Definitional Argument

In constructing criteria to define your contested term, you can either research how others have defined your term or you can make your own definitions. If you take the first approach, you turn to standard or specialized dictionaries, judicial opinions, or expert testimony to establish a definition based on the authority of others. A lawyer defining a wetland based on twenty-one consecutive days of saturated ground surface would be taking the first approach, using federal regulation as her source. The other approach is to use your own critical thinking to make your own definition, thereby defining the contested term yourself. Our definition of a socially responsible company, specifying three criteria, is an example of an individual's own definition created through critical thinking. This section explains these approaches in more detail.

Approach 1: Research How Others Have Defined the Term

When you take this approach, you search for authoritative definitions acceptable to your audience yet favorable to your case. Student writer Kathy Sullivan uses this approach in her argument that photographs displayed at the Oncore Bar are not obscene (see pp. 189–191). To define *obscenity,* she turns to *Black's Law Dictionary* and Pember's *Mass Media Laws.* (Specialized dictionaries are a standard part of the reference section of any library. See your reference librarian for assistance.) Other sources of specialized definitions are state and federal appellate court decisions, legislative and administrative statutes, and scholarly articles examining a given definitional conflict. Lawyers use this research strategy exhaustively in preparing court briefs. They begin by looking at the actual text of laws as passed by legislatures or written by administrative authorities. Then they look at all the court cases in which the laws have been tested and examine the ways courts have refined legal definitions and applied them to specific cases. Using these refined definitions, lawyers then apply them to their own case at hand.

If your research uncovers definitions that seem ambiguous or otherwise unfavorable to your case, you can sometimes appeal to the "original intentions" of those who defined the term. For example, if a scientist is dissatisfied with definitions of *wetland* based on consecutive days of saturated ground surface, she might proceed as follows: "The original intention of the Congress in passing the Clean Water Act was to preserve the environment." What Congress intended, she could then claim, was to prevent development of those wetland areas that provide crucial habitat for wildlife or that inhibit water pollution. She could then propose an alternative definition based on criteria other than consecutive days of ground saturation.

Approach 2: Create Your Own Extended Definition

Often, however, you need to create your own definition of the contested term.* An effective strategy is to establish initial criteria for your contested term by thinking of hypothetical cases that obviously fit the category you are trying to define and then by altering one or more variables until the hypothetical case obviously doesn't fit the category. You can then test and refine your criteria by applying them to borderline cases. For example, suppose you work at a homeless agency where you overhear street people discuss an incident that strikes you potentially as "police brutality." You wonder whether you should write to your local paper to bring attention to the incident.

A Possible Case of Police Brutality

Two police officers confront an inebriated homeless man who is shouting obscenities on a street corner. The officers tell the man to quiet down and move on, but he keeps shouting obscenities. When the officers attempt to put the man into the police car, he resists and takes a wild swing at one of the officers. As eyewitnesses later testified, this officer shouted obscenities back at the drunk man, pinned his arms behind his back in order to handcuff him, and lifted him forcefully by the arms. The man screamed in pain and was later discovered to have a dislocated shoulder. Is this officer guilty of police brutality?

To your way of thinking, this officer seems guilty: An inebriated man is too uncoordinated to be a threat in a fight, and two police officers ought to be able to arrest him without dislocating his shoulder. But a friend argues that because the man took a

---

*The defining strategies and collaborative exercises in this section are based on the work of George Hillocks and his research associates at the University of Chicago. See George Hillocks Jr., Elizabeth A. Kahn, and Larry R. Johannessen, "Teaching Defining Strategies as a Mode of Inquiry: Some Effects on Student Writing," *Research in the Teaching of English* 17 (Oct. 1983): 275–84. See also Larry R. Johannessen, Elizabeth A. Kahn, and Carolyn Calhoun Walter, *Designing and Sequencing Prewriting Activities* (Urbana: NCTE, 1982).

swing at the officer, the police were justified in using force. The dislocated shoulder was simply an accidental result of using justified force.

To make your case, you need to develop a definition of "police brutality." You can begin by creating a hypothetical case that is obviously an instance of "police brutality":

A Clear Case of Police Brutality

A police officer confronts a drunk man shouting obscenities and begins hitting him in the face with his police baton. *[This is an obvious incidence of police brutality because the officer intentionally tries to hurt the drunk man without justification; hitting him with the baton is not necessary for making an arrest or getting the man into a police car.]*

You could then vary the hypothetical case until it is clearly *not* an instance of police brutality.

Cases That Are Clearly Not Police Brutality

Case 1: The police officer handcuffs the drunk man, who, in being helped into the police car, accidentally slips on the curb and dislocates his arm while falling. *[Here the injury occurs accidentally; the police officer does not act intentionally and is not negligent.]*

Case 2: The police officer confronts an armed robber fleeing from a scene and tackles him from behind, wrestling the gun away from him. In this struggle, the officer pins the robber's arm behind his back with such force that the robber's shoulder is dislocated. *[Here aggressive use of force is justified because the robber was armed, dangerous, and resisting arrest.]*

Using these hypothetical cases, you decide that the defining criteria for police brutality are (1) *intention* and (2) use of *excessive force*—that is, force beyond what was required by the immediate situation. After more contemplation, you are convinced that the officer was guilty of police brutality and have a clearer idea of how to make your argument. Here is how you might write the "match" part of your argument.

Match Argument Using Your Definition

If we define police brutality as the *intentional* use of *excessive* force, then the police officer is guilty. His action was intentional because he was purposefully responding to the homeless man's drunken swing and was angry enough to be shouting obscenities back at the drunk (according to the eyewitnesses). Second, he used excessive force in applying the handcuffs. A drunk man taking a wild swing hardly poses a serious danger to two police officers. Putting handcuffs on the drunk may have been justified, but lifting the man's arm violently enough to dislocate a shoulder indicates excessive force. The officer lifted the man's arms violently not because he needed to but because he was angry, and acting out of anger is no justification for that violence. In fact, we can charge police officers with "police brutality" precisely to protect us from being victims of police anger. It is the job of the court system to punish us, not the police's job. Because this officer acted intentionally and applied excessive force out of anger, he should be charged with police brutality.

The strategy we have demonstrated—developing criteria by imagining hypothetical cases that clearly do and do not belong to the contested category—gives you a systematic procedure for developing a definition for your argument.

■ ■ ■ **FOR CLASS DISCUSSION** Developing a Definition

1. Suppose you wanted to define the concept "courage." Working in groups, try to decide whether each of the following cases is an example of courage:

   a. A neighbor rushes into a burning house to rescue a child from certain death and emerges, coughing and choking, with the child in his arms. Is the neighbor courageous?

   b. A firefighter rushes into a burning house to rescue a child from certain death and emerges with the child in her arms. The firefighter is wearing protective clothing and a gas mask. When a newspaper reporter calls her courageous, she says, "Hey, this is my job." Is the firefighter courageous?

   c. A teenager rushes into a burning house to recover a memento given to him by his girlfriend, the first love of his life. Is the teenager courageous?

   d. A parent rushes into a burning house to save a trapped child. The fire marshal tells the parent to wait because there is no chance the child can be reached from the first floor. The fire marshal wants to try cutting a hole in the roof to reach the child. The parent rushes into the house anyway and is burned to death. Was the parent courageous?

2. As you make your decisions on each of these cases, create and refine the criteria you use.

3. Make up your own series of controversial cases, like those above for "courage," for one or more of the following concepts:

   a. cruelty to animals

   b. child abuse

   c. true athlete

   d. sexual harassment

   e. free speech protected by the First Amendment

Based on your controversial cases, construct a definition of your chosen term. Follow the strategy demonstrated in the "police brutality" example (p. 184) of using a clear case that meets the criteria and then negative cases that do not meet the criteria. ■ ■ ■

Conducting the Match Part of a Definitional Argument

In conducting a match argument, you need to show that your contested case does or does not meet the criteria you established in your definition, supplying evidence and examples showing why the case meets or does not meet the criteria. In essence, you support the match part of your argument in much the same way you would support a simple categorical claim.

For example, if you were developing the argument that the Hercules Shoe Company is not socially responsible because it treats its workers unjustly, your match section would provide evidence of this injustice. You might supply data about the percentage of shoes produced in East Asia, about the low wages paid these workers, and about the working conditions in these factories. You might also describe the suffering of displaced American workers when Hercules closed its American factories and moved operations to Asia, where the labor was non-union and cheap. The match section should also summarize and respond to opposing views.

WRITING ASSIGNMENT A Definitional Argument

Write an essay in which you argue that a borderline or contested case fits (or does not fit) within a given category. In the opening of your essay, introduce the borderline case you will examine and pose your definitional question. In the first part of your argument, define the boundaries of your category (criteria) by reporting a definition used by others or by developing your own extended definition. In the second part of your argument (the match), show how your borderline case meets (or doesn't meet) your definitional criteria.

Exploring Ideas

Ideally, in writing this argument you will join an ongoing conversation about a definitional issue that interests you. What cultural and social issues that concern you involve disputed definitions? In the public arena, you are likely to find numerous examples simply by looking through news stories—the strategy used by student writer Kathy Sullivan, who became interested in the controversy over allegedly obscene photographs in a gay bar (see pp. 189–191). Other students have addressed definitional issues such as these: Is using TiVo to avoid TV commercials a form of theft? Is spanking a form of child abuse? Are cheerleaders athletes? Is Wal-Mart a socially responsible company? Can a man be a feminist?

If you have trouble discovering a local or national issue that interests you, you can create fascinating definitional controversies among your classmates by asking whether certain borderline cases are "true" or "real" examples of some category: Are highly skilled video game players (race car drivers, synchronized swimmers, marbles players) true athletes? Is a chiropractor (acupuncturist, naturopathic physician) a "real doctor"? Listen to the various voices in the controversy, and then write your own argument.

You can also stimulate definitional controversies by brainstorming borderline cases for such terms as *courage* (Is mountain climbing an act of courage?) *cruelty to animals* (Are rodeos [zoos, catch-and-release trout fishing, use of animals for medical research] cruelty to animals?).

As you explore your definitional issue, try to determine how others have defined your category. If no stable definition emerges from your search, create your own definition by deciding what criteria must be met for a contested case to fit within your category. Try using the strategy for creating criteria that we discussed on pages 183–184 with reference to police brutality. Once you have determined your criteria, freewrite for five or ten minutes, exploring whether your contested case meets each of the criteria.

Identifying Your Audience and Determining What's at Stake

Before drafting your argument, identify your targeted audience and determine what's at stake. Consider your responses to the following questions:

- What audience are you targeting? What background do they need to understand your issue? How much do they already care about it?
- Before they read your argument, what stance on your issue do you imagine them holding? What change do you want to bring about in their view?
- What will they find new or surprising about your argument?
- What objections might they raise? What counterarguments or alternative points of view will you need to address?
- Why does your argument matter? Who might be threatened or made uncomfortable by your views? What is at stake?

Organizing a Definitional Argument

As you compose a first draft of your essay, you may find it helpful to know typical structures for definitional arguments. There are two basic approaches, as shown in Organization Plan 1 and Organization Plan 2. You can can either discuss the criteria and the match separately or interweave the discussion.

Questioning and Critiquing a Definitional Argument

A powerful way to stimulate global revision of a draft is to role-play a skeptical audience. The following questions will help you strengthen your own argument or rebut the definitional arguments of others. In critiquing a definitional argument, you need to appreciate its criteria-match structure because you can question your criteria argument, your match argument, or both.

Questioning Your Criteria

- Could a skeptic claim that your criteria are not the right ones? Could he or she offer different criteria or point out missing criteria?
- Could a skeptic point out possible bad consequences of accepting your criteria?
- Could a skeptic cite unusual circumstances that weaken your criteria?
- Could a skeptic point out bias or slant in your definition?

Questioning Your Match

- Could a skeptic argue that your examples or data don't meet the STAR criteria (see Chapter 5, pp. 69–70) for evidence?
- Could a skeptic point out counterexamples or alternative data that cast doubt on your argument?
- Could a skeptic reframe the way you have viewed your borderline case? ▪

Organization Plan 1: Definitional Argument with Criteria and Match in Separate Sections

Introduce the issue and state your claim.

- Engage reader's interest in your definitional issue and show why it is controversial or problematic.
- Show what's at stake.
- Provide background information needed by your audience.
- State your claim.

Present your criteria.

- State and develop criterion 1.
- State and develop criterion 2.
- Continue with the rest of your criteria.
- Anticipate and respond to possible objections to the criteria.

Present your match argument.

- Consider restating your claim for clarity.
- Argue that your case meets (does not meet) criterion 1.
- Argue that your case meets (does not meet) criterion 2.
- Continue with the rest of your match argument.
- Anticipate and respond to possible objections to the match argument.

Conclude.

- Perhaps sum up your argument.
- Help reader return to the "big picture of what's at stake.
- End with something memorable.

Organization Plan 2: Definitional Argument with Criteria and Match Interwoven

Introduce the issue and state your claim.	• Engage reader's interest in your definitional issue and show why it is problematic or controversial. • Show what's at stake. • Provide background information needed by your audience. • State your claim.

↓

Present series of criterion-match arguments.	• State and develop criterion 1 and argue that your case meets (does not meet) the criterion. • State and develop criterion 2 and argue that your case meets (does not meet) the criterion. • Continue with the rest of your criterion-match arguments.

↓

Respond to possible objections to your argument.	• Anticipate and summarize possible objections. • Respond to the objections through rebuttal or concession.

↓

Conclude.	• Perhaps sum up your argument. • Help reader return to the "big picture" of what's at stake. • End with something memorable.

Our reading, by student Kathy Sullivan, was written for the definition   **READING**
assignment on page 186. The definitional issue that she addresses—
"Are the Menasee photographs obscene?"—was a local controversy in the state of
Washington when the state liquor control board threatened to revoke the liquor
license of a Seattle gay bar, the Oncore, unless it removed a series of photographs that
the board deemed obscene.

Oncore, Obscenity, and the Liquor Control Board

KATHY SULLIVAN (STUDENT)

In early May, Geoff Menasee, a Seattle artist, exhibited a series of photographs with the
theme of "safe sex" on the walls of an inner city, predominantly homosexual restaurant
and lounge called the Oncore. Before hanging the photographs, Menasee had to consult
with the Washington State Liquor Control Board because, under the current state law, art
work containing material that may be considered indecent has to be approved by the board
before it can be exhibited. Of the almost thirty photographs, six were rejected by the board
because they partially exposed "private parts" of the male anatomy. Menasee went ahead
and displayed the entire series of photographs, placing Band-Aids over the "indecent"
areas, but the customers continually removed the Band-Aids.

The liquor control board's ruling on this issue has caused controversy in the Seattle
community. The *Seattle Times* has provided news coverage, and a "Town Meeting" seg-
ment was filmed at the restaurant. The central question is this: Should an establishment
that caters to a predominantly homosexual clientele be enjoined from displaying pictures
promoting "safe sex" on the grounds that the photographs are obscene?

Before I can answer this question, I must first determine whether the art work should
truly be classified as obscene. To make that determination, I will use the definition of
obscenity in *Black's Law Dictionary:*

> Material is "obscene" if to the average person, applying contemporary community standards,
> the dominant theme of material taken as a whole appeals to prurient interest, if it is utterly with-
> out redeeming social importance, if it goes substantially beyond customary limits of candor in
> description or representation, if it is characterized by patent offensiveness, and if it is hard core
> pornography.

An additional criterion is provided by Pember's *Mass Media Laws:* "A work is obscene if it
has a tendency to deprave and corrupt those whose minds are open to such immoral
influences (children for example) and into whose hands it might happen to fall" (394). The
art work in question should not be prohibited from display at predominantly homosexual
establishments like the Oncore because it does not meet the above criteria for obscenity.

First of all, to the average person applying contemporary community standards, the predominant theme of Menasee's photographs is not an appeal to prurient interests. The first

element in this criterion is "average person." According to Rocky Breckner, manager of the Oncore, 90 percent of the clientele at the Oncore is made up of young white homosexual males. This group therefore constitutes the "average person" viewing the exhibit. "Contemporary community standards" would ordinarily be the standards of the Seattle community. However, this art work is aimed at a particular group of people—the homosexual community. Therefore, the "community standards" involved here are those of the gay community rather than the city at large. Since the Oncore is not an art museum or gallery, which attracts a broad spectrum of people, it is appropriate to restrict the scope of "community standards" to that group who voluntarily patronize the Oncore.

5   Second, the predominant theme of the photographs is not "prurient interest" nor do the photographs go "substantially beyond customary limits of candor." There are no explicit sexual acts found in the photographs; instead, their theme is the prevention of AIDS through the practice of safe sex. Homosexual displays of affection could be viewed as "prurient interest" by the larger community, but same-sex relationships are the norm for the group at whom the exhibit is aimed. If the exhibit were displayed at McDonald's or even the Red Robin it might go "substantially beyond customary limits of candor," but it is unlikely that the clientele of the Oncore would find the art work offensive. The manager stated that he received very few complaints about the exhibit and its contents.

Nor is the material pornographic. The liquor control board prohibited the six photographs based on their visible display of body parts such as pubic hair and naked buttocks, not on the basis of sexual acts or homosexual orientation. The board admitted that the photographs depicted no explicit sexual acts. Hence, it can be concluded that they did not consider the suggestion of same-sex affection to be hard-core pornography. Their sole objection was that body parts were visible. But visible genitalia in art work are not necessarily pornographic. Since other art work, such as Michelangelo's sculptures, explicitly depict both male and female genitalia, it is arguable that pubic hair and buttocks are not patently offensive.

It must be conceded that the art work has the potential of being viewed by children, which would violate Pember's criterion. But once again the incidence of minors frequenting this establishment is very small.

But the most important reason for saying these photographs are not obscene is that they serve an important social purpose. One of Black's criteria is that obscene material is "utterly without redeeming social importance." But these photographs have the explicit purpose of promoting safe sex as a defense against AIDS. Recent statistics reported in the *Seattle Times* show that AIDS is now the leading cause of death of men under forty in the Seattle area. Any methods that can promote the message of safe sex in today's society have strong redeeming social significance.

Those who believe that all art containing "indecent" material should be banned or covered from public view would most likely believe that Menasee's work is obscene. They would disagree that the environment and the clientele should be the major determining factor when using criteria to evaluate art. However, in the case of this exhibit I feel that the audience and the environment of the display are factors of overriding importance. Therefore, the exhibit should have been allowed to be displayed because it is not obscene.

12 Causal Arguments

CASE 1   What Causes Global Warming?

One of the early clues linking global warming to atmospheric carbon dioxide (CO_2) came from side-by-side comparisons of graphs plotting atmospheric carbon dioxide and global temperatures over time. These graphs show that increases in global temperature parallel increases in the percentage of carbon dioxide in the atmosphere. These graphs, however, show only a correlation, or link, between increased carbon dioxide and higher average temperature. It's possible that the increase in carbon dioxide has caused global temperatures to rise. But it's also possible that the causal direction is the other way around—an increase in global temperature has caused the earth to release more carbon dioxide. Furthermore, it's possible that some third phenomenon causes an increase in both atmospheric carbon dioxide and global temperature. To show that atmospheric carbon dioxide contributes to global warming, scientists used a model showing how increased carbon dioxide causes an increase in global temperature. Their model compares the earth to a greenhouse with carbon dioxide acting as glass windows. Carbon dioxide, like glass in a greenhouse, lets some of the earth's heat radiate into space but also reflects some of it back to the earth. The higher the concentration of carbon dioxide, the more heat is reflected back to the earth.

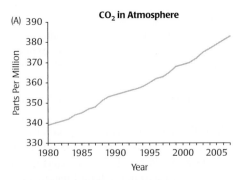

Source: Data from Dr. Pieter Tans, NOAA/ESRL

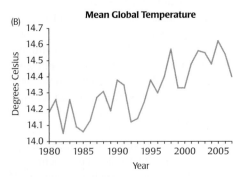

Source: Data from NASA Goddard Institute for Space Studies Surface Temperature Analysis

> **CASE 2   What Has Caused the Crime Rate to Decline Since the Early 1990s?**
>
> Beginning in the 1990s, the crime rate in the United States dropped precipitously. For example, the number of murders in New York City decreased from 2,245 in 1990 to 494 in 2007. Similar reductions for all kinds of crime were reported across the nation. What caused this sudden and unexpected decline? Many causal theories were debated in social science journals and the popular media. Among the proposed causes were innovative policing strategies, increased incarceration of criminals, an aging population, tougher gun control laws, a strong economy, and more police officers. However, economist Steven Levitt proposed that the primary cause was *Roe v. Wade,* the 1973 Supreme Court decision that legalized abortion.* According to Levitt's controversial theory, the crime rate began dropping because the greatest source of criminals—unwanted children entering their teens and twenties—were largely absent from the cohort of young people coming of age in the 1990s and 2000s; they had been aborted rather than brought up in the crime-producing conditions of unstable families, poverty, and neglect.

An Overview of Causal Arguments

We encounter causal issues all the time. What caused the sudden decline in the U.S. crime rate beginning in the 1990s? What are the causes of global warming? Why did rap music become popular? Why are white teenage girls seven times more likely to smoke than African-American teenage girls? Why do couples who live together before marriage have a higher divorce rate than those who don't? In addition to asking causal questions like these, we pose consequence questions as well: What might be the consequences of closing our borders to immigrants or of overturning *Roe v. Wade*? What have been the consequences—expected or unexpected—of the invasion of Iraq or the popularity of YouTube? What might be the consequences—expected or unexpected—of aggressively combating global warming as opposed to adapting to it? Often, arguments about causes and consequences have important stakes because they shape our view of reality and influence government policies and individual decisions.

Typically, causal arguments try to show how one event brings about another. When causal investigation focuses on material objects—for example, one billiard ball striking another—the notion of causality appears fairly straightforward. But when humans become the focus of a causal argument, the nature of causality becomes more vexing. If we say that something happened that "caused" a person to act in a certain way, what do we mean? Do we mean that she was "forced" to act in a certain way, thereby negating her free will (as in an undiagnosed brain tumor caused her to act erratically), or do we mean more simply that she was "motivated" to act in a certain way (as in her anger at her parents caused her to act erratically)? When we argue about causality in human beings, we must guard against confusing these two senses of

---

*Steven D. Levitt and Stephen J. Dubner, "Where Have All the Criminals Gone?," *Freakonomics: A Rogue Economist Explores the Hidden Side of Everything* (New York: Harper Collins, 2005), 117–144.

"cause" or assuming that human behavior can be predicted or controlled in the same way that nonhuman behavior can. A rock dropped from a roof will always fall at thirty-two feet per second squared, and a rat zapped for turning left in a maze will always quit turning left. But if we raise interest rates, will consumers save more money? If so, how much? This is the sort of question we debate endlessly.

Kinds of Causal Arguments

Arguments about causality can take a variety of forms. Here are three typical kinds.

- ■ *Speculations about possible causes.* Sometimes arguers speculate about possible causes of a phenomenon. For example, in 1999 at Columbine High School in Littleton, Colorado, two male students opened fire on their classmates, killing thirteen people, wounding twenty-three others, and then shooting themselves. Afterward, social scientists and media commentators spent months analyzing the massacre, trying to determine what caused it. Figure 12.1 illustrates some of the proposed theories. At stake was not only our desire to understand the sociocultural sources of school violence but also our desire to institute policies to prevent future school shootings. If a primary cause is the availability of guns, then we might push for more stringent gun control laws. But if the primary cause is the disintegration of the traditional family, inadequate funding for school counselors, or the dangerous side effects of Prozac, then we might seek different solutions.
- ■ *Arguments for an unexpected or surprising cause.* Besides sorting out possible causes of a phenomenon, sometimes arguers try to persuade readers to see the plausibility of an unexpected or surprising cause. This was the strategy used by

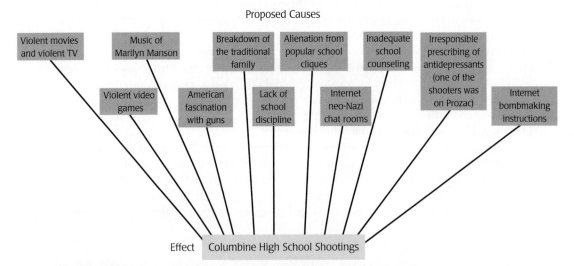

FIGURE 12.1 Speculation about possible causes: Columbine High School Massacre

Many youngsters are left alone for long periods of time (because both parents are working).

They play violent video games obsessively.

Their feelings of resentment and powerlessness "pour into the killing games."

The video games break down a natural aversion to killing, analogous to psychological techniques employed by the military.

Realistic touches in modern video games blur the "boundary between fantasy and reality."

Youngsters begin identifying not with conventional heroes but with sociopaths who get their kicks from blowing away ordinary people ("pedestrians, marching bands, an elderly woman with a walker").

Having enjoyed random violence in the video games, vulnerable youngsters act out the same adrenaline rush in real life.

FIGURE 12.2   Argument for a surprising cause: Role of violent video games in the Columbine massacre

syndicated columnist John Leo, who wanted readers to consider violent video games as a contributing cause to the Columbine massacre.* After suggesting that the Littleton killings were partly choreographed on video game models, Leo suggested the causal chain shown in Figure 12.2.

- ▪ ***Predictions of consequences.*** Still another frequently encountered kind of causal argument predicts the consequences of current, planned, or proposed actions or events. Consequence arguments have high stakes because we often judge actions on whether their benefits outweigh their costs. As we will see in Chapter 15,

---

*John Leo, "Kill-for-Kicks Video Games Desensitizing Our Children," *Seattle Times*, 27 Apr. 1999, B4.

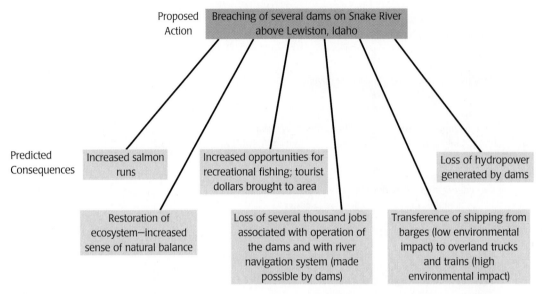

FIGURE 12.3 Predictions about consequences: Breaching dams on the Snake River

proposal arguments usually require writers to predict the consequences of a proposed action, do a cost/benefit analysis, and persuade readers that no unforeseen negative consequences will result. Figure 12.3 shows the consequence arguments considered by environmentalists who proposed eliminating several dams on the Snake River in order to save salmon runs.

Toulmin Framework for a Causal Argument

Because causal arguments can involve lengthy or complex causal chains, they are often harder to summarize in *because* clauses than are other kinds of arguments. Likewise, they are not as likely to yield quick analysis through the Toulmin schema. Nevertheless, a causal argument can usually be stated as a claim with *because* clauses. Typically, a *because* clause pinpoints one or two key elements in the causal chain rather than summarizes every link. John Leo's argument linking the Columbine massacre to violent videogames could be summarized in the following claim with a *because* clause:

> Violent video games may have been a contributing cause to the Littleton massacre because playing these games can make random, sociopathic violence seem pleasurable.

Once stated as an enthymeme, the argument can be analyzed using Toulmin's schema. It is easiest to apply Toulmin's schema to causal arguments if you think of the grounds as the observable phenomena at any point in the causal chain and the warrants as the shareable assumptions about causality that join links together.

Toulmin Analysis of the Violent Video Games Argument

ENTHYMEME

CLAIM Violent video games may have been a contributing cause to the Columbine school shooting

REASON because playing these games can make random, sociopathic violence seem pleasurable

Qualifiers

GROUNDS

- Evidence that the killers, like many young people, played violent video games

- Evidence that the games are violent

- Evidence that the games involve random, sociopathic violence (not good guys versus bad guys) such as killing ordinary people—marching bands, little old ladies, etc.

- Evidence that young people derive pleasure from these games

CONDITIONS OF REBUTTAL
Attacking the reason and grounds

- Perhaps the killers didn't play violent video games.

- Perhaps the video games are no more violent than traditional kids' games such as cops and robbers.

- Perhaps the video games do not feature sociopathic killing.

WARRANT

If young people derive pleasure from random, sociopathic killing in video games, they can transfer this pleasure to real life, thus leading to the Columbine shooting.

BACKING

- Testimony from psychologists

- Evidence that violent video games desensitize people to violence

- Analogy to military training in which video games are used to "make killing a reflex action"

- Evidence that the distinction between fantasy and reality becomes especially blurred for unstable young people

CONDITIONS OF REBUTTAL
Attacking the warrant and backing

- Perhaps kids are fully capable of distinguishing fantasy from reality.

- Perhaps the games are just fun with no transference to real life.

- Perhaps the games are substantially different from military training games.

■ ■ ■   **FOR CLASS DISCUSSION**   Developing Causal Chains

1. Working individually or in small groups, create a causal chain to show how the item on the left could help lead to the item on the right.

   a. High price of oil   Redesign of cities

   b. Invention of the automobile   Changes in sexual mores

      c. Invention of the telephone   Loss of sense of community
                                                       in neighborhoods

      d. Origin of rap in the black urban   The popularity of rap spreads from
         music scene   urban black audiences to white
                                                       middle-class youth culture

      e. Development of way to prevent   Liberalization of euthanasia laws
         rejections in transplant operations

  2. For each of your causal chains, compose a claim with an attached *because* clause summarizing one or two key links in the causal chain—for example, "The high price of oil is causing homeowners to move from the suburbs into new high-density urban communities because the expense of gasoline is making people value easy access to their work."

Two Methods for Arguing That One Event Causes Another

One of the first things you need to do when preparing a causal argument is to note exactly what sort of causal relationship you are dealing with—a onetime phenomenon, a recurring phenomenon, or a puzzling trend. Here are some examples.

Kind of Phenomenon	Examples
Onetime phenomenon	▪ 2007 collapse of a freeway bridge in Minneapolis, Minnesota ▪ Firing of a popular teacher at your university
Recurring phenomenon	▪ Eating disorders ▪ Road rage
Puzzling trend	▪ Rising popularity of extreme sports ▪ Increases in diagnosis of autism

With recurring phenomena or with trends, one has the luxury of being able to study multiple cases, often over time. You can interview people, make repeated observations, or study the conditions in which the puzzling phenomenon occurs. But with a onetime occurrence, one's approach is more like that of a detective than a scientist. Because one can't repeat the event with different variables, one must rely only on the immediate evidence at hand, which can quickly disappear.

Having briefly stated these words of caution, let's turn now to two main ways that you can argue that one event causes another.

EXAMINING VISUAL ARGUMENTS

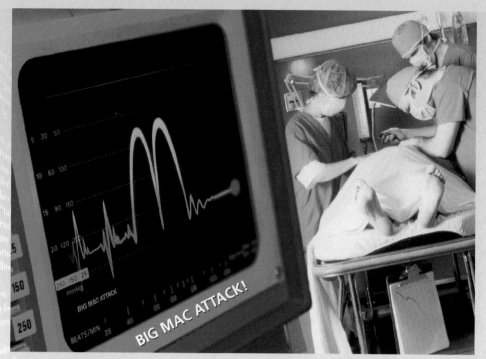

A Causal Claim

This spoof ad by Adbusters makes a causal argument against fast-food restaurants. How does the ad work visually to suggest the links in a causal chain? Place into your own words the argument implied by this ad. According to its Web site, Adbusters is "a global network of artists, activists, writers, pranksters, educators and entrepreneurs who want to advance the new social activist movement of the information age."

First Method: Explain the Causal Mechanism Directly

The most convincing kind of causal argument identifies every link in the causal chain, showing how an initiating cause leads step by step to an observed effect. A causes B, which causes C, which causes D. In some cases, all you have to do is fill in the missing links. In other cases—when your assumptions about how one step leads to the next may seem questionable to your audience—you have to argue for the causal connection with more vigor.

A careful spelling out of each step in the causal chain is the technique used by science writer Robert S. Devine in the following passage from his article "The Trouble with Dams." Although the benefits of dams are widely understood, the negative effects are less commonly known. In this article, Devine tries to persuade readers that dams have serious negative consequences. In the following passage, he explains how dams reduce salmon flows by slowing the migration of smolts (newly hatched young salmon) to the sea.

Causal Argument Describing a Causal Chain

Such transformations lie at the heart of the ongoing environmental harm done by dams. Rivers are rivers because they flow, and the nature of their flows defines much of their character. When dams alter flows, they alter the essence of rivers.

Consider the erstwhile river behind Lower Granite [a dam on Idaho's Snake River]. Although I was there in the springtime, when I looked at the water it was moving too slowly to merit the word "flow"—and Lower Granite Lake isn't even one of the region's enormous storage reservoirs, which bring currents to a virtual halt. In the past, spring snowmelt sent powerful currents down the Snake during April and May. Nowadays hydropower operators of the Columbia and Snake systems store the runoff behind the dams and release it during the winter, when demand—and the price—for electricity rises. Over the ages, however, many populations of salmon have adapted to the spring surge. The smolts used the strong flows to migrate, drifting downstream with the current. During the journey smolts' bodies undergo physiological changes that require them to reach salt water quickly. Before dams backed up the Snake, smolts coming down from Idaho got to the sea in six to twenty days; now it takes from sixty to ninety days, and few of the young salmon reach salt water in time. The emasculated current is the single largest reason that the number of wild adult salmon migrating up the Snake each year has crashed from pre-development runs of 100,000–200,000 to what was projected to be 150–75 this year.*

This tightly constructed passage connects various causal chains to explain the decline of salmon runs:

Smolts use river flow to reach the sea → dams restrict flow of river → a trip that before development took 6–20 days now takes 60–90 days → migrating smolts undergo physiological changes that demand quick access to salt water → delayed migration time kills the smolts.

Describing each link in the causal chain—and making each link seem as plausible as possible—is the most persuasive means of convincing readers that X causes Y.

Second Method: Infer Causal Links Using Inductive Reasoning

If we can't explain a causal link directly, we often employ a reasoning strategy called *induction*. Through induction, we infer a general conclusion based on a limited number of specific cases. For example, if on several occasions you got a headache after drinking red wine but not after drinking white wine, you would be likely to conclude inductively that red wine causes you to get headaches, although you can't explain directly how it does so. However, because there are almost always numerous variables involved, inductive reasoning gives only probable truths, not certain ones.

Three ways of thinking inductively   When your brain thinks inductively, it sorts through data looking for patterns of similarity and difference. In this section, we

---

*Robert S. Devine, "The Trouble with Dams," *Atlantic* (August 1995), 64–75. The example quotation is from page 70.

explain three ways of thinking inductively: looking for a common element; looking for a single difference; and looking for correlations.

1. ***Look for a common element.*** One kind of inductive thinking places you on a search for a common element that can explain recurrences of the same phenomenon. For example, psychologists attempting to understand the causes of anorexia have discovered that many anorexics (but not all) come from perfectionist, highly work-oriented homes that emphasize duty and responsibility. This common element is thus a suspected causal factor leading to anorexia.
2. ***Look for a single difference.*** Another approach is to look for a single difference that might explain the appearance of a new phenomenon. When infant death rates in the state of Washington shot up in July and August 1986, one event stood out making these two months different: increased radioactive fallout over Washington from the April Chernobyl nuclear meltdown in the Ukraine. This single difference led some researchers to suspect radiation as a possible cause of the increase in infant deaths.
3. ***Look for correlations.*** Still another method of induction is *correlation,* which expresses a statistical relationship between two phenomena: When A occurs, B is likely to occur also although it is not clear whether A causes B, B causes A, or some third factor C causes both A and B. For example, there is a fairly strong correlation between nearsightedness and intelligence. It could be that high intelligence causes people to read more, thus ruining their eyes (high intelligence causes nearsightedness). Or it could be that nearsightedness causes people to read more, thus raising their intelligence (nearsightedness causes high intelligence). Or it could be that some unknown phenomenon causes both nearsightedness and high intelligence. So, keep in mind that correlation is not causation—it simply suggests possible causation.

Beware of common inductive fallacies that can lead you to wrong conclusions
Largely because of its power, informal induction can often lead you to wrong conclusions. You should be aware of two common fallacies of inductive reasoning that can tempt you into erroneous assumptions about causality. (Both fallacies are treated more fully in Appendix 1.)

- *Post hoc fallacy:* The *post hoc, ergo propter hoc* fallacy ("after this, therefore because of this") mistakes sequence for cause. Just because event A regularly precedes event B doesn't mean that event A causes event B. The same reasoning that tells us that flipping a switch causes the light to go on can make us believe that low levels of radioactive fallout from the Chernobyl nuclear disaster caused a sudden rise in infant death rates in the state of Washington. The nuclear disaster clearly preceded the rise in death rates. But did it clearly *cause* it? Our point is that precedence alone is no proof of causality and that we are guilty of this fallacy whenever we are swayed to believe that one thing causes another just because it comes first.
- *Hasty generalization:* The *hasty generalization* fallacy occurs when you make a generalization based on too few cases or too little consideration of alternative explanations: You flip the switch, but the light bulb doesn't go on. You conclude—too hastily—that the light bulb has burned out. (Perhaps the power has gone off or

the switch is broken.) How many trials does it take before you can make a justified generalization rather than a hasty generalization? It is difficult to say for sure.

Both the *post hoc* fallacy and the hasty generalization fallacy remind us that induction requires a leap from individual cases to a general principle and that it is always possible to leap too soon.

■ ■ ■ **FOR CLASS DISCUSSION**   **Developing Plausible Causal Chains Based on Correlations**
Working individually or in small groups, develop plausible causal chains that might explain the relationship between the following pairs of phenomena:

a. A person who registers low stress level   Does daily meditation
   on electrochemical stress meter

b. Someone who grew up in a house   Is more likely to have higher SAT scores
   with two bathrooms   than a person who grew up in a
      one-bathroom home

c. A member of the National   Supports the death penalty
   Rifle Association

■ ■ ■

Glossary of Terms Encountered in Causal Arguments

Because causal arguments often are easier to conduct if writer and reader share a few specialized terms, we offer the following glossary for your convenience.

■ *Fallacy of oversimplified cause.* One of the great temptations when establishing causal relationships is to look for *the* cause of something. Most phenomena, especially the ones we argue about, have multiple causes. When you make a causal argument, be especially careful how you use words such as "all" or "some." For example, to say that *all* the blame for recent school shootings comes from the shooters' playing violent video games is to claim that violent video games are *the* cause of school shootings—a universal statement. An argument will be stronger and more accurate if the arguer makes a less sweeping statement: *Some* of the blame for school shootings can be attributed to violent video games. Arguers sometimes deliberately mix up these quantifiers to misrepresent and dismiss opposing views. For example, someone might argue that because violent video games aren't the sole cause of students' violent behavior, they are not an influential factor at all. Something that is not a total cause can still be a partial cause.

■ *Immediate and remote causes.* Every causal chain extends backward indefinitely into the past. An immediate cause is the closest in time to the event examined. Consider the factors leading to the fatal plane crash of John F. Kennedy, Jr., in July 1999. When Kennedy's plane crashed at night into the Atlantic Ocean south of Martha's Vineyard, experts speculated that the *immediate* cause was Kennedy's becoming disoriented in the night haze, losing visual control of the plane, and sending the plane into a fatal dive. A slightly less immediate cause was his decision to make an over water flight at night without being licensed for instrument flying.

Further back in time were all the factors that made Kennedy the kind of risk taker who took chances with his own life. For example, several months earlier he had broken his ankle in a hang gliding accident. Many commentators said that the numerous tragedies that befell the Kennedy family helped shape his risk-taking personality. Such causes going back into the past are considered *remote causes.*

■ ***Precipitating and contributing causes.*** These terms refer to a main cause emerging out of a background of subsidiary causes. If, for example, a husband and wife decide to separate, the *precipitating cause* may be a stormy fight over money, after which one of the partners (or both) says, "I've had enough." In contrast, *contributing causes* would be all the background factors that are dooming the marriage—preoccupation with their careers, disagreement about priorities, in-law problems, and so forth. Note that contributing causes and the precipitating cause all exist at the same time.

■ ***Constraints.*** Sometimes an effect occurs because some stabilizing factor—a *constraint*—is removed. In other words, the presence of a constraint may keep a certain effect from occurring. For example, in the marriage we have been discussing, the presence of children in the home might be a constraint against divorce; as soon as the children graduate from high school and leave home, the marriage may well dissolve.

■ ***Necessary and sufficient causes.*** A *necessary cause* is one that has to be present for a given effect to occur. For example, fertility drugs are necessary to cause the conception of septuplets. Every couple who has septuplets must have used fertility drugs. In contrast, a *sufficient cause* is one that always produces or guarantees a given effect. Smoking more than a pack of cigarettes per day is sufficient to raise the cost of one's life insurance policy. This statement means that if you are a smoker, no matter how healthy you appear to be, life insurance companies will always place you in a higher risk bracket and charge you a higher premium. In some cases, a single cause can be both necessary and sufficient. For example, lack of ascorbic acid is both a necessary and a sufficient cause of scurvy. (Think of those old-time sailors who didn't eat fruit for months.) It is a necessary cause because you can't get scurvy any other way except through absence of ascorbic acid; it is a sufficient cause because the absence of ascorbic acid always causes scurvy.

■ ■ ■   **FOR CLASS DISCUSSION**   Brainstorming Causes and Constraints

For the following events, try to think of as many causes as possible by brainstorming possible *immediate causes, remote causes, precipitating causes, contributing causes,* and *constraints:*

1. Working individually, make a list of different kinds of causes/constraints for one of the following:

   a. Your decision to attend your present college

   b. An important event in your life or your family (a job change, a major move, etc.)

2. Working as a group, make a list of different kinds of causes/constraints for one of the following:

   a. Why women's fashion and beauty magazines are the most frequently purchased magazines in college bookstores

   b. Why American students consistently score below Asian and European students in academic achievement

WRITING ASSIGNMENT A Causal Argument

Choose an issue about the causes or consequences of a trend, event, or other phenomenon. Write an argument that persuades an audience to accept your explanation of the causes or consequences of your chosen phenomenon. Within your essay you should examine alternative hypotheses or opposing views and explain your reasons for rejecting them. You can imagine your issue either as a puzzle or as a disagreement. If a puzzle, your task will be to create a convincing case for an audience that doesn't have an answer to your causal question already in mind. If a disagreement, your task will be more overtly persuasive because your goal will be to change your audience's views.

Exploring Ideas

Arguments about causes and consequences abound in public, professional, or personal life, so you shouldn't have difficulty finding a causal issue worth investigating and arguing. In response to a public controversy over why women are underrepresented on science and math faculties, student writer Julee Christianson contributed her own argument to the conversation by claiming that culture, not biology, is the reason (see pp. 208–213). Other students have focused on causal issues such as these: Why do kids join gangs? What causes anorexia? What are the consequences of violent video games on children? What are the consequences of mandatory drug testing (written by a student who has to take amphetamines for narcolepsy)?

If you have trouble finding a causal issue to write about, you can often create provocative controversies among your classmates through the following strategies:

- *Make a list of unusual likes and dislikes.* Think about unusual things that people like or dislike. You could summarize the conventional explanations that people give for an unusual pleasure or aversion and then argue for a surprising or unexpected cause. What attracts people to extreme sports? How do you explain the popularity of the Hummer or the tricked-out Cadillac Escalade as dream cars for urban youth?
- *Make a list of puzzling events or trends.* Another strategy is to make a list of puzzling phenomena and try to explain their causes. Start with onetime events (a cheating scandal at your school, the public's puzzling first reaction to a film, book, or new TV show). Then list puzzling recurring events (failure of knowledgeable teenagers to practice safe sex; use of steroids among athletes). Finally, list some recent trends (growth of naturopathic medicine; teen interest in the gothic). Engage classmates in discussions of one or more of the items on your list. Look for places of disagreement as entry points into the conversation.
- *Brainstorm consequences of a recent or proposed action.* Arguments about consequences are among the most interesting and important of causal disputes. If you can argue for an unanticipated consequence of a real, hypothetical, or proposed action—for example, a bad consequence of an apparently positive event or a good consequence of an apparently negative event—you can make an important contribution to the conversation. What might be the consequences,

for example, of some of the following: requiring a passing grade on a high-stakes test for graduation from high school; depleting the world's oil supply; legalizing marijuana; overturning *Roe v. Wade;* any similar recent, hypothetical, or proposed event?

Identifying Your Audience and Determining What's at Stake

Before drafting your argument, identify your targeted audience and determine what's at stake. Consider your responses to the following questions:

- What audience are you targeting? What background do they need to understand your issue? How much do they already care about it?
- Before they read your argument, what stance on your issue do you imagine them holding? What change do you want to bring about in their view?
- What will they find new or surprising about your argument?
- What objections might they raise? What counterarguments or alternative points of view will you need to address?
- Why does your argument matter? Who might be threatened or made uncomfortable by your views? What is at stake?

Organizing a Causal Argument

At the outset, it is useful to know some of the standard ways that a causal argument can be organized. Later, you may decide on a different organizational pattern, but the standard ways shown in Organization Plans 1, 2, and 3 on pages 206–207 will help you get started.

Plans 2 and 3 are similar in that they examine numerous possible causes or consequences. Plan 2, however, tries to establish the relative importance of each cause or consequence, whereas plan 3 aims at rejecting the causes or consequences normally assumed by the audience and argues for an unexpected surprising cause or consequence. Plan 3 can also be used when your purpose is to change your audience's mind about a cause or consequence.

Questioning and Critiquing a Causal Argument

Knowing how to question and critique a causal argument will help you anticipate opposing views in order to strengthen your own. It will also help you rebut another person's causal argument. Here are some useful questions to ask:

- When you explain the links in a causal chain, can a skeptic point out weaknesses in any of the links?
- If you speculate about the causes of a phenomenon, could a skeptic argue for different causes or arrange your causes in a different order of importance?
- If you argue for a surprising cause or a surprising consequence of a phenomenon, could a skeptic point out alternative explanations that would undercut your argument?

Organization Plan 1: Argument Explaining Links in a Causal Chain

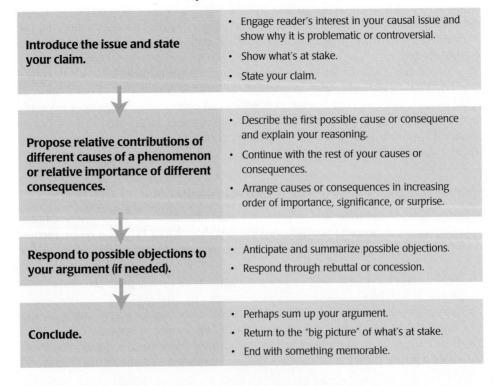

Introduce the issue and state your claim.
- Engage reader's interest in your causal issue and show why it is controversial or problematic.
- Show what's at stake.
- State your claim.

Explain the links in the chain going from cause to effect.
- Explain the links and their connections in order.
- Anticipate and respond to possible objections if needed.

Conclude.
- Perhaps sum up your argument.
- Return to the "big picture" of what's at stake.
- End with something memorable.

Organization Plan 2: Argument Proposing Multiple Causes or Consequences of a Phenomenon

Introduce the issue and state your claim.
- Engage reader's interest in your causal issue and show why it is problematic or controversial.
- Show what's at stake.
- State your claim.

Propose relative contributions of different causes of a phenomenon or relative importance of different consequences.
- Describe the first possible cause or consequence and explain your reasoning.
- Continue with the rest of your causes or consequences.
- Arrange causes or consequences in increasing order of importance, significance, or surprise.

Respond to possible objections to your argument (if needed).
- Anticipate and summarize possible objections.
- Respond through rebuttal or concession.

Conclude.
- Perhaps sum up your argument.
- Return to the "big picture" of what's at stake.
- End with something memorable.

Organization Plan 3: Argument Proposing a Surprising Cause or Consequence

Introduce the issue and state your claim.	• Engage reader's interest in your causal issue and show why it is problematic or controversial. • Show what's at stake. • State your claim.

↓

Reject commonly assumed causes or consequences.	• Describe the first commonly assumed cause or consequence and show why you don't think the explanation is adequate. • Continue with the rest of your commonly assumed causes or consequences.

↓

Argue for your surprising cause or consequence.	• Describe your surprising cause or consequence. • Explain your causal reasoning. • Anticipate and respond to possible objections if needed.

↓

Conclude.	• Perhaps sum up your argument. • Return to the "big picture" of what's at stake. • End with something memorable.

- If your argument depends on inferences from data, could a skeptic question the way the data were gathered or interpreted? Could a skeptic claim that the data weren't relevant (for example, research done with lab animals might not apply to humans)?
- If your causal argument depends on a correlation between one phenomenon and another, could a skeptic argue that the direction of causality should be reversed or that an unidentified third phenomenon is the real cause? ■

Reading

Student Julee Christianson wrote this causal argument in response to the assignment in this chapter. Julee was entering an intense public debate about the underrepresentation of women in science, a controversy initiated by Lawrence Summers, then president of Harvard, who suggested there might be fewer women than men on prestigious science faculties because women have less innate talent for science and math. A furious reaction ensued. The Web site of the Women in Science and Engineering Leadership Institute has extensive coverage of the controversy, including Summers' original speech (http://wiseli.engr.wisc.edu/news/Summers.htm). Julee's paper is documented and formatted in the style of the American Psychological Association. For more on APA style, see Appendix 2.

APA

Why Lawrence Summers Was Wrong:
Culture Rather Than Biology Explains the
Underrepresentation of Women in Science and Mathematics
Julee Christianson
English 260
February 20, 2008

Why Lawrence Summers Was Wrong:

Culture Rather Than Biology Explains the

Underrepresentation of Women in Science and Mathematics

In 2005, Harvard University's president, Lawrence H. Summers, gave a controversial speech that suggested that the underrepresentation of women in tenured positions in math and science departments was partly caused by biological differences. In his address, Summers proposed three hypotheses explaining why women shy away from math and science careers. First, he gave a "high-powered job hypothesis," which stated that women naturally want to start a family and therefore will not have the time or desire to commit to the high-stress workload required for research in math and science. His second hypothesis was that genetic differences between the sexes cause more males than females to have high aptitude for math and science. Lastly, he mentioned the hypothesis that women are under-represented because of discrimination, but he dismissed discrimination as a significant factor. It was Summers' second hypothesis about biological differences that started a heated national debate. The academic world seems split over this nature/nurture issue. Although there is some evidence that biology plays a role in determining math ability, I argue that culture plays a much larger role, both in the way that women are socialized and in the continued existence of male discrimination against women in male-dominated fields.

Evidence supporting the role of biology in determining math ability is effectively presented by Steven Pinker (2005), a Harvard psychologist who agrees with Summers and focuses extensively on Summers' "variability" argument. According to Pinker, "in many traits, men show greater variance than women, and are disproportionately found at both the low and high ends of the distribution." He explains that males and females have similar average scores on math tests but that there are more males than females in the top and the bottom percentiles. This greater variance means that there are disproportionately more male than female math geniuses (and math dunces) and thus more male than female candidates for top math and science positions at major research universities. Pinker explains this greater variance through evolutionary biology: men can pass on their genes to dozens of offspring, whereas women can pass on their genes to only a few. Pinker also argues that men and women have different brain structures that result in different kinds of thinking. For example, Pinker cites research that shows that on average men are better at mental rotation of figures and mathematical word problems, while women are better at remembering locations, doing mathematical calculations, reading faces, spelling, and using language. Not only do males and females think differently, but they release different hormones. These hormones help shape gender because males release more testosterone and females more estrogen, meaning that men are more aggressive and apt to take risks, while women "are more solicitous to their children." One example Pinker uses to support his biological hypothesis is the case of males born with abnormal genitals and raised as females. These children have more testosterone than normal female children, and many times they show characteristically male interests and behavior. Pinker uses these cases as evidence that no matter how a child is raised, the child's biology determines the child's interests.

Although Pinker demonstrates that biology plays some role in determining math aptitude, he almost completely ignores the much larger role of discrimination and socialization in shaping the career paths of women. According to an editorial in *Nature Neuroscience,* "[t]he evidence to support [Summers'] hypothesis of 'innate difference' turns out to be quite slim" (Separating science, 2005, p. 253). The editorial reports that intercultural studies of the variance between boys and girls scores on math tests show significant differences between countries. For example, in Iceland girls outscore boys on math tests. The editorial also says that aptitude tests are not very good at predicting the future success of students and that the "SATs tend to underpredict female and over-predict male academic performance" (p. 253). The editorial doesn't deny that men and women's brains work differently, but states that the differences are too small to be blamed for the underrepresentation of women in math and science careers.

If biology doesn't explain the low number of women choosing math and science careers, then what is the cause? Many believe the cause is culture, especially the gender roles children are taught at a very young age. One such believer is Deborah L. Rhode, an attorney and social scientist who specializes in ethics and gender, law, and public policy. In her book, *Speaking of Sex: The Denial of Gender Inequality*, Rhode (1997) describes the different gender roles females and males are expected to follow from a very young age. Gender roles are portrayed in children's books and television shows. These gender roles are represented by male characters as heroes and problem solvers, while the female characters are the "damsels in distress" (p. 34). Another example of gender roles is that only a very small number of these shows and books portray working mothers or stay-at-home fathers. Rhode also discussed how movies and popular music, especially rap and heavy metal, encourage violence and objectify women. As girls grow up, they face more and more gender stereotypes from toys to magazines. Parents give their boys interactive, problem-solving toys such as chemistry sets and telescopes, while girls are left with dolls. Although more organizations such as the Girl Scouts of America (2004), who sponsor the Web site *girlsgotech.org*, are trying to interest girls in science and math and advertise careers in those fields to girls, the societal forces working against this encouragement are also still pervasive. For example, magazines for teenage girls encourage attracting male attention and the importance of looks, while being smart and successful is considered unattractive. Because adolescents face so many gender stereotypes, it is no wonder that they shape the career paths they chose later in life. The gender roles engraved in our adolescents' minds cause discrimination against women later in life. Once women are socialized to see themselves as dependent and not as smart as males, it becomes very difficult to break away from these gender stereotypes. With gender bias so apparent in our society, it is hard for females to have high enough self-confidence to continue to compete with males in many fields.

5   The effect of socialization begins at a very early age. In one study, Melissa W. Clearfield and Naree M. Nelson (2006) show how parents unconsciously send gendered messages to their infants and toddlers. This study examined differences in mothers' speech patterns and play behaviors based on the gender of infants ranging from six months to fourteen months. Although there was no difference in the actual play behavior of male and female infants, the researchers discovered interesting differences in the way mothers interacted with daughters versus sons. Mothers of daughters tended to ask their daughters more questions, encouraging social interaction, whereas mothers of sons were less verbal, encouraging their sons to be more independent. The researchers concluded that "the mothers in our study may have been teaching their infants about gender roles through modeling and reinforcement.... Thus girls may acquire the knowledge that they are 'supposed' to engage in higher levels of interaction with other people and display more verbal behavior than boys.... In contrast, the boys were reinforced for exploring on their own" (p. 136).

One of the strongest arguments against the biological hypothesis comes from a transgendered Stanford neurobiologist who has been a scientist first as a woman and then as a man. In his article "Does gender matter?" Ben A. Barres states that "there is little evidence that gender differences in [mathematical] abilities exist, are innate or are even relevant to the lack of advancement of women in science" (2006, p. 134). Barres provides much anecdotal evidence of the way women are discriminated against in this male-dominated field. Barres notes that simply putting a male name rather than a female name on an article or resume increases its perceived value. He also describes research showing that men and women do equally well in gender-blind academic competitions but that men win disproportionately in contests where gender is revealed. As Barres says, "the bar is unconsciously raised so high for women and minority candidates that few emerge as winners" (p. 134). In one study reported by Barres, women applying for a research grant needed more than twice the productivity of men in order to be considered equally competent. As a female-to-male trans-gendered person, Barres has personally experienced discrimination when trying to succeed in the science and math fields. When in college, Barres was told that her boyfriend must have done her homework, and she later lost a prestigious fellowship competition to a male even though she was told her application was stronger and she had published "six high-impact papers," while the man who won only published one. Barres even notices subtle differences, such as the fact that he can now finish a sentence without being interrupted by a male.

Barres urges women to stand up publicly against discrimination. One woman he particularly admires as a strong female role model is MIT biologist Nancy Hopkins, who sued the MIT administration for discrimination based on the lesser amount of lab space allocated to female scientists. The evidence from this study was so strong that even the president of MIT publicly admitted that discrimination was a problem (p. 134). Barres wants more women to follow Hopkins' lead. He believes that women often don't realize they are being discriminated against because they have faith that the world is equal. Barres explains this tendency as a "denial of personal disadvantage" (p. 134). Very few women will admit to seeing or experiencing discrimination. Until discrimination and sexism are addressed, women will continue to be oppressed.

As a society, we should not accept Lawrence Summers' hypothesis that biological differences are the reason women are not found in high-prestige tenured jobs in math and science. In fact, in another generation the gap between men and women in math and science might completely disappear. In 2003–2004, women received close to one-third of all doctorates in mathematics, up from fifteen percent of doctorates in the early 1980s (American Mathematical Society, 2005). Although more recent data are not yet available, the signs point to a steadily increasing number of women entering the fields of math, science, and engineering. Blaming biology for the lack of women in these fields and refusing to fault our culture is taking the easy way out. Our culture can change.

Why Summers Was Wrong   6

References

American Mathematical Society. (2005, July 6). Women in mathematics: Study shows gains. Retrieved from http://www.ams.org/

Barres, B. A. (2006). Does gender matter? *Nature, 44*(7), 133–136.

Clearfield, M. W., & Nelson, N. M. (2006). Sex differences in mothers' speech and play behavior with 6-, 9-, and 14-month-old infants. *Sex Roles, 54*(1–2), 127–137.

Girl Scouts of the United States of America. (2004). *Girlsgotech.* Retrieved from http://www.girlsgotech.org

Pinker, S. (2005, Feb. 7). The science of difference: Sex ed. *The New Republic.* Retrieved from http://www.tnr.com/

Rhode, D. L. (1997). *Speaking of sex: The denial of gender inequality.* Cambridge, MA: Harvard University Press.

Separating science from stereotype [Editorial]. (2005). *Nature Neuroscience, 8*(3), 253.

Summers, L. H. (2005, Jan. 14). Remarks at NBER conference on diversifying the science and engineering workforce. Retrieved from http://www.president.harvard.edu/speeches/2005/nber.html

APA

13 Resemblance Arguments

CASE 1   How Serious Is College Debt?

In this graduation day cartoon by political cartoonist Matt Davies, the burden of college debt is likened to the plight of an oarless rower pumping madly to stay afloat in a sinking boat. Sharpened by a pun on "pomp and circumstance," the cartoon's argument depends on a visual analogy between paying off loans and pumping water from a boat. Humorously we fill in the unstated assumptions: without the debt, this happy grad would be rowing swiftly toward his destination of, say, a new car, a satisfying job, a house, and a bunch of money bags at his feet. Cartoonists frequently use visual analogies to make their argumentative claims.

CASE 2   Was the September 11, 2001, Terrorist Attack More Like a Criminal Act, an Act of War, or a Natural Disaster or Disease?

Following the September 11, 2001, terrorist attack on the World Trade Center and the Pentagon, media analysts tried to make sense of the horror by comparing it to different kinds of previous events. Some commentators likened it to Timothy McVeigh's bombing of the Alfred P. Murrah Federal Building in Oklahoma City in 1995—an argument that framed the terrorists as criminals who must be brought to justice. Others compared it to the 1941 Japanese attack on Pearl Harbor, an argument suggesting that the United States should declare war on some as-yet-to-be-defined enemy. Still others likened the event to an earthquake or an epidemic, arguing that terrorists will exist as long as the right conditions breed them and that it is useless to fight them using the strategies of conventional war. Under this analogy, the "war on terror" is a metaphorical war like the "war on poverty" or the "war against cancer." Clearly each of these resemblance arguments had high-stakes consequences. The Bush administration chose the Pearl Harbor argument and went to war. Critics of the war continued to say that war was an inappropriate strategy for fighting the "disease of terrorism."

An Overview of Resemblance Arguments

Resemblance arguments support a claim by comparing one thing to another with the intention of transferring the audience's understanding of (or feelings about) the second thing back to the first. Thus our dismay at seeing a graduate slowly sinking in his swamped rowboat is transferred to the issue of the burden of high education debts. The persuasive power of resemblance arguments comes from their ability to clarify an audience's conception of contested issues while conveying powerful emotions. The risk of a resemblance argument is that the differences between the two things being compared often are so significant that the argument may collapse under close examination. Thus, the cartoon may misrepresent the relationship between college debt and a graduate's future success by not showing the higher earnings that college graduates can expect to receive over a lifetime.

Toulmin Framework for a Resemblance Argument

Like most other argument types, resemblance arguments can be analyzed using the Toulmin schema. Suppose you want to find a startling way to warn teenage girls away from excessive dieting. Simultaneously, you want to argue that excessive dieting is partially caused by a patriarchal construction of beauty that keeps women submissive and powerless. You decide to create a resemblance argument claiming that women's obsessive dieting is like foot binding in ancient China. This argument can be displayed in Toulmin terms as follows:

ENTHYMEME

CLAIM Women's obsessive dieting in America serves the same harmful function as foot binding in ancient China

REASON because both practices keep women childlike, docile, dependent, and unthreatening to men.

GROUNDS

• Evidence that women, in attempting to imitate society's image of the "perfect woman," damage themselves (Chinese women were physically maimed; American women are psychologically maimed and often weakened by inadequate diet or constant worry about being fat.)

• Evidence that both practices make women childlike rather than grown-up (men call beautiful women "babes" or "dolls"; anorexia stops menstruation.)

• Evidence that women obsessed with beauty end up satisfied with less pay and subordinate positions in society as long as they are regarded as feminine and pretty.

CONDITIONS OF REBUTTAL
Attacking the reason and grounds

• Women who diet are concerned with health, not pursuit of beauty.

• Concern for healthy weight is "rational," not "obsessive."

• Thin women are often powerful athletes, not at all like Chinese victims of foot binding who can hardly walk.

• Dieting does not cause crippling deformity; a concern for beauty does not make a woman subordinate or satisfied with less pay.

• Dieting is a woman's choice—not something forced on her as a child.

WARRANT

Practices that are like ancient Chinese foot binding are bad.

BACKING

• Arguments that the subordinate position of women evidenced in both foot binding and obsession with weight is related to patriarchal construction of women's roles

• Arguments for why women should free themselves from patriarchal views

CONDITIONS OF REBUTTAL
Attacking the warrant and backing

• Perhaps arguments could be made that Chinese foot binding was not as repressive and patriarchal as the analogy implies (?). [We can't imagine a contemporary argument supporting foot binding.]

• Arguments supporting patriarchy and women's subordination

QUALIFIER: Perhaps the writer should say *"Under certain conditions* obsessive dieting can even seem like Chinese foot binding."*

Arguments by Analogy

The use of *analogies* can constitute the most imaginative form of argument. If you don't like your new boss, you can say that she's like a Marine drill sergeant, the cowardly captain of a sinking ship, or a mother hen. Each of these analogies suggests a different management style, clarifying the nature of your dislike while conveying an emotional charge. The ubiquity of analogies undoubtedly stems from their power to clarify the writer's understanding of an issue through comparisons that grip the audience.

Analogies have the power to get an audience's attention like virtually no other persuasive strategy. But seldom are they sufficient in themselves to provide full understanding. At some point with every analogy you need to ask yourself, "How far can I legitimately go with this? At what point are the similarities between the two things I am comparing going to be overwhelmed by their differences?" Analogies are useful attention-getting devices, but they can conceal and distort as well as clarify.

With this caveat, let's look at the uses of both undeveloped and extended analogies.

Using Undeveloped Analogies

Typically, writers use short, *undeveloped analogies* to drive home a point (and evoke an emotion) and then quickly abandon the analogy before the reader's awareness of disanalogies begins to set in. Suppose, for example, that you oppose taxpayer subsidies for the fine arts such as opera on the grounds that these are simply entertainments preferred by rich people. You might say: "Don't give my tax dollars to opera unless you also fund Monster Truck Rallies. Opera is simply a Monster Truck Rally for the rich." Your goal is to point out the hidden class bias in taxpayer support of opera and therefore win your audience to your side: Just as they would oppose a "National Endowment for Monster Truck Rallies," they ought to oppose a National Endowment for the Arts. But you don't want to linger too long on the analogy lest your audience begin pointing out important differences between subsidies for the arts and subsidies for monster truck rallies.

Using Extended Analogies

Sometimes writers elaborate an analogy so that it takes on a major role in the argument. As an example of a claim based on an extended analogy, consider the following excerpt from a professor's argument opposing a proposal to require a writing proficiency exam for graduation. In the following portion of his argument, the professor compares development of writing skills to the development of physical fitness.

> A writing proficiency exam gives the wrong symbolic messages about writing. It suggests that writing is simply a skill, rather than an active way of thinking and learning. It suggests that once a student demonstrates proficiency then he or she doesn't need to do any more writing.
>
> Imagine two universities concerned with the physical fitness of their students. One university requires a junior-level physical fitness exam in which students must run a mile in less than 10 minutes, a fitness level it considers minimally competent. Students at this university see the physical fitness exam as a one-time hurdle. As many as 70 percent of them can pass the exam with no practice; another 10–20 percent need a few months' training; and a few hopeless couch potatoes must go through exhaustive remediation.

After passing the exam, any student can settle back into a routine of TV and potato chips having been certified as "physically fit."

The second university, however, believing in true physical fitness for its students, is not interested in minimal competency. Consequently, it creates programs in which its students exercise 30 minutes every day for the entire four years of the undergraduate curriculum. There is little doubt which university will have the most physically fit students. At the second university, fitness becomes a way of life with everyone developing his or her full potential. Similarly, if we want to improve our students' writing abilities, we should require writing in every course throughout the curriculum.

If you choose to write an extended analogy such as this, you will focus on the points of comparison that serve your purposes. The writer's purpose in the preceding case is to support the achievement of mastery rather than minimalist standards as the goal of the university's writing program. Whatever other disanalogous elements are involved (for example, writing requires the use of intellect, which may or may not be strengthened by daily exercise), the comparison reveals vividly that a commitment to mastery involves more than a minimalist test. Typically, then, in developing your analogy, you are not developing all possible points of comparison so much as you are bringing out those similarities consistent with the point you are trying to make.

■ ■ ■ **FOR CLASS DISCUSSION** Developing Analogies

The following is a two-part exercise to help you clarify for yourself how analogies function in the context of arguments. Part 1 is to be done outside class; part 2 is to be done in class.

PART 1 Think of an analogy that expresses your point of view toward each of the following topics. Your analogy can urge your readers toward either a positive view of the topic or a negative view, depending on the rhetorical effect you seek. Write your analogy in the following one-sentence format:

_____ is like _____: A, B, C...(in which the first term is the contested topic being discussed; the second term is the analogy; and A, B, and C are the points of comparison).

Example

Topic: Cramming for an exam

Negative analogy: Cramming for an exam is like pumping iron for ten hours straight to prepare for a weight-lifting contest: exhausting and counterproductive.

Positive analogy: Cramming for an exam is like carbohydrate loading before a big race: it gives you the mental food you need for the exam, such as a full supply of concepts and details all fresh in your mind.

1. Using spanking to discipline children
2. Using racial profiling for airport security

3. Using steroids to increase athletic performance
4. Paying college athletes
5. Eating at fast-food restaurants

An effective analogy should influence both your audience's feelings toward the issue and your audience's understanding of the issue. For example, the writer of the negative analogy in the "cramming for an exam" illustration obviously believes that pumping iron for ten hours before a weight-lifting match is stupid. This feeling of stupidity is then transferred to the original topic—cramming for an exam. But the analogy also clarifies understanding. The writer imagines the mind as a muscle (which gets exhausted after too much exercise and which is better developed through some exercise every day rather than a lot all at once) rather than as a large container (into which lots of stuff can be "crammed").

PART 2   Bring your analogies to class and compare them to those of your classmates. Select the best analogies for each of the topics and be ready to say why you think they are good.

Arguments by Precedent

Precedent arguments are like analogy arguments in that they compare two phenomena. In precedent arguments, however, the second part of the comparison is usually a past event often involving a moral, legal, or political decision. An argument by precedent tries to show that a similar decision should (or should not) be reached for the present case because the situation for the present case is similar (or not similar) to that of the previous case.

A classic example of a precedent argument is the following excerpt from a speech by President Lyndon Johnson in the early years of the Vietnam War:

> Nor would surrender in Vietnam bring peace because we learned from Hitler at Munich that success only feeds the appetite of aggression. The battle would be renewed in one country and then another country, bringing with it perhaps even larger and crueler conflict, as we have learned from the lessons of history.

Here the audience recalls what happened at Munich: France and Britain tried to appease Germany's Hitler by yielding to his demand for a large part of Czechoslovakia, but Hitler continued his aggression anyway, using Czechoslovakia as a staging area to invade Poland. By arguing that surrender in Vietnam would lead to the same consequences, Johnson brings to his argument about Vietnam the whole weight of his audience's unhappy knowledge of World War II. Administration white papers developed Johnson's precedent argument by pointing out the similarity of Hitler's promises and those of the Viet Cong: You give us this and we will ask for no more. But Hitler didn't keep his promise. Why should the Viet Cong?

Johnson's Munich precedent persuaded many Americans during the early years of the war and helps explain U.S. involvement in Southeast Asia. Yet many

EXAMINING VISUAL ARGUMENTS

"AS A MATTER OF FACT, WE JUST BOUGHT ANOTHER SUV...."   www.IBDeditorials.com/cartoons

A Resemblance Claim

This political cartoon by Pulitzer Prize–winning cartoonist Michael Ramirez uses an analogy to link our desire for petroleum to Adam and Eve's desire for the apple leading to a fall from Paradise. Explore how this resemblance argument might create a clarifying lens for viewing our love affair with SUVs and other gas guzzling vehicles.

1. How was life during the era of cheap oil like Paradise?
2. To what extent are Americans "seduced" by gasoline?
3. Is the cartoonist correct in suggesting a theological dimension to the oil crisis?

scholars attacked Johnson's reasoning. For example, historian Howard Zinn rebutted Johnson's argument by claiming three crucial differences between Europe in 1939 and Southeast Asia in 1965. First, Zinn argued, the Czechs were being attacked from outside by an external aggressor (Germany), whereas Vietnam was under attack in a civil war. Second, Czechoslovakia was a prosperous, effective democracy, whereas the official Vietnam government was corrupt and unpopular. Third, Hitler wanted Czechoslovakia as a base for attacking Poland, whereas the Viet Cong and North Vietnamese wanted reunification of their country as an end in itself.*

---

*Based on the summary of Zinn's argument in J. Michael Sproule, *Argument: Language and Its Influence* (New York: McGraw-Hill, 1980), 149–50.

The Munich example shows again how arguments of resemblance depend on emphasizing the similarities between two phenomena and playing down the dissimilarities.

■ ■ ■   **FOR CLASS DISCUSSION**   Using Claims of Precedent

1. Consider the following claims of precedent, and evaluate how effective you think each precedent might be in establishing the claim. How would you develop the argument? How would you cast doubt on it?

   a. Gays should be allowed to serve openly in the U.S. military because they are allowed to serve openly in the militaries of most other Western countries.

   b. Postwar democracy can be created successfully in Iraq because it was created successfully in Germany and Japan following World War II.

2. Advocates for "right to die" legislation legalizing active euthanasia under certain conditions often point to the Netherlands as a country where acceptance of euthanasia works effectively. Assume for the moment that your state has a ballot initiative legalizing euthanasia. Assume further that you are being hired as a lobbyist for (against) the measure and have been assigned to do research on euthanasia in the Netherlands. Working in small groups, make a list of research questions you would want to ask. Your long-range rhetorical goal is to use your research to support (or attack) the ballot initiative by making a precedence argument focusing on the Netherlands.   ■ ■ ■

WRITING ASSIGNMENT   A Resemblance Argument

Write a letter to the editor of your campus or local newspaper or a slightly longer guest editorial in which you try to influence public opinion on some issue through the use of a persuasive analogy or precedent. Megan Matthews's argument against the Navy's use of low-frequency sonar to locate submarines is a student piece written for this assignment (see p. 223).

Exploring Ideas

Because letters to the editor and guest editorials typically are short, writers often lack space to develop full arguments. Thus, arguments from analogy or precedent are often effective in these situations.

Newspaper editors usually print letters or guest editorials only on current issues. For this assignment, look through the most recent back issues of your campus or local newspaper, paying particular attention to topics debated on the op-ed pages. Join one of the ongoing conversations about an existing issue, or draw attention to a current problem or situation that annoys you. In your letter or guest editorial, air your views. As part of your argument, include a persuasive analogy or precedent.

Identifying Your Audience and Determining What's at Stake

Before drafting your argument, identify your targeted audience and determine what's at stake. Consider your responses to the following questions:

- What audience are you targeting? What quick background could you sketch to help them understand your issue? How much do they already care about it?
- Before they read your argument, what stance on your issue do you imagine them holding? What change do you want to bring about in their view?
- What will they find new or surprising about your resemblance argument?
- If you are arguing from precedent, will your audience be familiar with the precedent, or will you have to explain it?
- What dissimilarities or disanalogies might they identify? What clarifications or counterarguments do you need to address to anticipate objections?
- Why does your argument matter? Who might be threatened or made uncomfortable by your views? What is at stake?

Organizing a Resemblance Argument

The most typical way to develop a resemblance argument is shown in the organization plan below. Of course, this structure can be varied in many ways, depending on

Organization Plan for a Resemblance Argument

Introduce the issue and state your claim.	• Engage readers' interest in the issue to which you will apply your analogy or precedent. • Show how your issue is controversial or problematic and explain what's at stake. • State your claim.
Develop your analogy or precedent.	• Present the analogy or precedent. • Draw the explicit parallels you want to highlight between your issue and the analogy or precedent. • Help readers transfer insights or emotions derived from the analogy or precedent back to your issue.
Respond to possible objections (if needed).	• Anticipate disanalogies, counter-arguments, or other objections. • Respond to them as appropriate.
Conclude.	• Perhaps sum up your argument. • Help reader return to the "big picture" of what's at stake. • End with something memorable.

your issue and rhetorical context. Sometimes writers open an argument with the analogy, which serves as an attention grabber.

Questioning and Critiquing a Resemblance Argument

Once you have written a draft of your letter or guest editorial, you can test its effectiveness by role-playing a skeptical audience. What follows are some typical questions audiences will raise about arguments of resemblance.

- *Will a skeptic say I am putting too much persuasive weight on my analogy or precedent?* The most common mistake people make with resemblance arguments is expecting them to do too much. Too often, an analogy is mistakenly treated as a logical proof rather than a playful figure suggesting tentative but significant insights. The best way to guard against this charge is to qualify your argument and to find other means of persuasion to supplement an analogy or precedent argument.
- *Will a skeptic point out disanalogies in my resemblance argument?* To refute a resemblance argument, you can highlight significant differences between the two things being compared rather than similarities. As one example, we have already shown you how Howard Zinn identified disanalogies between Europe in 1939 and Southeast Asia in 1965. ■

Our first reading is a letter to the editor by student Megan Matthews written for the assignment on page 221. The letter responds to a news story about whales damaged by Navy sonar. Notice how Megan uses an analogy to help readers imagine the effect of human-produced sea noise on marine mammals.

READINGS

Whales Need Silence

MEGAN MATTHEWS (STUDENT)

Re: "Whales beach themselves following NATO exercise" (news story, September 26). Imagine that you are forced to live in an apartment located next to Interstate 5 with its constant roar of engines and tires against concrete, its blaring horns and piercing sirens. When you open your windows in the summer, you have to shout to be heard. What if you had to leave your windows open all the time? What if your only housing alternatives were next to other freeways?

Seems impossible? Not for whales, dolphins, and other marine mammals. Jacques Cousteau's "world of silence" has been turned into an underwater freeway by the rumbling of cargo ships, the explosions of undersea mineral explorations, and the cacophony of the blasting devices used by fisheries. Now the Navy is adding a more powerful and dangerous source of sound with its low-frequency active sonar (LFA) for detecting enemy submarines. Low-frequency waves travel farther than high-frequency waves, which is why the bumping bass of a car stereo reverberates after the car passes you. In this case, 215 dB "pings" reflect off submarines—and whales—hundreds of miles away. The recent beaching incident in the Canary Islands reflects the danger that Navy sonar systems pose to whales.

Marine mammals depend on sound to avoid predators, to communicate across great distances between pods and prospective mates, and to establish mother-calf bonds. The extreme noise of Navy sonar apparently kills whales outright, while background "freeway" noise throughout the oceans may be threatening their ability to survive as communities.

Congress should not fund further implementation of LFA, which springs from an outdated Cold War model of warfare; the risks to our *environmental* security are too great.

Our second and third readings are a political cartoon and a letter to the editor written in response. The cartoon, by Pulitzer Prize winner Clay Bennett, first appeared in the *Chattanooga Times Free Press* on June 18, 2008, and was reprinted in the *Seattle Times.* The occasion was a California Supreme Court decision legalizing gay marriage in California. The responding letter to the editor, by Beth Reis, appeared in the *Seattle Times* on June 20, 2008.

Just Emancipated

CLAY BENNETT

Toon Offensive

BETH REIS

Don't get me wrong. I'm excited about California recognizing same-sex couples' right to marriage equality. I was a plaintiff in a Washington state marriage lawsuit. But the cartoon car with the words "just emancipated" on it, equating this development to the ending of slavery, especially on Juneteenth—the anniversary of the freeing of slaves after generations of brutality, forced labor, and families being separated and sold—is so offensive!

Yes, I feel a little more equal under the law this week. Yes, it matters that some people are now first-class citizens, entitled to the same rights and held to the same responsibilities as other couples. Yes, the word *marriage* is honorable and understandable and right.

But, please: How is that like outlawing slavery, exactly 146 years ago today? How is it like 143 years ago, when Texans were told that for the last three years they'd been enslaved illegally and were actually free? How is it like being told, nearly a century later, that they could finally vote?

I am proud to be gay, but not at all proud to have this week's small victory equated with the emancipation of slaves and the enfranchisement of their descendants.

For additional writing, reading, and research resources, go to www.mycomplab.com

14 Evaluation and Ethical Arguments

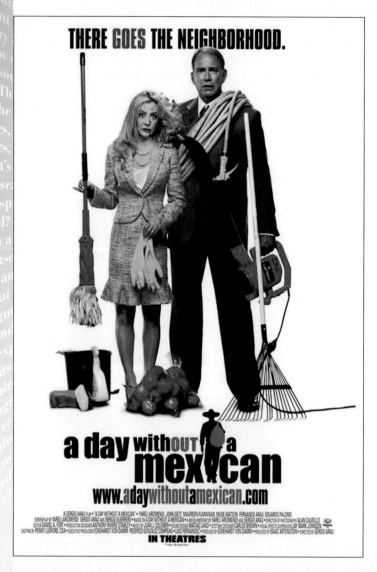

As we explored in Chapter 2, the United States has been embroiled in an ongoing controversy over the influx of illegal immigrants, mostly from Mexico and Central America. While some Americans want to offer citizenship as soon as possible to these immigrants, others want to close off the border between Mexico and the United States and to reduce the number of undocumented workers through deportation or through a crackdown on employers. This marketing image for the movie *A Day Without a Mexican* makes a humorous evaluation argument in favor of Mexican immigrants. It argues that the labor provided by immigrants is valuable—so valuable, in fact, that Californians could hardly endure a day without them. The image of the wealthy white couple having to do their own housekeeping, yard work, and tomato picking is an ironic reminder that the standard of living many Americans take for granted depends on the cheap labor of immigrants.

> **CASE 2   What Is a "Good Organ" for a Transplant? How Can a Diseased Person Ethically Find an Organ Donor?**
>
> In the United States, some 87,000 sick people have been waiting as long as six years for an organ transplant, with a portion of these dying before they can find a donor. The problem of organ short-ages raises two kinds of evaluation issues. First, doctors are reevaluating the criteria by which they judge a "good organ"—that is, a good lung, kidney, or liver suitable for transplanting. Formerly, people who were elderly or obese or who had engaged in risky behaviors or experienced heart failure or other medical conditions were not considered sources of good organs. Now doctors are reconsidering these sources as well as exploring the use of organs from pigs. Second, the shortage of organs for donation has raised numerous ethical issues: Is it ethical for people to bypass the national waiting list for organs by advertising on billboards and Web sites (see a billboard advertising for a liver on p. 163)? Is it morally right for people to sell their organs? Is it right for patients and families to buy organs or in any way remunerate living organ donors? Some states are passing laws that allow some financial compensation to living organ donors.

An Overview of Evaluation Arguments

In our roles as citizens and professionals, we are continually expected to make difficult evaluations and to persuade others to accept them. In this chapter, we explain strategies for conducting two different kinds of evaluation arguments. First, we examine categorical evaluations of the kind "Is this thing a good member of its class?"* (Is Joe a good commit-tee chair?) In such an evaluation, the writer determines the extent to which a given something fulfills the qualities or standards of its class. Second, we examine ethical argu-ments of the kind "Is this action right (wrong)?" (Was it right or wrong to drop atomic bombs on Hiroshima and Nagasaki in World War II?) In these arguments, the writer evaluates a given act from the perspective of some system of morality or ethics.

Criteria-Match Structure of Categorical Evaluations

A categorical evaluation follows the same criteria-match structure that we examined in definitional arguments (see Chapter 11). A typical claim for such an argument has the following structure:

> This thing/phenomenon is (is not) a good member of its class because it meets (fails to meet) criteria A, B, and C.

The main conceptual difference between an evaluation argument and a definition argument involves the second term ("a good member of its class"). In a definition argu-ment, one argues whether a particular thing belongs to a certain class or category. (Is this swampy area a *wetland?*) In an evaluation argument, we know what category

---

*In addition to the term *good,* a number of other evaluative terms involve the same kind of thinking—*effective, successful, workable, excellent, valuable,* and so forth.

something belongs to. For example, we know that this 2002 Ford Escort is a *used car*. For an evaluation argument, the question is whether this 2002 Ford Escort is a *good used car*. Or, to place the question within a rhetorical context, "Is this Ford Escort a *good used car for me to buy for college?*"

Toulmin Framework for an Evaluation Argument

To illustrate the criteria-match structure of an evaluation argument, let's continue with the Ford Escort example. Suppose you get in a debate with Parent or Significant Other about the car you should buy for college. Let's say that Parent or Significant Other argues that the following criteria are particularly important: (1) initial value for the

Toulmin Analysis of the Ford Escort Argument

ENTHYMEME

CLAIM The Ford Escort is a good used car for you at college

REASON because it provides the most initial value for the money.

GROUNDS

- Evidence that Escorts are dependable

- Evidence that Escorts are not in very high demand, so you can get a 2002 Escort for $5,000 less than a 2002 Honda Civic with the same mileage

- Evidence that a 2002 Civic for the same price would have double the miles

- Low initial mileage means years of dependable use without large repair bills.

CONDITIONS OF REBUTTAL
Attacking the reason and grounds

A 2002 Escort is not as great a value as it seems:

- My research suggests there are high maintenance costs after 60,000 miles.

- The initial savings may be blown on high repair costs.

WARRANT

High value for the initial money is an important criterian for buying your college car.

BACKING

Arguments showing why it is important to get high value for money:

- Money saved on the car can be used for other college expenses.

- Buying in this thrifty way meets our family's image of being careful shoppers.

CONDITIONS OF REBUTTAL
Attacking the warrant and backing

Other criteria are more important to me:

- Great handling and acceleration

- The fun of driving

- The status of having a cool car

money, (2) dependability, (3) safety, and (4) low maintenance costs. (Note: You would strenuously reject these criteria if you were looking for a muscle car, coolness, or driving excitement. This is why establishing criteria is a crucial part of evaluation arguments.) A Toulmin analysis of how Parent or Significant Other might make the case for "initial value for the money" is shown on page 228. Note how the warrant is a criterion while the stated reason and grounds assert that the specific case meets the criterion.

As the Toulmin analysis shows, Parent or Significant Other must argue that getting high value for the money is important (the criterion argument), and that the Ford Escort meets this criterion better than competing choices (the match argument). If you don't want a Ford Escort, you've either got to argue for other criteria (attacking the warrant) or accept the criterion but argue that projected maintenance costs undermine the car's initial value (attacking the reason and grounds).

Conducting a Categorical Evaluation Argument

Now that you understand the basic criteria-match structure of a categorical evaluation, let's look at some thinking strategies you can use to develop your criteria and to argue whether the thing you are evaluating meets the criteria.

Developing Your Criteria

To help develop your criteria, we suggest a three-step thinking process: (1) place the thing you are evaluating in the smallest relevant category so that you don't compare apples to oranges, (2) develop criteria for your evaluation based on the purpose or function of this category, and (3) determine the relative weight of your criteria. Let's look at each of these steps in turn.

Step 1: Place the Thing You Are Evaluating in the Smallest Relevant Category
Placing your contested thing in the smallest category is a crucial first step. Suppose, for example, that you want one of your professors to write you a letter of recommendation for a summer job. The professor will need to know what kind of summer job. Are you applying to become a camp counselor, a law office intern, a retail sales clerk, or a tour guide at a wild animal park? Each of these jobs has different criteria for excellence. Or, suppose lately that you have been thinking about problems created by e-mail. To create a stable context for your evaluation, you need to place e-mail in its smallest relevant category. You might choose to evaluate e-mail as medium for business communication (where e-mail might be contrasted with direct personal contact, with phone conversations or with snail mail), as a medium for staying in touch with high school friends (in contrast, say, to text messaging or Facebook), or as a medium for carrying on a long-distance romance (in contrast, say, to old-fashioned "love letters"). Again, criteria will vary across these different categories.

By placing your contested thing in the smallest relevant class you avoid the apples-and-oranges problem. That is, to give a fair evaluation to a perfectly good apple, you need to judge it under the class "apple" and not under the next larger class—"fruit"—or a neighboring class such as "orange." And to be even more precise, you may wish to evaluate your apple in the class "eating apple" as opposed to "pie apple" because the latter class is supposedly tarter and the former class juicier and sweeter.

Step 2: Develop Criteria for Your Evaluation Based on the Purpose or Function of This Category   Suppose that the summer job you are applying for is tour guide at a wild animal park. The tour guide drives the tour buses, makes people feel welcome, gives them interesting information about the wild animals, and so forth. Criteria for a good tour guide would thus include reliability and responsibility, a friendly demeanor, good speaking skills, and knowledge of the animals. In our e-mail example, suppose that you want to evaluate e-mail as a medium for business communication. The purpose of this class is to provide a quick, reliable, and efficient means of communication that improves productivity, minimizes misunderstandings, protects confidentiality, and so forth. Based on these purposes, you might establish the following criteria:

A good medium for business communication:

- Is easy to use, quick, and reliable
- Increases employee productivity
- Prevents misunderstandings
- Maintains confidentiality where needed

Step 3: Determine the Relative Weight of Your Criteria   In some evaluations, all criteria are equally important. However, sometimes a phenomenon to be evaluated is strong in one criterion but weak in another—a situation that forces the evaluator to decide which criterion takes precedence. For example, the supervisor interviewing candidates for tour guide at the wild animal park might find one candidate who is very knowledgeable about the wildlife but doesn't have good speaking skills. The supervisor needs to decide which of these two criteria gets more weight.

Making Your Match Argument

Once you've established and weighed your criteria, you'll need to use examples and other evidence to show that the thing being evaluated meets or does not meet the criteria. For example, your professor could argue that you would be a good wildlife park tour guide because you have strong interpersonal skills (based on your work on a college orientation committee), that you have good speaking skills (based on a speech you gave in her class), and that you know quite a bit about animals and ecology (based on your major in environmental science).

In our e-mail example, you might establish the following working thesis:

Despite being easy to learn, quick, and reliable, e-mail is not an effective medium for business communication because it reduces worker productivity, leads to frequent misunderstandings, and often disregards confidentiality.

EXAMINING VISUAL ARGUMENTS

An Evaluation Claim

This photograph of the "News Team" from *The Daily Show* makes an ironic evaluation argument. On the one hand, it argues that the news you get from *The Daily Show* is just as good (or better than) the news you get on regular news shows. On the other hand, it argues that *The Daily Show* is a spoof. How does this photograph serve to parody network news? What features make it similar to photographs for conventional network news teams? What features make it ironic? Do you think *The Daily Show* is a good source for news?

You could develop your last three points as follows:

- *E-mail reduces worker productivity.* You can use personal anecdotes and research data to show how checking e-mail is addictive and how it eats into worker time (one research article says that the average worker devotes 10 minutes of every working hour to reading and responding to e-mail). You might also show how e-mail frequently diverts workers from high-priority to low-priority tasks.
- *E-mail often leads to misunderstandings.* Because an e-mail message often is composed rapidly without revision, it can cause people to state ideas imprecisely, to write something they would never say face-to-face, or to convey an unintended tone. You could give a personal example of a high-consequence misunderstanding caused by e-mail.

231

■ *E-mail often disregards confidentiality.* You could provide anecdotal or research evidence of cases in which a person hit the "reply to all" button rather than the "reply" button, sending a message intended for one person to a whole group. Stories also abound of employers who read employees' e-mail messages or workers who forward e-mails without permission from the sender. Perhaps most troubling is the way that e-mail messages are archived forever—so that messages that you thought were deleted might show up years later in a lawsuit.

As these examples illustrate, the key to a successful match argument is to use sufficient examples and other evidence to show how your contested phenomenon meets or does not meet each of your criteria.

■ ■ ■ **FOR CLASS DISCUSSION**   Developing Criteria and Match Arguments

The following small-group exercise can be accomplished in one or two class hours. It gives you a good model of the process you can go through in order to write your own categorical evaluation.

1. Choose a specific controversial person, thing, or event to evaluate. Try brainstorming controversial members of the following categories: *people* (athletes, political leaders, musicians, clergy, businesspeople); *science and technology* (weapons systems, spreadsheets, automotive advancements, treatments for diseases); *media* (a newspaper, a magazine or journal, a TV program, a radio station, a Web site); *government and world affairs* (an economic policy, a Supreme Court decision, a law or legal practice, a foreign policy); *the arts* (a movie, a book, a building, a painting, a piece of music); *your college or university* (a course, a teacher, a textbook, a curriculum, the financial aid system); *the world of work* (a job, a dress policy, a merit pay system, a hiring policy, a supervisor); or any other categories of your choice.

2. Place your controversial person or thing within the smallest relevant class, thus providing a rhetorical context for your argument and showing what is at stake. Do you want to evaluate Harvey's Hamburger Haven in the broad category of *restaurants,* in the narrow category of *hamburger joints,* or in a different narrow category such as *late-night study places*? If you are evaluating a recent film, are you evaluating it as a *chick flick,* as a possible *Academy Award nominee,* or as a *political filmmaking statement*?

3. Make a list of the purposes or functions of that class, and then list the criteria that a good member of that class would need to have in order to accomplish the purpose or function. (What is the purpose or function of a late-night study place or a chick flick? What criteria for excellence can you derive from these purposes or functions?)

4. If necessary, rank your criteria from most to least important. (For a late-night study place, what is more important: good ambience, Wi-Fi availability, good coffee, or convenient location?)

5. Provide examples and other evidence to show how your contested something matches or does not match each of your criteria. (As a late-night study place, Carol's Coffee Closet beats out Harvey's Hamburger Haven. Although Harvey's Hamburger Haven has the most convenient location, Carol's Coffee Closet has Wi-Fi, an ambience conducive to studying, and excellent coffee.)

■ ■ ■

An Overview of Ethical Arguments

A second kind of evaluation argument focuses on moral or ethical issues, which often can merge or overlap with categorical evaluations. For example, many apparently straightforward categorical evaluations can turn out to have an ethical dimension. Consider again the criteria for buying a car. Most people would base their evaluations on cost, safety, comfort, and so forth. But some might feel morally obligated to buy the most fuel-efficient car or to buy an American car. Depending on how large a role ethical considerations play in the evaluation, we might choose to call this an ethical argument based on moral considerations rather than a categorical evaluation based on the purposes of a class or category.

It is uncertainty about "purpose" that makes ethical evaluations particularly complex. In making a categorical evaluation, we assume that every class or category of being has a purpose, that the purpose should be defined as narrowly as possible, and that the criteria for judgment derive directly from that purpose. For example, the purpose of a computer repairperson is to analyze the problem with my computer, fix it, and do so in a timely and cost-efficient manner. Once I formulate this purpose, it is easy for me to define criteria for a good computer repairperson. In ethical evaluations, however, the place of purpose is much fuzzier. In making ethical evaluations, we don't analyze the function of the class "manager" or a "judge" or a "computer repairperson." Who people are or what their social function is makes no difference to our ethical assessment of their actions or traits of character. A morally bad person may be a good judge, and a morally good person may be terrible at repairing computers and even worse at being a manager.

As the discussion so far has suggested, disagreements about ethical issues often stem from different value systems that make the issue irresolvable. It is precisely this problem—the lack of shared assumptions about value—that makes it so important to confront issues of ethics with rational deliberation. The arguments you produce may not persuade others to your view, but they should make others think seriously about it, and they should help you work out more clearly the reasons and warrants for your own beliefs. By writing about ethical issues, you see more clearly what you believe and why you believe it. Although the arguments demanded by ethical issues require rigorous thought, they force us to articulate our most deeply held beliefs and our richest feelings.

Major Ethical Systems

When we are faced with an ethical issue, we must move from arguments of good or bad to arguments of right or wrong. The terms *right* and *wrong* are clearly different from the terms *good* and *bad* when the latter terms mean simply "effective" (meets purposes of class, as in "This is a good laptop") or "ineffective" (fails to meet purposes of class, as in "This is a bad cookbook"). But *right* and *wrong* often also differ from what seems to be a moral use of the terms *good* and *bad*. We may say, for example, that sunshine is good because it brings pleasure and that cancer is bad because it brings pain and death, but that is not quite the same thing as saying that sunshine is "right" and cancer is "wrong." It is the problem of "right" and "wrong" that ethical arguments confront.

For example, from a nonethical standpoint, you could say that certain people are "good terrorists" in that they fully realize the purpose of the class "terrorist": they cause great anguish and damage with a minimum of resources, and they bring much attention to their cause. However, if we want to condemn terrorism on ethical grounds, we have to say that terrorism is wrong. The ethical question is not whether a person fulfills the purposes of the class "terrorist," but whether it is wrong for such a class to exist.

There are many schools of ethical thought—too many to cover in this brief overview—so we'll limit ourselves to two major systems: arguments from consequences and arguments from principles.

Consequences as the Base of Ethics

Perhaps the best-known example of evaluating acts according to their ethical consequences is utilitarianism, a down-to-earth philosophy that grew out of nineteenth-century British philosophers' concern to demystify ethics and make it work in the practical world. Jeremy Bentham, the originator of utilitarianism, developed the goal of the greatest good for the greatest number, or "greatest happiness," by which he meant the most pleasure for the least pain. John Stuart Mill, another British philosopher, built on Bentham's utilitarianism, using predicted consequences to determine the morality of a proposed action.

Mill's consequentialist approach allows you readily to assess a wide range of acts. You can apply the principle of utility—which says that an action is morally right if it produces a greater net value (benefits minus costs) than any available alternative action—to virtually any situation, and it will help you reach a decision. Obviously, however, it's not always easy to make the calculations called for by the principle, because, like any prediction of the future, an estimate of consequences is conjectural. In particular, it's often very hard to assess the long-term consequences of any action. Too often, utilitarianism seduces us into a short-term analysis of a moral problem simply because long-term consequences are difficult to predict.

Principles as the Base of Ethics

Any ethical system based on principles will ultimately rest on moral tenets that we are duty bound to uphold, no matter what the consequences. Sometimes the moral tenets come from religious faith—for example, the Ten Commandments. At other times, however, the principles are derived from philosophical reasoning, as in the case of German philosopher Immanuel Kant, who held that no one should ever use another person as a means to his own ends and that everyone should always act as if his acts were the basis of universal law. In other words, Kant held that we are duty bound to respect other people's sanctity and to act in the same way that we would want all other people to act. The great advantage of such a system is its clarity and precision. We are never overwhelmed by a multiplicity of contradictory and difficult-to-quantify consequences; we simply make sure we are following (or not violating) the principles of our ethical system and proceed accordingly.

Constructing an Ethical Argument

To show you how to conduct an ethical argument, let's now apply these two strategies to an example. In general, you can conduct an ethical evaluation by using the frame for either a principles-based argument or a consequences-based argument or a combination of both.

> *Principles-Based Frame:* An act is right (wrong) because it follows (violates) principles A, B, and C.
> *Consequences-Based Frame:* An act is right (wrong) because it will lead to consequences A, B, and C, which are good (bad).

To illustrate how these frames might help you develop an ethical argument, let's use them to develop arguments for or against capital punishment.

Constructing a Principles-based Argument

A principles-based argument looks at capital punishment through the lens of one or more guiding principles. Kant's principle that we are duty bound not to violate the sanctity of other human lives could lead to arguments opposing capital punishment. One might argue as follows:

> *Principles-based argument opposing capital punishment:* The death penalty is wrong because it violates the principle of the sanctity of human life.

You could support this principle either by summarizing Kant's argument that one should not violate the selfhood of another person or by pointing to certain religious systems such as Judeo-Christian ethics, where one is told "Vengeance is mine, saith the Lord" or "Thou shalt not kill." To develop this argument further, you might examine two exceptions in which principles-based ethicists may allow killing—self-defense and war—and show how capital punishment does not fall in either category.

Principles-based arguments can also be developed to support capital punishment. You may be surprised to learn that Kant himself—despite his arguments for the sanctity of life—supported capital punishment. To make such an argument, Kant evoked a different principle about the suitability of the punishment to the crime:

> There is no sameness of kind between death and remaining alive even under the most miserable conditions, and consequently there is no equality between the crime and the retribution unless the criminal is judicially condemned and put to death.

Stated as an enthymeme, Kant's argument is as follows:

> *Principles-based argument supporting capital punishment:* Capital punishment is right because it follows the principle that punishments should be proportionate to the crime.

In developing this argument, Kant's burden is to show why the principle of proportionate retribution outweighs the principle of the supreme worth of the individual. Our point is that a principles-based argument can be made both for and against capital punishment. The arguer's duty is to make clear what principle is being evoked and then to show why this principle is more important than opposing principles.

Constructing a Consequences-based Argument

Unlike a principles-based argument, which appeals to certain guiding maxims or rules, a consequences-based argument looks at the consequences of a decision and measures the positive benefits against the negative costs. Here is the frame that an arguer might use to oppose capital punishment on the basis of negative consequences:

> *Consequences-based argument opposing capital punishment:* Capital punishment is wrong because it leads to the following negative consequences:

- The possibility of executing an innocent person
- The possibility that a murderer who may repent and be redeemed is denied that chance
- The excessive legal and political costs of trials and appeals
- The unfair distribution of executions so that one's chances of being put to death are much greater if one is a minority or is poor

To develop this argument, the reader would need to provide facts, statistics, and other evidence to support each of the stated reasons.

A different arguer might use a consequences-based approach to support capital punishment:

> *Consequences-based argument supporting capital punishment:* Capital punishment is right because it leads to the following positive consequences:

- It may deter violent crime and slow down the rate of murder.
- It saves the cost of lifelong imprisonment.
- It stops criminals who are menaces to society from committing more murders.
- It helps grieving families reach closure and sends a message to victims' families that society recognizes their pain.

It should be evident, then, that adopting an ethical system doesn't lead to automatic answers to one's ethical dilemmas. A system offers a way of proceeding—a way of conducting an argument—but it doesn't relieve you of personal responsibility for thinking through your values and taking a stand. When you face an ethical dilemma, we encourage you to consider both the relevant principles and the possible consequences the dilemma entails. In many arguments, you can use both principles-based and consequences-based reasoning as long as irreconcilable contradictions don't present themselves.

■ ■ ■ **FOR CLASS DISCUSSION**   Developing Ethical Arguments

Working as individuals or in small groups, construct an ethical argument (based on principles, consequences, or both) for or against the following actions:

1. Eating meat
2. Buying a hybrid car
3. Legalizing assisted suicide for the terminally ill
4. Selling organs
5. Generating state revenue through lotteries

■ ■ ■

Common Problems in Making Evaluation Arguments

When conducting evaluation arguments (whether categorical or ethical), writers can bump up against recurring problems unique to evaluation. In some cases, these problems complicate the establishment of criteria; in other cases, they complicate the match argument. Let's look briefly at some of these common problems.

■ *The problem of standards—what is commonplace versus what is ideal:* In various forms, we experience the dilemma of the commonplace versus the ideal all the time. Is it fair to get a ticket for going seventy miles per hour on a sixty-five-mile-per-hour freeway when most of the drivers go seventy miles per hour or faster? (Does what is *commonplace*—going seventy—override what is *ideal*—obeying the law?) Is it better for high schools to pass out free contraceptives to students because students are having sex anyway (what's *commonplace*), or is it better not to pass them out in order to support abstinence (what's *ideal*)?

■ *The problem of mitigating circumstances:* This problem occurs when an arguer claims that unusual circumstances should alter our usual standards of judgment. Ordinarily, it is fair for a teacher to reduce a grade if you turn in a paper late. But what if you were up all night taking care of a crying baby? Does that count as a *mitigating circumstance* to waive the ordinary criterion? When you argue for mitigating circumstances, you will likely assume an especially heavy burden of proof. People assume the rightness of usual standards of judgment unless there are compelling arguments for abnormal circumstances.

■ *The problem of choosing between two goods or two bads:* Often an evaluation issue forces us between a rock and a hard place. Should we cut pay or cut people? Put our parents in a nursing home or let them stay at home where they have become a danger to themselves? In such cases, one has to weigh conflicting criteria, knowing that the choices are too much alike—either both bad or both good.

■ *The problem of seductive empirical measures:* The need to make high-stakes evaluations has led many people to seek quantifiable criteria that can be weighed mathematically. Thus we use grade point averages to select scholarship winners, student evaluation scores to decide merit pay for teachers, and combined scores of judges to judge figure skaters. In some cases, empirical measures can be quite acceptable, but they are often dangerous because they discount important nonquantifiable traits. The problem with empirical measures is that they seduce us into believing that complex judgments can be made mathematically, thus rescuing us from the messiness of alternative points of view and conflicting criteria.

■ *The problem of cost:* A final problem in evaluation arguments is cost. Something may be the best possible member of its class, but if it costs too much, we have to go for second or third best. We can avoid this problem somewhat by placing items into different classes on the basis of cost. For example, a Mercedes will exceed a Kia on almost any criterion, but if we can't afford more than a Kia, the comparison is pointless. It is better to compare a Mercedes to a Lexus and a Kia to an equivalent Ford. Whether costs are expressed in dollars, personal discomfort, moral repugnance, or some other terms, our final evaluation of an item must take cost into account.

WRITING ASSIGNMENT   An Evaluation or Ethical Argument

Write an argument in which you try to change your reader's mind about the value, worth, or ethics of something. Choose a phenomenon to be evaluated that is controversial so that your readers are likely at first to disagree with your evaluation or at least to be surprised by it. Somewhere in your essay you should summarize alternative views and either refute them or concede to them (see Chapter 7).

Exploring Ideas

Evaluation issues are all around us. Think of disagreements about the value of a person, thing, action, or phenomenon within the various communities to which you belong—your dorm, home, or apartment community; your school community, including clubs or organizations; your academic community, including classes you are currently taking; your work community; and your city, state, national, and world communities. For further ideas, look at the categories listed in the For Class Discussion exercise on page 232. Once you have settled on a controversial thing to be evaluated, place it in its smallest relevant category, determine the purposes of that category, and develop your criteria. If you are making an ethical evaluation, consider your argument from the perspective of both principles and consequences.

Identifying Your Audience and Determining What's at Stake

Before drafting your argument, identify your targeted audience and determine what's at stake. Consider your responses to the following questions:

■ What audience are you targeting? What background do they need to understand your issue? How much do they already care about it?

■ Before they read your evaluation argument, what stance on your issue do you imagine them holding? What change do you want to bring about in their view?

■ What will they find new or surprising about your argument?

■ What objections might they raise? What counter-arguments or alternative points of view will you need to address?

■ Why does your evaluation matter? Who might be threatened or made uncomfortable by your views? What is at stake?

Organizing an Evaluation Argument

As you write a draft, you may find useful the following prototypical structures for evaluation arguments shown in Organization Plans 1 and 2 below and on page 240. Of course, you can always alter these plans if another structure better fits your material.

Questioning and Critiquing a Categorical Evaluation Argument

Here is a list of questions you can use to critique a categorical evaluation argument:
Will a skeptic accept my criteria? Many evaluative arguments are weak because the writers have simply assumed that readers will accept their criteria. Whenever your audience's acceptance of your criteria is in doubt, you will need to argue for your criteria explicitly.

Organization Plan 1: Criteria and Match in Separate Sections

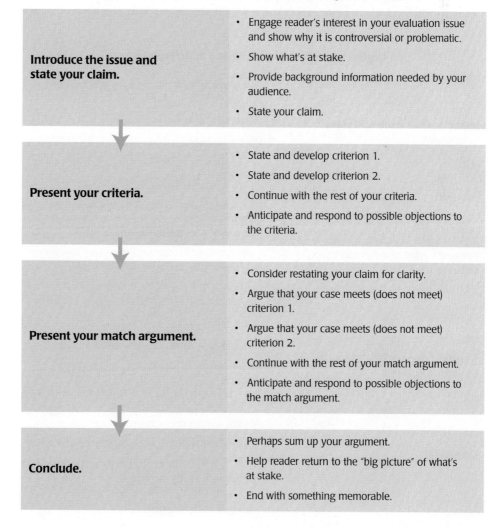

Introduce the issue and state your claim.

- Engage reader's interest in your evaluation issue and show why it is controversial or problematic.
- Show what's at stake.
- Provide background information needed by your audience.
- State your claim.

Present your criteria.

- State and develop criterion 1.
- State and develop criterion 2.
- Continue with the rest of your criteria.
- Anticipate and respond to possible objections to the criteria.

Present your match argument.

- Consider restating your claim for clarity.
- Argue that your case meets (does not meet) criterion 1.
- Argue that your case meets (does not meet) criterion 2.
- Continue with the rest of your match argument.
- Anticipate and respond to possible objections to the match argument.

Conclude.

- Perhaps sum up your argument.
- Help reader return to the "big picture" of what's at stake.
- End with something memorable.

Are my criteria based on the "smallest relevant class"? For example, the 1999 film *The Blair Witch Project* will certainly be a failure if you evaluate it in the general class "movies," in which it would have to compete with *Citizen Kane* and other great classics. But if you evaluate it as a "horror film" or a "low-budget film," it will have a greater chance for success and hence of yielding an arguable evaluation.

Will a skeptic accept my general weighting of criteria? Another vulnerable spot in an evaluation argument is the relative weight of the criteria. How much anyone weights a given criterion usually is a function of his or her own interests relative to your contested something. You should always ask whether some particular group might not have good reasons for weighting the criteria differently.

Will a skeptic question my standard of reference? In questioning an argument's criteria, a skeptic can also focus on the standard of reference used—what's commonplace versus what's ideal. If you have argued that your something is bad because it doesn't live up to what's ideal, you can expect some readers to defend it on the basis of what's

Organization Plan 2: Criteria and Match Interwoven

Introduce the issue and state your claim.	• Engage reader's interest in your evaluation issue and show why it is controversial or problematic. • Show what's at stake. • Provide background information needed by your audience. • State your claim.
Present series of criterion-match arguments.	• State and develop criterion 1 and argue that your case meets (does not meet) the criterion. • State and develop criterion 2 and argue that your case meets (does not meet) the criterion. • Continue with the rest of your criterion-match arguments.
Respond to possible objections to your argument.	• Anticipate and summarize possible objections. • Respond to the objections through rebuttal or concession.
Conclude.	• Perhaps sum up your argument. • Help reader return to the "big picture" of what's at stake. • End with something memorable.

commonplace. Similarly, if you argue that your something is good because it is better than its competitors, you can expect some readers to point out how short it falls from what is ideal.

Will a skeptic criticize my use of empirical measures? The desire to quantify criteria through empirical measures is always open to criticism. As we have discussed earlier, what's most measurable isn't always significant when it comes to assessing the worth of something. A ninety-five-mile-per-hour fastball certainly is an impressive empirical measure of a pitcher's ability—but if the pitcher doesn't strike batters out, that measure is a misleading gauge of performance.

Will a skeptic accept my criteria but reject my match argument? The other major way of testing an evaluation argument is to anticipate how readers may object to your stated reasons and grounds. Will readers challenge you by showing that you have cherry-picked your examples and evidence? Will they provide counterexamples and counterevidence?

Critiquing an Ethical Argument

Ethical arguments can be critiqued through appeals to consequences or principles. If an argument appeals primarily to principles, it can be vulnerable to a simple cost analysis. What are the costs of adhering to this principle? There will undoubtedly be some, or else there would be no real argument. If the argument is based strictly on consequences, we should ask whether it violates any rules or principles, particularly such commandments as the Golden Rule—"Do unto others as you would have others do unto you"—which most members of our audience adhere to. By failing to mention these alternative ways of thinking about ethical issues, we undercut not only our argument but our credibility as well.

Let's now consider some of the more subtle weaknesses of arguments based on principle. In practice, people will sometimes take rigidly "principled" positions because they fear "slippery slopes." If one has an absolutist commitment to the sanctity of life, for example, consider the slippery slope leading from birth control to euthanasia. Once we allow birth control in the form of condoms or the pill, the principled absolutist would say, then we will be forced to accept birth control "abortions" in the first hours after conception (IUDs, "morning after" pills), and then abortions in the first trimester, and then in the second or even the third trimester. And once we have violated the sanctity of human life by allowing abortions, it is only a short step to euthanasia and finally to killing off all undesirables.

One way to refute a slippery-slope argument of this sort is to try to dig a foothold into the side of the hill to show that you don't necessarily have to slide all the way to the bottom. You would thus have to argue that allowing birth control does not mean allowing abortions (by arguing for differences between a fetus after conception and sperm and egg before conception), or that allowing abortions does not mean allowing euthanasia (by arguing for differences between a fetus and a person already living in the world).

Arguments based on consequences have different kinds of difficulties. Have you calculated the consequences accurately? Have you considered all of the possible consequences, particularly unintended ones? Do you offer evidence that the predicted consequences will in fact come to pass? Do you show convincingly that the consequences of any given action are a net good or evil? ■

Our first reading, by student writer Sam Isaacson, was written for the   **READINGS**
assignment on page 238. It joins a conversation about whether the legalization of same-sex marriage would be good for our society. However, Isaacson, a gay
writer, limits the question to whether legalization of same-sex marriage would be *good
for the gay community.* As he considered the audience for his essay, Isaacson's decision
was to address this paper to the readers of a gay magazine such as *Harvard Gay and
Lesbian Review* or *The Advocate.*

Would Legalization of Gay Marriage Be Good for the Gay Community?

SAM ISAACSON (STUDENT)

For those of us who have been out for a while, nothing seems shocking about a gay
pride parade. Yet at this year's parade, I was struck by the contrast between two groups—
the float for the Toys in Babeland store (with swooning drag queens and leather-clad,
whipwielding, topless dykes) and the Northwest chapters of Integrity and Dignity
(Episcopal and Catholic organizations for lesbians and gays), whose marchers looked as
conservative as the congregation of any American church.

These stark differences in dress are representative of larger philosophical differences in
the gay community. At stake is whether or not we gays and lesbians should act "normal."
Labeled as deviants by many in straight society, we're faced with various opposing methods of response. One option is to insist that we are normal and work to integrate gays into
the cultural mainstream. Another response is to form an alternative gay culture with its
own customs and values; this culture would honor deviancy in response to a society which
seeks to label some as "normal" and some as "abnormal." For the purposes of this paper I
will refer to those who favor the first response as "integrationists" and those who favor the
second response as "liberationists." Politically, this ideological clash is most evident in the
issue of whether legalization of same-sex marriage would be good for the gay community.
Nearly all integrationists would say yes, but many liberationists would say no. My belief is
that while we must take the objections of the liberationists seriously, legalization of
same-sex marriage would benefit both gays and society in general.

Let us first look at what is so threatening about gay marriage to many liberationists.
Many liberationists fear that legalizing gay marriage will reinforce current social pressures
that say monogamous marriage is the normal and right way to live. In straight society, those
who choose not to marry are often viewed as self-indulgent, likely promiscuous, and shal-
low—and it is no coincidence these are some of the same stereotypes gays struggle against.
If gays begin to marry, married life will be all the more the norm and subject those outside
of marriage to even greater marginalization. As homosexuals, liberationists argue, we
should be particularly sensitive to the tyranny of the majority. Our sympathies should lie
with the deviants—the transsexual, the fetishist, the drag queen, and the leather-dyke. By
choosing marriage, gays take the easy route into "normal" society; we not only abandon the

sexual minorities of our community, we strengthen society's narrow notions of what is "normal" and thereby further confine both straights and gays.

Additionally, liberationists worry that by winning the right to marry gays and lesbians will lose the distinctive and positive characteristics of gay culture. Many gay writers have commented on how as a marginalized group gays have been forced to create different forms of relationships that often allow for a greater and often more fulfilling range of life experiences. Writer Edmund White, for instance, has observed that there is a greater fluidity in the relationships of gays than straights. Gays, he says, are more likely than straights to stay friends with old lovers, are more likely to form close friendships outside the romantic relationship, and are generally less likely to become compartmentalized into isolated couples. It has also been noted that gay relationships are often characterized by more equality and better communication than are straight relationships. Liberationists make the reasonable assumption that if gays win the right to marry they will be subject to the same social pressure to marry that straights are subject to. As more gays are pressured into traditional life patterns, liberationists fear the gay sensibility will be swallowed up by the established attitudes of the broader culture. All of society would be the poorer if this were to happen.

5   I must admit that I concur with many of the arguments of the liberationists that I have outlined above. I do think if given the right, gays would feel social pressure to marry; I agree that gays should be especially sensitive to the most marginalized elements of society; and I also agree that the unique perspectives on human relationships that the gay community offers should not be sacrificed. However, despite these beliefs, I feel that legalizing gay marriage would bring valuable benefits to gays and society as a whole.

First of all, I think it is important to put the attacks the liberationists make on marriage into perspective. The liberationist critique of marriage claims that marriage in itself is a harmful institution (for straights as well as gays) because it needlessly limits and normalizes personal freedom. But it seems clear to me that marriage in some form is necessary for the well-being of society. Children need a stable environment in which to be raised. Studies have shown that children whose parents divorce often suffer long-term effects from the trauma. Studies have also shown that people tend to be happier in stable long-term relationships. We need to have someone to look over us when we're old, when we become depressed, when we fall ill. All people, gay or straight, parents or nonparents, benefit from the stabilizing force of marriage.

Second, we in the gay community should not be too quick to overlook the real benefits that legalizing gay marriage will bring. We are currently denied numerous legal rights of marriage that the straight community enjoys: tax benefits, insurance benefits, inheritance rights, and the right to have a voice in medical treatment or funeral arrangements for a dying partner.

Further, just as important as the legal impacts of being denied the right to marriage is the socially symbolic weight this denial carries. We are sent the message that while gay sex in the privacy of one's home will be tolerated, gay love will not be respected. We are told that it is not important to society whether we form long-term relationships or not. We are told that we are not worthy of forming families of our own. By gaining the same recognitions by the state of our relationships and all the legal and social weight that recognition carries, the new message will be that gay love is just as meaningful as straight love.

Finally, let me address what I think is at the heart of the liberationist argument against marriage—the fear of losing social diversity and our unique gay voice. The liberationists are wary of society's normalizing forces. They fear that if gays win the right to marry gay relationships will simply become imitations of straight relationships—the richness gained through the gay experience will be lost. I feel, however, this argument unintentionally plays into the hands of conservatives. Conservatives argue that marriage is, by definition, the union between man and woman. As a consequence, to the broad culture gay marriage can only be a mockery of marriage. As gays and lesbians we need to argue that conservatives are imposing arbitrary standards on what is normal and not normal in society. To fight the conservative agenda, we must suggest instead that marriage is, in essence, a contract of love and commitment between two people. The liberationists, I think, unwittingly feed into conservative identification and classification by pigeonholing gays as outsiders. Reacting against social norms is simply another way of being held hostage by them.

10   We need to understand that the gay experience and voice will not be lost by gaining the right to marry. Gays will always be the minority by simple biological fact and this will always color the identity of any gay person. But we can only make our voice heard if we are seen as full-fledged members of society. Otherwise we will remain an isolated and marginalized group. And only when we have the right to marry will we have any say in the nature and significance of marriage as an institution. This is not being apologetic to the straight culture, but is a demand that we not be excluded from the central institutions of Western culture. We can help merge the fluidity of gay relationships with the traditionally more compartmentalized married relationship. Further, liberationists should realize that the decision *not* to marry makes a statement only if one has the ability to choose marriage. What would be most radical, most transforming, is two women or two men joined together in the eyes of society.

Our second reading was posted on the Web site of the Ayn Rand Institute in July 2005. The Ayn Rand Institute in Irvine, California, is an educational organization dedicated to the philosophy of novelist-philosopher Ayn Rand, who believed in "reason, rational self-interest, individual rights and free-market capitalism" (from the Web site, www.aynrand.org). This institute seeks to educate the public about Rand's philosophy, called Objectivism, and to promote a culture informed by its values. The author of this piece, David Holcberg, works for the institute as a media research specialist. In this argument, Holcberg joins the national and global debate about trading and selling human organs.

Human Organs for Sale?

DAVID HOLCBERG

As athletes who have received organ transplants gathered for the 2005 World Transplant Games in the city of London, Canada, a record 87,000 individuals who did not share these athletes' good fortune stood on the U.S. national waiting list for organs. Of the 82,000 waiting for kidneys or livers, about 6,000 will die in the next twelve months. Yet no one is considering a simple way to save many of these people: legalize trade in human organs.

Let's consider it.

Millions of Americans have exercised their right to give away their organs by signing organ donation cards. But very few made the legal arrangements necessary to ensure that their organs can be harvested after death. Many more would make such arrangements if their families were to be paid for the donated organs. It may work as a type of life insurance for the benefit of the deceased's family and would create a mutually advantageous situation: the deceased's family gets needed money while the transplant patient gets a vital organ.

A few people, on the other hand, may choose to sell an organ (or part of one) during their lifetime. This may seem like a radical idea, but it need not be an irrational one.

5   According to the Mayo Clinic, the extraction of a section of liver, for example, carries a risk to the donor's life of less than 1 percent—not negligible, but not overwhelming. In the case of a kidney donation, the *New England Journal of Medicine* reports that the risk to the donor's life is even smaller; just 0.03 percent. Moreover, liver donors can usually count on their healthy liver's ability to regenerate and regain full function. And donors of kidneys usually live normal lives with no reduction of life expectancy.

A person may reasonably decide, after considering all the relevant facts (including the pain, risk and inconvenience of surgery), that selling an organ is actually in his own best interest. A father, for example, may decide that one of his kidneys is worth selling to pay for the best medical treatment available for his child.

But those who object to a free market in organs would deny this father the right to act on his own judgment. Poor people, they claim, are incapable of making rational choices and so must be protected from themselves. The fact, however, is that human beings (poor or rich) do have the capacity to reason, and should be free to exercise it. So long as a person respects the rights of others, he ought to be free to live his life and use his mind and body as he judges best, without interference from the government or anybody else.

Of course, the decision to sell an organ (or part of an organ) is a very serious one, and should not be taken lightly. That some people might make irrational choices, however, is no reason to violate the rights of everyone. If the law recognizes our right to give away an organ, it should also recognize our right to sell an organ.

The objection that people would murder to sell their victims' organs should be dismissed as the scaremongering that it is. (Indeed, the financial lure of such difficult-to-execute criminal action is today far greater than it would be if patients could legally and openly buy the organs they need.)

10   Opponents of a free market in organs argue as well that it would benefit only those who could afford to pay—not necessarily those in most desperate need. This objection should also be rejected. Need does not give anyone the right to damage the lives of other people, by prohibiting a seller from getting the best price for his organ, or a buyer from purchasing an organ to further his life. Those who can afford to buy organs would benefit at no one's expense but their own. Those unable to pay would still be able to rely on charity, as they do today. And a free market would enhance the ability of charitable organizations to procure organs for them.

Ask yourself: if your life depended on getting an organ, say a kidney or a liver, wouldn't you be willing to pay for one? And if you could find a willing seller, shouldn't you have the right to buy it from him?

The right to buy an organ is part of your right to life. The right to life is the right to take all actions a rational being requires to sustain and enhance his life. Your right to life becomes meaningless when the law forbids you to buy a kidney or liver that would preserve your life.

If the government upheld the rights of potential buyers and sellers of organs, many of the 87,000 people now waiting for organs would be spared hideous suffering and an early death. How many?

Let's find out.

 For additional writing, reading, and research resources, go to www.mycomplab.com

Proposal Arguments

15

CASE 1 How Can the United States Reduce Its Dependence on Foreign Oil?

In 2008, the United States imported approximately 70 percent of its oil, much of it from the Middle East. Not only did this dependency threaten our economy and harm the environment, it also threatened national security. The Republican Party proposed addressing this problem by drilling for more domestic oil in offshore sites and in the Arctic National Wildlife Refuge. However, in the summer of 2008 Texas billionaire oilman T. Boone Pickens, one of the staunchest mainstays of the Republican Party, surprised the nation by rejecting the "drilling" plan and proposing instead the "Pickens Plan"—a multibillion-dollar proposal to build enough wind towers and transmission lines to supply 20 percent of the nation's electricity. Massive use of wind power, Pickens claimed, would free up natural gas to fuel automobiles rather than to generate electricity. Using clean-burning natural gas in cars would substantially reduce our oil imports while lowering Americans' carbon footprint. The Web site for the Pickens Plan illustrates a proposal argument in multimedia style using photographs, videos, graphics, and text.

CASE 2 How Can America's Army Recruit Enough Soldiers?

The U.S. Army has had trouble meeting its monthly recruiting goals, leading to a deepening crisis in supplying enough soldiers to meet conflicts throughout the world. To address this crisis, analysts proposed a number of possible solutions: increase the number of recruiters; improve recruitment methods; expand the pool of possible recruits by lowering standards or increasing the upper age limit; double the size of enlistment bonuses for prized recruits from $20,000 to $40,000; eliminate the ban on gay soldiers; keep more first-term soldiers by reducing the discharge rate for drug abuse, poor conduct, or failure to meet fitness standards; reinstitute a lottery draft; or mandate a period of national service for all Americans on graduation from high school (with military service one of the options).

An Overview of Proposal Arguments

Although proposal arguments are the last type we examine, they are among the most common arguments that you will encounter or be called on to write. Their essence is that they call for action. In reading a proposal, the audience is enjoined to make a decision and then to act on it—to *do* something. Proposal arguments are sometimes called *should* or *ought* arguments because those helping verbs express the obligation to act: "We *should* do this [action]" or "We *ought* to do this [action]."

For instructional purposes, we will distinguish between two kinds of proposal arguments, even though they are closely related and involve the same basic arguing strategies. The first kind we will call *practical proposals,* which propose an action to solve some kind of local or immediate problem. A student's proposal to change the billing procedures for scholarship students would be an example of a practical proposal, as would an engineering firm's proposal for the design of a new bridge planned by a city government. The second kind we will call *policy proposals,* in which the writer offers a broad plan of action to solve major social, economic, or political problems affecting the common good. An argument that the United States should adopt a national health insurance plan or that the electoral college should be abolished would be an example of a policy proposal.

Toulmin Framework for a Proposal Argument

The Toulmin schema is particularly useful for proposal arguments because it helps you find good reasons and link them to your audience's beliefs, assumptions, and values. Suppose that your university is debating whether to banish fraternities and sororities. Suppose further that you are in favor of banishing the Greek system. One of your arguments is that eliminating the Greek system will improve your university's academic reputation. The chart on page 249 shows how you might use the Toulmin schema to make this line of reasoning as persuasive as possible.

Special Concerns for Proposal Arguments

In their call for action, proposal arguments entail certain emphases and audience concerns that you don't generally face with other kinds of arguments. Let's look briefly at some of these special concerns.

- *The need for presence.* To persuade people to *act* on your proposal, particularly if the personal or financial cost of acting is high, you must give your argument presence as well as intellectual force. By *presence*, we mean an argument's ability to grip your readers' hearts and imaginations as well as their intellects. You can give presence to an argument through appeals to *pathos* such as effective use of details,

Toulmin Analysis of the Greek System Argument

ENTHYMEME

CLAIM Our university should eliminate the Greek system

REASON because doing so will improve our university's academic reputation.

GROUNDS

Evidence that eliminating the Greek system will improve our academic reputation.

- Excessive party atmosphere of some Greek houses emphasizes social life rather than studying—we are known as a party school.
- Last year the average GPA of students in fraternities and sororities was lower than the GPA of non-Greek students.
- New pledges have so many house duties and initiation rites that their studies suffer.
- Many new students think about rush more than about the academic life.

WARRANT

It is good for our university to achieve a better academic reputation.

BACKING

- The school would attract more serious students, leading to increased prestige.
- Campus would be more academically focused and attract better faculty.
- Losing the "party-school" reputation would put us in better light for taxpayers and legislators.
- Students would graduate with more skills and knowledge.

CONDITIONS OF REBUTTAL
Attacking the reason and grounds

- Many of the best students are Greeks. Last year's highest-GPA award went to a sorority woman, and several other Greeks won prestigious graduate school scholarships.
- Statistics on grades are misleading. Many houses had much higher average GPA than the university average. Total GPA was brought down by a few rowdy houses.
- Many other high-prestige universities have Greek systems.
- There are ways to tone down the party atmosphere on campus without abolishing the Greek system.
- Greeks contribute significantly to the community through service projects.

CONDITIONS OF REBUTTAL
Attacking the warrant and backing

- No one will argue that it is not good to have a strong academic reputation.
- However, skeptics may say that eliminating sororities and fraternities won't improve the university's academic reputation but will hurt its social life and its wide range of living options.

provocative statistics, dialogue, illustrative narratives, and compelling examples that show the reader the seriousness of the problem you are addressing or the consequences of not acting on your proposal.

- *The need to overcome people's natural conservatism.* Another difficulty with proposals is the innate conservatism of all human beings, whatever their political persuasion, as suggested by the popular adage "If it ain't broke, don't fix it." The difficulty of proving that something needs fixing is compounded by the fact that frequently the status quo appears to be working. So sometimes when writing a proposal, you can't argue that what we have is bad, but only that what we could have would be better. Often, then, a proposal argument will be based not on present evils but on the evils of lost potential. And getting an audience to accept lost potential may be difficult indeed, given the inherently abstract nature of potentiality.

■ *The difficulty of predicting future consequences.* Further, most proposal makers will be forced to predict consequences of their proposed action. As the "law of unintended consequences" suggests, few major decisions lead neatly to their anticipated results without surprises along the way. So when we claim that our proposal will lead to good consequences, we can expect our audience to be skeptical.

■ *The problem of evaluating consequences.* A final problem for proposal writers is the difficulty of evaluating consequences. In government and industry, managers often use a *cost-benefit analysis* to reduce all consequences to a single-scale comparison, usually money. Although this scale may work well in some circumstances, it can lead to grotesquely inappropriate conclusions in other situations. Just how does one balance the environmental benefits of high gasoline prices against the suffering of drivers who can't afford to get to work or the benefits of pollution-free nuclear power against the costs of a potential nuclear accident? Also, what will be a cost for one group will often be a benefit for others. For example, if Social Security benefits are cut, those on Social Security will suffer, but current workers who pay for it with taxes will take home a larger paycheck.

These, then, are some of the general difficulties facing someone who sets out to write a proposal argument. Although these difficulties may seem daunting, the rest of this chapter offers strategies to help you overcome them and produce a successful proposal.

Developing a Proposal Argument

Writers of proposal arguments must focus in turn on three main phases or stages of the argument: showing that a problem exists, explaining the proposed solution, and offering a justification.

Convincing Your Readers That a Problem Exists

There is one argumentative strategy generic to all proposal arguments: calling your reader's attention to a problem. In some situations, your intended audience may already be aware of the problem and may have even asked for solutions. In such cases, you do not need to develop the problem extensively or motivate your audience to solve it. But in most situations, awakening your readers to the existence of a problem—a problem they may well not have recognized before—is your first important challenge. You must give your problem presence through anecdotes, telling statistics, or other means that show readers how the problem affects people or otherwise has important stakes. Your goal is to gain your readers' intellectual assent to the depth, range, and potential seriousness of the problem and thereby motivate them to want to solve it.

Typically, the arguer develops the problem in one of two places in a proposal argument—either in the introduction prior to the presentation of the arguer's proposal claim or in the body of the paper as the first main reason justifying the proposal claim. In the second instance, the writer's first *because* clause has the following structure: "We should do this action *because* it addresses a serious problem."

Here is how one student writer gave presence to a proposal, addressed to the chair of the mathematics department at her school, calling for redesign of the first-year calculus curriculum in order to slow its pace. She wants the chair to see a problem from her perspective.

Example Passage Giving Presence to a Problem

For me, who wants to become a high school math teacher, the problem with introductory calculus is not its difficulty but its pace. My own experience in the Calculus 134 and 135 sequence last year showed me that it was not the learning of calculus that was difficult for me. I was able to catch on to the new concepts. My problem was that it went too fast. Just as I was assimilating new concepts and feeling the need to reinforce them, the class was on to a new topic before I had full mastery of the old concept....Part of the reason for the fast pace is that calculus is a feeder course for computer science and engineering. If prospective engineering students can't learn the calculus rapidly, they drop out of the program. The high dropout rate benefits the Engineering School because they use the math course to weed out an overabundance of engineering applicants. Thus the pace of the calculus course is geared to the needs of the engineering curriculum, not to the needs of someone like me who wants to be a high school mathematics teacher and who believes that my own difficulties with math—combined with my love for it—might make me an excellent math teacher.

By describing the fast pace of the math curriculum from the perspective of a future math teacher rather than an engineering student, this writer brings visibility to a problem. What before didn't look like a problem (it is good to weed out weak engineering majors) suddenly became a problem (it is bad to weed out future math teachers). Establishing herself as a serious student genuinely interested in learning calculus, she gave presence to the problem by calling attention to it in a new way.

Showing the Specifics of Your Proposal

Having decided that there is a problem to be solved, you should lay out your thesis, which is a proposal for solving the problem. Your goal now is to stress the feasibility of your solution, including costs. The art of proposal making is the art of the possible. To be sure, not all proposals require elaborate descriptions of the implementation process. If you are proposing, for example, that a local PTA chapter buy new tumbling mats for the junior high gym classes, the procedures for buying the mats will probably be irrelevant. But in many arguments the specifics of your proposal—the actual step-by-step methods of implementing it—may be instrumental in winning your audience's support.

You will also need to show how your proposal will solve the problem either partially or wholly. Sometimes you may first need to convince your reader that the problem is solvable, not something intractably rooted in "the way things are," such as earthquakes or jealousy. In other words, expect that some members of your audience will be skeptical about the ability of any proposal to solve the problem you are addressing. You may well need, therefore, to "listen" to this point of view in your refutation section and to argue that your problem is at least partially solvable.

In order to persuade your audience that your proposal can work, you can follow any one of several approaches. A typical approach is to lay out a causal argument showing how one consequence will lead to another until your solution is effected. Another approach is to turn to resemblance arguments, either analogy or precedent. You try to show how similar proposals have been successful elsewhere. Or, if similar things have failed in the past, you try to show how the present situation is different.

The Justification: Convincing Your Readers That Your Proposal Should Be Enacted

The justification phase of a proposal argument will need extensive development in some arguments and minimal development in others, again depending on your particular problem and the rhetorical context of your proposal. If your audience already acknowledges the seriousness of the problem you are addressing and has simply been waiting for the right solution to come along, then your argument will be successful so long as you can convince your audience that your solution will work and that it won't cost too much. Such arguments depend on the clarity of your proposal and the feasibility of its being implemented.

But what if the costs are high? What if your readers don't think the problem is serious? What if they don't appreciate the benefits of solving the problem or the bad consequences of not solving it? In such cases you have to develop persuasive reasons for enacting your proposal. You may also have to determine who has the power to act on your proposal and apply arguments directly to that person's or agency's immediate interests. You need to know to whom or to what your power source is beholden or responsive and what values your power source holds that can be appealed to. You're looking, in short, for the best pressure points.

Proposal Arguments as Advocacy Posters or Advertisements

A frequently encountered kind of proposal argument is the one-page newspaper or magazine advertisement often purchased by advocacy groups to promote a cause. Such arguments also appear as Web pages or as posters or fliers. These condensed advocacy arguments are marked by their bold, abbreviated, tightly planned format. The creators of these arguments know they must work fast to capture our attention, give presence to a problem, advocate a solution, and enlist our support. Advocacy advertisements frequently use photographs, images, or icons that appeal to a reader's emotions and imagination. In addition to images, they often use different type sizes and styles. Large-type text in these documents frequently takes the form of slogans or condensed thesis statements written in an arresting style. To outline and justify their solutions, creators of advocacy ads often put main supporting reasons in bulleted lists and sometimes enclose carefully selected facts and quotations in boxed sidebars. To add an authoritative *ethos,* the arguments often include fine-print footnotes and bibliographies. (For more detailed discussion of how advocacy posters and advertisements use images and arrange text for rhetorical effect, see Chapter 9 on visual argument.)

Another prominent feature of these condensed, highly visual arguments is their appeal to the audience through a direct call for a course of action: go to an advocacy Web site to find more information on how to support a cause; cut out a postcardlike form to send to a decision maker; vote for or against the proposition or the candidate; write a letter to a political representative; or donate money to a cause.

An example of a student-produced advocacy advertisement is shown in Figure 15.1. Here student Lisa Blattner joins a heated debate in her city on whether to close down

What Is Left for Teenagers to Do When the Teen Ordinance Bans Them from Dance Clubs?

Take Ecstasy
at Raves   Drink at Places with   Roam the Streets
                           No Adult Supervision

Is There an Answer to These Problems?

Yes! Through your support of the All Ages Dance Ordinance, teens will have a safe place to go where:

- **No hard drugs, like ecstasy and cocaine, are present**
- **Responsible adults are watching over everyone**
- **All of their friends can hang out in one place indoors, instead of outside with drug dealers, criminals, and prostitutes**

Give Your Child a Safe Place to Have Fun at Night

Let the Seattle City Committee Know That You Support the All Ages Dance Ordinance

FIGURE 15.1 Student advocacy advertisement

all-ages dance clubs. Frustrated because the evening dance options for under-twenty-one youth were threatened in Seattle, Lisa directed her ad toward the general readership of regional newspapers with the special intention of reaching adult voters and parents. Lisa's ad uses three documentary-like, emotionally loaded, and disturbing photographs to give immediacy and presence to the problem. The verbal text in the ad states the proposal claim and provides three reasons in support of the claim. Notice how the reasons also pick up the ideas in the three photo images. The final lines of text memorably reiterate the claim and call readers to action. The success of this ad derives from the collaboration of layout, photos, and verbal text in conveying a clear, direct argument.

Now that you have been introduced to the main elements of a proposal argument, including condensed visual arguments, we explain in the next two sections two invention strategies you can use to generate persuasive reasons for a proposal argument and to anticipate your audience's doubts and reservations. We call these the "claim-type strategy" and the "stock issues strategy."

Using the Claim-Types Strategy to Develop a Proposal Argument

In Chapter 10, we explained how claim-type theory can help you generate ideas for an argument. Specifically, we explained how evaluation and proposal claims often depend for their supporting reasons on claims about category, cause, or resemblance. This fact leads to a powerful idea-generating strategy based on arguments from category (which also includes argument from principle), on arguments from consequences, or on arguments from resemblance. This "claim-types" strategy is illustrated in the following chart:

Explanation of Claim-Types Strategy for Supporting a Proposal Claim

Claim Type	Generic Template	Example from Biotechnology Issue
Argument from principle or category	We should do this action ■ because doing so adheres to this good principle [or] ■ because this action belongs to this good category	We should support genetically modified foods ■ because doing so values scientific reason over emotion [or] ■ because genetically modified foods are safe
Argument from consequences	■ because this action will lead to these good consequences	■ because biotech crops can reduce world hunger ■ because biotech crops can improve the environment by reducing use of pesticides
Argument from resemblance	■ because this action has been done successfully elsewhere [or] ■ because this action is like this other good action	■ because genetic modification is like natural crossbreeding that has been accelerated [or] ■ because genetic modification of food is like scientific advancements in medicine

Before we give you some simple strategies for using this approach, let's illustrate it with another example.

Insurance companies should pay for long-term psychological counseling for anorexia (proposal claim)

- because paying for such counseling is a demonstration of commitment to women's health. (principle/category)
- because paying for such counseling may save insurance companies from much more extensive medical costs at a later date. (consequence)
- because paying for anorexia counseling is like paying for alcoholism or drug counseling, which is already covered by insurance. (resemblance)

Note how each of these supporting reasons appeals to the value system of the audience. The writer hopes to show that covering the cost of counseling is within the class of things that the audience already values (commitment to women's health), will lead to consequences desired by the audience (reduced long-term costs), and is similar to something the audience already values (drug and alcohol counseling). The claim-types strategy for generating ideas is easy to apply in practice. The following chart shows you how.

Suggestions for Applying the Claim-Types Strategy to Your Proposal

Claim Type	Your Goal	Thinking Strategy
Argument from principle or category	Show how your proposed action follows a principle valued by your audience or belongs to a category valued by your audience.	▪ Think of how your proposed action adheres to a rule or principle. ▪ Use this template: "because doing this action is _____" and then fill in the blank with a noun or adjective: *kind, just, loving, courageous, merciful, legal, fair, democratic, constitutional, an act of hope, an illustration of the golden rule, faithful to the principle of limited government.* ▪ If you are opposing a proposal, search for negative rather than positive principles/categories.
Argument from consequences	Show how your proposed action will lead to consequences valued by your audience.	▪ Brainstorm consequences of your proposal and identify those that audience will agree are good. ▪ If you are opposing a proposal, search for negative consequences.

(Continued)

Claim Type	Your Goal	Thinking Strategy
Argument from resemblance	Show how your proposed action has been done successfully elsewhere or is like another action valued by your audience.	▪ Brainstorm places or times when your proposal (or something similar to it) has been done successfully. ▪ Brainstorm analogies that compare your proposed action to something the audience already values. ▪ If you are opposing a proposal, think of places or times where similar actions have failed or construct a negative analogy.

■ ■ ■ **FOR CLASS DISCUSSION** Generating Ideas Using the Claim-Types Strategy

1. Working individually or in small groups, use the strategies of principle/category, consequence, and resemblance to create *because* clauses that support each of the following claims. Try to have at least one *because* clause from each of the categories, but generate as many reasons as possible. Don't worry about whether any individual reason exactly fits the category. The purpose is to stimulate thinking, not fill in the slots.

Example

People should not own pit bulls (proposal claim)

- because pit bulls are vicious. (category)
- because owning a pit bull leads to conflicts with neighbors. (consequence)
- because owning a pit bull is like having a shell-shocked roommate—mostly they're lovely companions, but they can turn violent if startled. (resemblance)

   a. Marijuana should be legalized.

   b. Division I college athletes should receive salaries.

   c. High schools should pass out free contraceptives.

   d. Violent video games should be made illegal.

   e. Parents should be heavily taxed for having more than two children.

2. Repeat the first exercise, taking a different position on each issue.   ■ ■ ■

Using the "Stock Issues" Strategy to Develop a Proposal Argument

Another effective way to generate ideas for a proposal argument is to ask yourself a series of questions based on the "stock issues" strategy. Suppose, for example, you wanted to develop the following argument: "In order to solve the problem of students who won't take risks with their writing, the faculty should adopt a pass/fail method of grading in all

*When
your right
to an abortion
is taken away,
what are you
going to
do*

Reproductive rights are under attack. The Pro-Choice Public Education Project. It's pro-choice or no choice.
1(688)253-CHOICE or www.protect.choice.org

A Proposal Claim

This ad attempts to counter the influence of the pro-life movement's campaign against abortion rights. Sponsored by the Planned Parenthood Responsible Choices Action Network, the ad appeared in a number of liberal magazines. What policy proposal does this ad make? How would you convert its visual argument into a verbal argument? What action is it asking people to take? How does the image of the coat hanger/question mark appeal simultaneously to both *pathos* and *logos*? How would you evaluate the overall effectiveness of this ad in motivating pro-choice advocates to take action? How might pro-life advocates respond to this ad?

writing courses." The stock issues strategy invites the writer to consider "stock" ways (that is, common, usual, frequently repeated ways) that such arguments can be conducted.

Stock issue 1: *Is there really a problem here that needs to be solved?* Is it really true that a large number of student writers won't take risks in their writing? Is this problem more serious than other writing problems such as undeveloped ideas, lack of organization, and poor sentence structure? This stock issue invites the writer to convince her audience that a true problem exists. Conversely, an opponent to the proposal may argue that a true problem does not exist.

Stock issue 2: *Will the proposed solution really solve this problem?* Is it true that a pass/fail grading system will cause students to take more risks with their writing? Will more interesting, surprising, and creative essays result from pass/fail grading? Or will students simply put less effort into their writing? This stock issue prompts a supporter to demonstrate that the proposal will solve the problem; in contrast, it prompts the opponent to show that the proposal won't work.

Stock issue 3: *Can the problem be solved more simply without disturbing the status quo?* An opponent of the proposal may agree that a problem exists and that the proposed solution might solve it. However, the opponent may say, "Are there not less radical ways to solve this problem? If we want more creative and risk-taking student essays, can't we just change our grading criteria so that we reward risky papers and penalize conventional ones?" This stock issue prompts supporters to show that *only* the proposed solution will solve the problem and that no minor tinkering with the status quo will be adequate. Conversely, opponents will argue that the problem can be solved without acting on the proposal.

Stock issue 4: *Is the proposed solution really practical? Does it stand a chance of actually being enacted?* Here an opponent to the proposal may agree that the proposal would work but that it involves pie-in-the-sky idealism. Nobody will vote to change the existing system so radically; therefore, it is a waste of our time to debate it. Following this prompt, supporters would have to argue that pass/fail grading is workable and that enough faculty members are disposed to it that the proposal is worth debating. Opponents may argue that the faculty is so traditional that pass/fail has utterly no chance of being accepted, despite its merits.

Stock issue 5: *What will be the unforeseen positive and negative consequences of the proposal?* Suppose we do adopt a pass/fail system. What positive or negative consequences may occur that are different from what we at first predicted? Using this prompt, an opponent may argue that pass/fail grading will reduce the effort put forth by students and that the long-range effect will be writing of even lower quality than we have now. Supporters would try to find positive consequences—perhaps a new love of writing for its own sake rather than the sake of a grade.

■ ■ ■ **FOR CLASS DISCUSSION** **Brainstorming Ideas for a Proposal**

The following collaborative task takes approximately two class days to complete. The exercise takes you through the process of creating a proposal argument.

1. In small groups, identify and list several major problems facing students in your college or university.

2. Decide among yourselves which are the most important of these problems and rank them in order of importance.

3. Take your group's number one problem and explore answers to the following questions. Group recorders should be prepared to present your group's answers to the class as a whole:

   a. Why is the problem a problem?

   b. For whom is the problem a problem?

   c. How will these people suffer if the problem is not solved? (Give specific examples.)

   d. Who has the power to solve the problem?

   e. Why hasn't the problem been solved up to this point?

   f. How can the problem be solved? (That is, create a proposal.)

   g. What are the probable benefits of acting on your proposal?

   h. What costs are associated with your proposal?

   i. Who will bear those costs?

   j. Why should this proposal be enacted?

   k. Why is it better than alternative proposals?

4. As a group, draft an outline for a proposal argument in which you

   a. describe the problem and its significance.

   b. propose your solution to the problem.

   c. justify your proposal by showing how the benefits of adopting that proposal outweigh the costs.

5. Recorders for each group should write their group's outline on the board and be prepared to explain it to the class.

WRITING ASSIGNMENT   A Proposal Argument

Option 1: A Practical Proposal Addressing a Local Problem   Write a practical proposal offering a solution to a local problem. Your proposal should have three main sections: (1) description of the problem, (2) proposed solution, and (3) justification. You may include additional sections or subsections as needed. Longer proposals often include an *abstract* at the beginning of the proposal to provide a summary overview of the whole argument. (Sometimes called the *executive summary,* this abstract may be the only portion of the proposal read by high-level managers.) Sometimes proposals are accompanied by a *letter of transmittal*—a one-page business letter that introduces the proposal to its intended audience and provides some needed background about the writer.

Option 2: A Policy Proposal as a Guest Editorial   Write a two- to three-page policy proposal suitable for publication as a feature editorial in a college or city newspaper or in some publication associated with a particular group or activity such as a church newsletter or employee bulletin. The voice and style of your argument should be aimed at general readers of your chosen publication. Your editorial should have the following features:

1. The identification of a problem (Persuade your audience that this is a genuine problem that needs solving; give it presence.)
2. A proposal for action that will help alleviate the problem
3. A justification of your solution (the reasons why your audience should accept your proposal and act on it)

Option 3: A Researched Argument Proposing Public Policy   Write an eight- to twelve-page proposal argument as a formal research paper, using research data for development and support. In business and professional life, this kind of research proposal is often called a *white paper,* which recommends a course of action internally within an organization or externally to a client or stakeholder. An example of a researched policy proposal is student writer Juan Vazquez's "Why the United States Should Adopt Nuclear Power" on pages 265–270.

Option 4: A One-Page Advocacy Advertisement   Using the strategies of visual argument discussed in Chapter 9 and on pages 252–253 of this chapter, create a one-page advocacy advertisement urging action on a public issue. Your advertisement should be designed for publication in a newspaper or for distribution as a poster or flier. An example of a student-produced advocacy advertisement is shown in Figure 15.1 on page 253.

Exploring Ideas

Because *should* or *ought* issues are among the most common sources of arguments, you may already have ideas for proposal issues. To think of ideas for practical proposals, try making an idea map of local problems you would like to see solved. For initial spokes, try trigger words such as the following:

- Problems at my university (dorms, parking, registration system, financial aid, campus appearance, clubs, curriculum, intramural program, athletic teams)
- Problems in my city or town (dangerous intersections, ugly areas, inadequate lighting, parks, police policy, public transportation, schools)
- Problems at my place of work (office design, flow of customer traffic, merchandise display, company policies)
- Problems related to my future career, hobbies, recreational time, life as a consumer, life as a homeowner

If you can offer a solution to the problem you identify, you may make a valuable contribution to some phase of public life.

To find a topic for policy proposals, stay in touch with the news, which will keep you aware of current debates on regional and national issues. Also, visit the Web sites of your congressional representatives to see what issues they are currently investigating and debating. You might think of your policy proposal as a white paper for one of your legislators.

Once you have decided on a proposal issue, we recommend you explore it by trying one or more of the following activities:

- Explore ideas by using the claim-types strategy (see pp. 254–256).
- Explore ideas by using the "stock issues" strategy (see pp. 256–258).
- Explore ideas using the eleven questions (a–k) on page 259.

Identifying Your Audience and Determining What's at Stake

Before drafting your argument, identify your targeted audience and determine what's at stake. Consider your responses to the following questions:

- What audience are you targeting? What background do they need to understand your problem? How much do they already care about it? How could you motivate them to care?
- After they read your argument, what stance do you imagine them holding? What change do you want to bring about in their view or their behavior?
- What will they find uncomfortable or threatening about your proposal? Particularly, what costs will they incur by acting on your proposal?
- What objections might they raise? What counterarguments or alternative solutions will you need to address?
- Why does your proposal matter? What is at stake?

Organizing a Proposal Argument

When you write your draft, you may find it helpful to have at hand an organization plan for a proposal argument. The plan on page 262 shows a typical structure for a proposal argument. In some cases, you may want to summarize and rebut opposing views before you present the justification for your own proposal.

Designing a One-Page Advocacy Advertisement

As an alternative to a traditional written argument, your instructor may ask you to create a one-page advocacy advertisement. The first stage of your invention process should be the same as for a longer proposal argument. Choose a controversial public issue that needs immediate attention or a neglected issue about which you want to arouse public passion. As with a longer proposal argument, consider your audience in order to identify the values and beliefs on which you will base your appeal.

When you construct your argument, the limited space available demands efficiency in your choice of words and in your use of document design. Your goal is to have a memorable impact on your reader in order to promote the action you advocate. The following questions may help you design and revise your advocacy ad.

1. How could photos or other graphic elements establish and give presence to the problem?
2. How can type size, style, and layout be used to present the core of your proposal, including the justifying reasons, in the most powerful way for the intended audience?

Organization Plan for a Proposal Argument

Introduce and develop the problem.	• Engage reader's interest in your problem. • Provide background, including previous attempts to solve the problem. • Give the problem "presence" by showing who is affected and what is at stake. • Argue that the problem is solvable (optional).
Present your proposed solution to the problem.	• First, state your proposal concisely to serve as your thesis statement or claim. • Then, explain the specifics of your proposal.
Justify your proposed solution through a series of supporting reasons.	• Restate your claim and forecast your supporting reasons. • Present and develop reason 1. • Present and develop reason 2. • Present and develop additional reasons.
Respond to objections or to alternative proposals.	• Anticipate and summarize possible objections or alternative ways to solve the problem. • Respond appropriately through rebuttal or concession.
Conclude.	• Sum up your argument and help reader return to the "big picture" of what's at stake. • Call readers to action. • End with something memorable.

3. Can any part of this argument be presented as a slogan or memorable catch-phrase? What key phrases could highlight the parts or the main points of this argument?

4. How can document design clarify the course of action and the direct demand on the audience this argument is proposing?

5. How can use of color enhance the overall impact of your advocacy argument? (Note: One-page advertisements are expensive to reproduce in color, but you might make effective use of color if your advocacy ad were to appear as a poster or Web page.)

Questioning and Critiquing a Proposal Argument

As we've suggested, proposal arguments need to overcome the innate conservatism of people, the difficulty of anticipating all the consequences of a proposal, and so forth. What questions, then, can we ask about proposal arguments to help us anticipate these problems?

Will a skeptic deny that my problem is really a problem? The first question to ask of your proposal is "What's so wrong with the status quo that change is necessary?" The second question is "Who loses if the status quo is changed?" Be certain not to overlook this second question. Most proposal makers can demonstrate that some sort of problem exists, but often it is a problem only for certain groups of people. Solving the problem will thus prove a benefit to some people but a cost to others. If audience members examine the problem from the perspective of the potential losers rather than the winners, they often can raise doubts about your proposal.

Will a skeptic doubt the effectiveness of my solution? Assuming that you've convinced your audience that a significant problem exists and is worth solving, you then have to convince readers that your solution will work. Skeptics are likely to raise at least two kinds of questions about your proposed solution. First, they may doubt that you have adequately identified the cause of the problem. Perhaps you have mistaken a symptom for a cause or confused two commonly associated but essentially unlinked phenomena for a cause-effect relationship. For example, will paying teachers higher salaries improve the quality of teaching or merely attract greedier rather than brighter people? Maybe more good teachers would be attracted and retained if they were given some other benefit (fewer students? fewer classes? more sabbaticals? more autonomy? more prestige?). Second, skeptics are likely to invoke the phenomenon of unintended consequences—solving one problem merely creates a sequence of new problems. ("Now that we've raised teachers' salaries, we don't have enough tax dollars for highway maintenance; not only that, now firefighters and police are also demanding higher salaries.") As you anticipate audience objections, look again at the potential negative consequences of your proposed solution.

Will a skeptic think my proposal costs too much? The most commonly asked question of any proposal is simply, "Do the benefits of enacting the proposal outweigh the costs?" As we saw earlier, you can't foresee all the consequences of any proposal. It's easy, before the fact, to underestimate the costs and exaggerate the benefits of a proposal. So, in asking how much your proposal will cost, we urge you to make an honest estimate. Will your audience discover costs you hadn't anticipated—extra financial costs or unexpected psychological or environmental or aesthetic costs? As much as you can, anticipate these objections.

Will a skeptic suggest counterproposals? Once you've convinced readers that a problem exists, they are likely to suggest alternative solutions different from yours. If readers acknowledge the seriousness of the problem, yet object to your proposal, they are faced with a dilemma: either they have to offer their own counterproposals or they have to argue that the problem is simply in the nature of things and hence unsolvable. So, given the likelihood that you'll be faced with a counterproposal, it only makes sense to anticipate it and to work out a refutation of it before you have it thrown at you. And who knows, you may end up liking the counterproposal better and changing your mind about what to propose! ■

Our reading, by student writer Juan Vazquez, is a researched public   **READING**
policy proposal written in response to the option 3 assignment on
page 260. Vazquez's argument is based on library and Internet research he conducted into the problem of fossil fuels and climate change. It is formatted as a
formal research paper using the documentation style of the Modern Language
Association (MLA). An explanation of this format is given in Appendix 2.

Juan Vazquez
Professor Bean
English 210
July 15, 2008

Why the United States Should Adopt Nuclear Power

Thousands of studies conducted by scientists to measure climate change over the last one hundred years have accumulated substantial evidence that global warming is occurring unequivocally. According to the NASA *Earth Observatory* web site, greenhouse gas emissions have caused the average surface temperature of the Earth to increase by 0.6 to 0.9 degrees Celsius between 1906 and 2006. If fossil fuel energy continues to be burned relentlessly, scientists are predicting that the average surface temperatures could rise between 2°C and 6°C by the end of the twenty-first century (Riebeek). A prevalent consensus among scientists is that humans are a major culprit in global warming by burning fossil fuels such as coal and petroleum, with coal-fired power plants being one of the major problems. Lately, discussion has focused on what governments in developed countries can do to tackle climate change.

One solution, advocated by scientist William Sweet writing for the magazine *Discover*, is that the United States should expand its long-ignored nuclear power industry. However, many people—especially environmentalists—are afraid of nuclear power and believe that we can solve global warming through other alternatives. Despite these fears and counter-arguments, I believe that Sweet is right about nuclear energy. The United States should as quickly as possible phase out coal-burning power plants and replace them with nuclear power and other green technologies.

Before we look at the advantages of nuclear power, it is important to see why many people are opposed to it. First, opponents argue that nuclear power plants aren't safe. They regularly cite the Three Mile Island accident in 1979 and the disastrous Chernobyl meltdown in 1986. A more exhaustive list of recent small scale but worrisome nuclear accidents is provided by an editorial from the *Los Angeles Times,* which describes how a July 2007 magnitude 6.8 earthquake in Japan "caused dozens of problems at the world's biggest nuclear plant, leading to releases of radioactive elements into the air and ocean and an indefinite shutdown" ("No to Nukes"). Opponents also argue that nuclear plants are attractive terrorist targets. A properly placed explosive could spew radioactive

Vazquez 2

material over wide swathes of densely populated areas. Nuclear power plants also provide opportunities for terrorists to steal plutonium for making their own nuclear weapons.

Second, while agreeing that nuclear power plants don't produce greenhouse gases, opponents remind us that radioactive waste cannot be stored safely and that radioactive waste remains hazardous for tens of thousands of years. The heavy walled concrete containers use to enclose nuclear waste will eventually develop cracks. If the planned disposal facility at Yucca Mountain, Nevada—where wastes would be stored in concrete and steel containers deep underground—ever becomes operational, it would ease the waste issue for the United States but would not eliminate it. The dangerous nuclear waste would still have to be trucked to Nevada, and even the Nevada site might not be completely impervious to earthquake damage or to the possibility that future generations would dig it up accidentally.

Finally, opponents claim that nuclear power plants are extremely expensive and the process of building them is extremely slow so that this method won't provide any short-term solutions for climate change. According to the "No to Nukes" editorial from the *Los Angeles Times*, the average nuclear plant is estimated to cost about $4 billion, making nuclear-generated energy about 25% to 75% more expensive than old-fashioned coal. At the same time, the regulatory process for building nuclear power plants is slow and unpredictable, making investors hesitant about supplying the capital needed. Opponents of nuclear energy argue that these high costs and long waiting period would make it impossible to launch a massive construction of nuclear power plants that would have an immediate impact on global warming.

So in the face of these risks, why should we support Sweet's proposal for expanding nuclear technology? One answer is that some of the fears about nuclear plants are overstated, fabricated, or politicized. It is true that in the past there have been accidents at nuclear power plants, but improvements in technology make such disasters in the future very unlikely. According to Sweet, changes in the design of nuclear reactors in the United States make them "virtually immune to the type of accident that occurred at Chernobyl in April 1986" (62). Furthermore, Sweet points out, the oft-cited Three Mile Island accident didn't injure a single person and led to a better regulatory system that makes new reactors much safer than old ones. According to Sweet, today's "coal fired power plants routinely kill tens of thousands of people in the United States each year by way of lung cancer, bronchitis, and other ailments; the U.S. nuclear economy kills virtually no one in a

5

normal year" (62). In addition, management of power plants has improved. As for the fear of terrorist threats and nuclear proliferation, these concerns have been blown out of proportion. As Sweet argues, if any terrorists are seeking to produce bombs, their access to plutonium will not depend on how many nuclear power plants the U.S. is building. Because nuclear power plants must be housed within concrete containment barriers to prevent damage from earthquakes, hurricanes, and floods, they are also resistant to terrorist attacks. A study carried out by the Electric Power Research Institute and reported in a major study of nuclear power by scientists from MIT showed that an airplane crashing into a U.S. nuclear power plant would not breech the containment barriers (*Future of Nuclear Power* 50). Moreover, nuclear scientists say that the safe containment of nuclear waste is not a technical problem but a political problem.

　　Although nuclear reactors are not risk free, they are much safer for people's health and for the environment than are coal-fired plants with their pollution-spewing greenhouse gases. According to the MIT study on nuclear power, since the first commercial nuclear reactor was built in the United States in 1957 (there are now currently 100 nuclear reactors in the United States), there has been only one accident that caused core damage (Three Mile Island). Using statistical analysis, the researchers estimate the current safety regulations and design specifications will limit core damage frequency to about 1 accident per 10,000 reactor years. They also believe that the technology exists to reduce the rate of serious accidents to 1 in 100,000 reactor-years (*Future of Nuclear Power* 48). The benefits of nuclear power for reducing global warming therefore outweigh the real but very low risks of using nuclear energy.

　　As to the problem of nuclear power's expense, it is true that nuclear plants are more expensive than coal, but it is important to understand that the high initial cost of building a nuclear power plant is being compared to the artificially low cost of coal power. If we were to tax coal-burning plants through a cap and trade system so that coal plants would have to pay for social and environmental costs of pollution and production of greenhouse gases, nuclear power would become more competitive. As Sweet argues, we need a tax or equivalent trading scheme that would increase the cost of coal-generated electricity to encourage a switch from cheap coal to more environmental friendly nuclear power plants.

　　Nuclear power plants are not the perfect or sole alternative to burning coal to generate energy, but they are certainly the most effective for combating global warming. Without nuclear power plants, we can't generate enough electricity to meet U.S. demands while also reducing carbon emissions. There are other alternatives such as wind

MLA

technology, but this is also more expensive than coal and not nearly as reliable as nuclear power. Wind turbines only generate energy about a third of the time, which would not be enough to meet peak demands, and the problem of building enough wind towers and creating a huge distribution system to transmit the power from remote windy regions to cities where the power is needed is overwhelming. Currently wind power generates less than 1% of the nation's electricity whereas nuclear power currently generates 20 percent (Sweet). According to Jesse Asubel, head of the Program for the Human Environment at Rockefeller University, "To reach the scale at which they would contribute importantly to meeting global energy demand, renewable sources of energy such as wind, water, and biomass cause serious environmental harm. Measuring renewables in watts per square meter, nuclear has astronomical advantages over its competitors."

To combat global warming we need to invest in strategies that could make a large difference fairly quickly. The common belief that we can slow global warming by switching to fluorescent light bulbs, taking the bus to work, and advocating for wind or solar energy is simply wrong. According to science writer Matt Jenkins, the climate problem is solvable. "But tackling it is going to be a lot harder than you've been led to believe" (39). Jenkins summarizes the work of Princeton researchers Stephen Pacala and Robert Socolow, who have identified a "package of greenhouse gas reduction measures" (44), each measure of which they call a "stabilization wedge." Each wedge would reduce carbon gas emissions by one gigaton. Pacala and Socolow have identified 15 possible stabilization wedges and have shown that adopting 7 of these wedges will reduce carbon emissions to the levels needed to halt global warming. One of Pacala and Socolow's wedges could be achieved by raising the fuel economy of 2 billion cars from 30 mpg to 60 mpg (Jenkins 44). Another wedge would come from building 50 times more wind turbines than currently exist in the world or 700 times more solar panels. In contrast, we could achieve a wedge simply by doubling the number of nuclear power plants in the world. Nuclear power is clearly not the only solution to climate change. In Pacala and Socolow's scheme, it is at most one-seventh of the solution, still forcing us to take drastic measures to conserve energy, stop the destruction of rain forests, develop clean-burning coal, and create highly fuel-efficient automobiles. But nuclear energy produces the quickest, surest, and most dramatic reduction of the world's carbon footprint. If we do not take advantage of its availability, we will need to get equivalent carbon-free power from other sources, which may not be possible and will certainly be more expensive. Therefore

10

expanded use of nuclear technology has to be part of the solution to stop global warming. We should also note that other countries are already way ahead of us in the use of nuclear technology. France gets almost 80% of its electricity from nuclear power and Sweden almost 50% ("World Statistics"). These countries have accepted the minimal risks of nuclear power in favor of a reduced carbon footprint and a safer environment.

In sum, we should support Sweet's proposal for adopting nuclear power plants as a major national policy. However, there are other questions that we need to pursue. Where are we going to get the other necessary wedges? Are we going to set gas mileage requirements of 60 mpg on the auto industry? Are we going to push research and development for ways to burn coal cleanly by sequestering carbon emissions in the ground? Are we going to stop destruction of the rain forests? Are we going to fill up our land with wind towers to get one more wedge? If all these questions make climate change seem unsolvable, it will be even more difficult if we cannot factor in nuclear technology as a major variable in the equation.

MLA

Works Cited

Ausubel, Jesse H. "Renewable and Nuclear Heresies." Canadian Nuclear Association. Ottowa, CA. 10 March 2005. Plenary Address. *Nuclear Green.* Web. 20 June 2008.

The Future of Nuclear Power: An Interdisciplinary MIT Study. Massachusetts Institute of Technology, 29 July 2003. Web. 20 June 2008.

Jenkins, Matt. "A Really Inconvenient Truth." *Miller McClune* April-May 2008: 38-49. Print.

"No to Nukes." Editorial. *Los Angeles Times.* Los Angeles Times, 23 July 2007. Web. 1 July 2008.

Riebeek, Holli. "Global Warming." *Earth Observatory.* NASA, 11 May 2007. Web. 18 June 2008.

Sweet, William. "Why Uranium Is the New Green." *Discover* Aug. 2007: 61-62. Print.

"World Statistics: Nuclear Energy around the World." *Resources and Stats.* Nuclear Energy Institute, 2008. Web. 19 June 2008.

MLA

Informal Fallacies

In this appendix, we look at ways of assessing the legitimacy of an argument within a real-world context of probabilities rather than within a mathematical world of certainty. Whereas formal logic is a kind of mathematics, the *informal fallacies* addressed in this appendix get embedded in everyday arguments, sometimes making fallacious reasoning seem deceptively persuasive, especially to unwary audiences. Fallacies of *pathos* rest on flaws in the way an argument appeals to the audience's emotions and values. Fallacies of *ethos* rest on flaws in the way the argument appeals to the character of opponents or of sources and witnesses within an argument. Fallacies of *logos* rest on flaws in the relationship among statements in an argument.

Fallacies of *Pathos*

Argument to the People (Appealing to Stirring Symbols) Arguments to the people appeal to the fundamental beliefs, biases, and prejudices of the audience in order to sway opinion through a feeling of solidarity among those of the group. Thus a "Support Our Troops" bumper sticker, often including the American flag, creates an initial feeling of solidarity among almost all citizens of good will. But the car owner may have the deeper intention of actually meaning "support our president" or "support the war in _____." The stirring symbol of the flag and the desire shared by most people to support our troops is used fallaciously to urge support of a particular political act. Arguments to the people often use visual rhetoric, as in the soaring eagle used in Wal-Mart corporate ads or images of happy families in marketing advertisements.

Appeal to Ignorance This fallacy persuades an audience to accept as true a claim that hasn't been proved false or vice versa. "Jones must have used steroids to get those bulging biceps because he can't prove that he hasn't used steroids." Appeals to ignorance are particularly common in the murky field of pseudo-science. "UFOs (ghosts, abominable snowmen) do exist because science hasn't proven that they don't exist." Sometimes, however, it is hard to draw a line between a fallacious appeal to ignorance and a legitimate appeal to precaution: "Genetically modified organisms must be dangerous to our health because science hasn't proven that they are safe."

Appeal to Popularity–Bandwagon   To board the bandwagon means (to use a more contemporary metaphor) to board the bus or train of what's popular. Appeals to popularity are fallacious because the popularity of something is irrelevant to its actual merits. "Living together before marriage is the right thing to do because most couples are now doing it." Bandwagon appeals are common in advertising where the claim that a product is popular substitutes for evidence of the product's excellence. There are times, however, where popularity may indeed be relevant: "Global warming is probably caused by human activity because a preponderance of scientists now hold this position." (Here we assume scientists haven't simply climbed on a bandwagon themselves, but have formed their opinions based on research data and well vetted, peer-reviewed papers.)

Appeal to Pity   Here the arguer appeals to the audience's sympathetic feelings in order to support a claim that should be decided on more relevant or objective grounds. "Honorable judge, I should not be fined $200 for speeding because I was distraught from hearing news of my brother's illness and was rushing to see him in the hospital." Here the argument is fallacious because the arguer's reason, while evoking sympathy, is not a relevant justification for speeding (as it might have been, for instance, if the arguer had been rushing an injured person to the emergency room).

Red Herring   This fallacy's funny name derives from the practice of using a red herring (a highly odiferous fish) to throw dogs off a scent that they are supposed to be tracking. It refers to the practice of throwing an audience off track by raising an unrelated or irrelevant point. "Debating a gas tax increase is valuable, but I really think there should be an extra tax on SUVs." Here the arguer, apparently uncomfortable with the gas tax issue, diverts the conversation to the emotional issue of SUVs.

Fallacies of *Ethos*

Appeal to False Authority   Arguers appeal to false authority when they use famous persons (often movie stars or celebrities) to testify on issues about which these persons have no special competence. "Joe Quarterback says Gooey Oil keeps his old tractor running sharp; therefore, Gooey Oil is a good oil." Real evidence about the quality of Gooey Oil would include technical data about the product rather than testimony from a hired celebrity.

Ad Hominem   Literally, *ad hominem* means "to the person." An *ad hominem* argument is directed at the character of an opponent rather than at the quality of the reasoning. Ideally, arguments are supposed to be *ad rem* ("to the thing"), that is, addressed to the specifics of the case itself. Thus an *ad rem* critique of a politician would focus on her voting record, the consistency and cogency of her public statements, her responsiveness to constituents, and so forth. An *ad hominem* argument would shift attention from her record to irrelevant features of her personality, life circumstances, or the company she keeps. "Senator Sweetwater's views on the gas tax should be discounted because her campaign was supported by the huge oil companies" or "Senator Sweetwater supports tax cuts for the wealthy because she is very wealthy herself and stands to gain." But not all *ad hominem* arguments are *ad hominem* fallacies. Lawyers, for example, when questioning expert witnesses who give damaging testimony, will often make an issue of their honesty, credibility, or personal investment in an outcome.

Poisoning the Well   This fallacy is closely related to *ad hominem*. Arguers poison the well when they discredit an opponent or an opposing view in advance. "Before I yield the floor to the next speaker, I must remind you that persons who oppose my plan do not have the best interests of working people in their hearts."

Straw Man   The straw man fallacy occurs when you oversimplify an opponent's argument to make it easier to refute or ridicule. Rather than summarizing an opposing view fairly and completely, you basically make up the argument you wish your opponent had made because it is so much easier to knock over, like knocking over a straw man or scarecrow in a corn field.

Fallacies of *Logos*

Hasty Generalization   This fallacy occurs when someone makes a broad generalization on the basis of too little evidence. Generally, the evidence needed to support a generalization persuasively must meet the STAR criteria (sufficiency, typicality, accuracy, and relevance) discussed in Chapter 5 (pp. 69–70). But what constitutes a sufficient amount of evidence? The generally accepted standards of sufficiency in any given field are difficult to determine. The Food and Drug Administration (FDA), for example, generally proceeds cautiously before certifying a drug as "safe." However, if people are harmed by the side effects of an FDA-approved drug, critics often accuse the FDA of having made a hasty generalization. At the same time, patients eager to have access to a new drug and manufacturers eager to sell a new product may lobby the FDA to quit "dragging its feet" and get the drug to market. Hence, the point at which a hasty generalization passes over into the realm of a prudent generalization is nearly always uncertain and contested.

Part for the Whole   Sometimes called by its Latin name *pars pro toto*, this fallacy is closely related to hasty generalization. In this fallacy, arguers pick out a part of the whole or a sample of the whole (often not a typical or representative part or sample) and then claim what is true of the part is true for the whole. If, say, individuals wanted to get rid of the National Endowment for the Arts (NEA), they might focus on several controversial programs funded by the NEA and use them as justification for wiping out all NEA programs. The flip side of this fallacy occurs when an arguer picks only the best examples to make a case and omits other examples that might weaken the case.

Post Hoc, Ergo Propter Hoc   The Latin name of this fallacy means "after this, therefore because of this." The fallacy occurs when a sequential relationship is mistaken for a causal relationship. (See Chapter 12, p. 201, where we discuss this fallacy in more depth.) For example, you may be guilty of this fallacy if you say "Cramming for a test really helps because last week I crammed for my psychology test and I got an A." When two events occur frequently in conjunction with each other, we've got a good case for a causal relationship. But until we can show how one causes the other and until we have ruled out other causes, we cannot be certain that a causal relationship is occurring. For example, the A on your psych test may have been the result of an easy exam. It is often difficult to tell when a *post hoc* fallacy occurs. When the New York police department changed its policing tactics in the early 1990s, the crime rate plummeted. Many experts attributed the declining crime rate to the new policing tactics, but some critics proposed other explanations (see p. 193).

Begging the Question—Circular Reasoning   Arguers beg the question when they provide a reason that simply restates the claim in different words. Here is an example: "Abortion is murder because it is the intentional taking of the life of a human being." Because "murder" is defined as "the intentional taking of the life of a human being," the argument is circular. It is tantamount to saying "Abortion is murder because it is murder."

False Dilemma—Either/Or   This fallacy occurs when an arguer oversimplifies a complex issue so that only two choices appear possible. Often one of the choices is made to seem unacceptable, so the only remaining option is the other choice. "It's my way or the highway" is a typical example of a false dilemma. Here is a more subtle one: "Either we allow embryonic stem cell research, or we condemn persons with diabetes, Parkinson's disease, or spinal injuries to a life without a cure." Clearly there may be other options here including other approaches to curing these diseases.

Slippery Slope   The slippery slope fallacy is based on the fear that once we put a foot on a slippery slope heading in the wrong direction we're doomed to slide right out of sight. The controlling metaphor is of a slick mountainside without places to hold on rather than of a staircase with numerous stopping places. Here is an example of a slippery slope: "Once we allow medical use of marijuana, we'll eventually legalize it for everyone, after which we're on a slippery slope toward social acceptance of cocaine and heroin."

False Analogy   In Chapter 13 on resemblance arguments, we explained that no analogy is perfect. Any two things being compared are similar in some ways and different in other ways. Whether an analogy is persuasive or false often depends on the audience's initial degree of skepticism. For example, persons opposed to gun control may find the following argument persuasive: "Banning guns on the basis that guns accidentally kill people is like banning cars on the basis that cars accidentally kill people." In contrast, supporters of gun control are likely to call this argument a false analogy on the basis of dissimilarities between cars and guns. (For example, they might say that banning cars would be far more disruptive on our society than would be banning guns.) Just when a persuasive analogy turns into a false analogy is difficult to say.

Non Sequitur   The name of this fallacy means "it does not follow." *Non sequitur* is a catchall term for any claim that doesn't follow from its premises or is supported by irrelevant premises. Sometimes the arguer seems to make an inexplicably illogical leap: "Genetically modified foods should be outlawed because they are not natural." (Should anything that is not natural be outlawed? In what way are they not natural?) At other times, there may be a gap in the chain of reasons: "Violent video games have some social value because the Army uses them for recruiting." (There may be an important idea emerging here, but too many logical steps are missing.) At still other times an arguer might support a claim with irrelevant reasons. "I should not receive a C in this course because I currently have a 3.8 GPA."

Loaded Label or Definition   Sometimes arguers will try to influence their audience's view of something by creating a loaded label or definition. For example, people who oppose the "estate tax" (which calls to mind rich people with estates) have relabeled it the "death tax" in order to give it a negative connotation without any markers of class or wealth. Or to take another example, proponents of organic foods could create definitions like the following: "Organic foods are safe and healthy foods grown without any pesticides, herbicides, or other unhealthy additives." "Safe" and "healthy" are evaluative terms used fallaciously in what purports to be a definition. The intended implication is that non-organic foods are not safe and healthy.

APPENDIX

2

A Concise Guide to Finding, Evaluating, and Documenting Sources

When you research material for your arguments, you must be able to find materials from licensed databases and the World Wide Web as well as from a library's print collection. In addition, you must be able to evaluate your sources, use them effectively in your own arguments (avoiding plagiarism), and cite and document them accurately so that readers can retrace your steps. This appendix provides brief instruction for finding, evaluating, and using sources and for citing and documenting them using both the MLA (Modern Language Association) and APA (American Psychological Association) systems.

Finding Print Articles: Searching a Licensed Database

For many research projects, useful sources are print articles from your library's periodical collection, including newspapers, scholarly journals, and magazines. Some of these articles are available free on the World Wide Web, but most of them are not. Rather, they may be located physically in your library's periodical collection or located electronically in vast databases leased by your library.

What Is a Licensed Database?

Electronic databases of periodical sources, called "licensed databases" (our preferred term), "general databases," or "subscription services," are produced by for-profit companies that index articles in thousands of periodicals and construct engines that can search the database by author, title, subject, key word, date, genre, and other variables. In most cases, the database contains an abstract of each article, and in many cases it contains the complete text of the article that you can download and print. Because access to these databases is restricted to fee-paying customers, they can't be searched through Web engines like Google or Yahoo! Most university libraries allow students to access these databases from a remote computer by using a pass code. You can therefore use the Internet to connect your computer to licensed databases as well as to the World Wide Web (see Figure A2.1).

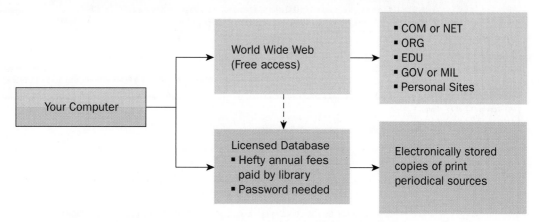

FIGURE A2.1 Licensed database versus free-access portions of Internet

An example of a licensed database leased by many college libraries is *EBSCOhost*, which includes citations and abstracts from most disciplines as well as the full text of many articles from over three thousand journals; its *Academic Search Elite* function covers material published as long ago as the early 1980s. Other important databases include *UMI ProQuest Direct, InfoTrac,* and *LexisNexis Academic Universe.* Generally, one of these databases will be the "default method" chosen by your library for most article searches. Your reference librarian will be able to direct you to the most useful licensed database for your purpose.

Illustration of a Database Search

As an illustration of a database search, we'll draw on the experience of student writer Megan Matthews as she researched the effect on sea mammals, particularly whales, of the Navy's experimental submarine-detecting sonar systems. Using the database EBSCOhost, Megan entered the key words *Navy sonar* AND *whales,* which revealed the five articles shown in Figure A2.2. As the Results list shows, this EBSCO database carries the full text of articles 1 and 3; for articles 2 and 4, Megan will have to check the library's catalog to locate the print periodical in the stacks. To get more information about article 3, "Sonic Blast," Megan clicked on its title, which revealed the screen shown in Figure A2.3. This screen gives full citation information and provides a brief abstract of the article along with its length, 2/3 page. If she were interested in reading it, Megan could click on the Full Text link to see the whole article.

After you've identified articles you'd like to read, locate physically all those available in your library's periodical collection. (This way you won't lose important contextual cues for evaluating them.) For those unavailable in your library, print, download, or e-mail them from the database or order them through interlibrary loan.

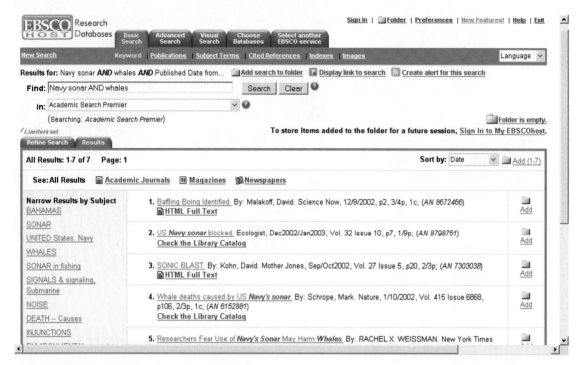

FIGURE A2.2 Results list from a search using EBSCOhost

FIGURE A2.3 Sample display for an article on EBSCOhost

Finding Cyberspace Sources: Searching the World Wide Web

To understand the logic of Web search engines, you need to keep in mind that the Internet has restricted sections open only to those with special access rights as well as a "free access" section. (See again Figure A2.1.) Web engines such as Google or Yahoo! search only the free access portion of the Internet. When you type key words into a Web search engine, it searches for matches in material posted on the World Wide Web by all the users of the world's networked computers—government agencies, corporations, advocacy groups, information services, individuals with their own Web sites, and hosts of others.

The following example will quickly show you the difference between a licensed database search and a Web search. When Megan entered the key words *Navy sonar* AND *whales* into EBSCOhost, she received five "hits"—the titles of five articles on this subject appearing in print periodicals. In contrast, when she entered the same key words into the Web search engine Yahoo!, she received 709,000 hits; when she tried Google, she got even more. The Web search engines are picking up, in addition to articles that someone may have posted on the Web, all references to Navy sonar and whales that appear in advocacy Web sites, government publications, newspapers, blogs, chat rooms, students papers posted on the Web, and so forth.

Although the hits from a Web search frequently include useless, shoddy, trivial, or irrelevant material, the Web's resources for researchers are breathtaking. At your fingertips you have access to government documents and statistics, legislative and corporate white papers, court cases, persuasive appeals of advocacy groups, consumer information—the list seems endless.

The World Wide Web can be searched by a variety of engines that collect and categorize individual Web files and search them for key words. Most of these engines will find not only text files but also graphic, audio, and video files. Some engines look through the titles of files, whereas others scan the entire text of documents. Different engines search the Web in different ways, so it is important that you try a variety of search engines when you look for information. Again, if you are in doubt, your reference librarians can help you choose the most productive search engine for your needs.

Evaluating Sources

When you read sources for your research project—whether published in print or in cyberspace—you need to evaluate them as you proceed. Clues needed for evaluating a source often come indirectly. For example, when you look at an article in a magazine (rather than downloaded from a computer), the features of the magazine itself—its format, its table of contents, its editorial information, its advertisements, its use of photographs, the length and range and style of its articles—can help you infer valuable information about the article's author, intended audience, and political bias. In contrast, when you print materials from a licensed database or from the Web, these contextual clues are lost: a mindless rant from Joe's Web page can have the same appearance as a downloaded article from a serious journal.

When you evaluate a source, begin by asking yourself questions about an author's angle of vision, degree of advocacy, reliability, and credibility.

Angle of Vision

By "angle of vision," we mean the way that a piece of writing gets shaped by the underlying values, assumptions, and beliefs of the author so that the text reflects a certain perspective, worldview, or belief system. The angle of vision is revealed by internal factors such as the author's word choice (especially note connotations of words), selection and omission of details, overt statements, figurative language, and grammatical emphasis and by external factors such as the politics of the author, the genre of the source, the politics of the publisher, and so forth. When reading a source, see if you can detect underlying assumptions or beliefs that suggest a writer's values or political views.

You can also get useful clues about a writer's angle of vision by looking at external data. What are the writer's credentials? Is the writer affiliated with an advocacy group or known for a certain ideology? (If you know nothing about an author who seems important to your research, try keying the author's name into a Web search engine. You might discover useful information about the author's other publications or about the author's reputation in various circles.) Also pay attention to publishing data. Where was this source originally published? What is the reputation and editorial slant of the publication in which the source appears? For example, editorial slants of magazines can range from very liberal to very conservative. Likewise, publications affiliated with advocacy organizations (the Sierra Club, the National Rifle Association) will have a clear editorial bias.

Degree of Advocacy

By "degree of advocacy" we mean the extent to which an author unabashedly takes a persuasive stance on a contested position as opposed to adopting a more neutral, objective, or exploratory stance. When a writer strongly advocates a position, you need to weigh carefully the writer's selection of evidence, interpretation of data, and fairness to opposing views. Although objectivity is itself an "angle of vision" and no one can be completely neutral, it is always useful to seek out authors who offer a balanced assessment of the evidence. Evidence from a more detached and neutral writer may be more trusted by your readers than the arguments of a committed advocate. For example, if you want to persuade corporate executives of the dangers of global warming, evidence from scholarly journals may be more persuasive than evidence from an environmentalist Web site or from a freelance writer in a leftist popular magazine like *Mother Jones*.

Reliability

"Reliability" refers to the accuracy of factual data in a source as determined by external validation. If you check a writer's "facts" against other sources, are they correct? Does the writer distort facts, take them out of context, or otherwise use them unreasonably? In some controversies, key data are highly disputed—for example, the number of homeless persons in the United States, the frequency of date rape, or the risk factors for many diseases. A reliable writer will acknowledge these controversies and not treat disputed data as fact. Furthermore, if you check the sources used by a reliable writer, they will reveal accurate and careful research—respected primary sources rather than hearsay or secondhand reports.

Credibility

"Credibility" is similar to "reliability" except that it is based on internal rather than external factors. It refers to the reader's trust in the writer's honesty, goodwill, and trustworthiness and is derived from the writer's tone, reasonableness, fairness in summarizing opposing views, and respect for different perspectives. Audiences differ in how much credibility they will grant to certain authors. Nevertheless, a writer can achieve a reputation for credibility, even among bitter political opponents, by applying to issues a sense of moral courage, integrity, and consistency of principle.

Evaluating Web Sites

If some of your sources come from Web sites, you also need to become skilled in evaluating the Web site itself. The Web is a great vehicle for democracy, giving voice to the otherwise voiceless. Anyone with a cause and a rudimentary knowledge of Web page design can create a Web site. Before the invention of the Web, persons with a message would have to stand on street corners passing out fliers or invest in newsletters or advocacy advertisements. The Web, in contrast, is cheap. The result is a rhetorical medium that differs in significant ways from print.

Analyzing the Purpose of a Site and Your Own Research Purpose

When you do research on the Web, your first question should be, Who placed this piece on the Web and why? You can begin answering this question by analyzing the site's home page, where you often will find navigational buttons linking to "Mission," "About us," or other identifying information about the site's sponsors. You can also get hints about the site's purpose by asking, What kind of Web site is it? As we explained earlier, different kinds of Web sites have different purposes, often revealed by the domain identifier following the server name (.com, .net, .org, .gov, .mil). As you evaluate the Web site, also consider your own purpose for using it. For instance, are you trying to get an initial understanding of various points of view on an issue, or are you looking for reliable information? An advocacy site may be an excellent place for researching a point of view but a doubtful source of data and evidence for your own argument.

Sorting Sites by Domain Type

One powerful research strategy for evaluating Web sites is to use the "advanced search" feature of a search engine to sort sites by domain type. As an example, consider again Megan's research dilemma when she plugged *Navy sonar* AND *whales* into Yahoo! and received 709,000 hits. How could she begin to navigate through such a huge number? Using Yahoo!'s "advanced search" feature, Megan sorted through her hits by domain, selecting one type of domain at a time:

- The **.com sites** were primarily the sites of newspapers, news services, and whale watching tourist sites. These sites tended to repeat the same news stories and offer superficial coverage.
- The **.org sites** were primarily the sites of environmental advocacy groups, such as the National Resources Defense Council, the Sierra Club, the League for Coastal Protection, the Cetacean Society International—all dedicated to protecting marine life. These advocacy sites were strongly pro-whale; in their arguments against Navy sonar, they either discounted or ignored issues of national security.
- The **.edu sites** of colleges and universities were primarily references to course descriptions and syllabi that included this controversy as a source of study. Megan didn't find these helpful.
- The **.gov sites** revealed documents on whales and sonar submitted to congressional hearings; they also revealed key government agencies involved in the sonar dispute: the National Marine Fisheries Service and the National Oceanic and Atmospheric Administration.
- The **.mil sites** gave access to white papers and other documents provided by the Navy to justify its use of low-frequency sonar.

Criteria for Evaluating a Web Site

Given this overview of the territory, Megan still had to decide which specific sites to use for her research. We offer the following criteria developed by scholars and librarians as points to consider when you are using Web sites.

1. Authority

- Is the author or sponsor of the Web site clearly identified?
- Does the site identify the occupation, position, education, experience, and credentials of the site's authors?
- Does the introductory material reveal the author's or sponsor's motivation for publishing this information on the Web?
- Does the site provide contact information for the author or sponsor such as an e-mail or organization address?

2. Objectivity or Clear Disclosure of Advocacy

- Is the site's purpose (to inform, explain, or persuade) clear?
- Is the site explicit about declaring its author's or sponsor's point of view?
- Does the site indicate whether authors are affiliated with a specific organization, institution, or association?
- Does the site indicate whether it is directed toward a specific audience?

3. Coverage

- Are the topics covered by the site clear?
- Does the site exhibit suitable depth and comprehensiveness for its purpose?
- Is sufficient evidence provided to support the ideas and opinions presented?

4. Accuracy

- Are the sources of information stated? Can you tell whether this information is original or taken from someplace else?
- Does the information appear to be accurate? Can you verify this information by comparing this source with other sources in the field?

5. Currency

- Are dates included in the Web site?
- Do the dates apply to the material itself or to its placement on the Web? Is the site regularly revised and updated?
- Is the information current, or at least still relevant, for the site's purpose?

To illustrate how these criteria can help you evaluate a Web site, consider how they could be applied to "Environmental Groups Sue to Stop Global Deployment of Navy Low Frequency Sonar System," a press release Megan found on the site of the National Resources Defense Council (see Figure A2.4). Is the article trustworthy and reliable, or is it from a fringe environmental group likely to suppress or distort evidence? Using the criteria for evaluating Web sites, Megan was able to identify the strengths and weaknesses of this site in light of her research purpose.

1. *Authority.* The sponsor of the site is clearly the NRDC. Because the NRDC presents the material as a press release, Megan assumed that their motivation is to provide information for the news media that favors their position on the sonar issue. The site does provide contact information so that journalists and others can get in touch with NRDC staff.
2. *Objectivity or clear disclosure of advocacy.* What type of site is NRDC.org? The site is clearly that of an advocacy group, as indicated by the logo and motto in the left-hand panel: "The Earth's Best Defense." Megan located the home page, clicked on "About Us," and discovered that the National Resources

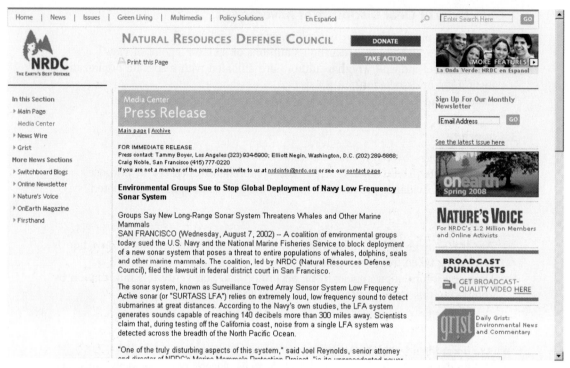

FIGURE A2.4 First screen from article on NRDC Web site

Defense Council has been around for almost forty years. The "About Us" section states:

NRDC is the nation's most effective environmental action group, combining the grassroots power of 1.2 million members and online activists with the courtroom clout and expertise of more than 350 lawyers, scientists and other professionals.

The site does very well on the criterion "clear disclosure of advocacy."

3. *Coverage.* The site is unusually broad and deep. It covers hundreds of different environmental issues and has multimedia features, blogs, games for children, and in-depth technical articles written for specialists.

4. *Accuracy.* Megan also determined that the site was accurate. Technical articles had bibliographies, and references to factual data had notes about sources. She discovered that information on this site corroborated well with references to the same data from other sites.

5. *Currency.* The site was current. News items within the site had clear indications of dates. This is an active, ongoing site.

Megan concluded that the site was an excellent source for both arguments and data from a pro-environmental perspective. She could use it to understand potential dangers of Navy sonar to whales and other marine life. However, the site was not helpful for understanding the national security and Navy reasons for needing low-frequency sonar.

Using Sources and Avoiding Plagiarism

Once you have evaluated a source and determined that it is worth using in your own argument, you need to learn how to use the source, how to avoid plagiarism, and how to cite and document it properly. We now turn to these concerns.

Using Sources for Your Own Purposes

To illustrate the purposeful use of sources, we will use the following short argument from the Web site of the American Council on Science and Health—a conservative organization of doctors and scientists devoted to providing scientific information on health issues and to exposing health fads and myths. Please read the argument carefully in preparation for the discussions that follow.

Is Vegetarianism Healthier Than Nonvegetarianism?

Many people become vegetarians because they believe, in error, that vegetarianism is uniquely conducive to good health. The findings of several large epidemiologic studies indeed suggest that the death and chronic-disease rates of vegetarians—primarily vegetarians who consume dairy products or both dairy products and eggs—are lower than those of meat eaters....

The health of vegetarians may be better than that of nonvegetarians partly because of nondietary factors: Many vegetarians are health-conscious. They exercise regularly, maintain a desirable body weight, and abstain from smoking. Although most epidemiologists have attempted to take such factors into account in their analyses, it is possible that they did not adequately control their studies for nondietary effects.

People who are vegetarians by choice may differ from the general population in other ways relevant to health. For example, in Western countries most vegetarians are more affluent than nonvegetarians and thus have better living conditions and more access to medical care.

An authoritative review of vegetarianism and chronic diseases classified the evidence for various alleged health benefits of vegetarianism:

- The evidence is "strong" that vegetarians have (a) a lower risk of becoming alcoholic, constipated, or obese and (b) a lower risk of developing lung cancer.
- The evidence is "good" that vegetarians have a lower risk of developing adult-onset diabetes mellitus, coronary artery disease, hypertension, and gallstones.
- The evidence is "fair to poor" that vegetarianism decreases risk of breast cancer, colon cancer, diverticular disease, kidney-stone formation, osteoporosis, and tooth decay.

For some of the diseases mentioned above, the practice of vegetarianism itself probably is the main protective factor. For example, the low incidence of constipation among vegetarians is almost certainly due to their high intakes of fiber-rich foods. For other conditions, nondietary factors may be more important than diet. For example, the low incidence of lung cancer among vegetarians is attributable primarily to their extremely low rate of cigarette smoking. Diet is but one of many risk factors for most chronic diseases.

What we want to show you is that the way you use this article depends on your own research question and purpose. Sometimes you may decide to summarize a source completely—particularly if the source represents an opposing or alternative view that you intend to address. (See Chapter 2, pp. 27–29.) At other times you may choose to use only parts of a source. To illustrate how your rhetorical purpose governs your use of a source, we show you three different hypothetical examples:

■ *Writer 1, arguing for an alternative treatment for alcoholism:* On some occasions, you will draw details from a source for use in a different context.

Another approach to fighting alcoholism is through naturopathy, holistic medicine, and vegetarianism. Vegetarians generally have better health than the rest of the population and particularly have, according to the American Council on Science and Health, "a lower risk of becoming alcoholic."[1] This lower risk has been borne out by other studies showing that the benefits of the holistic health movement are particularly strong for persons with addictive tendencies.... [goes on to other arguments and sources]

■ *Writer 2, arguing for the value of vegetarianism:* Sometimes you can use part of a source for direct support of your own claim. In this case, a summary of relevant parts of the argument can be used as evidence.

Not only will a vegetarian diet help stop cruelty to animals, but it is also good for your health. According to the American Council on Science and Health, vegetarians have longer life expectancy than nonvegetarians and suffer from fewer chronic diseases. The Council summarizes evidence from the scientific literature strongly showing that vegetarians have reduced risk of lung cancer, obesity, constipation, and alcoholism. They also cite good evidence that they have a reduced risk of adult-onset diabetes, high blood pressure, gallstones, or hardening of the arteries. Although the evidence isn't nearly as strong, vegetarianism may also lower the risk of certain cancers, kidney stones, loss of bone density, and tooth decay.

■ *Writer 3, arguing for a skeptical view of vegetarianism:* Here Writer 3 uses portions of the article consciously excluded by Writer 2.

The link between vegetarianism and death rates is a classic instance of correlation rather than causation. While it is true that vegetarians have a longer life expectancy than nonvegetarians and suffer from fewer chronic diseases, the American Council on Science and

---

[1]If the writer had found this quotation in a print source such as a book or magazine, the page number would be placed in parentheses immediately after the quotation (9). Because the writer found this passage in a Web site, no page citation is possible. If this were an actual essay, rather than a hypothetical illustration, readers would find full information about the source in the bibliography at the end. In this case, the author would be listed as "American Council on Science and Health," indicated in the attributive tag preceding the quotation.

Health has shown that the causes can mostly be explained by factors other than diet. As the Council suggests, vegetarians are apt to be more health conscious than nonvegetarians and thus get more exercise, stay slender, and avoid smoking. The Council points out that vegetarians also tend to be wealthier than nonvegetarians and see their doctors more regularly. In short, they live longer because they take better care of themselves, not because they avoid meat.

Avoiding Plagiarism

Plagiarism, a form of academic cheating, is always a serious academic offense. You can plagiarize in one of two ways: (1) By borrowing another person's ideas without indicating the borrowing with attributive tags in the text and a proper citation or (2) by borrowing another person's language without putting the borrowed language in quotation marks or using a block indentation. The first kind of plagiarism usually is outright cheating; the writer usually knows he is stealing material and tries to disguise it.

The second kind of plagiarism, which often begins in a hazy never-never land between paraphrasing and copying, is much more common than the first, perhaps because inexperienced writers don't understand that you must indicate the borrowing of language through quotation marks just as you must acknowledge the borrowing of ideas through citation. It is not enough to change the order of phrases in a sentence or to replace a few words with synonyms. Thus, in our classes, we would fail a paper that included the following passage.

Writer 4: Plagiarism

The link between vegetarianism and death rates is a classic instance of correlation rather than causation. While it is true that vegetarians have a longer life expectancy than nonvegetarians and suffer from fewer chronic diseases, the American Council on Science and Health has shown that the health of vegetarians may be better than that of nonvegetarians partly because of nondietary factors. Many vegetarians are very conscious of their health. They exercise regularly, keep a desirable body weight, and abstain from smoking. The Council points out that in Western countries most vegetarians are more affluent than nonvegetarians and thus have better living conditions and more access to medical care. In short, they live longer because they take better care of themselves, not because they avoid meat.

The best way to avoid plagiarism is to be especially careful at the note-taking stage. If you copy from your source, copy exactly, word for word, and put quotation marks around the copied material. If you paraphrase or summarize material, change the grammatical structure and wording so that you don't follow the writer's original language.

■ ■ ■ **FOR CLASS DISCUSSION**   **What Is Plagiarism?**

Do you think it was fair to flunk Writer 4's essay? He claimed he wasn't cheating because he used attributive tags to indicate his source throughout this passage, and he listed the American Council on Science and Health article accurately in his "Works

Cited" list (bibliography) at the end of his paper. Before answering, compare Writer 4's passage with the original article on page 285; also compare the passage with Writer 3's passage on page 286. What justification could an instructor use for giving a high grade to Writer 3 and a failing grade to Writer 4?   ■ ■ ■

Citing Sources in Your Text in MLA Style

When academic writers cite sources, they use the conventions appropriate to their discipline. In this section, we will explain briefly the MLA style used in the humanities. (We explain the APA system used in the social sciences later in this appendix.) Our discussion of MLA style and our citation examples are based on the new seventh edition of the *MLA Handbook for Writers of Research Papers,* published in 2009, and used by undergraduates. The major changes in style in this edition of the handbook include

- italicizing, rather than underlining, all titles of longer works;
- citing both volume and issue numbers in all journal entries;
- adding the medium of publication (Print, Web, Audio, CD, Film, etc.) to every works-cited entry; and
- a simplified style for all online citations

Visit the MLA Web site for further information about style changes (http://www.mla.org).

In the MLA system of in-text citation, you place the author's last name and the page number of the cited source in parentheses, usually at the end of the material you wish to cite. (If the author's name is mentioned in a preceding attributive tag, such as "according to Karnow" or "Karnow says," only the page number is placed in parentheses. In the following examples, note that the citation precedes the period. If you are citing a quotation, the parenthetical citation follows the quotation mark but precedes the final period.

> The Spanish tried to reduce the status of Filipina women who had been able to do business, get divorced, and sometimes become village chiefs (Karnow 41).

> According to Karnow, the Spanish tried to reduce the status of Filipina women who had been able to do business, get divorced, and sometimes become village chiefs (41).

> "And, to this day," Karnow continues, "women play a decisive role in Filipino families" (41).

A reader who wishes to look up the source will find the bibliographic information in the Works Cited section by looking for the entry under "Karnow." If more than one work by Karnow was used in the paper, the writer would also include an abbreviated title of the book or article following Karnow's name in the in-text citation.

> (Karnow, *In Our Image* 41)

When citing sources and page numbers, you should know about two special cases:

Citing from an Indirect Source   Occasionally you may wish to use a quotation that you have seen cited in one of your sources. You read Jones, who has a nice quotation from Smith, and you want to use Smith's quotation. To do so, quote Smith, but then cite Jones in your text preceded by the terms "qtd in." List only Jones in your "Works Cited."

> According to the ex-mayor of Gotham City, Rupert Smith, "the rate of crime was at an all-time low" during his term of office (qtd. in Jones 25).

Citing a Work without Page Numbers   If the work you are citing in your paper has no page numbers but does have numbered paragraphs, use *par.* or *pars.* and give the number of the paragraph(s): (Helvarg, par. 10). If the source has neither page nor paragraph numbers, as is typical of many Web sources in HTML format, do not give any numbers in the in-text citation but cite the source in its entirety. (Do not use the page numbers from an HTML printout because they will not be consistent from printer to printer.)

Documenting Sources in a "Works Cited" List (MLA)

MLA Format for the "Works Cited" List

In the MLA system, you place a complete bibliography, titled "Works Cited," at the end of the paper. The list includes all the sources that you mention in your paper. However, it does not include works you read but did not use. Entries in the Works Cited follow these general guidelines:

- Entries are arranged alphabetically by author, or by title if there is no author.
- Entries must include the publication medium of the source you consulted, for example: *Print, Web, DVD, Performance, Oil on canvas,* and so on.
- If there is more than one entry by the same author, the second and subsequent entries begin with three hyphens followed by a period and the title.

> Smith, Roberta. *Body Image in Non-Western Cultures.* London: Bonanza, 1999. Print.
> ---. *Body Image in Western Cultures, 1750-Present.* London: Bonanza, 1995. Print.
> ---. "Eating Disorders Reconsidered." *Journal of Appetite Studies* 45.3 (1999): 295–300. Print.

For an example of how to format a "Works Cited" page in MLA style, see the last page of Juan Vazquez's researched argument (p. 270). The remaining pages in this section show examples of MLA "Works Cited" entries for different kinds of sources.

MLA Quick Reference Guide for the Most Common Citations

Table A2.1 provides MLA models for the most common kinds of citations. This table will help you distinguish the forest from the trees when you try to cite sources. All the major categories of sources are displayed in this table.

TABLE A2.1 Quick Reference Guide for MLA Citations

Kind of Source	Basic Citation Model
Print Sources When You Have Used the Original Print Version	
Article in scholarly journal	Pollay, Richard W., Jung S. Lee, and David Carter-Whitney. "Separate, but Not Equal: Racial Segmentation in Cigarette Advertising." *Journal of Advertising* 21.1 (1992): 45–57. Print.
Article in magazine or newspaper	Beam, Alex. "The Mad Poets Society." *Atlantic Monthly* July–Aug. 2001: 96–103. Print. Lemonick, Michael D. "Teens Before Their Time." *Time* 30 Oct. 2000: 66–74. Print. Liptak, Adam. "In Abortion Rulings, Idea of Marriage is Pivotal." *New York Times* 2 Nov. 2005: A1. Print.
Book	Tannen, Deborah. *The Argument Culture: Moving From Debate to Dialogue.* New York: Random, 1998. Print.
Article in anthology with an editor	Shamoon, Linda. "International E-mail Debate." *Electronic Communication Across the Curriculum*. Ed. Donna Reiss, Dickie Self, and Art Young. Urbana: NCTE, 1998. 151–61. Print.
Print Sources That You Have Downloaded from a Database	
Article downloaded from database	Beckham II, Jack M. "Placing *Touch of Evil, The Border,* and *Traffic* in the American Imagination." *Journal of Popular Film & Television* 33.3 (2005): 130–41. *Academic Search Premier*. Web. 16 July 2008.*
Other Internet and Web Sources	
Home page (use for citing an entire Web site)	*MyNRA*. National Rifle Association, 2005. Web. 3 Aug. 2007.
Document within a Web site	Marks, John. "Overview: Letter from the President." *Search for Common Ground*. Search for Common Ground, 25 June 2004. Web. 18 July 2008.°
Article from scholarly Web journal	Welch, John R., and Ramon Riley. "Reclaiming Land and Spirit in the Western Apache Homeland." *American Indian Quarterly* 25.4 (2001): n. pag. Web. 19 Dec. 2005.†
News article downloaded from Web	Bounds, Amy. "Thinking Like Scientists." *Daily Camera* [Boulder]. Scripps Interactive Newspapers Group, 26 June 2007. Web. 27 June 2007.‡
Blog posting	Wright, Jeremy. "*MySpace* Is the New Blogosphere." *Ensight.org*. N. p., 21 Feb. 2006. Web. 6 June 2007. <http://www.ensight.org/archives/2006/02/21/myspaceis-the-new-blogosphere/>.§
Miscellaneous Sources	
Interview	Van der Peet, Rob. Personal interview. 24 June 2009.
Lecture, address, or speech	Sharples, Mike. "Authors of the Future." Conference of European Teachers of Academic Writing. U of Groningen. Groningen, Neth. 20 June 2001. Lecture.

*Give print publication information first, then the name of the database, italicized. Web is the medium of publication; 16 July 2008 is the date the source was accessed.

°The Web site name is italicized; the sponsor is in regular type.

†When there are no page numbers for a scholarly article, use *n. pag.*

‡If the location of the newspaper is not clear from its name, give the city in brackets.

§If readers may have difficulty finding an Internet source, give the URL in angle brackets at the end of the citation.

Formatting an Academic Paper in MLA Style

An example research paper in MLA style is shown on pages 265–270. Here are the distinctive formatting features of MLA papers.

- Double-space throughout including block quotations and the Works Cited list.
- Use one-inch margins top and bottom, left and right. Indent one-half inch or five spaces from the left margin at the beginning of each paragraph.
- Number pages consecutively throughout the manuscript including the Works Cited list, which begins on a new page. Page numbers go in the upper right-hand corner, flush with the right margin, and one-half inch from the top of the page. The page number should be preceded by your last name. The text begins one inch from the top of the page.
- Do *not* create a separate title page. Type your name, professor's name, course number, and date in the upper left-hand corner of your paper (all double-spaced), beginning one inch from the top of the page; then double-space and type your title, centered, without underlines or any distinctive fonts (capitalize the first word and important words only); then double-space and begin your text.
- Start a new page for the Works Cited list. Type "Works Cited" centered, one inch from the top of the page in the same font as the rest of the paper; do not enclose it in quotation marks. Use hanging indentation of one-half inch for each entry longer than one line. Format entries according to the instructions in Table A2.1.

Student Example of an MLA-Style Research Paper

For an illustration of a student research paper written in MLA style, see Juan Vazquez's researched policy proposal on pages 265–270.

Citing Sources in Your Text in APA Style

Our discussion of APA style is based on the *Publication Manual of the American Psychological Association,* 5th ed. (2001), and the *APA Style Guide to Electronic References* (2007).

To cite sources in the body of your paper in the APA system, you follow procedures very similar to those in the MLA system except that you also include the year of the source and you place a "p." or "pp." before the page number. The author's last name, date, and page numbers are separated by commas. When the author is mentioned in an attributive tag, place only the date and page number in parentheses, usually directly after the author's name.

> The Spanish tried to reduce the status of Filipina women who had been able to do business, get divorced, and sometimes become village chiefs (Karnow, 1989, p. 41).

> According to Karnow (1989, p. 41), the Spanish tried to reduce the status of Filipina women who had been able to do business, get divorced, and sometimes become village chiefs.

If your readers wish to follow up on this source, they will look for "Karnow" in the References section at the end of the essay. If Karnow had more than one entry in the References section, they would look for the 1989 source. If Karnow had published more than one work in 1989, you would add a lower case "a" to the date of the first one and a lowercase "b" to the date of the second one. Your in-text parenthetical citation would then be either

(Karnow, 1989a)

or

(Karnow, 1989b)

APA style also makes provision for quoting or using data from an indirect source (see p. 289). In your parenthetical citation use "as cited in" rather than the MLA's "qtd in."

According to the ex-mayor of Gotham City, Rupert Smith, "the rate of crime was at an all-time low" during his term of office (as cited in Jones, 1995, p. 25).

Documenting Sources in a "References" List (APA)

Like the MLA system, the APA system includes a complete bibliography, called "References," at the end of the paper. Entries are listed alphabetically, with a similar kind of hanging indentation to that used in MLA style. If you list more than one item for an author, repeat the author's name each time and arrange the items in chronological order beginning with the earliest. If two works appeared in the same year, arrange them alphabetically, adding an "a" and a "b" after the year for purposes of in-text citation. Here is a hypothetical illustration:

Smith, R. (1995). *Body image in Western cultures, 1750–present.* London: Bonanza Press.
Smith, R. (1999a). *Body image in non-Western cultures.* London: Bonanza Press.
Smith, R. (1999b). Eating disorders reconsidered. *Journal of Appetite Studies, 45,* 295–300.

APA Quick Reference Guide for the Most Common Citations

Table A2.2 provides examples in APA style for the most common kinds of citations to be placed in a "References" list at the end of the paper.

TABLE A2.2   Quick Reference Guide for APA Citations

Kind of Source	Basic Citation Model
Print Sources When You Have Used the Original Print Version	
Article in scholarly journal	Pollay, R. W., Lee, J.S., & Carter-Whitney, D. (1992). Separate, but not equal: Racial segmentation in cigarette advertising. *Journal of Advertising*, 21(1), 45–57.
Article in magazine or newspaper	Beam, A. (2001, July–August). The mad poets society. *Atlantic Monthly*, 288, 96–103.
	Lemonick, M. D. (2000, October 30). Teens before their time. *Time*, 156, 66–74.
	Cauvin, H. E. (2001, July 18). Political climate complicates food shortage in Zimbabwe. *The New York Times*, p. A13.
Book	Tannen, D. (1998). *The argument culture: Moving from debate to dialogue.* New York: Random House.
Article in anthology with an editor	Shamoon, L. (1998). International e-mail debate. In D. Reiss, D. Self, & A. Young (Eds.), *Electronic communication across the curriculum* (pp. 151–161). Urbana, IL: National Council of Teachers of English.
Print Sources That You Have Downloaded from a Database	
Article without digital object identifier (DOI)	Beckham II, J. M. (2008). Placing *Touch of evil, The border,* and *Traffic* in the American imagination. *Journal of Popular Film & Television 33*(3), 130–141. Retrieved from Academic Search Premier database.
Article with DOI	Adelt, U. (2008). Trying to find an identity: Eric Clapton's changing conception of "blackness." *Popular Music & Society 31*, 433–452. doi: 10.1080/03007760802052809
Other Internet and Web Sources	
Document within a Web site	Marks, J. Overview: Letter from the president. Retrieved 2004, June 25 from the Search for Common Ground Web site: http://www.sfcg.org/sfcg/sfcg_overview.html
Article from scholarly Web journal	Welch, J. R., & Riley, R. (2001). Reclaiming land and spirit in the western Apache homeland. *American Indian Quarterly, 25,* 5–14. Retrieved from http://muse.jhu.edu/journals/american_indian_quarterly/v025/25.1welch.pdf
News article downloaded from Web	Thevenot, B. (2004, July 31). Once in a blue moon. *Times Picayune* [New Orleans]. Retrieved from http://www.nola.com/t-p/
Blog posting	Wright, J. (2006, Feb. 21). *MySpace* is the new blogosphere. Message archived at Ensight.org web site: http://www.ensight.org/archives/2006/02/21/myspace-is-the-newblogosphere/
Miscellaneous Sources	
Interview, personal communication	R. Van der Peet (personal communication, June 24, 2009) stated that...[In-text citation only; not included in References]
Lecture, address, or speech	According to Mike Sharples (lecture given at the Conference of European Teachers of Academic Writing, Groningen, June 20, 2001), authors...[in-text citation only; not included in references]

Student Example of an APA-Style Research Paper

An example of a paper in APA style is Julee Christianson's researched argument on pages 208–213.

Credits

Text

Page 5. Dr. Louis Sullivan, "Let the Facts Decide, Not Fear…Veto AB1108." Copyright © Louis Sullivan. Reprinted with permission.

Page 12. Brent Schotenboer, "College Athletes Caught in Tangled Web." *San Diego Union Tribune,* May 24, 2006. Copyright © 2006. Used with permission.

Pages 18, 19. Michael Banks, student writing. Reprinted with the permission of the author.

Page 26. John F. Kavanaugh, "Amnesty?" *America,* March 10, 2008. Copyright © 2008. All rights reserved. Reprinted by permission of America Press.

Page 29, 30. Michael Banks, student writing. Reprinted with the permission of the author.

Page 32. Fred Reed, "Why Blame Mexico?" *The American Conservative,* March 10, 2008. Copyright © 2008. Reprinted by permission.

Page 37. Michael Banks, "Should the United States Grant Legal Status to Undocumented Immigrant Workers?" Reprinted with the permission of the author.

Pages 53, 67. Carmen Tieu, student writing. Reprinted with the permission of the author.

Page 84. Carmen Tieu, "Why Violent Video Games Are Good for Girls." Reprinted with the permission of the author.

Page 104. John Tierney, "Recycling Is Garbage," *New York Times Magazine,* June 30, 1996, p. 28. Copyright © 1996 John Tierney. Used with permission.

Page 107. Ellen Goodman, "Minneapolis Pornography Ordinance." *The Boston Globe.* Copyright © 1985 The Washington Post Writers Group. Reprinted with permission.

Page 111. David Langley, "'Half-Criminals' or Urban Athletes? A Plea for Fair Treatment of Skateboarders." Reprinted with the permission of the author.

Page 114. Rebekah Taylor, "A Letter to Jim." Reprinted with the permission of the author.

Page 122. Kathryn Jean Lopez, "Eggheads." *National Review,* September 1, 1998. Copyright © 1998 by National Review, Inc., 215 Lexington Ave., New York, NY 10016. Reprinted by permission.

Page 130. Ellen Goodman, "Womb for Rent, for a Price." *The Washington Post,* February 11, 2008. Copyright © 2008 Washington Post Writers Group. Used with permission.

Page 131. Zachary Stumps, "A Rhetorical Analysis of Ellen Goodman's 'Womb for Rent, for a Price.'" Reprinted with the permission of the author.

Page 151. Athletes Against Steroids web page. © 2008 Athletes Against Steroids. Used with permission.

Page 171. Aaron Friedman, "All that Noise for Nothing," *The New York Times,* December 11, 2003. Copyright © 2003 New York Times Company, Inc. Used with permission.

Page 189. Kathy Sullivan, "Oncore, Obscenity, and the Liquor Control Board." Reprinted with the permission of the author.

Page 208. Julee Christianson, "Why Lawrence Summers Was Wrong." Reprinted with the permission of the author.

Page 223. Megan Matthews, "Whales Need Silence." Reprinted with the permission of the author.

Page 225. Beth Reis, letter to the editor, June 20, 2008. Copyright © 2008. Used with permission.

Page 242. Sam Isaacson, "Would Legalization of Gay Marriage Be Good for the Gay Community?" Reprinted with the permission of the author.

Page 244. David Holcberg, "Human Organs for Sale," July 21, 2005. © 2005 The Ayn Rand Institute. Reproduced by permission.

Page 265. Juan Vazquez, "Why the United States Should Adopt Nuclear Power." Reprinted with the permission of the author.

Page 278. Figures A2.2, A2.3 © 2008 EBSCO Publishing.

Page 284. Figure A2.4 reprinted with permission from the Natural Resources Defense Council.

Page 285. Excerpt from "Is Vegetarianism Healthier than Nonvegetarianism?" *Priorities,* Vol. 9, No. 3, 1997. Copyright © 1997 American Council on Science and Health (ACSH.org). Used with permission.

Images

Page 1. Everett Collection

Page 4. United Steelworkers

Page 5. Jonathan Ernst/Reuters/Corbis

Page 17. (top). Khalil Bendib

Page 17. (bottom). Kenny Be

Page 43. Courtesy Eidos Interactive

Page 75 (top). Tom Reese/The Seattle Times

Page 75 (bottom). Honolulu star

Page 93. Alex Quesada/Polaris

Page 94. Advertising Archives

Page 117. Advertising Archives

Page 138. Courtesy The Seattle Field Division of the Drug Enforcement Administration and NW-HIDTA, and the Seattle Times (ad design)

Page 140. Courtesy EarthJustice

Page 143. Courtesy Save the Children

Page 145. Laura Rauch/AP (Kerry), AP (Clinton), Ron Haviv/VII/AP (Obama), Bill Ray/Time Life Pictures/Getty Images (Reagan)

Page 146. Courtesy Brave New Films

Page 150. By Permission of Steve Benson and Creators Syndicate, Inc.

Page 163. Pat Sullivan/AP

Page 173. Courtesy of ConocoPhillips Company

Page 199. Courtesy www.adbusters.org

Page 214. Matt Davies © 2007 The Journal News/TMS Reprints

Page 220. By Permission of Michael Ramiriez and Creators Syndicate, Inc.

Page 224. Clay Bennett

Page 226. Neal Peters Collection

Page 231. Courtesy Comedy Central

Page 247. Courtesy pickensplan.com

Page 257. Courtesy of Devito/Verdi, New York, NY

Index